Putting on the Polish

A Guide to Image Enhancement

For Men and Women

Putting on the Polish

A Guide to Image Enhancement

for Men and Women

Detselig Enterprises Ltd.

Calgary, Alberta, Canada

© 1992, 1993 **Decima Malet-Veale**
West Vancouver, B.C.

Canadian Cataloguing in Publication Data
Malet-Veale, Decima, 1927-
  Putting on the polish

  Originally published: West Vancouver, B.C. :
West Vancouver Productions, 1992.
  ISBN 1-55059-074-x

  1. Clothing and dress.   2. Beauty, Personal.
3. Grooming for men.   4. Business etiquette.
1. Title.
RA776.98.M34   1993   646.7'042   C93-091825-8

Detselig Enterprises Ltd.
210, 1220 Kensington Rd. N.W.
Calgary, Alberta, Canada T2N 3P5

Printed in Canada   SAN 115-0324   ISBN 1-55059-074-x

Dedicated to:

My Dear Departed Mom:
> A long ago graduate of South Africa's Templestow Academy for Young Ladies. Trained as a concert pianist, she held several music degrees and as a piano teacher gave many people the gift of music appreciation. I thank her for providing me with an appreciation for gracious living and I thank her for her kindness and tireless assistance to so many underprivileged.

My Brother & Sister-In-Law:
> Neville and Winnifred Malet-Veale.
> Always there to encourage and help me and whose faith in me made this book possible. Both so special to our entire family.

My Dear Husband Frank:
> Who for many years and through many adversities has held my hand and whose loyalty has been my salvation.

My Special Friends:
> Marilyn (Thomas) Ward
> Who has been my dear friend and trusted confidant.
>
> Edith Weber
> Who, first as my C.G.I.T. leader, later as my lifetime mentor, became my precious and lifelong friend.
>
> Ursula Petrov
> Who, in my depths of despair, gave me the courage to persevere.

*Each one a superb example of polished grooming
and gracious behavior.*

TABLE OF CONTENTS

CHAPTER 4: EFFECTIVE COMMUNICATION

CHAPTER 5: SOCIAL ETIQUETTE

CHAPTER 8: CORRESPONDING WITH POLISH

INTRODUCTION

Comparing diamonds to people in the great mosaic of humanity, we find some polished, some needing a little attention, and some downright "in the rough," but *all* very *valuable*. We find, too, that society can make us feel somewhat "flawed" if we unwittingly and outwardly display a lack of polish. It's unfortunate that society in general does not seek to find the precious gem beneath. However, since our world insists on this evaluation of our worth, then, our jobs, our social acceptance, and sometimes our very survival depend on the perfection of our image.

The 1990's will be a time of "Putting on the Polish." Don't let a lack of knowledge of the social graces and of image enhancement categorize you as something less than you have the potential and the desire to be.

Now, too, in the 1990's, the rules of etiquette have changed considerably, due to far more mobility among the world's people, and thus more blending of various racial customs and proprieties. Also, business etiquette has been revamped, since women have become a significant factor in the business world. "Putting on the Polish" reflects the underlying principles that emerged after surveying many authorities on the subjects discussed within these covers.

Leading Image Consultants say they are appalled at the lack of good manners of many people in senior and high profile corporate and social positions. This has probably occurred as a result of the "Hippie" years when "getting back to Nature" and bare essentials was the mode of the day. Anything hinting of "class" was ridiculed, and that generation was deprived of the opportunity to learn about the decencies that for centuries have proven to be the answer to making day to day living much more pleasant.

Ah, but the *good news* is that "polish" has regained its shine. Social concern and consideration for others is the order of the '90's. Even *better news* is that the assistance to learn about that polish is right at your fingertips and can result in *the best news of all: that it's all within your power to be what ever you want to be.*

Please regard "Putting on the Polish" as a current guide featuring everything from *WARDROBE SELECTION* to *GROOMING HINTS*; from *TABLE MANNERS* to *BUSINESS* and *SOCIAL ETIQUETTE*. This is information compiled to help man, woman, and child feel confident and aware of acceptable behavior.

Attention to every facet of you the valuable gem.

"Putting on the Polish" the contemporary way!

CHAPTER ONE

FIRST

IMPRESSIONS

CHAPTER ONE

FIRST IMPRESSIONS

Behind the 8 Ball

Be you man or woman, when people first meet you they make 8 decisions about you based on your appearance.

They assume: — your economic level
                 — your intellectual level
                 — your reliability
                 — your social position
                 — your level of refinement
                 — your moral standards
                 — your present success
                 — your potential for progress

Be you *man* or *woman,* your success or failure is greatly influenced by other people and their first impressions of you. It is to your advantage to do everything possible to ensure those impressions are favorable and to have people react positively to-ward you.

The 8 decisions that affect those crucial first impressions involve topics in order of initial impact.

They are: **1 Posture (Attitude)**
                2 Grooming, Hair Style, & Apparel
                3 Accessories
                4 Personality
                5 Confidence/Poise
                6 Speech
                7 Social Etiquette
                8 Business Etiquette

To get out from "behind the 8 ball" is within your power.

Number 1 impact on "first impression" is POSTURE/ATTITUDE.

Posture immediately reflects a person's *attitude*. Good grooming is usually listed as *the* prime concern of image enhancement, but even meticulous grooming and the finest of apparel won't redeem a slouching or hang-dog stance. With shoulders back (then dropped for a look of ease), head held up with the chin back, (imagine being suspended by the hair on the top of your head), tummy and posterior tucked in, and an even-paced, smooth gait as you walk, you'll project an attitude of poise and confidence. *Posture* reveals *Class*, the way you sit, the way you stand, the way you move, all have a profound and immediate effect on *first impressions*.

Number 2 impact on "first impression" is GROOMING, which includes: HAIR STYLE & APPAREL.

The *cleanliness* of yourself, your apparel, and your abode should be your prime concern. Practising all the rules of wardrobe selection, etiquette, etc., will mean nothing if everything about you is not *clean*. First impressions, as ruthless as they can sometimes be, will always be tolerant of many flaws if the person being evaluated is very *clean* with a *tidy hair style*.

Actually, grooming and apparel go hand in hand, and one cannot separate the two when considering first impressions or any other social or business contacts. Apparel, whether of high quality or inferior grade, will be of no significance if the person wearing it is not well groomed.

Your posture, the clothing you wear, and your hair style have the greatest impact on first impressions. For *men* and for *women*, clothing projects an image affecting most of the above 8 determining factors and on the 8 topics listed above.

The *quality* of your clothing influences every one of these 8 decisions. You are immediately slotted as to your worth not just in dollars but in all facets of your character by the *quality* of the clothes you wear.

Don't let this dismay you if you are working with a limited budget. With relatively small expenditure, whether you learn the tricks of purchasing good second hand clothes or prefer new clothes only, it is quite realistic to own and to proudly enjoy a quality wardrobe if you heed the guidance on *wardrobe investment* and *clothing care* in the following chapters of "Putting on the Polish".

The *appropriateness of your apparel to the occasion* is another immediate impression. Even the finest of quality won't excuse apparel regarded to be too fussy for a casual or business situation or too casual for a dress-up function. Clothing inappropriate to the occasion indicates lack of awareness of social and business custom. Here's where this book, "Putting on the Polish", will be of crucial importance.

The *suitability of your clothes to your body shape* shouts a message loud and clear that something is very right or very wrong. Often, in an endeavor to be in step with the fashion of the day, you may be tempted to forget your body build and choose a style or design quite out of proportion and unattractive to your body structure. "Putting on the Polish" covers this topic with illustrations of body types and suggestions for both *men* and *women*.

The *suitability of your apparel to your personality*. Must you always fit the "mold" of social and business customs? Where's the opportunity to be unique and still be favorably received? "Putting on the Polish" encourages individuality in some very clever ways but also shows how to avoid the pitfalls.

Number 3 impact on "first impression" is ACCESSORIES.
You'll be surprised to learn the substantial benefits of sensible accessorizing. Creative and smart application of accessories can extend your wardrobe in ways you'll find exciting and fashionable and, best of all, not too costly.

The *quality and suitability of your accessories* can enhance or undermine your otherwise well chosen apparel. From scarfs to ties, from belts to jewelry, from briefcases to pens and handbags, how to effectively and acceptably accessorize is given extensive coverage. *Men* and *women* will benefit from the contemporary guidance provided in this personal development publication, "Putting on the Polish".

Number 4 impact on "first impression" is PERSONALITY.

In what way can reading a book teach you how to improve your personality? Well, I agree that one's personality is almost an innate characteristic, but there are some undesirable traits to try to eliminate if they have become part of your personality. "Putting on the Polish" pays attention to *every* facet of your being.

Number 5 impact on "first impression" is CONFIDENCE/POISE.

Following the guidance in this book will increase your confidence and, with a few hints about "kinesics" (the study of communication through body movement), you'll feel *so* confident and poised you'll be able to forget about yourself and give full attention to the people you meet. *That is real polish!*

Number 6 impact on "first impression" is SPEECH.

How many times have you wished some public speakers would pay as much attention to the *sound* of their voice as to the gist of their speech? Nasal, high pitched, sing-song, rasping, these people that want so badly to have us listen and agree with them do not seem to be aware that their voice is *dis*agreeable to our eardrums. Not only public speakers but many of our friends and acquaintances never give a thought to the *sound of their voice*. We can be impressed with someone's appearance and then they open their mouth and ruin the whole image. You'll learn from this author, a former radio and television commentator, how to project a sound that communicates well and makes people want to listen to you. Does that *sound encouraging?*

Number 7 impact on "First impression" is SOCIAL ETIQUETTE.

Many people these days are rushing to enroll in "etiquette" classes. There are several reasons for the popularity of this instruction. Two reasons being (a) the fact that the "Hippie" era of the 60's did not provide the guidance one used to get as a child and social graces were put on the back burner but now *that* generation is of quite another attitude, anxious to learn correct behavior and (b) new immigrants want to learn appropriate customs.

Etiquette is not a facade of snobbery, it is a concern for other people's feelings and comfort. Do we need a book to teach us this if we are basically considerate people? Yes, because what might not seem important to one person can be quite objectionable to another. Knowing this in advance is what practising etiquette is all about. An action we find upsetting and annoying in a person is usually not due to their disregard for etiquette but is due to their not being aware of the most acceptable behavior. "Putting on the Polish" is published for that express reason, it provides an opportunity to learn how to enhance your image and how *not* to offend socially or personally.

Number 8 impact on "First impression" is
BUSINESS ETIQUETTE.

This guidance doesn't only concern office personnel. In addition to corporate and business procedures there are basic rules such as correct telephone etiquette that everyone would do well to learn and to practise. *Customer, employer, and employee all respond with pleasure to a courteous environment.* If it's career success you are seeking you'll find it more quickly when your behavior and attitude enhance the corporate image.

There they are, the determining factors that influence first impressions and put you behind the 8 ball. However, you can take a cue from the following pages and rack up a winning score. The Game of Life is really much easier when we know what's expected of us and we're then able to nurture goodwill with our friends and associates. It's all just a simple matter of "Putting on the Polish." Extensive guidance on these 8 topics will be found in the following pages.

POLISH PERSONIFIED!

CHAPTER TWO

GROOMING

CHAPTER TWO

GROOMING

Hair—Get a head start

Of all aspects of one's appearance, hair has the most impact.

STYLE:
First and foremost a good cut

Most people are quite capable of and prefer to look after the shampooing and conditioning of their hair themselves, as often there isn't time to spend in a salon. This book will assist you in doing that most effectively. However, there are very few people that can expertly *cut* their own hair. This brings us to the greatest concern of all in achieving a polished image: *the selection of a hairstylist.* Many tears have been shed as a result of inept operators that mistakenly call themselves stylists. The most often expressed complaint by both men and women is that they cannot find a good hair stylist. There are two sides to this subject, however, the customer's side and the stylist's.

The customer should:

(a) Ask about the hairdresser's credentials. What training has he or she had? It is not unusual for a hairdresser, with little or no professional training, to simply go from shampooing heads to styling hair. Small wonder the results are unseemly and tears are useless. A poor shampoo or set is disappointing, but a bad hair cut is almost soul shattering.

Two ways to find a qualified stylist are:
> (1) When you see a person with a hair cut and style that appeals to you, ask him or her if they'd mind telling you the name of their hairstylist. Usually, even a stranger will not be offended by

your query if asked discreetly.

(2) Select a reputable salon and ask the salon manager if you may watch some of the shop's stylists as they perform their work, so you are better able to determine who you want to engage for yourself. This takes time but is very rewarding both for you and for the salon which will gain a long term customer.

After finding that stylist, allow him or her two or three appointments with you to achieve the results you want. Your hair may need growth time to be gradually shaped for a particular style. Also, each person's hair is *unique,* and it is only fair to let a hairdresser work with your hair a time or two to get experience with your particular needs.

(b) Be prepared to pay for expert hair care. If you just want a haircut to get it out of the way, you shouldn't waste your time reading this book, however, if you're serious about getting a polished image, a prime requisite will be to find an expert hair stylist and set up your budget to include the cost of a hair cut on a three to four week basis for a man and, depending on the style, anywhere from three weeks to two months for a hair trim for a woman. This is the maximum. There is nothing more relaxing than letting your hair stylist take complete care of your hair with weekly visits to the salon if time and budget permit. That'll polish your appearance *and* your morale! On the other hand, having a polished image doesn't rely on spending a lot of money. Ask your stylist to give you a cut that you yourself can easily maintain, and by following the guidance in this book, "Putting on the Polish," you'll find beautiful, well conditioned hair can be yours quite inexpensively.

(c) Never expect a hair style that isn't possible. Be realistic as to what can be done with the amount and type of hair with which you are blessed. A competent hairdresser will cut a style that pleases you, suits your features and *size,* and is easy to maintain.

(d) Pay heed to research on hair care. You should be aware, for instance, that, when cutting the hair, a competent hairdresser uses *scissors* on *dry* hair. The only exception to this is for very short styles that can only be shaped by means of a razor. Other than that, a razor

cut leaves the hair shaft with an angled end which easily splits and within days is damaged. Dry hair falls in its natural growth way and a good scissor cut on dry hair keeps its shape. When wet, hair strands tend to stick to-gether and, if cut that way, will bounce back to their natural fall when dry. Thus the style that was cut disappears leaving an unmanageable and unsightly result. You may get an argument about this from many hairdressers but highly qualified, world renowned, hair consultants verify the benefits of scissor cutting the hair.

When the hair is washed at home or in the salon, the water should not be too hot or too cold. Shampoo should first be diluted with water. Ask what brand of conditioning rinse is used and whether that rinse is of the type that remains on the hair or if it must be left on a few minutes to penetrate the hair shaft and then be rinsed away. This is important because it alerts the hairdresser to check the type of rinse and to use it correctly. If necessary, *be demanding.*

Part of a good cut is the style of the cut. Properly barbered hair will fall naturally into place and look tidy with no help from rollers, irons, or hair spray. With this basic shape, lift, volume, and curl, etc., can be applied to add other dimension by using rollers, irons and/or hairspray, gel, or mousse. Before being a slave to *trendy styles* consider the following: If you're planning on having a permanent wave and wearing a "wash and wear" style, *please believe that a polished appearance never is achieved with this tousled look.* Some control is a must. Get that control with the use of a few rollers or a curling iron to give some line to your hairstyle. A curling iron or a few rollers used to style the hair around the face will give a finished set and yet retain the curly just-out-of-the-shower natural look. A perm is great for giving body and curl to your hair, but to simply wash it and "scrunch" it gives a harsh, common appearance.

Hair style and body proportions:

Consider your *body size.* For example a very short, close cropped hair style on a large person will emphasize body size just as a very long, very full hairstyle will overwhelm a small person. No matter how attractive to the face a hair style may be, if it is out of proportion to the overall body structure it won't do much to enhance your total image.

This isn't to say a large person can't wear a short hair style, it simply means to keep that style full and in better balance with your size. A very tall person needs some length to the hair to avoid looking like a bean pole. A short, stout person looks best with a short hair style but it must have a bit of fullness to balance the body's stockiness. A small person can add height by wearing an upswept hairstyle but shouldn't get carried away and pile that hair too high. When choosing a hair style, consider the entire body proportions and keep an over-all balance. Men, too, should keep this in mind and if an old-fashioned slicked back hair style gives the look of a "pinhead" on a big frame, ask your hairstylist if it is possible to have a style with more volume. It stands to reason one must have the type and quantity of hair that is required for certain styles, but consult a capable stylist and take advantage of their advice and expertise.

Long hair styles:

Long hair that must be constantly handled to keep it out of your face is unsightly and disconcerting when conversing with people. Also, we sometimes see someone with long, luxurious, hair that is shiny and of good quality but it is *just* that and really not doing anything for the appearance of the owner, in fact is actually a detriment to their appearance. So you've grown your hair very, very long. It's untidy, it's uncomfortable, it doesn't enhance your features and, to those over 40, it's aging. What is it doing for you? This should be considered by both men and women. The 1960's showed us that some men can grow marvelous hair; long, wavy, gorgeous, and, though styles have changed, are you one of those men that have kept this long style and hate to part with those shoulder-length locks? Well, in my opinion, you *should* keep this hair. . . . *in a box!* Cut it off and frame it, it'll be more admired in a glass case than dragging down your polished appearance and, particularly in business, affecting your credibility.

Some men lose their hair except for a fringe around the edges and they let this hair grow and grow, twisting it in grotesque strands over the bald spot. Please, sir, if this is you, you are far more presentable exposing your bald pate and not detracting from your handsome face. Just to convince you that bald is beautiful, how about Sean Connery? He (bald)headed into the 1990's being voted the sexiest looking man. We agree. Just a word of advice, however, use a bronzer or get a bit of a tan on that "crowning glory." Carefully, that's *carefully*, and gradually, let the sun do it's wonders. Be sure to use a moisturizing tanning lotion. Treating your scalp properly is as important as treating the hair that isn't there!

For a woman, long hair of reasonable length can be easily controlled and majestic when classically styled, whether worn down (out of the eyes!) or worn up in a chignon, top knot, French braids, whatever. The look is always sophisticated and polished. Don't leave long strands hanging down around the hairline. This seldom looks tidy and is *never* appropriate for business. Everyone admires long hair that is in good condition, well cut, and attractively styled. Long hair just hanging about the face is unsightly, is *aging* and can be damaging to the complexion.

To review hair styling:
- *Hair style*, more than any other feature, has the greatest effect on a person's appearance.
- First and foremost a good cut.
- Careful choice of a hairstylist.
- Hair should be cut when *dry*.
- Hair should be *scissor* cut. (Unless very short style.)
- Hair styles should be in proportion to body structure.
- Trendy, off-beat hair styles detract from a polished image.
- Be sure to tidy the hair at the back of the head too.
- Hair is electrically charged and so it attracts odors and pollutants, therefore, *hair must be shampooed often.*

HAIR CARE:
Letting first impressions go to your head
Men, and women too, live in fear of losing their hair, and *most people want all the knowledge they can get to retain this physical feature.* There is so much concern about hair and so much to learn about hair care, it is little wonder it has such an effect on appearance and is referred to as being one's "crowning glory." *Style*, condition, color, and even *scent*, all directly influence the grooming of your hair. It is fortunate that the human body is constantly pushing out new little hair cells or, due to the way we abuse it, there would be few of us with any

hair on our heads. Even with care, some people, because of heredity and/or a health condition, lose their hair. A great deal can be done to save your hair and to promote healthy growth. So let's discuss hair care under the following topics:

(1) Structure: The rise and the fall of a human hair.
Each person's hair is absolutely unique. Hair differs widely in number, color, thickness, degree of curl and substance. The average is about 90,000 to 150,000 hairs per head with Redheads averaging about 90,000, Brunettes 110,000, and *natural* Blondes with up to 140,000 or more hairs per head. (Ah, those fortunate blondes, they not only have more fun, they also have more hair!)

The thickness of a single hair varies from 1/140 to 1/500 of an inch in diameter. Even hairs sharing the same head vary widely in each hair's thickness and should be treated accordingly. Usually an individual's hair will be replaced at least 12 times during a lifetime. It is normal to lose about 40 to 100 hairs a day. If the hair is very long it looks like much more is being lost and the owner becomes unduly concerned. Each hair grows about 1/4 to 1/2 inch per month, lives 2–6 years and eventually is pushed out and is replaced by a new one. It grows most rapidly at night, but don't ask me to tell you who it was that sat up all those nights watching hair grow, so we'd have this profound knowledge. Perhaps it's a result of "hair-raising" nightmares! Hair also grows more rapidly in the summertime, on women, and particularly between the ages of 15 through 25. After the hair reaches a length of about 10 inches it slows down to about half of its previous growth. Often people think something is wrong when their hair doesn't grow as well as it did in their youth. This slower growth is quite normal. Also, contrary to general belief, hair does not grow faster when it is frequently cut. Snipping away split ends as soon as they appear, however, stops the hair shafts from splitting further and breaking off and so they retain their length, and thus the assumption that the hair is growing faster.

Before the hair cell emerges from the scalp, your genes have established its color and structure and the nourishment it has received from your body has determined its quality. Your hair reflects the condition of your health and depends on adequate diet, rest, and even on your emotional state. Once grown, the hair shaft itself is dead tissue. The growing part of the hair lies within a tubular indentation of the skin called the follicle, hair inside this follicle is called the hair root. Only this part of the hair is "alive." The visible part outside the follicle is called the hair shaft. The hair shaft is dead tissue and that's why any damage to which you expose your hair cannot be undone and won't heal as does an injury to living tissue such as your skin. Though dead, the hair shaft, when placed under a microscope, reveals quite a story. Pathologists can determine what chemicals have been internally consumed by a person; for instance, what amount of such things as zinc, iron, arsenic (!) or any other substances that have entered the body intentionally or unintentionally, and they can even determine, quite specifically, over what period of time that substance was consumed. Murders have been solved by the use of hair analysis. Those little hair cells that the body produces and pushes out of the pores, one at a time, are silent but obvious "tattletales."

Each hair follicle is supplied with one to six sebaceous glands that produce oil. This natural oil lubricates the hair giving it lustre and protection. Though beneficial to the hair, it can, if not treated correctly, create problems. If allowed to build up, this oil can adversely affect the hair root and also can cause or aggravate acne and/or complexion eruptions on the face and back. Hair *cleanliness* is not only more attractive but is essential. Proper shampooing and conditioning are vital. Less oil is secreted with advancing age but with diets rich in carbohydrates and fats, and also during puberty, the oily secretion increases. Learning about the hair is a complicated matter, but a most rewarding endeavor. To achieve its best appearance means not only providing care to the hair you've grown but, even more importantly, giving attention to the process of helping your body to grow a healthy head of hair. A balanced diet is imperative. To have strong, healthy hair we must *grow* it that way. Hair and nails are almost totally protein so foods rich in protein are beneficial. When it comes to our hair it is particularly true that, indeed, *we are what we eat!*

HAIR CARE:
Cleanliness is next to godliness
"But I'd rather be next to you!" That's what your special love will say when your hair is squeaky clean and so nice to see and to be near. But, many people, that wouldn't dream of going a day without a

shower, think nothing of neglecting to wash their hair much less often than that. If *hair* cleanliness is not part of your ritual, you're heading for trouble. Here's why:

- Hair is electrically charged; nothing attracts pollutants, (smoke, dust, odors, etc.) quite as readily as does hair. Add to that the oil that is continuously being supplied by all those sebaceous glands at the roots of the hair and the situation can get pretty "hairy."
- The way the hair shaft is formed by each cell pushing out the one before it, gives a scaly surface to each hair. This helps lint from clothing and bedding to cling to the hair, making frequent shampooing and brushing necessary.

About that shampoo:

There are shampoos manufactured for every condition and type of hair. Read the label and buy the shampoo that meets your needs. Here are some guidelines.

- *Shampoo for dry hair* is very mild and may have conditioning agents added.
- *Shampoo for oily hair* is more concentrated and is capable of removing excess oil. Not good for hair that is dry.
- *Deep cleansing shampoos* should be used occasionally to remove residue buildup from the hair shaft such as hair sprays, chlorine from swimming pools, certain conditioning buildups, that the regular shampoos have not removed. "Neutrogena" shampoo is a good one for this purpose. Try L'ANZA's *"Pree"* with an ingredient called "chelator" that removes chlorine from the hair. Be sure to condition the hair immediately after, these are very thorough washes.
- *Dandruff shampoos* should only be used in actual cases of dandruff. People often mistakenly assume that dry flaking scalp is dandruff. This is not true. Dandruff is caused by bacteria and is actually a skin disorder. *A dandruff shampoo is highly alkaline and may contain alcohol* to kill that bacteria but, if it's just a case of dry scalp, would only *increase* the flaking. Not washing the hair frequently and *rinsing it thoroughly to remove all detergent* allows this flaking to build up

and then bacteria can enter the picture and dandruff results. If the flaking is extreme it's best to have a dermatologist determine the exact condition before using "dandruff" shampoos and adding to the problem.

- *Shampoo for color treated hair*: These shampoos are slightly acidic to keep the hair cuticle (small scales on the surface of the hair shaft) closed. This protects the color.

How to shampoo the hair

You can't damage the hair by washing it frequently. More damage occurs from *not* washing the hair often enough. If the scalp pores become clogged with oil, perspiration, etc., the hair follicle can be damaged. Your hair will benefit from the following guidelines:

- *Always dilute the shampoo with water*. In a glass or cup mix about one measure of shampoo to seven measures of water. *Shampoo products are greatly concentrated and most people use far more than is required for a thorough washing*. That is often the cause of flaking that is thought to be dandruff. It is simply that using too much shampoo has resulted in not enough rinsing, then dry scalp and shampoo residue create the flakes. Diluted shampoo is much easier on the hair than a heavy shot of concentrated shampoo delivered to one area and then spread around from there.
- *Give the hair two washes*. With the first wash you should pay attention to the scalp. Wash the scalp to clean it and unclog those pores around the hair root. Massage the shampoo gently into the hair next to the scalp, giving extra attention to the spots where oil tends to accumulate (around the forehead, behind the ears, at the nape of the neck). This enables the oil glands around the hair follicles to function normally so they can more effectively nurture the hair root. It is at the roots of the hair that perspiration is most concentrated. Because perspiration is acidic and salty, it is not good to let it build up on the hair or the scalp. The first wash, then, loosens the accumulations at the scalp. Rinse this away with clear water. The combination of hair oil and perspiration creates a very unpleasant scent that requires thorough washing to remove. The second application of diluted shampoo assures that the hair is

thoroughly clean. What nicer compliment than to hear some-one say, "Mmmm! Your hair smells soooo nice."

Hair conditioners:

Conditioning agents can have quite an effect on the hair, but we must always keep in mind that none of them have the ability to "heal" this dead tissue. Some products make the claim that they correct split ends. This claim can be made, perhaps, by using certain ingredients that glue those split ends to-gether, but this is a very temporary measure and not one I recommend. Split ends, unless removed, split further. *There is only one cure for split ends—scissors!*

Conditioners can give the hair *body* by using ingredients that expand the hair shaft. This is a help for fine hair or for those that want to increase the volume of their hair. Conditioners also can provide beneficial oils and proteins to strengthen the hair shaft, relieve dryness, and give the hair shine. Most conditioning products employ the use of anti-static ingredients that make the hair easier to control. This cuts down on the hair's tendency to attract pollutants. There are so many products with varying degrees of effectiveness that it really is a matter of experimenting to find what is best for your particular and, I repeat, *unique* hair. If you find that your hair is getting limp and stringy, it often is the result of *too much conditioning*. Perhaps it's time for a deep cleansing shampoo to remove the build-up.

Hair sprays and styling products:

Though soft, easy-flowing hair styles are the most attractive, we often find that the hair needs a little assistance to hold that shape. Humid climates demand the use of holding sprays. It's a matter of using them judiciously and being sure to use sprays that are not damaging to the hair. There is a good deal of alcohol in most hair sprays and this is drying to the hair. Also, you should look for setting and holding products that are *water soluble*. This means that with each shampoo they'll be washed away and not build up on the hair. Try not to get these products on your clothes as they can discolor fabrics and are very damaging to furs. When using hair sprays, gels, and mousses it is important to comb them out *carefully* or the hair shaft is easily torn. To endeavor to describe every type of hair spray would be too difficult. Again, it's a matter of experimentation. *Price of the product is not always indicative of it's quality.*

Let me caution you. In the interests of selling the particular products that they themselves stock, hair salon operators and staff often tell the public that these products are superior to those sold in drug and department stores and that is why they are only available in a *professional* hair salon. Are these products so exclusive they could not bear the shame of being seen in the ordinary store? Really? I'm inclined to believe that most manufacturers of these so-called exclusive products would give their eyeteeth to be on the drug and department store shelves with the opportunity for greatly increased sales. It may be that they haven't been made available there because the retailer does not deem that product's sales volumes large enough to list. There *are* a very few exceptions, I agree, where the product has costly ingredients and therefore priced beyond what the general retailer wishes to stock. Then again, perhaps that price is high because sales are limited and the producer has to make a profit. How can you determine which of these products does indeed warrant the price, and the exclusive sale? *You'll find out only by trying the product. If it meets its claim to superior performance, that's the criterion to consider.* The hair care industry is a huge one. Shelves after shelves are provided for merchandising hair care products. Every day manufacturers try to get their foot in the door to introduce some new product to get a piece of the lucrative market. Many do introduce products through beauty salons and, through this means, if they are indeed quality products, eventually become very popular in salons *and* in stores. Whether from a hair salon or from a store, I rely on the experience of the well known, long-established product manufacturers because I feel their researchers are most likely to provide the best and most apt to be the first to discover any new hair care improvements.

HAIR COLORING PRODUCTS:

If you plan to color your hair, it is imperative that you learn the basics of hair coloring products and the procedure to follow. Whether you do it yourself or have it done in a salon you should have some knowledge of what is being applied to your hair. It is not as simple as looking at the picture on the product package and deciding that's the color for you. *Remember that a person's hair is unique and color products are going to perform differently on each head of hair.*

There are *two* classifications of color products for the hair: *Permanent* color products and *temporary* color products.

Permanent color products:

Permanent hair color products need a developing agent, peroxide, to penetrate through the outer layer of the hair to the cortex (centre layer) where they are oxidized and change the pigmentation (color) of the hair. This process involves lifting the small scales (the cuticle) of each hair's surface so the color can be deposited inside the hair shaft. Be aware that this is very harsh treatment and the hair requires careful conditioning to restore this cuticle to its normal position against the hair shaft. To-day's permanent hair coloring products are as gentle as possible on the hair. It is wise to use products produced by manufacturers with many years experience in the hair color business. CLAIROL, to name one such company, has introduced product innovations and improvements since 1932. Products now are so perfected that even permanent hair coloring products actually enhance the hair, providing natural looking color and effective conditioning. Permanent hair coloring requires great care. Do-It-Yourself products are designed to be used by people with no coloring experience so exact directions are included. *It is important to do exactly as the directions indicate.*

Pointers about permanent hair color products

Color lasts until it is cut off or changed by another color application. As the hair grows out, there will be a line of demarcation between the natural color of the new growth and the changed color. It is necessary to "re-touch" this new growth about every three weeks depending on how fast the hair grows. To avoid overlapping of color, or missing spots, is very difficult to do yourself and should be done by a professional hair dresser. This is *permanent* color.

- Cannot be washed out.
- Can be used to cover grey hair.
- Can change a hair shade completely.
- Can brighten, lighten, or deepen an existing shade.
- Can be changed by another process i.e. lightening/darkening
- Color goes *inside* the hair shaft by the use of peroxide.
- Conditioning agents also are carried to *inside* the hair shaft

giving the hair extra strength and more body.

- *Only* permanent color products can *lighten* the hair. Products that just coat the hair shaft cannot lighten it.
- *When selecting a permanent color product*, it is safest to stay within your own natural color shade range or to go a bit lighter.
- Use shampoos and conditioners made for color treated hair to retain the color and help to keep it from fading.
- If you're planning to have a perm it should be done *before* coloring your hair as perms temporarily soften the hair shaft and the color tends to be lost. Wait at least a week after a perm to apply color.
- Protect your hair from the sun to help save color.
- Color treated hair must be treated with penetrating conditioners every few weeks (Vidal Sasoon's Protein Pac Treatment is a good one) and a one or two minute conditioning rinse every time the hair is shampooed.

Temporary color products:

Temporary colorings deposit color on the *outside* of the hair shaft. This color will wash out with the first shampoo, or, depending on the type of temporary color product, will gradually wash away over four to six shampoos.

Color agents that wash out with each shampoo are usually used to refresh tinted or toned hair between touch-ups; to tone down brassiness; or to remove yellow and give highlights to gray hair. *These products have no peroxide.* I might warn you that if you are caught in a rainstorm or if you perspire profusely, you might find this kind of color tends to "run." I've found it also can discolor pillowcases and head scarves. It serves its purpose but it is, after all, a very temporary coating on the hair shaft and should be treated accordingly.

Long lasting temporary color

Color agents that last for several shampoos are often called "Semi-Permanent" color. This rather contradictory term indicates that the product, though temporary, lasts for a longer time. *The person who knows and uses these products correctly, finds how great they are for many reasons.*

- Without peroxide, they gently penetrate the hair cuticle layer to "glow from within" like natural hair colors.
- They do not alter the natural hair color pigment.
- They blend in gray hair to match the natural hair color.
- They will last through three to five shampoos.
- These colors gradually fade naturally, so you are never a slave to touching up the new growth. When this color is washed away, it is time to apply a fresh application to the entire head of hair instead of just the new growth. This temporary color is a Do-It-Yourself product all the way. I highly recommend such products as L'OREAL's *Avantage* and CLAIROL's *Loving Care* for men or women. These products are as simple to apply as a shampoo and truly enhance your hair color whether you use them to cover gray or just to add highlights and body to your hair. Men might prefer a product that's called "CLAIROL INSTANT" that works in the same way as the above mentioned color products but is in a package directed to the men's market. Terrific! Man or woman, be the best you can be!
- These products *do not* contain *peroxide* or *ammonia*.
- In selecting temporary hair color, choose a color at least two shades lighter than your own. Think of it this way, with the color that's in the product added to your own color, you'll have darker hair than you intended.
- Don't be concerned that by selecting a lighter color, you will lighten your hair. *It is impossible to lighten your hair with a temporary color product*. All that would happen is you'd get attractive highlights. Also, if you select a shade that turns out not to be as dark as you wanted, it's a simple matter to apply a darker shade later. However, if you choose a shade that turns out darker than you wanted, you'll be a few weeks waiting for it to wash away. If you do not want red highlights, be sure to choose an "ash" shade. Most drug store cosmeticians are knowledgeable about these products, *ask!*

To be a blonde
Requires totally removing the existing natural color pigment from the hair. This entails lifting the hair cuticle to allow an oxidizing agent (peroxide) to penetrate the hair shaft and bleach out the natural color.

As with bleaching a fabric, after a few applications the fabric is weakened and holey, so it is with your hair, each lightening application damages the hair making it more and more porous.

Why then would we subject our hair to such harsh treatment? For the same reason we wear high heels and ruin our poor feet, we like the look! (At least we can grow *new* hair but our ever-suffering feet must stagger along in perpetual deformity.) There should be limits to the extent we'll carry our pursuit of beauty but, since most of us get more pleasure than pain out of looking our best, I'm sure there'll be "Bottle Blondes" till the end of time. If it's your desire to be a blonde (your desire, and my desire, and most people's at some time or another!), I strongly recommend that you should know a lot about the process before you try to do it yourself. We've all seen the unsightly yellow shades and straw-like disasters of incorrect blonding attempts. It would bore most readers for me to give the many pages necessary to explain the steps to follow to become a blonde, so I'll only give you the major points to consider.

If you do decide to lighten your hair, may I suggest you *first take into consideration the color of your skin and eyes and your natural hair shade*. Blonde hair won't complement some complexions. Being a blonde involves more than just hair color, it is a combination of fair skin, light eyebrows, etc., for a total blonde image.

Become a blonde *gradually*. Have your hair "streaked" professionally. This suits more complexions. Some men, too, like this effect of light highlights in their hair. *Gradual* lightening is not so shocking to your admiring public. It is also much easier on your hair and on your personality!

Other than streaking, a radical change of hair shade will require retouching at the roots about every ten days. Because the hair shaft is new and soft at the roots and because it is right next to the warm scalp, lightening products develop much more rapidly in this area. It is important to *apply the lightener quickly without overlapping on to the already lightened part of the hair shaft*. Trying to get the lightener on that small width (about 1/8 to 1/4 of an inch) is beyond the ability of most people. To avoid having hair breakage, and an over porous condition of your hair, *you really require professional attention for root retouch*. Being a "Bottle Blonde" is a costly endeavor. Much more frequent conditioning is required. Doing it yourself, if you apply lightening agents time after time, eventually your hair (if you have any left!) will be all one shade. This looks very artificial as natural hair is never all one color throughout. Because I know how complicated the blonding process can be, how much damage you can do to your hair, and how unsightly can be the results, *I urge you to enlist the service of a capable color professional.* Processed correctly and given the right care, blonde can be absolutely *beautiful* and well worth the investment. *But . . . can you handle all that fun?*

HAIR CARE IN GENERAL:

- Dry the hair as much as possible with a towel before using a blow-dryer.
- Use a blow-dryer on the lowest setting. Too much heat can break delicate hair strands. Dry underneath layers first.
- For straight hair, begin blow drying the hair from the roots and gradually work to the ends. Ends dry rapidly.
- Keep the blow-dryer moving at all times with the nozzle held at least 10 inches from the hair.
- To give your hair more fullness, blow dry your hair with your head turned upside down until you hair is almost dry then finish by blow-drying it in your final style.
- Never brush wet hair. Wet hair stretches more easily and can break. Using a wide toothed comb, begin at the ends and work towards the scalp to avoid breakage.
- Have hair ends trimmed every six to eight weeks.
- When at the beach, massage conditioner onto your hair and leave it there to keep the sun from drying your hair.
- *Use a styling product with sunscreen* to protect your hair.
- Use shampoos made for color-treated hair. They are somewhat acidic and help keep the hair cuticle closed.
- Wear a swim hat when using a chlorinated swimming pool. Hair, especially blonde hair, can take on a green cast from the chlorine. If you don't wear a cap, wash, or at least rinse, your hair immediately after your swim.
- Wash your hair frequently. Hair is more damaged by oil build-up and pollutants than by too much washing.
- Dilute your shampoo before applying to the hair. Mix one cap of shampoo to six caps of water in a glass.

- With each wash, *two* diluted shampooings are essential.
- To lock in shine, follow the shampoo with a lukewarm rinse then with a cool water rinse.
- Pay attention to the back of your head. Some people comb and tidy the hair at the front of their head but neglect the back. Hang a mirror on the wall or door opposite to the mirror you use when combing your hair so you get a view of the back of your head. Tidy it!
- Don't use nylon or metal bristle brushes they can cut the hair cuticle. Natural bristle brushes are best.
- Check your combs to be sure they don't have sharp teeth or broken edges that can damage the hair.
- Make sure your hair is dry and free of hair spray when using a curling iron as the hair may stick and scorch.
- Rubberbands can tear your hair. Use a coated elastic when you fasten your hair back.
- *Whatever hair product on your hair be sure to read the manufacturer's instructions and follow them exactly. Now you're really "Putting on the Polish"!*

Skin care

Skin is in! Just everybody is wearing it!

Usually it fits pretty well, except maybe for the odd wrinkle here and there. It doesn't come unfastened, thanks to that one strategically placed little button. Style? Well, it's *always* in style. Comes in different colors, too, but you don't get your pick so you can't do much about that. As for pattern and *quality* of the skin, those are very much within your ability to influence.

When your skin breaks out in those unsightly little patterns just at the time you're wanting to look your best, there is no polish thick enough to cover the problem. Wearing a mask may be your last resort. Hold on now, don't get your birthday suit in a knot! A mask just might be the answer to the problem of those "patterns." Not a Halloween

mask; we want to discuss a more realistic solution: the facial masks
that help to eliminate "pattern" problems before they happen.

Skin is the largest organ of the body. It has a job to do. We'll discuss all skin care topics and the effect they have on the *skin.* Yes, indeed, skin *is* "in" and we want to make sure you're wearing the most
beautiful skin possible.

Saving face

How deep is the ocean? How high is the sky?

How *old* is a wrinkle? Is there some reason why?

Wrinkles can be any "age" and, yes, there are many reasons why.
First and foremost, the greatest cause of wrinkled skin depends not so
much on the number of years a person has lived but how much time
their skin has been exposed, and, worse, *over*-exposed, to the *Sun.*
This is called photo-aging. Surprisingly, children's skin is particularly vulnerable and most premature aging of the skin starts in child-
hood by overexposure to the sun. It isn't obvious *then* but later in life
this overexposure is the main reason for those wrinkles. The sun can
be so beneficial to our health and to our emotions that I'm not suggest-
ing shutting Old Sol out of our lives completely. Let's just learn to
protect our skin from the sun's damaging rays while we collect its important vitamins and its boost to our "sunny" dispositions.

Genetics, of course, influence the tendency of skin to lose its
elasticity. We can't change any pre-programming of our genes, however, what we sometimes blame on our heritage is actually just generations of bad habits and lack of care. Proper cleansing and protection
can improve skin immensely and avoid many of those things called
"wrinkles".

The younger you are when you begin to take care of your skin, the
more attractive and *healthy* it will be. At one time people were
thought to be conceited if they gave too much attention to the "outer"
appearance of their bodies. That was when we lived in a world less
encumbered with the pollutants that now attack us all. It no longer is
a matter of vanity but actually a matter of survival to learn good skin
care especially. Mothers and fathers should be aware of the changing
elements and begin protecting their children from the day they are
born. For instance, skin cancer used to be a rarity but statistics recently revealed in the U.S.A. show that one person in less than every

100 people will be afflicted with malignant skin melanoma by the end of this century. What shall we do? Manufacturers are creating more and more products; advertising agencies are getting more and more convincing; and the media are getting smarter and smarter at appealing to our "needs." We're confused. Just what *should* we be buying and how best can we care for our children and ourselves? A good way to tackle the situation is to heed the advice of those with professional experience. In the case of skin care that would be dermatologists. In writing this book, "Putting on the Polish," we follow the advice of leading dermatologists.

Skin cleansing

The most important care of the skin is, of course, to keep it meticulously *clean*. Does that mean expensive facials and a complicated skin care program with cleansing lotions, astringents, toners, et al? *No!* I have always been an advocate of using *soap and water. Most dermatologists agree that the cleanest skin is achieved that way. At one time beauty advisors from cosmetics companies fervently persuaded us *never* to use *soap and water on our faces. *Now,* realizing that more people are taking the advice of dermatologists, many leading cosmetics companies produce "cleansing bars" to be used with water. Cosmetic suppliers can no longer ignore the fact that people are more aware of good skin care and less inclined to believe everything the beauty industry claims or promises. They still try to convince us, however, that we *need* all the other paraphernalia to *properly* clean our faces. Nonsense!

We *are* often influenced by large price tags that *seem* to indicate great quality and the probability of miraculous results that are offered by certain fancy skin-care products. We all often fall for their lure, the look of the beautiful bottles and pretty pots is what we pay for, and *the prestige of owning such luxury products is all part of our lifestyle.*

The beauty industry is thriving because we want the dream that they promise: instant beauty. Every now and then we should pinch ourselves and find we really *are* just dreaming. *When a product is created that is truly of benefit, our governments' watchdogs will give it their endorsement, and, with eyes wide open, we'll see we aren't being fooled.* If it's the products' snazzy containers you like, I suggest you buy your other beauty items, like fragrance and grooming accessories, in fancy bottles to gussy up your decor. *Buy pure and simple and un-adulterated when you buy skin care.* I prefer Nature's own provision, *water,* and the aid of a cleansing bar. Think about it. Isn't it kind of ludicrous that some persons don't mind swimming in a chlorine-drenched pool, or of lying beneath the harsh rays of the sun but those same persons are afraid of using beneficial *soap and water on their face? Anyway, what we commonly refer to as "soap" is not soap at all. Soap is made by the action of an alkali on fat, which may remove too much of the skin's natural acid balance. When I refer to "soap" the little asterisk is there to let you know I mean a cleansing agent, a mild detergent. A detergent (to quote Webster) simply means a cleaning agent. There are many types and strengths of detergents. A facial cleansing bar is a very mild detergent. Both words, "soap" and "detergent", seem to inspire thoughts of harshness. Detergents don't always deserve that rating. They are quite a wonderful discovery. Detergents perform effectively in both hard or soft water, either in cold or hot water, and they rinse away easily, carrying impurities with them. Soaps leave a scum that dries the skin and clogs pores. So, even at the risk of endangering my credibility, I'll now refer to clean-ing agents as detergents. After all, I'm not meaning a laundry detergent, save that for your jeans. For your face, choose a nice mild detergent that won't shrink your genes!

When you are using a detergent and water, you are working with skin that's flexible because it is moist but when you use lotion cleansers *without water,* you are wiping and pulling at your skin, stretching delicate tissue when it is *least* flexible. Then, to remove the cleanser you use tissues that irritate the skin's surface and you pull and stretch the skin some more. After that, because the tissues couldn't possibly remove all the cleanser, you apply a product that can. That product may have alcohol that hardens the skin, as you wipe and pull and stretch that skin again. By now, you may even be filling your pores with all these things that are supposed to clean the skin not clog it more. Remember: *The less the skin is handled the bet-ter it'll be.*

Products such as PEARS' cleansing bar or one of NEUTROGENA's cleansing bars, specially formulated for your specific skin type, are ideal. If your budget allows and you get a *psychological* lift from using more expensive, "luxury" products, go right ahead, indulge yourself, a good one to try is CHANEL's Gentle Cleansing bar. These cleansers and water glide over *moist* skin, gently dissolving make-up and impurities. Use *tepid* water, never hot nor very cold, and after lightly working up a suds to clean the skin, be sure to rinse and rinse and rinse with clear tepid water. *Forty splashes will plump the skin with moisture.* The skin is left clean and *moist*, perfect for applying a product that will hold that beneficial moisture in the skin. That product is called a **moisturizer**. Apply it immediately after washing.

Cleansing and treatment of teen-age skin: (usually oily)
- Use a cleansing bar recommended for oily skin. (ALMAY's Oil Control Facial Soap or NEUTROGENA's Oily Skin Formula cleansing bar)
- Make it a habit to wash your face twice a day, in the morning and again at night before going to bed.
- Never go to bed with make-up on. Wash it away.
- Use a moisturizer that contains no oil: non-comedogenic.
- Place just enough moisturizer (about the size of a dime) and spread it gently over your face to moisturize the surface of the skin just until your body's natural oils and moisture can surface and replace what was removed in washing. Teen-age skin is young and healthy and if kept scrupulously clean, doesn't usually need anything else.
- Teen-age skin *does* need a sunscreen when exposed to the sun. *These are the most crucial years for protection.* Skin damaged by the sun can never be repaired.
- In removing mascara and eye make-up, do it *gently, wipe* don't rub. Mascara is usually not water soluble so use either cotton squares and baby oil or non-oily eye make-up remover pads. (MAX FACTOR; CLIFTON; ANDREA) I repeat, wipe gently. The skin around the eyes is very delicate and every push and pull will, in later years, remind you of any rough treatment you deliver now.
- If your natural oil accumulation is a problem and causes skin eruptions and/or acne, it is best to ask the guidance of a dermatologist as to what products to use. This may be a hormonal imbalance and no one but a qualified doctor should determine the treatment required.

- *Wash your hair frequently.* Oil build-up at the hair roots is often the cause of complexion problems.
- My special message to teenagers is that beauty is not just a *surface* condition. Attractive appearance is a result of *good health* and *proper care.* Poor dietary habits, layer upon layer of eye make-up, and radical hair styles will do nothing to enhance your image. The beauty of *youth* is what we'd all like to have. *You have it.* Guard it carefully. Display it well.

Cleansing and treatment of oily skin: (usually age 13–30)
- Most of the advice listed above for *teenage* skin cleansing and treatment is applicable to anyone with oily skin.

Cleansing and treatment of normal skin: (usually age 30–40)
- What we refer to as "normal" skin can often be a combination of dry and oily areas. Treat your skin accordingly. Apply emollients where it is dry (usually cheeks and eye areas) and oil-free moisturizer on what is called the oily "T-zone" (forehead, nose and chin).
- Use a mild cleansing bar. Glycerine bars like PEARS' or NEUTROGENA's Original Formula (unscented) are superb.
- Choose a water-based moisturizer that contains humectants. Ask a cosmetician to assist you if you need guidance.
- *Always choose a moisturizer that is non-comedogenic* (will not clog pores). (Pronounced non-*kom'*-e-doe-jen-ic)
- If you're going out in the sun, use a moisturizer or a make-up that contains a sun screen. (MAX FACTOR's Invisible Make-Up SPF6; CHANEL's Emulsion #1 SPF8; or a total sun block with NEUTROGENA's Paba-Free Sunblock)
- *Exercise.* Brisk walking is one of the best exercises to get the circulation moving. This gets more oxygen into the blood stream.
- Exercise makes a person perspire. This unclogs the pores and is a great skin cleanser. *Be sure to wash your face immediately after exercising and perspiring, as perspiration is salty and loaded with body impurities.* Wash it away and get your complexion glowing.

Cleansing and treatment of sensitive skin

- Whether skin is dry, oily, or normal, it can also be sensitive and react unfavorably to cleansers and cosmetics in general and/or with certain products in particular.
- Sensitive skin is prevalent among women because most women tend to use more color and treatment products than men, and also because women's skin is somewhat thinner and less oily than men's. Older women generally have what we refer to as sensitive skin due to lack of oil and thinning of the epidermis due to age.

Other causes:

Genetics: a person's genes basically determine their skin type. What is inherited can't be changed but can be catered to.

Medications: Almost every medication and/or drug (prescription or illicit) has an effect on the skin. Contraceptives; hormones such as estrogen; diuretics, tranquilizers; antibiotics; and antihistamines can make the skin extra sensitive to the sun and can create imbalance in body functions that in turn cause acne, inflammation, itching, and/or rashes and the least they do is leave the skin sensitive to the sun and cleansing and treatment products.

Environment: Any exposure to harsh weather, very dry climates, prolonged outdoor activity, all affect the skin and leave it in a sensitive condition.

Treatment:

- Read labels. Avoid products that contain known irritants such as PABA, lanolin, perfume, alcohol, mineral oil, or preservatives such as parabens.
- Hypoallergenic products such as ALMAY, CLINIQUE, MARCELLE, have been screened for known irritants and are least likely to cause problems for ALL types of skin.
- Do patch tests. The inside of the elbow reacts quickly to any chemicals that may be irritants. Apply some of the product here, cover it, wait 24 hours and if the skin is red or itchy don't use the product . . . you are allergic to it.

- Apply a moisturizer before any color foundation. Choose a water-based, oil-free foundation that has a sunscreen (Revlon's Springwater Makeup is great).
- Apply cosmetics with brushes, sponges, and FINGERS that are absolutely clean.
- Use cleansing bars or rinse-off cleansing lotions not soap or wipe off cleansers. Try Neutrogena's glycerine bar or Aveeno Cleansing Bar.
- If you use a toner use one that is alcohol free. Witch hazel is an excellent toner and costs very little. Most expensive toners are just witch hazel with some added ingredients that you don't need.
- Use eye make-up for sensitive eyes. Replace liquid eyeliners and mascaras every 3 to 4 months, they get contaminated.
- Use lipsticks that are hypoallergenic and free of indelible dyes. Physicians Formula Lipstick and Almay lipsticks are superb.
- Use hypoallergenic nail enamels. Many of our skin problems are a result of nail polishes that contain very strong irritants. I highly recommend Almay's.
- Take care with exfoliation. A washcloth or scrubbing grains may be too harsh if your skin tends to be dry or very sensitive. Though I recommend occasionally using a washcloth for exfoliation for most complexions, I don't advise anyone with dry or sensitive skin to use one.
- For troubled skin, the less you put on your face the better. If you're tempted to use a concealer, apply it after you've applied foundation. Cover Girl's Replenishing Concealer may do the trick.
- Apply liquid cosmetics with clean fingers not sponges. Sponges can collect germs. Wash your hands often.
- The less you touch your face the better it'll be.

Skin moisturizing

Air conditioning in our buildings and automobiles robs the skin of moisture. Pollutants in the air absorb moisture from the surface of the skin. Indoor heating units dry the skin as does the sun and cold weather. There are two types of moisturizers: *Humectants* and *Emollients*

HUMECTANTS

These are ingredients that attract and hold water on the surface of the skin for an extended period of time. *All skin types benefit from using a humectant.* Some common, *effective ones are glycerine, sorbitol, lactic acid and urea.*

EMOLLIENTS

These are ingredients that as closely as possible resemble the skin's natural oils. They form a barrier on the skin's surface that help to seal in moisture and to stop evaporation of that moisture. The most common of these are: lanolin, mineral oil, and petroleum jelly. Beware! Different skin types require specific ingredients in a moisturizing product. An oily skin *does not* require a product that contains an emollient, and a dry skin probably would respond better to one that *does* contain such an oily ingredient. Combination skin (part oily/part dry) responds favorably to using both: oily emollients on the dry part and non-oily humectants on the oily part.

Here are the major terms to look for in selecting an effective moisturizing product:
- *Non-comedogenic.* This means the product will not clog pores. (A comedo is a blackhead. *kom'*-e-doe)
- *Contains a humectant.* Holds moisture in the skin.
- *Contains a sunscreen.* Some high-SPF products are too heavy to wear under make-up. Look for oil-free sun screen formulations that are light enough to wear under make-up. (CLINIQUE's Oil-Free Sun Block SPF15)
- *Fragrance free.* Perfumes can cause allergies.
- *Moisturizers can agravate acne.* Ask a dermatologist to guide you if you have any troubled skin condition.

Don't be fooled by products that claim to:
- "repair," "rejuvenate," "rebuild," "replenish," "remove wrinkles," or to "remove cellulite." *No product available without prescription is able to achieve such results.*

- *be expensive because they are so beneficial.* The magazine "U.S. Consumer Reports" tested 48 moisturizers and found that the *least expensive* and *simplest formulae* were often the *most effective!* Such ingredients as collagen and emulsifiers *do not* increase the performance of a moisturizer. They *can* increase the clogging of pores and allergic problems.
- *have only "natural" ingredients.* Very complex chemicals are used to create so called "natural" cosmetics products. They are often more allergenic than products that use synthetic materials. Dermatologists agree that these products are often the worst offenders in creating skin problems. Then why would a manufacturer offer them for sale? Well, aren't we a society dedicated to *Nature's* products? *Ooooops!* Gullible public, fooled again!
- *Dermatologist Tested:* Because a cosmetics product claims to be dermatologist tested *does not mean* it is dermotologist *approved. There is a big difference!*

Skin and the sun: Sunscreens

Why are we human beings such obstinate creatures? When we're born dark skinned we want to be white, and when we're born fair skinned we do everything possible to be brown. Each skin color of every race is, or can be, beautiful in its own right. We're always living dangerously when we try to be something we aren't. *Getting a tan is living dangerously* and, I hasten to add, *those of you with dark skin,* who do not need a tan but who are outdoors in the sun, are also living dangerously if you don't protect your skin from the sun. There's not just the danger of premature wrinkles but the incidence of skin cancer which is more prevalent every year. This is one of the hazards of the 1990's. The earth's ozone layer allows an increase of ultra-violet rays. It's no use to say your parents had no problem with sun damage or to make comparisons of any kind from the past. This is *now* and our world and climatic conditions have changed dramatically. All people, fair skinned or dark, shall have to protect ourselves from ultra-violet rays and pollutants. We must re-evaluate our habits and adjust our lifestyles to effectively cope with "what's out there". "Putting on the Polish" requires healthy skin. *Sunscreens are essential to skin protection.*

You still insist on having a tan? Well, I have to agree that white skin bared in a swimsuit or shorts looks quite "naked!" without a tan. However, more and more fair skinned fashion models, in the interests of skin protection, are being shown without a tan, so perhaps as we get accustomed to seeing white skin without a tan it won't seem so "nude." At present we are so keen on admiring and being admired because of a tan, we try to ignore the hazards.

Good news! One of the benefits of the 1990's is that as a result of space travel and of in-depth study of the atmosphere, scientists and researchers know how to better deal with the elements. Excellent skin protection has been developed and is available. Use it. Get that tan if you must but even for every day outdoor activities it is important to use a sunscreen. Keep in mind that when you are young, people will say, "What a gorgeous tan!" but a few years later they'll say, "Look at that old walnut!"

Here's how to enjoy the sun

- Man, woman, and child should use a sunscreen *but never use any sunscreen product on babies under one year old. The toxic effects of certain ingredients can harm babies.* Just be sure a baby is shielded from the sun and its bare skin is never exposed when outdoors.
- A moisturizer or plain oil *without sun screen ingredients* actually *encourages* sun burn and skin damage.
- Choose a sunscreen with an adequate SPF number. SPF means a Sun Protection Factor and the number indicates how long you can stay in the sun without burning. For example, if you usually burn in about half an hour, you could stay in the sun 6 times longer with an SPF6. If you burn in as little as 20 minutes an SPF6 will only protect you for two hours.
- *Choose a sunscreen with a Sun Screen Protection Factor of 15 (SPF15).* There are higher SPF's but the Food and Drug Administration confirms that even a sun-sensitive person is totally protected by a Sun Protection Factor 15 if the sunscreen stays on the skin throughout exposure to the sun.
- *An SPF higher than 15 won't give more protection but puts more chemicals on the skin which might cause irritation and clog pores.*
- If you are swimming, select a waterproof sunscreen that will

stay on the skin until removed with soap. Even perspiration and swimming won't remove it.

- Look for a sunscreen that shields against UVB and UVA rays (Neutrogen's Paba-Free Sunblock is excellent and stays at 15 even after 6 hours in water.)

- A sunscreen should be *non-comedogenic* which means it won't clog pores.

- Select a sunscreen that is fragrance free. Perfumes tend to cause allergies and to react unfavourably to the sun.

- Paba is a leading sunscreen ingredient, but very often people are allergic to this, and if paba is mixed with certain other chemicals, it can clog pores.

- Remember that ultra-violet rays can penetrate thin fabrics, even umbrellas. Be sure you're wearing a sunscreen. Ultra-violet (ultra-*violent?*) rays can penetrate water too, so, even when you are swimming, the sun is "out to getcha."

- Hazy, overcast days and winter days can be deceiving. Ultra-violet rays may be giving you the worst kind of zap. Just because the sun isn't hot or shining boldly from the heavens, doesn't mean it isn't up there sneaking a peek at unprotected skin. Skier, jogger, swimmer, stroller, protect thyself at *all* times.

- Your skin can become dehydrated if you drink alcoholic beverages while sitting in the sun for long periods of time. What has that to do with using a sunscreen? Nothing what-so-ever. I'm just being a spoil sport!

Head to toe skin care: Terrific! That's you all over!

The best way to "put on the polish" is with a small square item called a "washcloth." The body's skin is constantly flaking and shedding. If these flakes are allowed to build up, they prevent the skin's natural oil from coming to the surface to nourish the skin. These flakes also create an ideal breeding ground for bacteria to cause infections and acne. Gently removing these flakes keeps the skin's surface clean and the pores unimpeded from functioning at their best. That little rig known as a washcloth or facecloth can work wonders used with tepid water, a mild detergent and a light circular motion. Change that washcloth often and rinse it well after each use. Some people prefer a soft complexion brush for this washing, but those brushes often have bristles that tend to cut into tender skin and leave it open to infection. I like a *white 100% cotton* washcloth that can be bleached to disinfect it and keep it absolutely clean; save your color co-ordinated facecloths for display. For all-over skin exfoliating, (from the neck down, that is) use a loofa sponge. Ah! Invigorating! Rinse, rinse, rinse with *tepid* water, never hot or too cold and your skin will glow. If the water in the area where you live is hard, you may want to use a product that will neutralize or soften the water.

- *Exercise* keeps the blood circulating and carrying beneficial oxygen to the cells. Getting perspiration flowing through the pores clears them of impurities and oil build-up. It's wise to shower after exercising, because perspiration is salty and laden with these impurities and should not be left on the skin, wash it away.
- *Cotton balls:* What we refer to as "cotton" balls are often not cotton but are made of synthetic material that doesn't absorb and that scratches the skin. Look for *real cotton* squares at the cosmetics counter. (*Bonne Bell's are best.*)
- *Be well heeled!* Don't let heels and other parts of your feet get to a state of calluses and major problems. Use a buffer to remove rough skin and plenty of skin conditioning lotions or creams to keep your feet soft and pliable. This is much easier on your hosiery and certainly far more comfortable than dry, cracking skin. (*Buf-Puf* works wonders.)
- Skin is the largest organ of the body. Don't forget that *it is an organ and therefore has an important job to do.* It acts as a thermostat so care should be taken to see that its pores are not blocked. Protection is the key.
- Skin is *in!* Just everyone is wearing it. With attention, your skin is going to look so perfect people will ask, "*Wow!* Who is your tailor?"

Skin care and cosmetics

Cosmetics products fall into three main categories: *cleansing, treatment,* and *color.*

Cosmetics for cleansing

Earlier in this chapter I pointed out that glycerine cleansing bars and water are the most effective facial cleasers for women and for men too. If you don't agree or if you have a special skin problem, you should ask your dermatologist, who may recommend something more suited to your individual skin requirements or, perhaps, products that require a prescription. Other than that, I can only leave you to your own devices. (Wrinkle, wrinkle, little star!)

Cosmetics for treatment

Treatment products include complexion nourishing creams, moisturizing lotions, toners, astringents, masks, etc. and I suggest you may also need some *salt*. When you're considering most manufacturers' claims of miraculous results, be sure to take them with a grain of salt! *If and when a cosmetics company creates a product that will really erase all signs of age from a person's skin, the Food and Drug Administration will give it a seal of approval for* **prescription** *sale. So far there are none.* Save your money.

If a product penetrates the skin to the depth it must to have any effect on the cells, the FDA supervises its sale by requiring that it only be prescribed by a doctor. It then can be purchased only by prescription through the pharmacy department, not the cosmetics department. Retin-A has caused a great deal of interest and some favourable results, but I am not a doctor and won't advise you regarding this product. There are similar names being given to products to ride the shirt-tails of Retin-A's success but, I repeat, if it has a substantial effect on the skin it will be professionally supervised and not available at the cosmetics counter.

On some occasions when a customer has complained that a treatment product she has purchased has actually caused skin eruptions, I have heard cosmeticians make the comment, "Oh, don't worry about that, it has to get worse before it gets better." Reach for that salt! There's something in that product that may be quite wrong for you, don't be intimidated, ask for a refund, the face you save may be your own!

MOISTURIZERS

These are beneficial to the epidermis and I have discussed them earlier in quite specific depth because this is a treatment product that can be worthwhile. You might find, as I do, that it is better not to put any moisturizer on the eye*lid* as it tends to make the eyelid look puffy.

EYE CREAMS AND OILS

These relieve dryness in the eye area. Because the skin around the eyes is very thin and delicate, *has no sebaceous oil glands and very limited dermis support*, this area requires gentle care. The better treatment products to use are specially formulated creams and oils that are light and readily absorbed. These products must be fragrance free. When applying any treatment products around the sensitive eye area do not *rub*, but instead use a gentle patting motion with the fingertips only. The roots of eyelashes can be irritated and easily clogged by too much oil or cream—take care. (Young complexions should not require such products at all as they have oil enough.) It is best to use eye creams and eye oils at night upon retiring as for daytime wear they are too oily and will smudge your eye make-up. Use a lighter, protecting eye cream for day wear. At night, use products with *no* sunscreen, as the chemicals in sunscreens may irritate the eyes. *Fellows*, you could do with a few less "laugh lines" around your eyes, too, try an eye cream made especially for men.

ASTRINGENTS AND TONERS

These usually have an alcohol base and are quite harsh. If a very oily complexion needs such treatment it is best to have a dermatologist evaluate your skin type and condition and advise you what to purchase and how to apply it. Your pharmacist can also be helpful.

Men have used shaving lotions for many decades but few have questioned the effect these lotions have on the complexion. In the 1990's we know it isn't effeminate to pay attention to skin care, it is downright necessary to do so. After-shave lotions contain alcohol and give the skin a double whammy besides being very drying if used every day. Because most men have a lot of oil in their skin, this may not pose a problem. However, you , sir, may want to consider switching to a moisturizing, skin-conditioning, after-shaving balm that not only protects your complexion but is usually available in that same great fragrance that you (and she?) like so much. Or try a product such as Royal Copenhagen's After Shaving Balm that is effective and smells divine! Face up to it. What's effeminate about leading people around by the nose and having them enjoy it so much?

I've expressed some criticism of the cosmetics industry for making outlandish claims, but it is really our own fault for being gullible and probabably expecting too much. Could even our very own Fairy God-mothers deliver perpetual youth? We want a dream and the cosmetics manufacturers sometimes get carried away in their endeavor to see that dream realized. . . . "Step right up, folks, and buy this marvelous age slicer." *Actually, I think most cosmetics products do more for our morales than anything else on the market. Let's give thanks!*

COSMETICS FOR COLOR:

There are few people that have naturally perfect coloring, but cos-metics, skillfully applied, can achieve a natural, attractive ap-pearance. The most common mistake in wearing color is *"too much."* Strive for a natural look not a painted mask. Most eye make-up is far too heavily applied. Cosmetics were designed to provide the natural color we may lack, instead we see the bazaar look of a clown with bright red cheeks and doleful looking eyes. Surely women don't *want* to look so strange. Is it just a lack of know-how or have they become accustomed to the look and don't realize the adverse impact it is hav-ing on their viewing public?

How does one achieve a natural look? Practice! Do just one side of your face and compare it to the untouched side. Is there too stark a difference or could you use a bit more color? I suggest you go to some cosmetics departments and have a look at the cosmeticians. When you see one that you think has applied her make-up in a manner that is becoming and that you would like to emulate, ask her advice. Tell her the type of lifestyle you lead, busy mother at home with children or busy mother with children *and* a career or busy senior citizen man-aging to stay gorgeous, whatever, let her know your cosmetics re-quirements. *Explain that you are not buying today but want guidance and suggestions to consider.* Perhaps she would arrange a make-up application for you. The reason I say *not to buy* on this visit is because you'll be tempted to go home with a great bundle of beauty prepara-tions that you may or may not need. If you state this at the beginning of the discussion you won't feel obligated and the cosmetician is aware of your intentions. Also you may find that the routine this cos-sie is recommending does not appeal to you and you certainly don't want to purchase colors and treatment you will never use. We all see color in quite a different way. If all goes well and you have chosen a capable cosmetician she'll be happy when you return a few days later, after you've had time to evaluate the purchase, and she'll have made a loyal customer and a good friend. When I hired cosmeticians, I tried to have a "team," an older woman who could relate to the mature customer's problems of aging skin and who also knew how to guide the young person in early skin care and, as her team-mate, a young woman who could relate to the fashion-conscious youth market. If the older cosmetician has kept up with the times and looks fashionable and attractive, take advantage of her wealth of experience, she not only knows what products are available but she also has the experience to advise what is effective.

Here is a good time to make you aware that most cosmeticians work on a salary plus commission basis. Ah! Ha! Could that be why you go home with all those bottles and jars and sticks and pots, all that *unnecessary* folderol? A department store cosmetician is paid directly by the cosmetics manufacturer and she represents one line only. Occasionally she may look after more than one cosmetics line but most suppliers want undivided loyalty to their line. The cosmetics supplier even pays for the space where their line is merchandised in a department store. I point this out because if, on occasion, you have gone in with the intention to purchase a certain product and been talked into quite another, it may be that an enterprising cosmetician has switched you to her particular line. This doesn't usually happen in a drug or food store cosmetics department because the cosmetician gets a commission on most of the lines she sells so she usually is conversant on all lines and more likely to cater to *your* preferences. I have great respect for the drug store cosmetician, as she is trained on everything from cosmetics to fragrance to hair color products. For overall assistance, I can't resist recommending these dedicated, friendly cosmeticians who make you feel welcome and comfortable in addition to providing extensive product knowledge. Best of all, most of them *look* the part.

Make-Up Base or Foundation Base

This is colored liquid foundation that just about every woman can wear to advantage. Few people have flawless complexions. Make-up or Foundation Base covers any blotchiness and gives a soft glow of color. Some beauticians advise the use of a dry sponge to apply make-up base, but I find this can give too heavy a coverage and is difficult to blend around eyes and hairline. A light touch with the finger tips to spread the liquid thinly and evenly is what I recommend. Never rub base into the skin, it is meant to *cover* not to penetrate. A light blending of color to enhance your own.

Skin type (oily, dry, combination); skin color tone; and skin structure all must be considered when choosing a make-up base. Two things you should look for in a base are *non-comedogenic* and *sunscreen* (unless you're using a sunscreen in your moisturizer). It is a mistake to choose a make-up base in too heavy a consistency. If you're hoping that it'll give more coverage, it won't, it'll just look unnatural, tend to settle in facial lines and accent their presence. The sheerer the better. Also don't select a shade lighter than your natural color. Match the base as closely as possible to your face. Often you'll be advised to test the color on the inside of the wrist, but this area is usually much paler than the face because it hasn't had the same exposure to the sun. Test the make-up base on the *back* of the wrist which more closely resembles your facial color. A shade a trifle darker than your natural color is all right, as it tends to cover any color imperfections in the skin. Basic make-up depths of color are: Light, Medium, Dark, or Extra Dark. Basic make-up shade tone categories are: Pink, Peach, or Beige. A red, flushed complexion is helped with a beige tone base to counteract the over-rosy appearance. A sallow or olive complexion needs a warming rose or peach tone. A person with a natural skin tone can wear any of the three shade tone bases quite effectively.

To help determine what color base would be best for you, take a *pink* towel (or any piece of fabric with no shine) and hold it next to your face. If the color of your skin looks fine next to *pink*, then a *pink* tone base will be suitable for you. Do the same with a *peach* or *pale orange* fabric. Or, place your hands with one on each piece of fabric, compare and decide which color looks better against your skin, then choose that shade tone for your make-up base. You may want to choose two depths of color, one for daytime and something a bit darker for evening when artificial lighting tends to drain color from the face. Be alert to complexion changes, from summer to winter and from young to older.

If you change your haircolor you must remember to re-evaluate your complexion and what needs changing in the colors of your apparel.

Blusher

There are various forms of face blushers from cream type to liquid type to powder blush-ons. Powder blush-ons are the most popular and easiest to apply. Here again, you'll find either *pink* or *peach* are the basic shade tones in varying depths of color. If you have a peach tone make-up base, your blusher must be of peach tone too and a pink base requires a pink tone blusher. Keep lipsticks and all color cosmetics in the same tone for a blended look. In selecting and applying blush-on powder:

> *(1) Be sure the product has a good brush.* Some inexpensive blushers are excellent but they don't provide a good brush. It's best to invest in a good blusher brush with sable bristles, and then you can use less expensive blush-ons.
>
> *(2) Never take the brush directly from the compact to your face.* Pick up the powder with the brush and shake off excess, then lightly apply to the face.
>
> *(3) To apply blush, draw an imaginary line from the pupil of the eye down to-ward the tip of the nose. Start color beneath the cheek bone and sweep out to-ward top of ear.* (See Fig. D) Just give a hint of color, don't overdo. Then, with minimal powder on the brush, *blend lightly* over entire face and neck.

Eyebrow Color

Eyebrows have as much impact on the face as a picture frame has on a picture. Too heavy and dark, and they overpower and detract from the picture. Too fine a line, and they give the face a blank expression. It is far better to leave the brows in their natural state, as nature intended, than to tweeze the brows too sparsely or unevenly. The eyebrows have such an influence on one's facial expression they can completely change one's appearance. If you want to tidy up the stragglers you should tweeze the hairs *below* the browline only. *Never* pluck from above.

Here's how: Look straight ahead into a mirror. *The arch of the eyebrow should be directly above the outside edge of the iris.* A common

Figure (s)

FIG B

BEGIN BROW

FIG A

ARCH OF EYEBROW

FIG C

END BROW

FIG D

BLUSHER

mistake is to paint or shape the centre of the arch of the brow directly over the centre of the eye instead of further out from the bridge of the nose. Hold a pencil angled from the side of the nostril to the outside edge of the iris (Fig. A) and make a small dot on the browline as it is here where the arch should be. To find where the brow should begin, place a pencil straight up from the side of the nostril (Fig. B). This is where the brow should start. Now hold the pencil diagonally against the outer corner of the eyelid (Fig. C) and, pointing up to the brow bone, this is where the brow should end. If the eyebrows are scant and need defining, use a brow pencil. I much prefer a metal brow pencil with very fine lead refills (like an eversharp pencil). Revlon and Max Factor have these pencils and one will last you a lifetime, as you just buy refills and can change colors if you change your hair color. With these fine, specially made, leads you can draw small, short strokes to fill in the browline and shape it with a natural look instead of heavy lines that are too distinct. These leads come in black, charcoal, brown, and auburn. Charcoal is the most natural looking color for almost everyone. After defining the browline to the ideal shape for your face, take a brow brush and gently *blend the shading*. An expert beautician can somewhat alter brow shapes to compensate for certain facial flaws, such as, if eyes are too far apart, brows can be pencilled in slightly closer to the bridge of the nose than to the inner corner of the eye. Or, close-set eyes will seem further apart if you start the browline slightly back from the inner corner of the eyes. *The ideal distance between the eyebrows should be the width of an eye*. It is important to use very light strokes and keep the line subtle. When shading the outside end of the eyebrow, be sure not to drop the curve down too much or you'll create a woeful, unhappy expression. We warned you that the eyebrows are very important to your facial expression so tamper with care!

Eyeliner

Many beautiful faces are reduced to "ugly" because of badly applied eyeliner. Eyeliner was created to enhance and draw attention to the *eye* not to the eyeliner. A heavy black line closes the eye in and gives the illusion of *reducing* the size of the eye, just the opposite effect you want to achieve. There are few women that use eyeliner effectively. Most of us weren't blessed with long, thick eyelashes, I think the "dealers-out" of eyelashes gave the best ones to men, so usually our eyes need some added emphasis.

Eyes are the windows of the soul. Isn't that a beautiful description? Here's a good way to define your eyes without detracting from their beauty. Using the *eyebrow pencil* described above and a charcoal lead, draw a soft line beneath and right next to the eyelashes, never *inside* the lashes, this looks unnatural, as eyelashes don't grow out of the whites of the eyes! Only apply liner on *2/3 of the top eyelid* from the outside corner of the eyelid to just past the centre to-ward the nose. Apply liner to *half the lower lid* from the centre to *almost* the outside corner of the lower lid. (See illustration.) It is better not to carry liner right to the end but to leave an open space at the outside corners of the eyes to give a wide open look, not closed in by a heavy line of eyeliner. Widen the line a little at the outside corners. Use light strokes, as this is very thin skin that stretches easily, eventually creating wrinkles if not handled gently. Your eyeshadow will complete the shading and coloring. I should mention that, because eye make-up smudges so easily, it is a wise thing to take a Q-tip and carefully wipe around each eye to remove any excess oil *before* applying any eye make-up, then blot (don't wipe) with a tissue to clean the eyelashes. After liner application—blend, blend, blend.

Eye Shadow

Eye shadow was first created in blues and mauves, so adults could tint their eyelids to closely resemble the soft, almost transparent, pale blue beauty of a baby's eyelid. Delicate and appealing. Sadly, this was misconstrued and women carried the blue color over the lids and right up to their eyebrows. Oh! Those big blue eyes, so unattractive that someone recently named a book condemning the use of blue eyeshadow totally. I don't agree. Used correctly, a soft hint of blue can widen the eye and make the white of the eye look whiter. A hint of light blue shadow carefully *blended* just below the eye has the same effect. To magnify small eyes (whose eyes are ever too big?) concentrate the liner, shadow, and mascara to-ward the outer portions from the centre of the eye out. So much depends on your facial bone structure and shape of eyes and face that I won't attempt to describe the many ways eye make-up can be used to contour, to shade, to add width or length, and to camouflage the negative. Clever selection of color to co-ordinate with your apparel can be very dramatic also. The most important thing to remember is *never to overdo*. If you aren't sure, ask an expert's advice.

Your eyes are your biggest asset. They convey everything you are feeling—happiness, sadness, interest, anger, compassion—don't let an overabundance of eyemakeup distort these powerful expressions.

Mascara

There are many types of mascaras. *It is imperative that you be aware that mascara can quickly become contaminated, and you should replace your mascara every 3 or 4 months to be sure bacteria has not flourished. Many serious eye infections have resulted from mascara.* Under a microscope you would see that there are microorganisms (a very small living animal!) right next to the eye on every-one's eyelashes. These microorganisims get on the mascara brush and are inserted back into the tube. Most mascaras have preservatives to kill this bug, but the defense system can suffer from overload and finally become contaminated. Your eyes are too valuable. Don't take a chance. Replace that mascara often.

TYPES OF MASCARA:

Mascara for Sensitive Eyes: These mascaras have *no* short fibres for lenthening and therefore are the best ones for contact lens wearers. Also, contact lens wearers should be careful of waterproof mascara because if it gets on the lens it will stick and tears can't wash it away.

Waterproof, Smudgeproof Mascara: All mascaras will smudge if the area is too oily. Be sure to gently blot away excess oil from eyes before applying eye makeup. Roll a corner of a tissue to make a point and get up under and over the eyelashes to blot the oil. A Q-tip works well if you're careful not to let little bits of cotton catch on the eyelashes.

Conditioning Mascaras have built in moisturizers and protein. They remain soft and pliable, not brittle, this means less lash breakage.

Colorless Mascara gives the lashes shape and body, but if your lashes are pale, you'll need to apply a second mascara for color. This can give a spikey, unnatural look. Careful!

Lengthening & Thickening Mascaras have short fibres that cling to the lashes to give them length. Never apply more than one coat of this type of mascara. At all times strive for the natural look. Attention should not be drawn to thick, clumpy, eyelashes.

GENERAL INFO ABOUT MASCARA:

- A charcoal or black/brown mascara is best for all unless your hair is very black, then a black mascara probably won't be too harsh.
- To color lower lashes, hold the mascara wand in a vertical position and sweep *across* the lashes, then straight down. The eyelashes will return to their natural position.
- Use an eyelash brush to gently separate lashes and remove clumps. Some mascaras have a dual purpose brush.

MASCARA REMOVER

Use a mascara remover designed for the type of mascara you're using i.e. waterproof. Close your eyes and gently wipe remover along lashes from roots to tips. Then another gentle stroke should remove mascara from bottom lashes. I recommend Bonne Bell's cotton squares instead of harsh tissues or synthetic balls if you are using a liquid mascara remover. Clifton's Mascara Remover Pads are excellent, there are so many in a jar they go a long way. They go a long way to protect sensitive eye tissue, because they are so mild. Andrea's Eye Q's to remove waterproof mascara, or Biotherm's Bio Cils for regular mascara removal. These removers, particularly Clifton's, can be left on the eye*lids to soften and condition*.

Eyelash curlers

Some women say they are excellent and I second the motion, however, some say that an eyelash curler gives the lashes a 90 degree bend and they don't like the effect. The problem, most likely, is the wrong kind of curler. A curler should have a *soft* rubber inset that is removable and replaceable. If you get anything other than a natural-looking curve from a curler, it is either because you're using a curler that is all metal with no rubber, or the rubber needs replacing because the curling bar has broken a ridge in the rubber inset. Another problem may be that you're squeezing the curler too tightly. Used properly, a quality eyelash curler can sweep your lashes upward and make them more visible. Curl the lashes *before* applying mascara.

Lipstick

It can't be too often stressed that cosmetics are meant to enhance. Unfortunately, too often they take on a life of their own and instead of being supporting cast and bit players on the scene, they take over the show. Many a show has been ruined by "ham" performance. The same old problems: too much, too little, or poor direction. For example, white lipstick was created to be worn as a highlighter over other lipstick, to contour and give a rounded, what is called a pouting, look to the mouth. In ignorance or in a mistaken idea it was high fashion, some women wore it alone. Occasionally I still see this awful sight and am reminded of something out of a horror movie. What could one possibly find appealing about a foamy-looking white mouth? Bring on the straight jacket!

Few people have a healthy red color to their lips; most have a blue color that isn't very attractive. *Every woman benefits from a little color that a lipstick can provide. Now, lipsticks are even more important because many of them contain a sunscreen.* The tissue of the lips is very, very thin and sensitive. Perhaps you've had problems with wearing lipstick—an allergic reaction from mild to severe can often result. If your lips get cracked and pebbly looking and the area beneath your mouth is red and itchy or your eyelids are itchy, it is probably an allergic reaction to lipstick or to nail enamel. After several years of treatment by a dermatologist, I found this is what I, myself, was having a problem with, and ever since then I have used either Almay or Marcelle lipsticks and nail enamels and have never experienced the slightest reaction, because they are truly hypoallergenic. There used to be far more problems with lipstick when, in the interests of making the color stay on longer, manufacturers used indelible dyes that tended to make the lips peel and crack. That's no longer the case. In fact, manufacturers now put conditioning ingredients in lipstick formulae. Now, a good quality lipstick is not only beautifying, its good for you! It'll put a prettier smile on your mouth and a broad grin on your self-esteem.

Lipstick colors are either of *pink* variety or of *peach* variety. *Pinks* are of a red/blue blend ranging from light pinks to deeper rose and purple tones. *Peaches* are of the red/yellow blend ranging from light peach to deeper orange and coral tones. Be sure your lipstick shade co-ordinates with your apparel. If a certain shade of lipstick doesn't suit you, it follows that you shouldn't wear that shade of apparel either.

LIPSTICK POINTERS

- Don't paint beyond the natural lip line. Sometimes, women with thin lips believe they'll improve the shape by going beyond the natural lip line, but it just looks strange and draws attention to a negative. Women with full lips are not as likely to try to paint them narrower, as full lips are regarded as a plus feature. I have noticed that some female television commentators paint their lips (or their make-up artists do) inside the line, and it greatly detracts from their commentating as we watch the strange contortions this creates. It's a good revelation of what not to do.

- A lip brush or a lip pencil can be of help in outlining and in correcting small irregularities in the natural lip line. Some beauticians suggest a lip pencil of a darker color for outlining the lips but, in my opinion, this too distinctly defines the lip line and gives a "paint by number" look to the face. I recommend using a lip pencil in the same shade as the lipstick.

- To make teeth look their whitest, choose a true red lipstick or paler pink with a bluish cast. Orangey reds, corals, and brownish tones can emphasize yellow undertones in tooth enamel.

- Try using two colors to contour the lips. After applying the base color, use a highlighter or lighter shade in the centre of the mouth to give a fuller appearance and a youthful glow.

- To keep color on your lips longer, try putting on a coat of lipstick and carefully blotting most of it off, then applying more lipstick. A liquid lip stain as a base before applying your lipstick also works well. If you find an indelible dye doesn't irritate your lips, you'll appreciate the long lasting color of the COTY 24 line.

Masks

Masks can be beneficial to women and to men too, look what one did for Batman! A mask serves three purposes:

(1) Helps to lift excess oil and impurities from the facial pores.

(2) Acts as an exfoliant to remove flaking skin.

(3) Tones and invigorates facial tissue.

An important thing to remember when using a mask is not to put it on the area around the eyes. Pulling off a mask would stretch this delicate skin and be destructive. Remove a peel-off mask carefully, you want to lift any accumulation from the pores that is clinging to the dried mask, but you don't want to stretch the skin on your face. Some masks are designed to stimulate the complexion by stirring up the circulation. Test a bit of this type of product on the inside of your elbow first to be sure it will not be too irritating for your face. A weekly clay mask may be helpful for troubled skin.

Frequent skin eruptions indicate a problem that may not only be a surface reaction. It could be a hormonal imbalance or many other reasons. No product should be applied to a troubled complexion without first seeing a dermatologist to determine the cause of the problem.

Hair removal

There are now several methods of hair removal.

> (1) Removal at the skin's surface:
>> • Shaving
>> • Depilatories
> (2) Bleaching: Not actually removed but lightened.
> (3) Pulling out by the roots:
>> • Waxing
>> • Tweezing
>> • Rotary coil implement
> (4) Electrolysis: Permanent hair removal.

Shaving

> • Shaving does not make hair grow more coarse nor does shaving encourage hair growth as is commonly believed. The hair, when it first emerges from the skin, *seems* more coarse be

cause its end is bluntly cut and no longer has the wispy point that it had prior to shaving.

- Shaving cuts off hair at the skin's surface so it is only a matter of days before the hair needs shaving again.
- Shave against the direction of the hair growth. If using a blade razor, use a shaving foam or cream to help the razor glide over the skin smoothly and avoid nicks. Shaving cream softens the hair so it is more easily cut.
- An electric shaver may not cut the hair quite as close as a blade but it leaves the skin less irritated so can be used as frequently as necessary.
- It is best to shave underarms before going to bed at night and not to apply underarm deodorant until the next morning to avoid irritation from chemicals which, applied to freshly shaven skin, close the pores and create ingrown hairs.
- Shaving is the least expensive way of removing hair, but care must be taken as curly hair can easily become ingrown and infected. Change the razor blade often to be sure it is sharp and clean. Clean the head of an electric shaver very frequently, so it functions properly.

Depilatories

Chemicals in hair removal lotions, creams, foams, etc., come in various strengths to "melt" the hair below the skin's surface. The product is spread thickly over the area to be treated and left on for 6 to 10 minutes. It is then rinsed away with the melted hair.

- New growth is as soft as natural regrowth (no blunt ends) and lasts about two weeks.
- This method can be used on stomach, bikini line, legs, face, and arms, depending on the strength of the lotion.
- Be sure to use the gentlest strength for the face. Keep away from the eyes and eyebrows and protect the eyes when rinsing the product off.
- Always do a skin test for allergic reactions, these are strong chemicals. If you have no adverse effects, this is probably the best hair removal method available. The hair's root is not damaged and there is less probability of infection. Usually, it is not a painful procedure.
- It's quick, easy to do and is relatively inexpensive.

Bleaching

A specially formulated beaching agent is smoothed over the area to be treated and, after about 15 to 25 minutes, is rinsed off. The hair is lightened just to the surface of the skin and the regrowth will begin showing after about 4 days.

- When using bleaching products be careful of the eyes as these are very strong products and can damage your sight.
- If the hair is very dark and is not bleached enough it will be an orange color.
- If the hair is bleached very light, keep in mind that it will be very obvious against dark skin. There are only specific cases where bleaching is an effective method. Consider this method carefully.

Waxing

Hair removal by waxing, tweezing, or rotary coil, pulls the hair out by the roots. This can eventually damage or distort the hair follicle, so that future hair growth may grow in misshapen and unruly. There is much more possibility for infection, as you are leaving the pores wide open to bacteria.

- With waxing, warm wax is melted and then smoothed on with a spatula *(with the grain of the hair)*. If you use cold wax, it comes coated on strips that you press on the hair that is to be removed and then peel it off.
- Pull the wax off against the direction of the hair growth, and this removes the hair, root and all.
- Hair doesn't appear again for 6 to 8 weeks, *but* you have to let the hair grow to a length of 1/16 of an inch long before it can be waxed again or the wax has nothing on which to cling. Are you ready to go into hiding a lot?
- Warm wax treatments at home are messy and time consuming so it is better to go to a salon for this method.

Tweezing

You manually pull out each individual hair with tweezers, so this method is only used in small areas like eyebrow shaping or to remove stray hairs on face, stomach, or breasts.

- Treat the area afterwards, to cut down on infection.
- Results last about 2—3 weeks.

Rotary coil implement

This is an appliance that looks like an electric razor, but instead of shaving off the hair, it has a coil head that grasps the hairs and pulls them out by the roots.

- Use quick circular motions on the legs only.
- Results last 3 to 4 weeks, but there is an awkward growing out time between treatments, as the hair has to be at least 1/16 inch long for the appliance to perform.
- I say, "*Ouch!*"

Electrolysis

To permamently remove hair, there is a method that involves electricity. Every hair is zapped with electricity which kills the root, and the hair does not grow again. This has proven to be a boon to women who need this help. It is very time consuming, but once done is permanent. It takes several visits to a licensed practitioner to finally treat each and every hair but don't get discouraged, if the attendant is capable, you'll be pleased with the final results.

With any hair removal method you must be scrupulously clean. The root of each hair has direct contact with the blood stream, and there is danger, particularly with the methods that pull hairs out by the roots, leaving the pores open to infection.

I have great sympathy for women who must cope with this problem. Though I believe one should do as little as possible to disrupt the normal function of the human body, I'm glad there are products that are helpful in instances such as removing superfluous hair. Removing hair from face, arms and legs may be necessary. I have to say, however, that a woman doesn't project a polished image running around in a G-string...so.... maybe we shouldn't be depending on *certain* hair removal products but should shop for more adequate coverage in a swim suit!

Hygiene

Feminine hygiene & deodorant products

Listening to the advertisers of feminine hygiene products, we're convinced that women are closely related to that little black animal with the stripes down its back. All people, male and female, should strive to be clean, but these so-called feminine hygiene products are *unnecessary*. **An underarm deodorant** and frequent showering and bathing is sufficient. The human body is able to maintain its healthy balance if we don't interfere with its natural functions.

Oral hygiene

We've all been taught to brush our teeth and floss regularly. It goes without saying that regular visits to the dentist will keep on top of any problems. Try these hints:

- Brushing the teeth with baking soda can get rid of stains. Soda keeps teeth as white as they can naturally be.
- Use baking soda at least once a week or twice a day in place of your usual dentifrice. Freshens the breath too.
- A soaking of hot water laced with plenty of salt is good for the gums and disinfects any small abrasions in the mouth. Take a mug and fill it with water as hot as you can comfortably stand (not hot enough to burn you, of course), place two teaspoons of salt in the water, stir. Take a mouthful of this salt water and hold it in the mouth for half a minute. Swish it about to get it into all areas of the gums and teeth and gargle a little into the throat. Spit it out. Continue to do this until the cup is emptied. It's very healing. Repeat once a week.
- I wonder why mouth washes are blue or green. They make one look like a dragon every time the mouth is opened. I find it really funny to speak with someone who wields a green or blue tongue flipping about. LAVORIS™ or STERI/SOL™ are very effective and leave a nice rosy colored mouth.

Fingernails—The flags of good grooming

Your hands are always right out in front. Let me point out that we often use our hands to express ourselves, and we always place our hands in full view when we sign for something. Your hands silently convey a lot of information about you. Hand out a favorable message.

Here are some good "rules of thumb":
(1) Be sure your fingernails are clean. Expensive diamond rings or even a Rolex watch won't help your image if dirty, jagged fingernails share the territory.

- An effective cleaning method is to scrub your nails with a toothbrush and toothpaste.
- Don't use sharp objects to clean your nails, or you'll make scratches beneath the nail where dirt will collect and be difficult to remove. Use an orangewood stick tipped with a bit of absorbent cotton soaked in hydrogen peroxide to clean beneath the nails, helps whiten them too.

(2) Don't cut your nails with scissors or clippers. This encourages the nails to split and to crack.

(3) Invest in a good nail file to shape your nails, one made with diamond dust so fine it doesn't tear the nail. These are not expensive but are unsurpassed for efficiency. Never use a "scored" metal file. Use good quality, fine, not coarse, emery boards.

- File in one direction only, from the side to the tip of the nail. Finish with a very fine emery board. Revlon supplies an extra fine one. Look for them in the cosmetics departments of your drug or mega-food store. These emery boards are pale pink in color and come several to a package in a blister pack. You can get an absolutely smooth edge to your nails with this item. Choose the *finest* grain, not the coarse, to finish filing.
- Don't file too much off the sides of the nail as this weakens it. The curved part of the nail should start where the tip of the finger ends.

(4) Never cut the cuticle. The cuticle is the skin that grows around the

base of the nail. *This cuticle must be constantly pushed back, just after washing the hands while the skin is soft and pliable, to keep it from extending up the nail, causing hangnails and looking unsightly.* Don't let your manicurist cut this cuticle (change manicurists if this ever happens). Use a cuticle massage cream and, if necessary, a cuticle remover gel.

- Cuticle remover lotion has oils and nutrients to soften the cuticle and gently dissolve this dead skin.
- Handle the cuticle gently, as this is the root of the nail, it is here that the cells are renewed and the nail grows. Too much pressure can bruise the nailbed, and the nail will form badly.

(5) If you wear nail enamel, be sure it is in good repair. Remove it rather than wear it chipped or patched. Clear nail enamel is always attractive (for men too) and protects the nails. If your nails are short or bitten (tut! tut!), colored nail enamel will only draw attention to them but clear enamel improves their appearance.

(6) Allergic reaction to nail enamel happens quite frequently. Often, people are not aware that when they have itchy eyelids and/or red, itchy spots on their chin and neck it is because they are allergic to the ingredients in nail enamel. Because their hands are far from their face, they never suspect the real culprit. The blood stream beneath and at the base of the nails carries the offending toxin through the system and shows up in an allergic reaction on the eyelids and chin. This takes days and weeks to go away and, if the use of the irritating product is not discontinued, can advance into a weeping, peeling condition. Allergies cannot be treated lightly. After spending wads of money for dermatologists' services, it was finally determined that I was allergic to nail enamel. It was a great day for me to discover AL-MAY products, and for many years I've been able to use nothing but ALMAY nail enamels, because they are more hypo-allergenic with none of the chemicals that usually trigger reactions. I recommend this line wholeheartedly even for people without problems of allergy.

(7) The key word for "on the job" nails is conservatism. The length should be no longer than 1/4 inch past the end of the finger, for women, and just to the finger's end, for men. I might say here that I've

noticed that some men clip their nails right up to the quick. This can cause infections and really is not very attractive. Why not leave a small edge? Concerned that you might have to clean your nails too often? Ah! but well groomed nails look so terrific and say such nice things about you. . . . give it a try. I'm picking on you, sir, only because I want to see you looking as great as you have the potential to look. You must have heard about that survey that revealed the three things women notice first about a man. I'll let you guess number one, but number two is his hands and number three is the back of his neck. So there! Give yourself a hand that's a "10" (full marks—one for each fingernail).

(8) To remove nail enamel, use an oily nail polish remover and wash the hands immediately with fairly warm water to remove this harsh product as quickly as possible. Never leave polish remover on your nails, as it will dry them and crack them. Inexpensive polish remover is as good as *any*.

(9) Use cotton squares (Bonne Bell's) to remove nail enamel. Synthetic balls do not absorb the polish remover, so it slides under the nails carrying polish with it to discolor the skin beneath and around the nails.

(10) When you apply a protein conditioner to your hair, rub it into your fingernails too. Your nails and hair are of the same substance, so give your nails a treatment too.

(11) Occasionally, massage the roots of the fingernails with a little warm, pure olive oil. They'll thrive on the attention. There are excellent nail conditioners on the market. Get your cosmetician to help you with your selection.

(12) Buffing with a chamois nail buffer is good for the circulation and encourages strong nail growth.

(13) A nail that is lost as a result of an accident, takes anywhere from 4.5 to 6 months to renew itself. Use creams and nutrients to help it grow. It would be wise to protect it with a finger guard, or if it is damaged further it may grow back deformed.

(14) Artificial Nails: When your nails aren't looking their best, you may be tempted to use acrylic nails or nail extenders.

Sculptured nails are formed by mixing an acrylic powder with liquid acrylic to make a paste. This is pasted on to the existing nail base. I don't recommend that you do this yourself because, unless you are ambidextrous, one hand won't be very skillful. Have sculpturing done professionally.

These nails usually last 3 to 4 weeks before they'll need to be refurbished, *however,* this process can cause serious problems. Some people are allergic to the strong chemicals in the acrylics or in the glue used to attach tips in nail extension. The natural nail can become irritated. *There is a high occurrence of infection because acrylic nails, nail tips, and nail wraps move up as the nail grows, leaving a space at the end of the nail. As the artificial nail lifts from the natural nail, a space is created where dirt can get in and bacteria can thrive.* If this gap isn't cleaned immediately, a fungal infection is the result. Before having any artificial nail reglued, be sure to dip the finger in alcohol to prevent infection. *At the first sign of pain or infection, have the false nail removed and see a doctor.*

If only one or two of your natural nails are short and broken, giving your hand just an 8 or 9 points out of a possible 10, why not try good quality, reusable "stick-on" artificial nails? Revlon's Nylon Reusable Nails (Natural Length) are excellent. If you follow the directions exactly, you'll be pleasantly surprised how well the adhesive tabs hold these nails in place for at least a week, with care.

In my opinion, they look more natural than sculptured acrylic nails, and they do not cause half the problems. You can easily apply them yourself, for *much* less cost. You probably can't wear more than two or three at a time, as you'd be left kind of helpless if you have to cater to more than that many "handicapped" fingers. Stick on nails don't relate well to keyboards, that's asking too much of any adhesive

Artificial nails of all types require dedicated care and attention. Most of them don't contribute much to a polished image. Those shaped like long claws, look awful.

Hand lotions and creams

Of the huge selection available, it is simply a matter of finding which one does the most for *you.* A waterproof lotion or cream is superb used prior to doing household chores, to protect the hands from detergents.

Other than a protective lotion, I like to use a scented hand lotion that not only provides treatment, but lends a pleasant aroma. Most of the fine quality fragrance lines such as Chanel; Nina Ricci; Lanvin; Hermes; Oscar de la Renta; make a good quality hand lotion, and the fragrance is so delightful every time you use it. Much less expensive than perfumes and colognes and not nearly so intrusive, try a luxury hand lotion that gives you a psychological lift every time you use it. *Mmmmmmm!* "Royal Secret" by Germaine Monteil.

Fragrance—Leading people around by the nose?

Have you noticed how often, if you catch the scent of something, it will bring a sudden reminder of another time, another place, another occasion, or even of another person? The smell of freshly baked bread, for instance, reminds one of a warm kitchen and a cosy home. A whiff of pine needles, and a scene of carefree camping days flashes through one's mind. We closely associate smells with particular situations—the smell of onions frying, and we're immediately at the fair. These reminders can arouse pleasant or unpleasant memories.

Why are we so influenced by scent, and why does it make such a profound and permanent imprint on our memory? There's a very real explanation: *the olfactory nerve in the nose is the only nerve in the human body that is directly connected to the brain.* The word olfactory comes from the Latin word olfacere which means "to smell." Every scent that contacts the olfactory nerve has far more lasting effect than do the things we touch or hear or see. *You can understand then, how important the fragrance we impart can be.* A message sent directly to the brain, leaving a lasting imprint and impression. Engrave your personal signature pleasantly.

The market abounds in a variety of superb fragrance products from light colognes and after-shave lotions for men, to more concentrated colognes and perfumes for women. Take advantage of this captivating way to enhance another dimension of your image.

What you should know about fragrance.

After pointing out to you that the price difference in some skin care products is not always justified, you may wonder if the vast difference in the prices of various perfumes and fragrance lines is realistic. Can there really be that much difference in the value of a $10 bottle of perfume, to the dram of perfume selling for hundreds of dollars? *Yes! Most of the time.* Four factors actually affect the price. Rely on the first three factors, be cautious of the fourth. They are: (1) The quality of the ingredients. (2) The rarity of the ingredients and development expertise. (3) The packaging of the product. (4) The exclusiveness of the product, priced high to keep it prestigious.

(1) The quality of the product. Cheap fragrance (I usually use the word "inexpensive" when making reference to price, but when it comes to low price perfumes there is one word only, cheap!) smells *cheap.* Poorly formulated fragrances lose their character rapidly and tend to all smell alike (Phew!) after a short time. These scents are usually created by mixing synthetics with alcohol. These products come onto the market with a great advertising flourish, and in a few short years (months?) they vanish and, like prosaic people, we can't even remember their names.

As for the fragrances the industry calls The Imposters, well, as with any imposters, who has any faith in them after awhile? Their advertising says: "If you like Chanel #5, you'll love XYZ Imposter" or "If you like Georgio, you'll love XYZ Imposter." Actually, they don't even compare. Perhaps the ads should say: "If you like fooling yourself, go ahead and smell offensively!" Am I too harsh in my critique? You be the judge—if the advertising claims were true, wouldn't these inexpensive copies take over the market? Why is their popularity so fleeting? Take my word for it, you'll never put on the polish with a cheap fragrance. Better to go without, or invest in a good quality, lightly scented hand lotion that will please you and all those around you.

(2) The rarity of the ingredients and development expertise. Quality fragrance lines are made from such truly sensational ingredients as the attar (oil) distilled from millions of rose petals. Costly? Of course, but how very appealing. Not only are the floral, musk, citron, and

other components that are used in quality perfumes costly to obtain, but an important ingredient called a "fixative" is rarest and costliest of all. This fixative does just what the word indicates, it stabilizes the scent, so it holds its true characteristics. That fixative is *the* major difference between an inexpensive and a quality fragrance.

Most of the finest perfumes come from France. Grasse is renowned throughout the world for producing the finest quality essential oils. It's an expensive process. For example it takes 750 kilograms of jasmine petals to make one kilogram of essential oil which to-day costs about $40,000.00. The person who finally determines the exact blend is called a "nose", and this highly developed expertise is rare indeed. Probably the world's most famous "nose" is Jacques Polge, director of Chanel's laboratory of perfume. A perfume that is created with this combination of quality ingredients and scientific expertise has to reflect these costs in its price.

(3) Fragrance Packaging: Packaging doesn't only refer to the box in which the fragrance is packed. Mainly, packaging means the bottle holding the product. Fragrance manufacturers compete to have the most magnificent packaging and can win design awards for outstanding creations. We must pay for this elaborate presentation and, if our budget will allow, we willingly do so. These beautiful and valuable containers such as the swirled design of Nina Ricci's L'Air du Temps bottle of Lalique crystal with its dove-shaped stopper, are more than a bottle of perfume, they become a decorative treasure. Fragrance is a luxury. I object to unnecessary and elaborate packaging on products vital to our survival but these gorgeous bottles appeal to anyone's love of beauty and the product within deserves an elegant "etui." A product's packaging and a person's surroundings are very much a part of their total image.

(4) The exclusivity of the product. Not all expensive fragrances are created equal. Some very expensive perfumes are named for famous clothing designers or film stars. These are referred to as "celebrity" lines and you pay for the manufacturer's use of that famous name. In some instances the product *may* be of fine quality but the price is *always* exorbitant and often the fragrance is raucous and forceful, not

having had the benefit of being created by an expert "nose." So how do you determine whether the price is justified, that the fragrance will have the true characteristics of a fine perfume and that you're not just paying for a celebrity's name? I suggest that, before you pay a huge price for a perfume, you wait until it has been on the market for awhile. A truly fine fragrance never loses its popularity. Years become decades and still the lovely fragrance captures the public's favor. What better criterion in determining quality? *Excellence speaks for itself!*

The selection, care, and application of fragrance

HOW TO PURCHASE

- Shop for fragrance in stores that have busy fragrance departments so you're sure of getting *fresh stock*. Don't overlook discount operations, as these substantial price reductions make stock move quickly.
- *Never just smell the demonstration bottle*. It will tell you nothing about the actual scent. *Fragrance does not reveal its true character in a bottle or even sprayed on a tissue as some salesclerks sometimes try to demonstrate it. A perfume needs to develop with the heat of the body and the individual's particular body chemistry before all essences used in its formula come into play*. Perfumers refer to this as having a *top*, *middle*, and *bottom note*. When the scent is first applied, you will be aware of just the top note. As the scent develops with the warmth of your body and mixed with your body chemicals, the middle note becomes more intense. Finally, after a few hours of wear, when the fragrance starts to fade, the bottom note develops. A top quality fragrance, expertly formulated with effective ingredients, will retain its true character throughout this development. When you sniff the demonstration bottle you show your lack of knowledge of fragrance, and you don't get the true scent of that product.
- *Never test more than two fragrances at one time*. If you want to make a comparison, spray one scent on the inside of one wrist and another scent on the other wrist. Go do the rest of your

shopping and let these scents develop. What you have found to be a pleasant fragrance on someone else may not be at all pleasant on you. Each person's body chemistry can profoundly change a fragrance.

The reason you should not test more than two fragrances at one time is because these are very concentrated, and the olfactory nerve goes into overload and can't determine the difference in more than two at one time. Men should test aftershave lotions and colognes in this way, too. A fragrance can be distorted most disagreeably if worn by a person who smokes or has very oily skin. The combination of nicotine that the body exudes and the highly concentrated ingredients in a fragrance, can be objectionable. It is better to wear none at all.

• Because a fragrance has a "big" name and a lot of advertising, don't be fooled into thinking that everybody likes it so you should wear it. Some fragrances are very strong and quite intrusive, yet people buy them for the celebrity name only. *A scent's appeal or lack of appeal is an individual preference, so we must be careful to wear it very discreetly.*

• *Know the fragrance forms and how to use them.* Perfume; Perfume Oil; Perfumed Bath Oil; Eau De Toilette; Eau de Parfum; Cologne (Eau De Cologne); Toilet Water. Fragrance is available in various strengths to be used in a specific way. It may seem to you that you don't need every strength, but to get the most value for your dollar, to wear it properly and to enjoy it to its fullest, there are 5 steps to a fragrance ensemble.

THEY ARE:

Step One: Bath Oil and Scented Bath Soap leave a mantle of fragrance over the entire body.

Step Two: After the bath, Bath Powder or Lotion set the fragrance base and keep it going.

Step Three: Spray-on or Splash-on Cologne or Eau de Toilette give a light finishing touch and help the more expensive perfume, that you'll apply last, go further.

Step Four: Perfume or Perfume Oil is used as a climax to this ensemble, and these most intense versions bring the fragrance to its full potential and keep it lingering longer. Perfume and Perfume Oil should be used very sparingly.

Step Five: Touch Up. Every few hours a light touch-up refreshes the scent. This is a perfume in a convenient purse size container to carry along with you.

Wear a fragrance all in one scent. Don't use a soap in one scent and a body lotion or powder in another then apply a cologne or perfume in another. If you are going to use a perfume or cologne only, be sure your bath soap, talc, deodorant, and hand lotion are unscented, so as not to compete with the final touch. Otherwise, you'll defeat the purpose of your investment in a fine perfume or cologne.

A Fragrance Ensemble is all in one particular scent. *Perfume or perfume oil* is the most concentrated form of fragrance. It is meant to be applied sparingly to the pulse spots where it will develop quickly with the heat of the body; inside wrist, inside elbow, back of knees, base of throat, cleft of bosom, and *front* of ears (there are no pulse spots behind the ears).

Toilet water, eau de toilette, cologne, eau de perfume, are all lighter, less concentrated (diluted with alcohol) fragrance forms designed to impart a light scent over the entire body. There are no specific rules about levels of concentration, so you'll find that fragrances of this type vary from one product line to another. Usually when both eau de toilette and cologne are available in a line, the cologne is the lighter of the two. Eau de parfum is usually more intense and concentrated than either. Your salesclerk should be able to advise you and guide your selection. At least, having read this book, "Putting on the Polish," you'll be a more knowledgeable customer in making that selection.

A Fragrance Collection consists of sets of fragrance ensembles. Even if you don't invest in every item in an ensemble and you plan to wear fragrance, you should have at least two fragrances in your collection. Why? There are two reasons: (1) because you wear fragrance not just appeal to others but for the pleasure it gives you. If you wear the same fragrance day after day you get so accustomed to it that it almost doesn't register with your brain after a while, so you can't enjoy it as much. When you become less aware of the fragrance you're wearing, what do you do? You apply more fragrance, and more and more. That brings us to reason number (2) for having an alternative scent: the people around you are so overwhelmed that they almost suffocate in your presence, and you aren't even aware that you're wearing *too much*.

In adding to your fragrance collection, remember that the lasting popularity of well known, classic fragrances have never been over-shadowed by "celebrity" scents. We might be influenced to try these for a short time, but the long established favorites continue to keep more than their share of the market. When choosing fragrance you'll know that your dollar is well spent with any of the following classics:

CHANEL:

#5 (a leader since 1921) made in Grasse, France, from roses and jasmine. Could anyone object to this light, floral scent? Best of all, it seems to relate well to all types of body chemistry and, though it's aroma is a bit different on each person that wears it, it is always de-lightful.

#22 (created in 1922) a blend of white flowers only.

#19 (created in 1970) a woodsy-mossy scent.

Cristalle (created in 1975) a flowery-fruity fragrance.

Coco (created in 1984) to honor Coco Chanel.

LANVIN:

Arpege (1927) jasmine and rose with a wood base. Bottled in opa-que black glass, as all perfumes should be bottled, to protect it from light.

GUERLAIN:

Shalimar (1925) even the name is appealing, it means "abode of love" and is an oriental scent. Quite intense.

WORTH:

Je Riviens (1932)

CHRISTIAN DIOR:

Miss Dior (1947)

NINA RICCI:

L'Air du Temps (1948)

Other reliables are: *Ma Griffe* (My Signature) by CARVEN; *Caleche* by HERMES; *Ysatis* and *Givenchy 3* by GIVENCHY, *Bal A' Versailles* by JEAN DESPREZ; *Oscar* by DE LA RENTA. Newcomers, sure to be eventual classics, are these: *Panthere*, CARTIER's newest fragrance; and *Evere*, a blend of floral bouquets and oriental notes in a crystal bottle from the ERNO LASZLO INSTITUTE. These are favorites, you'll find many others. Some of which are: SALVADOR DALI'S: *Laguna*, ESTEE LAUDER'S: *Spellbound*, LIZ TAYLOR'S: *White Diamonds*, CALVIN KLINE'S: *Escape*, LANCOME'S: *Tresor*, GUCCI'S: *L'Art di Gucci*, CALVIN KLINE'S: *Obsession* (for him & for her), CHRISTIAN DIOR'S: *Poison*, GUY LAROCHE'S: *Drakkar Noir* for men, ESTEE LAUDER'S: *Aramis* for men. There's no greater enhancement to your image than the rapture you impart by wearing a lovely fragrance.

- Fragrance can be light, medium, or heavy. Florals usually appeal to everyone just as does nature's own garden of flowers. That is probably why Chanel #5 is so popular. Formulae with musk in the base are usually quite heavy and not favored by all. You've heard that somewhat crude rule for effective communication: KISS (Keep It Simple, Stupid), well, the rule for communicating with fragrance is KILL: (Keep It Light, Lady). Kill the urge to overindulge. See the chapters on etiquette for the etiquette of fragrance.
- Keep your fragrance products in a dark, cool place. Light and heat deteriorate delicate ingredients. When I see prestige fragrance displayed under hot lights in a store's showcase, I shudder at the abuse. Be sure you don't purchase any product that has been treated in this way.
- Avoid spraying fragrance on clothing. It can discolor fabric and is very hard on furs. Also don't apply fragrance where metal will touch it (your watch or jewelry), metal distorts the scent and perfume can discolor jewelry.
- Never use a fragrance in an endeavor to mask other odors. It doesn't mask the odor, it just tends to make it more foul. A splash of fragrance is no substitute for a bath and a deodorant!
- *Speaking of odors, please, oh please, don't refer to something that has a pleasant smell as an "odor." Say: fragrance; scent; perfume; bouquet; aroma; redolence.* Excuse me, but, to put it bluntly, the word "odor" stinks.

• When you're Putting on the Polish with perfume, it's better to have a little of the best than a lot of the inferior. You want to be a real *knockout*, but not by way of a powerfully fragrant punch on the nose!

CHAPTER THREE

DRESS

FOR

PROGRESS

CHAPTER THREE

DRESS FOR PROGRESS

Apparel for Women and for Men

Dressing for success has its pitfalls. What is success? To some it may mean landing a date with a good-looking co-worker. To others it may mean getting a lot of money (by fair means or foul!). To others it has quite different connotations. Dressing for success could be anything from a micro-mini skirt for a woman or a muscle-revealing tank top for a man to a severely tailored business suit for either.

Dressing for progress, however, means dressing for advancement, for betterment, for psychological and cultural development, for gain and for growth. This would rule *out* that micro-mini skirt or muscle-revealing tank top, and it would rule *in* standards of refinement. Progress is not as fleeting as success can sometimes be, so, as is the rule of stability and security, progress takes more commitment and endeavor to achieve.

In the 1980's some women thought that to assert themselves they had to dress like men. They strutted about in severely tailored suits; man tailored trousers; massive shoulder pads; big, B-I-I-I-G clothes. *Some* women followed that dress code, but others refused to, knowing it would only tend to indicate some kind of insecurity.

Welcome to the 1990's

- Women are not so insecure that we have to do anything so falsely dramatic to prove our worth.
- We know, as women, we're different than men. Just as capable, just as decisive, just as sensible—but different. We

recognize it and are secure in that difference. We now can let our apparel reflect that secure difference.

• Now we don't wear football player's shoulder pads to show that we can be effective *team* players whether at business or on the home front.

• Since women have begun to respect ourselves for what we are (terrific!), fashion designers can no longer con us into being slaves to certain skirt lengths, colors, or fashion trends. *We wear what most becomes and appeals to us and what best suits our lifestyles.*

• Men have always been out in the business world, and the old boys' school ties were there to help and guide them. Men's business apparel has changed very little, and that's because *they learned decades ago that good quality apparel of classic and traditional style never goes out of fashion and always is a wise investment.* Unfortunately, the Hippie era and the Let's Go Offbeat trend convinced some men that 5 o'clock shadow and slovenly clothing were "cool." Now, however, young men are realizing the importance of a professional image and are seeking the advice of image consultants.

• What I like best about the '90's is we've reached a stage where men in all classes of labor are respected. *Where men in all classes of labor respect themselves.* The tradesman and entrepreneur can now enjoy an income comparable to that of the lawyer or senior executive, and now he dresses to reflect that progress. If he doesn't, he should. The information on "First Impressions" that follows applies to men as well as to women.

These are the 1990's but certain things never change. First impressions are still crucial and apparel influences those first impressions with these 8 evaluations:

(1) *Your economic level* is determined by the *quality* of your clothes.

(2) *Your intellectual level* is determined by the *quality* of your clothes and the intelligence you've used in *selecting* your clothes.

(3) *Your reliability* is determined by the care and grooming of *all* your apparel. Well groomed clothes but run-down

unpolished shoes indicate a facade of quality, but what else are you hiding?

(4) Your social position is determined by the *quality* and *style* of your clothes. We tend to dress the way our peers and close associates dress.

(5) Your level of refinement is determined by the *quality* and *coordination* of your clothes and *accessories*.

(6) Your moral standards are decided by the *quality* and *style* of your clothes. *A person who cares about quality, applies that attitude to their morals as well as to their clothes.* Too short skirts and deeply plunging necklines on women, and skin tight pants on men reveal more than their anatomy when they dress daringly. Keep in mind that "the less one is revealed, the more one is revered!"

(7) Your present success is decided by the *quality* and *suitability* of your clothes to the occasion.

(8) Your potential for progress is decided by the *quality, style, coordination, care and suitability* of your *apparel* and is greatly influenced by your *confidence (which is greatly bolstered by being appropriately dressed).*

Therefore:
(1) Buy the best quality you can afford.
(2) Buy traditional, classic styles.

Dress for progress: *Look the part*
Behave the part
And you'll be the part!

Choosing a Clothing Consultant

• A knowledgeable Clothing Consultant can save you a lot of money, in addition to polishing your image. Because people are realizing how important this is, the popularity of Image

Consultants has risen. This is not a certified trade, however, so be careful who you engage to do the job.

- *This book, "Putting on the Polish," gives most of the information necessary to enhance your image. You shouldn't require an image consultant if you pay heed to the advice provided on these pages.* However, because of the many aspects involved in choosing a practical wardrobe: lifestyle, body shape, appeal, budget, etc., no printed word could be specific enough for every reader, so if you have need of more help in this area, a *clothing* consultant may be of service.

- *If you do engage the services of a clothing consultant, be sure to determine their credentials i.e. actual experience in determining the type of clothing you require.* For instance, a consultant with little or no experience as an employee in the corporate world often chooses clothing inappropriate for a business environment. A consultant closely attuned to high fashion may be too impressed with choosing the "flashy" as opposed to clothing selection of a more enduring, conservative styling and quality.

- *Ask for a pre-contract interview with the consultant.* In this interview ask for evidence of their performance, perhaps to see pictures of some of their past clients' "make-overs." Don't rule out a consultant if they decline to name names, as most clients want strict privacy and an ethical consultant will honor their request. *The appearance of the consultant will tell you a great deal as to his or her ability, as will the management and quality of the interview.*

- If, after engaging the consultant, the clothing selection doesn't appeal to you, *say so, and don't buy it*. No matter how correct it is alleged to be, if *you* don't like it it will undermine your confidence when you wear it. You needn't be intimidated by the consultant's objections, *a good consultant can find what is right for you and please your tastes also*. You must feel inspired and pleased about what the consultant selects for you to wear, or the entire assignment has lost its purpose.

- *Consultants are of various categories.* Clothing consultants, etiquette consultants, etc., each specialize in their particular service. An *image* consultant should be capable of *improving every facet of your image that needs a polish, from your voice to your shoelaces.*

- **With this book, "Putting on the Polish," you'll be able to initiate these improvements yourself in the privacy of your own home without anyone knowing you needed a little help. "Putting on the Polish" is your resident image consultant. Always right there to bolster your confidence.**

WOMEN OF THE 1990's

How to begin to develop an effective wardrobe

A man's or a woman's wardrobe investment is attuned to the kind of work they do. It stands to reason that someone in a high profile, public position would need more *dress clothes* than someone in an outdoor job who can wear jeans and workclothes much of the time.

(1) Determine your lifestyle and your body type.

Tastes, body shapes, and lifestyles change, and your closet probably has many items you will never wear again. Ask yourself what kind of an image you want to project. Please, *if it is not business-like, don't be influenced by what others are wearing in your work place. Too often we set our standards this way and neglect the opportunity to DRESS FOR PROGRESS, to stand out as someone with the potential for advancement. What do you want your image to be? One of progress? Then keep this image in mind as you sort through your present wardrobe. Evaluate each item as to how it relates to the look you want to develop.*

(2) Take an inventory of the apparel you now have. Make an inventory list under these headings:

Item	Color	Fabric	Fits? Yes/No	Color? Yes/No	Matches? Yes/No	Lifestyle Yes/No	Keep? Yes/No

Take all your clothes out of the closet, put them on the bed or wherever it is convenient. Take each piece of clothing, one at a time and, using your inventory list, evaluate it.

As you evaluate each piece, decide whether to keep it, store it, sell it, or give it away! Put the "keepers" back in the closet and put the other pieces in a pile to be attended to.

(3) Make a second inventory list showing, by item, what you have retained and what you want to work around to develop the ideal wardrobe.

(4) To develop a totally workable wardrobe where every piece co-ordinates each with the other, you must *first decide what your basic color is going to be*. It is best to choose either *black* or *grey* or *navy* or *beige*. This becomes the nucleus, the real *investment core* of your wardrobe. You'll find this way of planning your wardrobe will make it very easy to organize what you'll wear each day. It'll save you time and, for travel, clothes will be easy to select.

(5) Women: Work toward having:
- *2 suits*. Choose styles that can be worn as separates not always as a suit. Choose *one suit* in a *solid* of the *base* color you've decided to build around. The other suit should be of a color that can be worn with the *base* color and, if it's a patterned fabric, must have the *base* color as the *predominant* shade.
- *2 bottoms*. Choose either tailored slacks or skirts in a solid or in a patterned fabric, but they must co-ordinate with the *base* color of the 2 suits.
- *5 tops*. Choose solids or patterns, but they must co-ordinate with every part of the above pieces by matching or enhancing that piece of your wardrobe.

Properly chosen, these 11 pieces will give you 30 outfits.

The addition of belts, scarfs, vests, can change each outfit dramatically and extend these few pieces into more outfits.

By keeping to the rule of one *basic* color in your wardrobe it is possible to have a great variety of co-ordinated outfits. *Another example:*

3 Jackets + 4 Bottoms + 4 Tops = 60 Outfits.

It's simply a matter of working around that one *basic* color. There can be bright, contrasting colors in your co-ordinating *tops, as long as each piece goes with every item.*

- *Every woman's wardrobe should contain a good leather handbag.* If you can't afford to have several good quality handbags of different colors, choose a black one. It is more important that you have one good leather bag than it is to have several inexpensive plastic ones. Quality accessories can upgrade an outfit immensely.

- *Every woman's wardrobe should contain a pair of plain black leather pumps.* Nothing will detract from your image nor be more detrimental than poor quality shoes. Here again, if you can't afford several pairs of different *basic* colors, one pair of black pumps will be acceptable with all your business and dress clothes. Sports shoes and sandals can run the gamut of colors, but these, too, should be of the best quality you can afford. Not only for the sake of your feet and for the sake of your image, but also for the sake of your budget. Purchasing poor quality shoes is false economy. They don't wear well, they lose their shape and, because of the low grade of glue and material in their construction, no matter how clean you are, after a few wearings they take on a most unpleasant odor. Good quality shoes, given attention to replacement of worn heel lifts and plenty of protective polish, will last for years. Top quality leather shoes and handbags can weather the years and still retain their fine "character." They are sensible and necessary investments.

- *These are the essentials.* I'm not saying never buy a "fun" fashion in the fad of the day, if you love it and it gives you a lift and you can afford to be unrestrained, buy it. Ask yourself first, though, "How often will I wear it?" It may be very often if it is acceptable to your lifestyle, so, even if it's out of style in a short time, you may get plenty of wear from it while it's the fad. Don't sabotage your image by wearing an off-beat fashion creation where it isn't apropos of the circumstance—wear it, enjoy it, but only where it belongs and if it fits your polished image.

• *In choosing classic styles that are never outdated, be alert to these guidelines:*

Lapels: Choose medium width lapels. Not extra wide or extra narrow, these date a coat or jacket. (Approx. 3.5″)

Shoulders: Massive shoulder lines have never been attractive, and women that want the most for their clothing investment dollar steer clear of such fashions. The natural shoulder line with the usual padding is never outdated.

Skirt Length: A well dressed woman never wears a skirt that shows her knees. It isn't a matter of morals, it's a matter of knowing that knees are never very pretty and, more importantly, the natural break of the body line is *at* the knee not above it. Dresses and skirts are far more attractive and classic in appearance if worn just at or over the knee. Longer lengths almost to the ankle, come and go in fashion but are quite generally acceptable.

The long lengths can look a bit overwhelming for business wear (except in cold climates), but tall, slender women wear them quite elegantly. A small woman is lost in these lengths and, on a stout woman, long full skirts can add pounds.

Very short skirts are not in any circumstance associated with a polished image. *You'll never climb the corporate ladder in a mini-skirt.* If you want to show you are serious about your business career, you'll dress the part and be treated with the respect you so obviously deserve. Women should not complain if they present themselves as sex symbols but are indignant when not treated as business equals. If this advice seems Victorian and limiting to female freedom, please consider this: if a man wore a tank top or short shorts to his place of business, he wouldn't get anywhere either. There are rules that apply for women and also for men. Take your choice, adhere to those rules or be branded a bimbo! You may think that older women are just envious that they can't wear mini-skirts, that isn't the case. The truth is, we've been through that craze and *learned from experience* how demeaning they are and wish we'd never been foolish enough to wear them. If "sexy" is what you want to be, then *cover up*—wondering what's there is far more enticing than seeing it all flaunted and suffering from *observation overload!*

To enhance body shapes:

Accentuate the positive. Eliminate the negative.

PETITE WOMEN: (UNDER 5' 3")

- Accent the vertical.
- Wear an outfit in one color or mix of one color to create an unbroken line from shoulder to hemline.
- Wide belts of an accent color will shorten the appearance of the body line. Keep belt the same color tone as the outfit. An unbroken line *without* a belt is ideal.
- Keep a natural shoulder line. Wide, emphasized shoulders will give the illusion of a shorter body and will overwhelm the body line. Proportionately out of balance.
- Always keep the overall proportions in mind. Skirts too short or too long won't complement a petite body line.
- Wear simple, uncluttered, dresses enhanced with jewelry that isn't too chunky or you'll be lost in the regalia.
- Suit jackets are best kept short and single breasted with fitted lines instead of boxy.
- Slacks that have wide legs shorten the line and give a square, boxy look to the body. Straight, trimmer-legged styles are better for those with wide hips. Narrow, tapered styles look great on slender, petite figures.
- *No super-high heels.* Short women tend to compensate by wearing very high heels. This throws their body out of balance and also gives them a teetering carriage. Short, stout women look particularly "unbalanced" in spike heels.
- As discussed in the hair styling chapter, hair volume should be kept in proportion to a petite body structure. Neat, tidy,

close to the head styles will add height. Long hair will give the appearance of a shorter stature.

MEDIUM HEIGHT WOMEN: (5'4" TO 5'8")
- Accent the vertical.
- If you want to look taller, see the advice for petites as listed previously.
- Women of medium height are fortunate in that they can look tall by wearing higher heels, or can look petite by wearing flats. Those with well proportioned, slender, body measurements can wear most styles with little concern.
- Check the general rules we've mentioned under the topic "Silhouettes."

TALL WOMEN
Tall, very slender women should avoid a too thin, angular look.
- Belts of a contrasting color can break the monotony of a long body line and add "curve" to the waistline.
- If the top part of the body (the torso) is long and the legs short, wear blouses tucked in at the waistline with a wide belt the same color as the slacks or skirt of the outfit. Short, to the waist style jackets are also fine.
- If the top of the body is short and the legs long, wear blouses and sweaters *over* the skirt or slacks waistline, or wear a wide belt the same color as the blouse or sweater to give the torso length. Longer jackets look best.
- Tall women can wear a wide variety of styles but should be careful not to wear clothes that are too bulky or they can appear massive and masculine.
- Usually all one color on a tall woman is overwhelming. It is better to provide some contrast in color accents.
- Large, chunky jewelry suits a tall woman. Wide bracelets, not fine little narrow ones, look more in proportion to the body structure and are more noticeable.
- Sleeveless garments are usually not attractive for long arms. Long or three-quarter (push-up or roll-up) sleeves look best. For business wear, however, don't get too casual a look with roll-up sleeves or sleeveless apparel.

- Striped fabrics should be predominantly horizontal. Slacks should not have vertical stripes unless your legs are much shorter than your torso and you want them to appear longer. Long striped legs look like Uncle Sam in drag!

THE PLEASINGLY PLUMP:

- Don't wear skirts any shorter than just beneath the knee. Short skirts add *pounds* to the appearance because they cut the total body line, widening and shortening the look.
- Shoulder pads of *medium* thickness *do* help to give a balanced line to a wide-hipped person, but if the pads are too thick they can make the body look even larger. Take care.
- The appropriate *accessories* can work like magic wands to slenderize a large body:

  Belts: Take two, fasten them to-gether to give plenty of length, then wear them dropped low beneath the waist. This gives a long line to the upper body and slenderizes.

  Jewelry: If you have a full bustline, be sure your necklace doesn't end right at the fullest part. This accents and draws attention where you want to *de*-emphasize. Wear *long* strings of beads, chains, or oblong scarves tied long and low. This gives a long vertical line that is very slimming. If necessary, fasten two strings of beads or chains to-gether to get more length. Wear large, chunky jewelry, never small.

Typical silhouettes of women:

The clothes you wear can make you appear taller, shorter, thinner, or more shapely than you actually are. Over the decades, silhouettes have changed from bound in, flat-chested lines to voluptuous, rather chubby looks. *To-day's ideal figure is one with the hips two inches larger than the bust and a waist 10 inches smaller than the hips.* Though we might try for the ideal, to-day's woman would never wear anything like a bustle or bind in her natural curves to present a silhouette of the fashion of the day. We do what we can to achieve a balanced-looking figure but our key words are: *"comfortable"*; *"personable"*; *"unpretentious."*

- Most silhouettes are basically rectangles or triangles.

- Vertical lines make you look taller and more slender, carrying the eye upward. FIG. A
- Two or more verticals can do just the opposite, however. The separated lines draw the viewer's eyes across the figure making it seem wider and shorter. FIG. B

(Illustration A & B)

 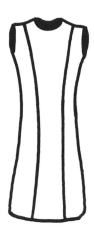

- Horizontal lines shorten and broaden the figure, especially when they divide a figure in half. FIG. C

(Illustration C & D)

A colored belt will shorten the figure even more. FIG. D

• A diagonal line can enhance any figure. Depending where the line begins and ends, it can lengthen the torso; emphasize hips; camouflage a thick or short waistline; etc. FIG. E

(Illustration E)

• A curved vertical line will create height. FIG. F

(Illustration F)

• A curved horizontal line will add width. FIG. G

(Illustration G)

• A deep "V" neckline will seem to lengthen a short neck or make a long neck look gangly. FIG. H
• Add a wide collar and you add weight and emphasize the shoulder area. FIG. I
• A "V" shaped yoke will make shoulders appear wider. FIG. J

(Illustration H, I, J)

• Pockets can draw attention to the hips. Vertical pockets make hips seem narrower. FIG. K.
  Patch pockets make hips look wider. FIG. L

(Illustration K, L)

- Darker shades slenderize.
- Bright or light colors enlarge a silhouette.
- Warm colors: reds, oranges, yellows, enlarge size.
- Cool colors: blues, greens, violets, are slimming.
- Contrasting colors cut height. Short figures should avoid such ensembles as a dark skirt and a light top.
- Tunic styles are especially good for tall women. Easy fitting tunic lines can improve the appearance of a tall, quite stout figure also.
- Large prints are not good on a small figure.
- Small prints are not the best choice for a large or tall figure.
- A large patterned plaid tends to enlarge a figure and plaids with bold color contrasts will do the same.
- A small or petite silhouette is overpowered by a very bold or large plaid or checked pattern. Small checks such as a shepherd's check can be worn quite well.
- The heavier or stout figure should choose accessories of a larger scale, more proportionate to their size.
- Short, close to the throat necklaces emphasize stoutness. It is better to wear necklaces of at least 36 inches in length to draw the eye vertically and create a more slender look.
- Heavier figures should avoid round shapes in accessories. Earrings should be large but long in shape, not round. Round shapes accent round lines.
- Stout women should avoid frilly collars and turtle neck or mandarin neck tops. The best necklines are long V shaped.

- The heavier figure requires clothing that is strongly constructed so as not to lose its original line. Look for well sewn, strong seams particularly at points of stress such as armholes, inseams, crotch, and waistline. Look for generous seam allowances.
- Women of all figure shapes and sizes, when shopping for clothes, should not limit themselves to looking for one size only. Styles can be so diverse and manufacturers' size measurements so dissimilar that a shopper is wise to look at a *range* of sizes. For example, if you wear a size 14 look at sizes 12, 14 and 16. Many beautiful garments get left on the stores' racks because they were not constructed true to realistic size measurements. If the size looks like it may be adequate for your needs, give it a try. Store salesclerks usually are familiar with their stock and can advise if a certain garment is of large or small fit. Carry a tape measure with you, use it.
- We sometimes are not aware that our figures have changed and we need a size smaller or larger than we think we do. This is particularly true of the aging figure. From age around 40—45 the spine begins to shorten and body measurements change quite rapidly.
- Many overweight people tend to wear their clothes too small and by doing this make themselves look much heavier than they actually are. A loose, easy fit is slenderizing and much more comfortable to wear.
- *Fabric texture* affects proportions, too.

  Fluffy and nubby finishes add pounds.

  Stiff fabrics tend to make one look larger.

  Soft, clinging fabrics reveal every curve and draw attention to any figure flaws. Avoid these.

  Soft fabrics that do not cling seem to flatter every silhouette. Good choices of these are:

  Challis: (pronounced "shall-ee") can be of wool, rayon, cotton, or acrylic content. Solid or pattern.

  Crepe: available in several weights of wool, rayon, silk, or polyester.

  Chiffon: a thin, gauzy material suited to dress-up occasions and evening wear. Drapes superbly, so is ideal for scarfs.

THE HALF SIZE FIGURE

The 5′2″ to 5′3″ figure might find that Half Size styles are a better fit. Half Size styles have a larger waistline; hip 7″ below waistline; shorter back to waist length (from bone on neck to waistline); and narrower shoulder width than a Misses.

THE MISSES FIGURE

This is considered *average size* in measurement. Shop for this sizing if you're about 5′5″ to 5′6″; hip 9″ below waist; well developed in proportion; and longer back neck to waist measurement.

THE WOMAN'S FIGURE

Shop for this size if you're 5′5″ to 5′6″; hip 9″ below waistline. This figure is similar to a Misses figure but is fuller.

THE PETITE FIGURE

This figure is about 5′1′ to 5′4″; hip 7″ below waist. Shorter and smaller over all with narrower shoulders than Misses figure.

THE JUNIOR FIGURE

This figure type is about 5′4″; hip 9″ below waist; well developed; has shorter back neck to waistline; and a higher bustline.

THE JUNIOR PETITE FIGURE

This figure is about 5′ to 5′1″; hip 7″ below waist; has a full figure; shorter than a Junior Figure but otherwise similar proportions.

YOUNG JUNIOR TEEN FIGURE

This figure type is about 5′1″ to 5′3″; hip 7″ below waistline; has a developing figure with a small high bustline; with a waist that is larger in proportion to the bust.

Purchasing women's apparel

The consistently well-dressed woman has learned to invest in quality as opposed to quantity. The two most important factors in developing a polished wardrobe are:

(1) *Buy the best quality you can afford.* This rule can't be too persistently stressed. That doesn't necessarily mean the highest *priced* apparel, it means learning how to recognize quality and the best value for your money.

(2) *Buy classical, perennial, styles* that are seen the world over as being exemplary. *Clothing of good quality, conservatively styled,* can be worn until it's threadbare and it'll still hold its shape and reflect a quiet dignity. What initially may seem an enormous price will prove to be very inexpensive when that cost is spread over the several years service you'll get from a garment of this caliber. *This is the most difficult thing to convince people to do, but once they've owned one or two garments of distinction they realize how valuable they are in appearance and in wise investment.* They never want mediocre goods again. *Excellence speaks for itself!*

How to recognize classic styling:

- *No unnecessary detailing:* no extra buttons or extra pockets or extra trim and appliques in the fashion fad of the day. Go for uncluttered styling.
- *Lapels on jackets and coats should be about 3 1/4 to 3 1/2 inches at the widest point.* This is a medium width and won't look dated when, and if, lapels are featured wider or narrower on fad fashions that come and go. This width will remain fashionable because it is standard. Your investment is secure.
- *No loud colors in the major pieces of a wardrobe.* Add bright, morale-boosting colors in accessories.
- *No extremes in length of skirt or width of slacks.* Skirt length just over the knee, and straight leg, medium width slacks never go out of style because they are considered classic and well-dressed.
- *No extremes in shoulder padding.* Wide, heavily padded shoulder styling cannot be easily changed without costly tailoring. This look has never been accepted as classic, that's why it comes and goes.
- *Solid colors and plain fabrics or very subdued patterns* are the most popular for classics, as they will mix and match and are the most versatile.
- *Quality buttons.* Pearl buttons as opposed to plastic on blouses and shirts. *Pure brass* buttons on suits and coats are the ulti-

mate quality. To identify pure brass, carry a small magnet with you when you shop. *Brass, gold, or copper will not adhere to a magnet*. Many quality garments do not have real brass buttons, so consider replacing these to upgrade a garment.

Buy major pieces of apparel in "all-seasons" weight: It's the *weight* and *weave* of a fabric that make it adaptable to wearing year round. With the superb heating systems we now have in buildings and vehicles; with underground parking; and various other conveniences, we seldom need heavy clothing other than coats and clothes for outdoor activities. It is more comfortable and *more economical* to "*layer-dress*," such as a V neck sweater or a sweater vest under a suit jacket, than to wear heavy, bulky winter clothes that are costly and worn only a few months. (See the information on wools, for "all-season" fabric weight.)

Buy major pieces of apparel in "all-seasons" colors: All-seasons' colors are: *Navy; Black; Grey; Tan (Khaki)*. You can adapt the look of each of these colors to Spring; Summer; Fall; and Winter by the blouses, shirts, sweaters, and accessories you wear with them. Your wardrobe should be built around one of these *basic* colors, anyway, so, by choosing fabrics in all-seasons weight, the money you've spent on expensive clothing is working for you all year around, not just a few months of each year. *All-seasons color* and *weight*, now *that's* what we mean by *investment dressing*.

Buy major pieces of apparel in the natural fibers: The best clothing investments are in natural fiber fabrics which are: *cotton, wool, silk, and linen*. There are varying grades of quality in these fabrics, however, so here are some guidelines:

COTTON:
- A hollow fiber that traps air, so therefore it insulates. Warm in winter, cool in summer. Purchase in 2 ply 100% cotton.
- Absorbs perspiration, helping your body's natural air conditioning system. Very comfortable to wear.
- *Sea Island Cotton* is of the ultimate quality in fineness, great durability, and vibrancy. This cotton washes perfectly and resists wrinkling. The best Sea Island cotton (and *all* top quality

cotton) has a *high yarn count* which means more threads per square inch.

- *Egyptian* and *Suprima* types of cotton are of finest quality and, as with *Sea Island* cotton, these are never blended with synthetics. The fine weaves of these cottons do not wrinkle easily so have no need for a blend with synthetics.
- *English two-ply Egyptian cotton* is available in a wide range of stripes, checks, and plains in *custom made blouses and shirts*. Women should consider these.
- The cotton garment you select should not have a high percentage of synthetic fiber in its content. Some synthetic fiber blended with cotton can help the garment retain its shape and keep it from creasing, but too high a percentage of a synthetic can cheapen the quality. Synthetic fibers tend to hold body heat and moisture and be uncomfortable to wear. Check the label to be sure you are getting what you want to live with. The more synthetic, the more pilling and the cheaper the quality of the garment.
- If there is *any* amount of synthetic blended with the cotton, do not add *chlorine* bleach to the laundry water. It will turn the garment yellow.
- A garment of pure cotton can be sterilized in boiling water so it is the *most antiseptic* of all fabrics. Such things as perspiration odors can be removed in this way if the garment is of *pre-shrunk pure* cotton.
- Cotton fabric is the least expensive in terms of up-keep. Wears very well and launders superbly.
- Dry cleaning can turn white cottons yellow, so it is best to buy whites that are *pre-shrunk* and *washable*.
- Be cautious of buying white cottons that have color contrasting trim, as this may limit laundering.
- Functional finishes of a number of types are applicable to cotton, perhaps even more than to other fabrics: wash and wear, durable press, soil release, flame retardation, water repellance, and shrinkage control. These finishes require specific laundering and cleaning procedures, check for instructions.
- When purchasing cotton apparel, look for those made by reliable suppliers. The *regular price* of the item will usually reflect the level of quality.

- Good quality *cotton knits* should have all seams stabilized with seam binding to keep the garment from stretching and sagging. Or, do this yourself!

WOOLS:
- *The air conditioned fabric. All-seasons' wear.*
- The kinky structure of wool traps air and makes it a good insulator for hot or cold weather. Light weight woven or knit wools can be worn year around.
- *The two basic types of wool: woolens and worsteds.*

  Woolens are produced by spinning the fiber into yarn after carding; the yarn has a soft, slightly hairy surface. Woolens are manufactured in both *woven* or *knit* form. Woolens are coarser and more prickly.

  Worsteds yarn has been *combed after carding* and the shorter fibers are removed producing a lighter, smoother yarn with a dry crisp hand. Worsteds are generally more expensive than woolen fabrics, and can be woven into the sheerest of voiles or the thickest of meltons. Light weight worsteds are year around favorites for both men's and women's wear.

TROPICAL WOOLS:
100% worsted wool fabric. All-seasons weight: about 8 ounces per square yard. Light enough to take advantage of wool's summertime cooling qualities. Perfect for blazers.

WORSTED WOOL GABARDINE:
Hard wearing twill construction. Worsted wool's weave is tight and smooth with a hard finish. Available in all-seasons' weight (about 8 oz.) and in heavier weight (12 oz.) for winter.

LUXURY WOOLS: *Cashmere; Camel Cloth; Alpaca; Mohair; Merino*

CASHMERE:
The world's most expensive fiber.
- A very fine hair from the fleece of the Himalayan mountain goat. The goats will only produce the cashmere fleece in their natural habitat, so efforts to cultivate these animals elsewhere

have not been successful. Very limited supply of pure cashmere.

- One male goat produces 4 ounces of cashmere per year (females only 2 ounces). It takes about a full year's growth from 2 to 4 goats to make 7 to 10 ounces of cashmere for one sweater. Very expensive.
- *Beware! Depending on how they are produced, the quality of cashmere products can differ extensively.* There are various grades of cashmere qualities and a range of prices from which to choose, so depend on an established, reputable shop when you purchase.
- With proper care, cashmere garments can last forever.
- Hand wash. (Woolite™ is not recommended for cashmere.)
- There may be some pilling with cashmere, but this can carefully be removed with a fabric brush.
- A good quality, solid shade, cashmere pullover is as elegant for evening as it is for daytime, social, or business wear. It exudes polish. Treat yourself!
- Cashmere is true luxury. It is understated elegance, appropriate for *all seasons*, in all climates, a timeless piece of fashion. A satisfying investment.

CAMEL CLOTH:
Made from the hair of the camel.

- The fabric is warm and soft and is often combined with other wools.
- Excellent for a quality look in top coats, blazers, and suits. Available in a variety of weights.

ALPACA:
Comes from the llamalike animal of the same name in South America.

- This fiber is strong, silky and luxurious.

MOHAIR:
Is the hair of the Angora goat.

- This fiber is strong and silky and is usually blended with other fibers both natural and synthetic.
- Items made with mohair can be quite "shaggy" looking but mohair is a high quality product.

M E R I N O :
A fine silky wool from the Merino sheep.
* It is woven into a fine, soft fabric resembling cashmere. Very
  luxurious and costly.

S I L K
The fiber of elegance, silk dates back at least to 2640 BC. Despite all
the advances in fiber technology which have given us a great variety
of excellent man made fibers, silk is still unsurpassed.
* *Just because the label says "pure silk," it doesn't mean that all
  pure silks are equal in quality.* This is a fabric thats quality
  can be quite deceiving, looking like top quality to the novice's
  eye but not behaving as a good silk should. The price tag will
  indicate, pretty closely, the quality of the garment. Some silks
  have "fillers" to compensate for a natural lack of crispness
  and this quickly leaves a low grade silk. Buy your silk apparel
  only at reputable outlets that you're sure will stand behind
  their goods.
* A good quality silk scarf should have all sides even and line
  up squarely. Patterns should be uniform and stripes or checks
  should parallel the sides exactly. Hems should be rolled and
  sewn with concealed slip-stitching, not folded and finished
  with a visible running stitch.
* Silk is warm and pleasant to the touch and is generally considered comfortable to wear.
* Silk is adversely affected by sunlight, deteriorating quite
  rapidly in fiber strength and in color.
* Silk is also adversely affected by perspiration and deodorants,
  so dress shields should be worn.
* Due to the triangular shape of silk fiber, it *reflects light* and
  possesses a natural luster. This contributes to the brilliance
  and depth of color of silk fabrics.
* Silk, because of this luster, is usually considered overdressed
  for business wear other than in ties or scarfs or as a blend with
  certain other fibers.
* When purchasing silk garments, check to see that seams are
  generous and buy the garment in quite a loose fit, as any strain
  such as at shoulders and back of armholes will separate the
  fabric immediately.

- Silk fabrics can be treated with a number of finishes including crease and stain resistance.
- Most silk is not washable, so up-keep is expensive.

LINEN

- Considered to be a luxury fabric, linen enjoys a good reputation for durability, for color retention and for richness of appearance.
- Of all fabrics, linen is the coolest for its weight.
- The main objection to pure linen is its unsightly tendency to crease badly. New processes of treating linen with blends of synthetics or other treatment have helped reduce this unsightly creasing, however. Since I dislike that creased look, this is a fabric I prefer blended unless it is of the lightest weight and weave and soft enough not to crease.
- A number of synthetics and linen/synthetic blends have been able to imitate linen very closely, but they do not have the absorbency and coolness, nor the rich appearance of high-quality linens. They *are* less expensive and don't crush as easily.
- Linens wash well and are usually colorfast.
- If the fabric is identified as "rayon linen," it is all rayon.
- Expect to pay a healthy price for a good linen.

SYNTHETIC FABRICS

Though the major pieces of a polished wardrobe should be invested in the natural fibers, there are some first-rate synthetics we wouldn't want to live without. More care must be taken in selecting synthetics because they range in quality and appearance from bargain-basement tacky (polyester knits) to excellent imitations of fine fabrics (polyester silks and rayon linens).

RAYON

Is derived mainly from wood pulp.

- Top quality rayons are quite appropriate to include in a distinguished wardrobe, notably the "imposters" that so closely resemble more expensive fabrics.
- Rayon has recently become very popular again, being shown in a wide variety of patterns and finishes.

- Rayon has a good ability to absorb moisture, which makes it comfortable to wear in all seasons and receptive to dyes in an infinite range of colors.
- Rayon drapes beautifully, so lends itself well to many styles and to many body shapes; stout or slender.
- *Rayon is not always washable.* Some rayon is very weak when wet. It is important to check the label.
- Rayon often is blended with wool or cotton and gives these fabrics a silky finish.
- The low priced rayons are poor quality and lose their shape besides looking cheap. Rayon blended with other fabrics is probably your best choice if you're considering buying rayon at all.

POLYESTER FABRICS

Derived from petroleum, coal, air and water, polyester has created whole new concepts in clothing: wash and wear, durable press, and crush proof. When making reference to anyone that looks cheaply dressed, they're said to have a *"polyester profile,"* and the word polyester has become taboo in creating a quality wardrobe. The addition of a small percentage of polyester fiber has great benefits in some garments, however, so it shouldn't be banished entirely. There are many different qualities of polyester, and to say banish them all, would hardly be sensible.

- Polyester blends with other fibers so unobtrusively, giving the fabric strength and durability without destroying its desirable features and often eliminating some of the fabric's faults, for example, wool's tendency to bag or linen's tendency to crease.
- "Silk" polyesters are expensive and are of such fine quality they have the appearance of luxury silk, with a lower price tag. This is fine for scarfs and some blouses and dresses, if the workmanship is impeccable.
- Though polyesters wash easily and dry quickly, their biggest drawback is the fact that oil and grease stains tend to cling firmly and permanently if not removed immediately with a cleaning fluid prior to laundering. Follow label instructions carefully.
- Closely woven or knit polyesters do not "breathe," so they are uncomfortable in hot weather; they also take on the odor of any

perspiration to which they are exposed, and this is almost impossible to remove.

- Polyester *knits* are not at all attractive and seem to scream "seedy." Banish them from your life!

General rules when purchasing apparel

- Check that the weave is firm and regular. See that the garment is not cut on the bias and hence will lose its shape. To do this, take the straight seam of the back of the jacket, for instance, and holding it from the center of the neckline to the hem, give it a slight pull. The fabric should resist stretching. These up and down lines should be cut on the straight of the fabric, not the bias.
- *Buy the best quality you can afford*. Better quality fabrics, with the exception of linen and some silks, wrinkle less.
- See that checks, plaids, stripes and patterns line up properly at the side, centre back, and front seams.
- Pattern on lapels should balance and match.
- The pattern on the two front panels of a jacket should line up across.
- Check the buttonholes for loose threads. This is a good indication of fine workmanship. Buttonholes should be firmly finished with *double stitched ends*. If these start to unravel it is often impossible to find matching thread for repairs.
- Crush a bit of the fabric up in your hand to see if it creases easily. Do this carefully with clean hands, *never* with your gloves on, have respect for the merchandise. After a brief squeeze, the fabric should quickly return to a smooth finish without creases.
- Check the structure of the garment. Is there substantial interfacing to support lapels, collar, and front panels of the garment?
- Check the seams. See that there is a generous seam allowance. If the fabric ravels easily, see that the seams are bound, serged, or adequately finished. See that the stitching on the seams is not so far spaced that seams look open and too loose.
- If the fabric is cotton, check to see that it is not too stiff. This indicates that a lot of "filler" or sizing (starch) has been used

in the production of the fabric to give it body. This will wash out at the first wearing, leaving a limp, poor quality rag. The finest of cottons are soft and almost silky with a very close weave not requiring filler.

- Consider other ways to change the appearance of a garment of simple styling, e.g. add a lace collar to a plain business dress or blouse, so it can be worn for more dressy occasions.

- A very high quality garment will have buttons and trim of equally high grade. Sometimes, you'll find a garment of good quality, but that has buttons and/or belt of a lesser quality. This is often done with the intention of having the customer replace the buttons and belt with something of their own choosing. To add a fine leather belt to a garment can increase the price beyond the popular price line, and the consumer could have added their own at much less cost. Consider this when you see a garment that you like but don't find the trim to be attractive. The switch of buttons and belt can make the garment *uniquely your own* and *upgrade* it considerably. If the belt is of the same fabric as the garment, however, be sure that another kind of belt would be appropriate before deciding to switch it.

- There should be *no plastic thread anywhere in the garment*. It can cut the fabric; can catch on your hosiery; jab your skin; and come unraveled. Awful!

- Linings should be attached at one or two spots at the bottom of the jacket or coat and in several points along the side seams. Lining is best when it is not attached all the way around as it doesn't wear well when so firmly anchored, it has no limited flexibility. On leather, suede, or fur jackets and coats, if the lining is attached all around it is usually a sure sign that the maker has something to hide. Perhaps the pelts have been pieced, not whole, or there are thin and thick spots in the pelts. You should be able to examine the backside of the garment's shell to check for flaws.

- Linings should be of top grade material, not synthetics. Synthetic fabrics don't breathe and can make a garment feel hot, clammy and uncomfortable.

- Beware the *"private label."* These are special purchases the retailer has a factory make up. Some stores have a factory sew a label into the same merchandise that several other stores carry as *their* "private label," under another name of course. This gives the retailer the opportunity to get a higher mark-up without the consumer having something to compare it to, and often there are better values than that private label is offering. If, however, the private label is under the *store's name* and the store has a reputation for carrying good quality merchandise, then that garment will be of the store's usual quality and a safe buy.

- It's a good practice to find a shop or shops that suit your budget and taste, and then become their loyal customer. *Getting established with a store is one of the best ways to develop shopping benefits.* When staff get to know your likes and dislikes and your figure type, they can serve you more efficiently and even give you a phone call when something ideal arrives in their stock. You'll get notice of up-coming sales events and often the opportunity to shop prior to the general public. Wise retailers value their regular customers and offer many "fringe benefits" to attract and keep them. Become one!

- When you're dressing for progress and refinement, search for the type of store that carries this style and quality of merchandise. This usually isn't the high fashion outlets, though some of these do carry a selection of classic styles as well. Stores establish reputations just as do people:

(a) loud and flashy

(b) dull and non-descript

(c) those that exude quality and quiet dignity. *These stores are free image consultants.* Because every day they are dealing with a propriety-conscious, fashion-aware clientele, they are able to offer capable guidance on investment dressing and on what is appropriate. The shopper can rely on their expertise. A reliable store has highly experienced, long term sales staff that is there to serve you year after year. Staff that will *honestly* guide your selection to ensure that it pleases you and does the most for your appearance. *A high quality store knows that their customer is their best advertisement and they'll work hard to help you project a superb image, not just for you but for themselves as well*. You'll feel confident that all your purchases are sensibly made.

- As beneficial as a sales person in a top quality store can be, there are others that do not have the exposure to what investment dressing really requires. That store may or may not have the apparel you want, but *don't be influenced by the salesperson's opinion if it doesn't seem to reflect what you know to be true*. For example: a salesperson (who probably has never worked in an office) insists that a certain garment is appropriate for business wear and you know that it would *not* be acceptable, or when, for example, a clerk advises that the suspenders you are buying for your husband should be *clip-on* suspenders when you know that only *button-on* suspenders have polish. Stick to your guns!

The best times and the best ways to shop

- First thing in the morning on a week day is the best *time* to shop, not only for sale merchandise but for general shopping too.
- The worst times are lunch hours and week-ends. There is limited store staff at lunch time and stores are extra busy at lunch hours and on week-ends.
- *Shop with your hair styled and looking your best*, or everything you try on will not appeal to you.
- *Shop in your best quality, appropriate clothing*. Sales staff will be more impressed with your ability to buy and will tend to show you more interest. More importantly, sales staff will be able to better determine what quality and style you prefer and can more easily assist you in finding what you require. We often are inclined to dress for comfort when we shop and we wear our sports clothes and jogging shoes, giving no indication of our general lifestyle.
- Even if you wear comfortable walking shoes in which to shop, be sure to *wear sheer hosiery and carry your dress shoes* with you to put on for the full effect when trying on clothes. Be sure to *wear a slip* or a half-slip.
- *Don't shop with children* when shopping for apparel for your

self. You deserve uninterrupted time to try on clothes without having to attend to little ones. Sales personnel can't properly serve you if they must baby-sit your babes while you shop.

- Use a credit card to shop. It's *faster* than having a cheque approved. Also, you won't have the cost of a cancelled cheque on your chequing account. I especially like the American Express credit card, for two reasons: (1) It must be paid in full every month and there is no temptation to involve interest charges and (2) if the item purchased is damaged, lost, or stolen within 90 days of purchase, it is fully insured by American Express.

- *Consider custom made shirts and blouses*. Many tailors are now offering these at prices quite comparable to ready-made. For the same price, you can have a blouse that fits perfectly, is exactly the color and fabric you want, and may even have your initials embroidered on the cuff or pocket. Elegant!

- When shopping for clothes, always remember *teamwork*. Just as a group of people working as a *team* on a project can be more effective, good clothes working as a *co-ordinated team* can produce more impact than individual parts hitting off in all (color) directions. *Think: Does this work with what I have?*

- *Check each apparel item for versatility*. For instance, a blazer suit can be worn as a separate blazer or as a two piece suit. A blazer can be worn for both casual wear or for business wear. An all-seasons' weight suit could be worn year round, but if it has a velvet collar (chesterfield style) that suit is limited to fall and winter wear.

- *Don't buy anything unless you truly love it*. Nothing is a bargain if it is seldom worn, and we won't wear what we don't enjoy. Love it or leave it.

- *Don't shop in a hurry*, and don't leave essential shopping until the last minute. For important social or business events, plan ahead, and give plenty of consideration to what you are going to wear. It's almost impossible to find what you need without time for extensive searching. You'll probably end up buying something less satisfying than you wanted. If that is the case, *don't buy it*. It would be better to wear something you already own that you like and are comfortable with than to buy a new

garment just to have something *new*. You may never wear it
again, and you won't enjoy wearing it even the first time.

- I'm reluctant to buy at a shop that has "overstuffed" racks.
  The *clothes get badly damaged and very worn* as, day after
  day, customers push and shove them against the jammed-in
  hangers. It is difficult to view the clothes and infuriating to
  have to struggle with each cramped item. Mention this to the
  store manager. When a store treats clothes in this manner they
  are ruined, and it is wise to shop elsewhere.

Designer Creations are not always the value the price tag would indicate. It annoys me to have a designer's name printed in a conspicuous place on an item. Do *you* want to pay to give that designer
free advertising space on *your* frame? It seems so tacky to broadcast
that you buy Mister or Madame Bigshot's creations. Putting on the
Polish doesn't mean flaunting fancy names. The only Gucci, Gucci, I
need in my life is to coo to a baby as I tickle its precious chin!

- There must be *some* quality to the garment or that designer
  would not want his or her name associated with it. Keep in
  mind that you do pay substantially for the name. *If you find
  that a certain clothes designer's fit, styling, and creativity, always appeal to you, then that designer's line does provide a
  benefit for which it is worth paying.*
- Designer labels once gave an assurance of *some* exclusivity.
  For an exorbitant price, it is still possible to get a "one-of-a-
  kind" creation from a designer, but most have recognized the
  vast consumer retail market and some of their products are
  now commonplace, mass produced. Prosaic.
- The astute shopper waits to see if a certain top designer's creation becomes a winner. You can be sure it will be quickly
  copied and available in excellent quality at a much lower
  price sans the designer label. Knock-offs, as they are called,
  are on the retail clothing store racks within days. Learn to be
  an observant and patient shopper.
- Some suppliers' lines provide "designer label" apparel that
  somewhat follows fashion trends but cleverly combines it with
  very wearable, classic styling, suitable also for business wear.
  Women refused to buy the foolishly fad clothes some desig-

ners tried to intimidate us into buying, and the suppliers had to provide something more realistic for to-day's pragmatic woman. There will always be the sensational, come-hither creations (and the right moment for them, we hope!) but designers are learning that most of our hard earned cash will be spent astutely.

- Lines such as those of "Anne Klein 11"; "Liz Claiborne"; " Mr Jax"; are basic. The shopper who is not sure which clothes would be good investments, can rely on these lines. If this is more than you want to pay, check the styling and fabrics of these lines and then shop around. You'll very likely find something similar at less cost. If you want the reassurance that you are indeed getting good quality and you haven't time to comparison shop, these lines are really quite fairly priced for designer presentations.

Imports

When shopping for apparel, *be careful with imports*. First of all, *the price is far more than the actual quality*. This is not an idle observation. Having, for many years, owned a top-label ladies' and men's wear store, I know that the *customary* way to price a garment is to take the wholesale cost, add on the various government taxes, shipping charges, and *import costs*, and, to arrive at the retail selling price, this total is then doubled. So, you can see, the *import costs are not only in the price of the garment but are doubled, and that has nothing to do with improving the quality of the item or of helping the customer relate quality to price*. You might think this way of pricing is at the stores' discretion, and that only greedy merchants would subscribe to such tactics. Not so. These imported goods represent very involved purchasing and that extra cost is often justified.

Additional processing costs and the difficulty of obtaining rare merchandise such as fine cashmeres, only available on an import basis, can skyrocket the price.

- To avoid paying import costs, you would have to purchase these items in the origin of their manufacture, and many people remember to do this when they travel. It's easy to see that the savings can be more than substantial.

- I point out this pricing structure because not *all* imported goods are of prestige or hard to obtain materials. If and when you are paying a premium for imports, *be sure that you could not get the same or better quality from the domestic market for much less money*.
- Another aspect of imported apparel, of which the shopper should be aware, is the *size measurements*. They can be much different from country to country of origin. Some proportions are quite unusual for the North American consumer, just as ours probably confuse our visiting tourists who shop here. The hang tags on some imported garments give comparison size details which are of great assistance to a consumer. The sales staff can advise you.
- There is a line of imports I have relied on for many years which is reasonably priced and which keeps pace with the good basic, attractive trappings we all need in our wardrobes. That line is "Ports International."

Sale merchandise

RECOGNIZE THE REASON FOR THE SALE

To balance stock:
A realistic reason. This type of sale merchandise will usually be found all year round on tables and racks through-out the store. Watch for these clearance items, there are good bargains here. Sizes and colors will be limited, since it is a clearance of leftovers from regular stock. Some items may be soiled or damaged. Some items may be in good depth in sizes and colors, but a large number is available simply because the store overbought. These sales are often called *"end of month"* sales, and this is a good time to be alert to the event.

To clear seasonal merchandise:
A realistic reason. These are the sales for which the public waits, knowing it is *regular, first grade merchandise*. Small boutiques and department stores don't have space to store even classics (that won't go out of style the next season), so they must be cleared to make space for the new season's stock. Also, in these days of high interest rates,

stores need regular stock turns for every invested dollar. End of season sales are usually staged twice a year, January and July, and last for about 4 weeks. Sizes and colors are limited, and some stock may be a bit shop worn, but the bargains are real.

Special purchase sales:
These sales are timed to bring in customers when sales volumes are at the lowest ebb. These are often manufacturers' clearance items. If you recognize this as apparel generally higher priced, it's worth the buy. If it looks like it has limited fashion endurance, forget it.

Impromptu sales:
These sales are well promoted, often with sensational advertising. They're usually staged when the store needs money. *If you are aware that the economy is slack and retail sales are suffering, you should be able to count on this type of sale to be quite worthwhile.* With so many retail stores in operation now, competition for business is intense. Impromptu sales have become so commonplace that the consumer doesn't believe they're real and even if they are, we don't rush to buy because, just like the busses, there'll be another one coming along in a minute or so. We've been conditioned not to buy anything at regular price, we wait until it's on sale.

BEWARE THE BAIT AND SWITCH ROUTINE
A store or a chain of stores may offer a name brand item at a great price reduction but have only a few available. This may be a bait and switch routine: "Sorry we're sold out of that one, but how about this more expensive one?" Stores of good reputation are never guilty of this. Trust them.

How to take advantage of a special sale:
- When you're aware of the date of an authentic sale, shop the afternoon or evening before the sale to spot the items you want to buy. Quite often the store will let you have them early, at the sale price (here's where the regular customer gets the breaks), and if they won't, you'll at least be able to capture these plums when the doors open on the morning of the sale. You'll have tried them on and know if the fit is right, so you'll just have to pay for them and go.

- If there's no way to determine what will be offered on sale, then you'll need to be a bright and early shopper. Go through the racks and gather up several items that look suitable. *Be sure to have a tape measure with you, so you can measure to see that these things may fit and save yourself the time of trying on the impossible.* You want to get the best selection possible, and other shoppers will be striving to do the same, time is of the essence.

- *Don't buy anything on sale you wouldn't otherwise buy.* Exceptions to this are expensive items you could not afford at the regular price. We've all purchased things because we recognize that they're a "real buy," but nothing is a real bargain if we never wear or use it. Resist the temptation.

- Make it a habit to purchase such things as underwear and hosiery when manufacturers' feature their semi-annual sales. Sensible planning can keep you well supplied with first quality goods at a much reduced price.

- Most retailers do not allow any returns on sale merchandise. *Be sure you have them write it on the bill* if they tell you they *do* allow returns. Many a misunderstanding has arisen over this. Be very sure you try everything on and check carefully for imperfections, if the sale is final.

- *Be alert to stores that set prices very high knowing only a few will sell at that price. Then, when they are reduced in price they are still at the normal mark-up.* Because so many shoppers now wait for sales and are not purchasing at the regular price, *this has become a practise with some stores.* When you comparison shop, it is obvious that this game is prevalent. These shops don't deserve your business.

- High fashion items are often available at a much reduced price. Stores bring them in to give dash and glamor to the store's image, but they seldom sell at their normal mark-up. If you're madly in love with it and can afford to be reckless, this is the time to buy it. Careful! Next year when it's out of favor it'll haunt you from the dark corners of your closet.

- *By the time a garment goes on sale it has often seen some hard wear. It has been tried on many, many times,* often more times than you'd put it on in a lifetime! Buttonholes may be soiled and stretched, there may be perspiration or cosmetics stains from all these try-ons. *Check carefully before you buy*.

- Garments that have been featured in a window display can have major damage from the sun or from display lights. The loveliest stock in the store is used to entice the potential customer to come in and buy. Look the garment over for faded streaks which might not be too obvious in a poorly lit dressing room.

- *Shoe sales* are usually terrific *if* you can find your size in the style you want. That's the purpose of the sale, the store is clearing broken size and style ranges. Be sure what you buy is comfortable, because these are almost always *non-returnable sales*.

- *Sales are the classic dresser's dream*. When you're buying traditional, conservatively styled clothes, you know they'll always be in fashion, and you're getting them at a bargain price. For example: If you can only afford to pay $200 for a suit, wait for a sale and get a $400 suit for that $200. It's simply a matter of careful shopping. *Buy the best quality you can afford, and buy it on sale*.

Secondhand—Resale—Consignment store shopping

Come now! Don't grimace! Many good bargains of top quality merchandise are available at re-sale shops. You can find very valuable, designer label garments, at exceptionally low price tags, perhaps only worn once by their wealthy previous owner. People put on weight; change their lifestyle (i.e. retire and don't need so many business clothes); move to a different climate; change their tastes. There are several feasible reasons for selling their *perfectly wearable clothing*. This becomes your lucky find. The secret to successful second-hand shopping is the same as regular shopping: *find the stores that carry only good quality merchandise*.

- You can tell at a glance if it's your kind of store. If it is a potpourri of junk mixed with finery, it'll be a waste of your time. It's obvious the operater does not have an eye for quality. The way stock is merchandised and displayed will reveal the store's reliability and expertise. *A reputable re-sale shop will be as tidy and attractive as any regular retail operation*. The stock will not be soiled, it will be merchandise the former owner will have grown out of or become tired of, you'll scarcely know the stock is secondhand.

- It takes time and patience to shop in re-sale stores. If you're looking for something specific, *ask*. Not all stock is on display. Get to know the staff, and they'll let you know when such an item is available.

- Find out from the store what days and hours they are open and which are the best days to shop. They are different than regular shops.

- Even if you don't buy secondhand clothing, it's a good idea to check these shops for such *accessories* as *belts* and *costume jewelry*.

- *If you see what you want, buy it*. Because it's a bargain it won't be available for long.

- *Be sure to try it on*. Sizes in re-sale shops are not always accurate and the item may have been altered.

- *Stains can't be removed*. Don't take a chance on even the smallest one. A polished image is what you want and that means no stains.

- *Do consider alterations*. If it's a good buy and you can use it, it's worth the alteration costs. Turn the garment inside out and check the seams. Are they wide enough to allow alterations? Don't plan to lengthen sleeves or hemlines. On a used garment, the previous fold line cannot be removed.

- Check for missing buttons. If they can be replaced, buy it. If they are "important" buttons, forget it.

- *Check the garment at points of wear*. Armholes, crotch areas, "seats" of skirts and slacks, hems of slacks, backs of suit jackets. You discard your own clothing when it becomes shiny from wear, why would you buy someone else's in that condition? A top quality consignment shop would not offer this for sale unless it has escaped their scrutiny.

- Check for perspiration stains and odors. Check armholes and crotch areas. This odor can never be removed even with dry cleaning. Sometimes perspiration has discolored the outside of the garment too. This is not for you.

- Be careful of down-filled clothing. If the down has shifted, don't buy the garment, you'll freeze!
- Salt stains on shoes and boots can usually be removed with a 50/50 solution of white vinegar and water.
- I don't recommend buying shoes or boots secondhand. If they look next-to-new they *may* be satisfactory.
- Re-sale stores of *high quality* are an ideal source for children's coats, jackets, and dress wear of very distinctive appearance at a bargain price. The entire family can put on the polish!
- Even if you don't care to wear secondhand clothes, you may find consignment shops a good way to dispose of your own cast-offs. Sell items you no longer need and earn money for something new for your wardrobe.

Coats—The status messengers

Research has shown that at a *first glance* people decide your socio-economic level and make up their minds about you with little change from that point. Wouldn't it be a shame to be perfectly dressed in good quality, appropriate clothes but to be evaluated unfavorably because you made the mistake of hiding them beneath a *second-rate coat?* A coat is an important messenger. Much of the time it is the only major part of your apparel that is showing. Be sure the message it delivers leaves a favorable impression. Consider the following guidelines:

STYLE

The most versatile and most exemplary styles from which to choose are:

- A cloth coat of medium weight, rich wool, with neatly tailored lines (*not* form fitted), single-breasted.
- A trench coat of top quality light weight wool worsted which will serve year round. One with a warm zip-in lining adapts it to even the coldest climate. This is a long, double-breasted coat with epaulets and loose shoulder yoke, made in water repellent fabric. A khaki shade is the most popular and probably the most practical for year around wear.

- A wraparound camel colored cloth coat of lightweight top quality wool or, if you should be so fortunate, one of the luxury fabrics: camel hair or alpaca in a light tan shade.
- A "Chesterfield" is one of my favorite styles but it isn't as versatile as the above three. This is a semi-fitted, straight cut, classic coat in single or double-breasted style with a black velvet collar. A Chesterfield style coat in charcoal grey or black worsted wool exudes elegance. This has long been a favorite for both men's and women's coats.
- A Balmacaan styled topcoat. This is a loose-fitting, raglan sleeved style that fits well over suits. It has a small collar and either single or fly-front button closure. Available in lightweight fabric or various weights of wool worsted usually treated to be rain repellant.
- A "Topper" which is a three-quarter or seven-eighth length coat. In a good lightweight worsted, this style of coat can fill many roles. Its a great traveller, as it can be worn over anything from casual sports clothes to very tailored suits and long evening dresses. Every wardrobe should have one in a solid color of *creamy white*, tan, or (perhaps) black.

DETAILING:

- Avoid extra pockets, fancy buckles, flashy buttons, elaborate top-stitching or pleating which will brand the coat as lower class.
- *It is important that the coat be long enough to cover the clothes beneath it*. Coats should always be purchased in lengths longer than dresses or skirts, therefore a good length is mid-calf. This is one reason why very long skirts are not appropriate for business wear. When you put a very long coat over them, you look like you're wearing a man's topcoat and too encumbered to get around and do your job. This is where a "Topper" style coat in 3/4 or 7/8 length looks better. In my opinion, nothing looks worse than a regular length coat worn over long, formal evening wear. Someone once referred to this as the "peasant formal" and that's probably a good name for it. Here again, a Topper style looks quite fine.

COLORS

Unless you can afford a number of styles and colors, you'd be wise to choose either a top quality *khaki* or *beige trench coat* or a plain tailored cloth coat in wool worsted in a solid color of *black, grey* or *tan*. When your budget will allow, treat yourself to that topper in light tan or creamy white. The ideal one will look and feel like cloud nine!

FUR COATS

I won't get into the controversy of whether or not it is cruelty to animals to wear furs, but I do think *a fur coat is out of place for business wear*. In this day and age of practicality we tend to look askance at anything that appears ostentatious. Far better to wear a top quality, distinctive cloth coat than a fur coat of mediocre or inferior status.

FAUX FUR COATS

A polished image doesn't need *anything* that's false. The new faux furs are quite realistic and the very expensive ones are rather attractive but please don't wear them for business. In fact they make terrific toss cushions and some snazzy accessories, let's confine them to that, shall we?

CONSTRUCTION

- A coat for fall and winter wear should have a layer of chamois across the back between the outer shell and the lining for added warmth.
- A classic coat will have standard shoulder lines with no extreme shoulder padding.
- The lining should be of durable, high quality material that complements the quality of the coat.

Accessories

BELTS

- It's better to own one or two good quality *leather* belts than several inexpensive ones that don't wear well. A belt can make or break an outfit.

- Look for *contour* belts that hug the natural line of the body and settle comfortably on the waistline. Any belt over an inch and a half wide should be contoured. Contour belts are not easy to find. It surprises me that manufacturers don't realize that women's waistlines are different than men's, who, due to their hip structure, need a straight line belt.
- A belt can be used to give a very different look to a garment: to brighten a plain dress with color.
- By wearing a belt the *same color as the blouse* or top you are wearing you will give a longer look to the upper body proportions.
- By wearing a belt the *same color as the skirt* or slacks you are wearing you will give a longer look to the lower body proportions.
- The heavier the waistline, the narrower the belt should be. A wide belt thickens the waistline.
- Short women should not shorten the look of the body by cutting it in half with a contrasting belt.
- A very long torso can be given a shorter look by breaking the long line with a belt of a contrasting color. A wide belt is especially effective.
- Belts should be worn so they just touch the waistline not cinched in so much that they pull the garment into unsightly gathers. A heavy or overweight body can look like an overstuffed duffelbag tied in the middle if a belt is worn too tightly.
- Handy as they are, I dislike belts with *velcro closings* because they grab on to the fabric of fine blouses and skirts and damage them. Be warned!
- The simpler the belt design, the more versatile it will be. Too much metal on a belt can look tacky.
- Belts of fabric or faux furs look terrific. Fabric readily molds to the body, is comfortable and any number of patterns can be used to give dash to an otherwise plain outfit. A leopard or a zebra print belt will go with almost every solid color outfit and look superb.
- Elasticized belts are trim looking and help to keep a blouse tucked in. Choose an elasticized belt of top quality or it can cheapen your outfit. Be sure it isn't too tight or it'll make your tummy bulge!

SCARFS

- Scarfs are those valuable little investments that never go out of fashion and that can extend your wardrobe in a hundred different ways. When your spirits need a lift and your budget can't take a major purchase, ta-dah!, a new scarf to the rescue.
- The superiority of a fine silk scarf can make an outfit come alive. To check its quality, see that the edges line up exactly when the scarf is folded in half. In the best scarfs those edges are rolled and slipped stitched, not hemmed with a machine running stitch.
- To own even one "Liberty" or "Hermes" silk scarf is to capture a little bit of heaven and wallow in its luxury.
- Scarfs can be more than an accent piece. A large square scarf can become a halter top to wear in summer or under a suit jacket as a blouse.

Here's how: Take a large (36″ to 40″) scarf, fold it in half into a triangle and tie the two top corners around your neck. (See diagram.) Fold up the lower hem and tie the two lower corners around your waist.

Figure(s)

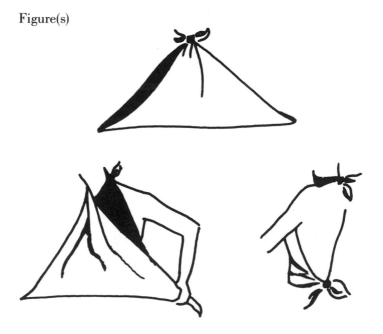

Another halter top can be made this way: Take a large scarf at least 30″ square and tie the two top corners around your neck forming a loosely draped cowl neckline. Fold the lower edge of the scarf up around the waistline and tie at the back. If you use a scarf with a bold border it will look like a set in waistband.

Illustrations

• Wear a scarf as a belt. A long oblong tied around the waist becomes a sash. Or a large square scarf could be folded into a triangle, tied around the waist, draped over one hip and knotted on the other hip.

- *The Safari Look*: Take a large square scarf (30″) and with the centre of one edge under the chin tie the two corners on top of your head. Take the lower two corners and wrap them around to the back of your head tucking under for a smooth fit. Place a hat over the scarf.

- For a perfect fill-in for a V neck, place a large square scarf on a flat surface with the wrong side up. Pick up the scarf almost in the centre and tie a small knot on this wrong side. With the knot on the inside, take opposite corners of the scarf and make a triangle. With the knotted part of the scarf under your chin, carry the two corners around your neck and tie (if the scarf is small), if the scarf is large enough, carry these two corners right around to the front and tie them under the front panel of the scarf. The knot beneath makes the folds of the scarf very full and provides an intricate design.

- To make a long tie that is very easy on a scarf, take a long oblong scarf and place it around your neck with one end about 3″ to 4″ inches longer than the other. On the longer end make a loose, overhand knot. Take the short end of the scarf and push it down through the loop of the knot in the long end. Slide this end through to where you want the tie to be. FIG. M

(Diagram)

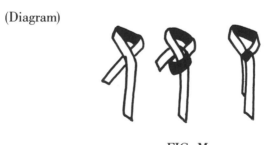

FIG. M

- To tie a square knot in a scarf, place one end *right* over left and the other end *left* over right and tie.

- Because tying can be hard on a silk scarf, here is a way to use a neck scarf without a knot. Fold a long oblong scarf in half, place it with the fold at the centre front of your neck. Pull the loose ends of the scarf through the loop that is formed by the fold. Draw up tightly to the neck. FIG. N

(Diagram)

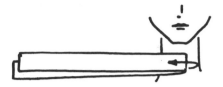

FIG. N

- A quick and easy neckline fill-in that stays in place and always looks tidy is to take an oblong scarf, place it around your neck with 1/3 on one side and 2/3 on the other. Tie a square knot. Take the longer end of the scarf up through and under the knot and spread that end of the scarf over the knot.

(Diagram)

- To give a little dash to a trench coat, tie a long oblong scarf around one epaulet and let it drape over the shoulder. It could also then be tied through the strap of your shoulder bag to keep it from sliding off your shoulder. Great help if you need your hands free and also as a security measure. FIG. O and P

(Figure O and P)

- Scarfs basically come in two shapes:
    Squares which are:
        small 24″ (60 cm)
        medium 24″ to 30″ (60cm to 75cm)
        large 34″ to 40″ (85cm to 100 cm)
    Oblongs which are:
        medium 11″ wide by 54″ long
- Silk scarfs drape the most beautifully and enhance an outfit. Silk is very delicate, however, constant tying can separate its weave, so it takes extra care.
- Don't think because a scarf is only a small part of your apparel that its quality is insignificant. That small part can have great impact, so it is very important to see that it is of good quality. There are exceptionally high grade synthetic scarfs which not only are beautiful but are easy to keep clean. Since a scarf is worn close to the face, it gets soiled with cosmetics. Better to have a scarf that is *clean* than one that constantly must be dry cleaned at great expense.
- A scarf is useful in helping to keep collars of suits and coats from getting soiled. It is easier and cheaper to clean a small scarf than a coat or suit.
- Be sure that the material of the scarf is appropriate for the material of your outfit. A wispy chiffon scarf looks too delicate for wear with heavy materials like denim or sports clothes of cotton, just as a wool scarf on a light weight dress fabric looks out of place.

- Choosing printed scarfs that combine *several* colors that complement *more than one* of your ensembles, extends your wardrobe most effectively.
- Since a scarf is worn close to your face, look in a mirror to make sure that it complements your complexion coloring.
- A scarf of medium or large size is much more versatile than a small scarf and comparatively of far more value for the price. There are ways of folding even very large scarfs for smaller needs but a small scarf is strictly limited.
- Scarfs can be used to camouflage figure problems. For example, a scarf placed around the neck and worn loose and long can accent vertical lines and give a longer look to the body.
- A scarf can be used to combine two pieces of apparel that otherwise may look unrelated. For example, a yellow blouse with a pink suit; a scarf with pink and yellow dominating in the pattern can make the two colors "gel".
- Arrange your scarfs by color in a drawer. For easy selection, place a piece of stiff cardboard inside each scarf and stand the scarfs on end instead of stacking them. Or use clip-on skirt hangers and hang your scarfs next to your clothes in the clothes closet. This way you can experiment with several different color combinations when selecting a scarf for an outfit. By hanging your scarfs they are never creased and it will eliminate a lot of ironing which is hard on delicate fabrics. *For travel*, I wrap tissue paper around the hanger and scarfs and roll up the entire thing. No creases when I arrive and those handy scarfs give many changes of outfits.
- Its very easy and much less expensive to make your own scarfs. You don't need a sewing machine because the finest scarfs have *rolled* and *hand sewn* edges. There are even border prints in silk or high quality polyester by the yard, in perfect size for making a scarf. Or purchase remnants of silk fabrics.
- Tuck a small scarf in the breast pocket of your suit and give it a burst of color. You could *hand-sew* a number of these in different colors. Keep an eye on the remnant tables in prestige fabric stores.
- Fine *cotton* scarfs look terrific with cotton or casual outfits. Tie

one to your handbag so it'll be handy to cover your hair to protect it from the sun or wind. Cotton *clings* and won't slide off
as silk tends to do.

GLOVES

- Carry your gloves holding their fingers in your hand and the
  rest of the glove draped over the back of your hand. This looks
  more polished than clutching the gloves in the middle with the
  fingers splayed in all directions. Evening gloves, in particular, should be carried in this way. (See diagram.)

- Gloves can give a finished look to an outfit besides adding
  colorful dash for *certain* ensembles. If you're using gloves to
  lend color, be careful not to overdo the number of your color
  accents.
- A good pair of *leather* gloves is a must for winter. Select those
  of very plain, slim-fitting design. If you're buying lined gloves
  choose a style with the most trim look, not those with bulky
  outside seams.
- Good quality fabric or finely knit gloves look more polished
  than do low grade leather or synthetics.
- Be sure your gloves are spotlessly clean. Leather gloves soil
  easily from body oils and hand lotions, treat them with care.
  Buy colors that don't show oil stains so readily: black, dark
  brown or dark taupe.
- Gloves aren't worn as much socially as they used to be, but
  they always have been and still *are required for very formal occasions.* Now, in the 90's, we're moving to-ward more polish
  and dignity in our social behavior and gloves are getting very
  popular again.

Let's brush up on our "hand in glove" rules:

- *Short, wrist length* gloves are worn with long sleeved or sleeve-less dresses.
- *Medium length,* to the elbow, preferably shirred, gloves are worn with 3/4 or elbow length sleeves.
- *Over the elbow length* gloves are worn with strapless or spaghetti strapped gowns. Mini-skirted dresses with long gloves look out of balance, more gloves than dress! If you bare your legs *why* cover your arms?
- Short, sheer or lace gloves are ideal for evening wear in black, white or beige. They also are a dandy camouflage for aging hands.
- *Never, but never, eat with your gloves on.* This is the utmost of "tasteless" behavior. Small gloves should be tucked into your handbag. Over the elbow gloves usually have a buttoned opening at the front of the wrist, this is so the wearer can take off part of the glove and tuck it into the wrist of the glove leaving the arms covered. Or, remove them entirely.

HANDBAGS:

- Every ensemble needs a good quality *leather* handbag. If your budget won't allow for more than one, then make it a black one.
- *Outsize handbags* can look cumbersome and detract from a clean-cut appearance. Do you really need to carry *all* of your worldly goods with you? Everywhere? Knocking into people in stores, on airlines, and in line-ups at check-out counters does nothing for your image. Is any performance more ludicrous than someone up to their shoulders in a handbag searching for something in its vast and mysterious bowels?
- *Do* be sure your handbag is of adequate size to carry the essentials. An overstuffed handbag is unsightly and it's beautiful lines can be ruined in this way.
- *Over-the-shoulder bags* may be handy but they're hard on the spine *and* on the posture. Even if the bag isn't heavy, we tend to hold up one shoulder to keep the strap from falling off and thus the spine is thrown out of kilter. Over a period of time these bags can create a serious back problem. Clothes don't drape properly with the body twisted sideways. The straps of

shoulder bags damage clothes. Handbags with convertible straps will give some relief from constant over the shoulder wear.

- There should be as little *metal hardware* as possible showing on a handbag.
- When purchasing a handbag, check to see that it has *at least one zippered compartment inside*. Small items like contact lens cases and lipsticks can fall out if the bag is of an envelope or fold over design.
- Handy as zippers are *inside* a bag, I'd rather not see zippers on the *outside* of a handbag for dress wear.
- A good quality handbag should be as well finished *inside* as it is outside. No plastic linings.
- *Keep your handbag well organized*. You should be able to put your hand on exactly what you want without searching around for it. Tissues neatly folded, and all unnecessary items cleared out regularly. A small cosmetics bag is useful to keep essentials to-gether and for easy transfer when you change handbags.
- Designer handbags are often made of plastic. A snazzy name doesn't always mean superb quality.
- *Your handbag says a lot about you*. Make it speak favorably. Buy a high quality, classic bag. It will give you distinguished service for many years.
- A useful gadget to have is a *handbag holder* that clips on to the side of a table. In such places as restaurants there is seldom a place to put a handbag.
- *There is much more leather in a handbag than there is in a pair of shoes. Expect to pay accordingly.*

BRIEFCASES:
- Quality leather is still the most favored material for a polished image.
- Hard structured lines in a briefcase are seldom necessary. Opt for a case with a foldover or zippered top and top handles, this design looks more professional.
- Women shouldn't carry both a handbag *and* a briefcase. One more piece of luggage and you'll have to hail a porter. Manu-

facturers have been alert to our needs, and many very handsome briefcases have a side pocket to accommodate small essentials that are usually carried in our handbag. A small
leather clutch bag that holds lipstick, comb, mirror, credit
cards, etc., is the handiest. Tuck it into your briefcase. When
you want to shop and not carry your briefcase into the stores
with you, this clutch bag is ideal.

PENS

Accessories include many things, and putting on the polish means not
to overlook any accessory as being insignificant. A good pen not only
ensures a tidy signature but is one of those small enhancements that
quietly announce your refinement.

- A nibbed pen lends the most character to your signature—
  accenting thin and thick lines. There are several designs,
  prices and finishes from which to choose.
- The *"Cross"* gold, ball point pen is quite popular, but the one
  that company has designed for women has no clip. This makes
  it very inconvenient for business use. It's a case of not being
  tuned in to the business woman's world.
- In this day of credit card purchasing and having to sign for
  this, that, and the other, a pen is often on display and does
  more than *write* a message, make sure its *visual* message ex-
  presses your sophistication.

PRESCRIPTION EYEGLASSES AND SUNGLASSES

There they are in the most conspicuous place they could possibly be
and most people don't give enough thought to what kind of an impact
the *glasses* they're wearing can have on their personal image. The
same persons that wouldn't think of wearing junk jewelry will wear
glasses of inferior quality and unflattering design.

- If you choose frames that have *any gold colored metal* on them
  it should be *carat gold*. Other metals soon discolor from wear
  and body contact and look unsightly and cheap. Your glasses
  are the most important "accessory" you wear and they should
  be of the same fine quality as your apparel. Carat gold on the
  fittings for glasses is not a great deal more expensive but will
  remain shiny and distinctive. It would be better to choose

chrome, enameled metal, or plastic than imitation gold.

- Good fit at the bridge of the nose is essential. Glasses should not slide down or pinch. To be constantly adjusting your glasses detracts from your poise and is annoying to you and to your observers.
- The frames of glasses should not rest on the cheeks. They leave marks and over a period of time can permanently mar the face. The glasses will steam up more readily, also.
- Side or temple pieces should be long enough to extend past the ear and not dig into the top of it. What's that do to your image? Gives it a pained frown!
- Frames should *follow* the line of the brow not *cross* it. Oversize frames should cover the brow.
- The *shape* of eyeglass frames can greatly affect your appearance. Your face shape should determine what style frames are best for you:

  Round Face: Look for thick, angular frames to lengthen a round face. Rimless or transparent frames are not good choices as they lack definition.

  Small Face: Don't hide your delicate features with heavy or large frames. Narrow metal frames look best, or anything with fine lines.

  Square Face: No wide, large frames—these will accent the squareness of the facial lines. Roundish frames can soften angular lines.

  A-Line Face: (Narrow at the temples, wide in the jawline.) To give width at the temples, choose glasses with a bar of metal or color at the top and clear at the bottom. Avoid rimless or wire frames.

  Long Face: Glasses with a bar at the top or large rectangular frames tend to shorten the length of the face. Don't choose glasses that extend beyond the sides of your face, or it will appear even narrower.
- Frames should never be jewelled or of faddish design. Side pieces that swoop and curve just add unnecessary detail that's too much. Classic lines are clean and simple.
- If you're in need of bi-focals, please wear them. It really is a funny sight to see little half-size reading glasses parked out on

the end of a person's nose. There stands that politician desperately trying to impress millions of viewers and he vainly refuses to put on proper glasses, choosing instead to look like a clown and peer over these little uglies. How much more distinguished and authoritative he'd look with conventional glasses. How polished!

SUNGLASSES

Because sunglasses have become a glamour accessory, we may not pay attention to the potential danger of certain types. People sometimes look for the design or the prestige celebrity name on the glasses not realizing the importance of the lenses.

Unless sunglasses have protection from ultra-violet rays they can cause severe eye damage. *Because the tinted lens cuts the light, the pupil of the eye opens wide to see. If the lens doesn't filter out ultra-violet rays the pupil is wide open and exposed to damage.* Not all sunglasses filter out these rays. The next time you try on sunglasses, check that little tag that hangs so annoyingly over your nose. It should tell you the type of lenses they are and if they'll do their job. Look for lenses that filter out 90% of UV rays.

Your prescription lenses should do the same. Let your optometrist know that you want this protection.

Here's some further guidance:

Polarized

These lenses *do not* protect from UV rays though some do have UV coating. Your optometrist can add this process to your polarized sunglasses.

Gradient

These lenses are dark at the top and gradually get lighter to-ward the bottom. This screens out overhead light but gives very little protection from UV rays.

Mirrored

These lenses are coated with a thin layer of steel alloy. They give good protection from glare and UV and IR rays because they bounce off up to 85% of light.

CONTACT LENSES

These I'll leave for you to discuss with a professional opthamologist. I'll only say I've worn contacts for thirty years and have never had a problem. When wearing glasses, one has to be careful of what earrings and hats one can wear. The head can get pretty cluttered! With contact lenses that poses no problem.

If contact lenses irritate your eyes, it is better not to wear them. There is nothing attractive about red, weepy eyes. A smart pair of top quality conventional glasses would be far more becoming and can provide an authoritative air.

SHOES

- Shoes of poor quality or wrong style can ruin the appearance of an otherwise perfect outfit.
- There are several grades of leather, and a consumer has to be particularly careful of inexpensive imports. When you consider that there are double import charges in that low price you can imagine how little quality you are getting.
- Not only the shell of the shoe should be leather but it's important that linings also be leather. Leather stretches, breathes, and absorbs perspiration, making shoes much more comfortable to wear.
- Check the stitching. Any loose thread ends can mean poor workmanship. Are joins tight and smooth?
- The shoe should *bend* easily. Leather soles are comfortable and pliable. To protect leather soles, have them treated with a thin rubber coating. This is great for wet weather and also makes the shoes skid-proof. Ask your shoe repair man about this process.
- To protect the heel of your shoe while driving your car, cut off the toe of a man's sock (one of those odd ones whose mate went to sock heaven) make a small slit for your shoe heel and slip the sock over your right shoe and foot. This really saves your shoe. Hang it on your rear view mirror to remind you to put it on. (People's curious stares as you walk down the street will remind you to take it off!)

(Illustration)

- Have heel lifts replaced frequently to avoid damaging the leather covering on the heel.
- Wear shoes that co-ordinate with the *type* of clothes you have on: not sports shoes with dress clothes and tailored business clothes; not strappy sandals with business suits.
- A plain pump with closed toe serves all purposes. Opened toed shoes are not the most appropriate for business wear.
- Polish! Polish! Polish! Here Putting on the Polish has meaning in the most literal sense. Polish protects shoes and puts a shine on good grooming.
- Any heel height from flat to medium high is fine for business wear. Heels higher than 2 1/2 inches are out of place with business wear and business bearing.
- Gold or silver metallic colored shoes should be reserved strictly for evening and *never* for business.
- The seasonal rule: *No white shoes before May 24th or after Sept. 1st.*

HOSIERY

- Hosiery should be of the same color *tone depth* as your shoes *or* skirt unless you choose a natural skintone shade. Dark shoes—dark hosiery. Light (beige, white) shoes—light hosiery. Never light shoes and dark stockings or dark shoes and white or pastel stockings. The only exception is if the hosiery is kept to the *same color depth as the skirt or dress*. To be well dressed, hosiery should carry the eye without a break, so the ideal is light colored clothing, light colored hosiery, and light colored shoes *or*: dark colored clothing, dark*ish* colored hosiery and dark shoes. *I can hear you gasp and say you don't agree,* you've seen the so-called fashion experts doing otherwise. True. You have. That doesn't make it any easier on the eye. In this book we're promoting polish. A light colored skirt, dark stockings and light colored shoes gives a broken line of color and detracts from the overall picture. Nothing looks more impeccable than shoes and hosiery that match in color tone: Black shoes with very *sheer*, medium to dark, black toned hosiery. Navy shoes with a hint-of-navy hosiery. Light grey shoes with light grey toned hosiery. Taupe shoes with taupe toned hosiery. Cream with ivory.

- In summer, various shades of "skin tone" are always attractive, giving a tanned, bare-legged look that goes with all summer clothing. This is the time, when you're wearing lighter colored clothes, that off-white and pastel hosiery blends with skirt and shoes and doesn't disrupt head-to-toe continuity.
- Lace or patterned hosiery is not appropriate for business or street wear. The worst look is white lace stockings worn with black shoes. Have mercy!
- Don't be influenced by off-beat presentations featured in fashion magazines. They aren't of the real world. Fortunately, they no longer have a stranglehold on our fashion decisions. These are the '90's. Our "follow-like-sheep" mentality is long gone. We're more influenced by people of quality in positions of importance because we know they didn't get there wearing kooky get-ups or purple panty-hose.
- Have an emergency pair of hosiery handy. In a small plastic bag they take only a little space in your desk drawer or handbag and can save the day when a glaring run enters the scene. It isn't so much how unsightly it *looks*, it's what it does to shatter your self-confidence that matters.
- Better quality hosiery is tailored to fit, with contoured feet, ankles and leg areas.
- If panty-hose creases at the ankles and feels twisted, they probably haven't been put on properly. It is important to keep the hosiery legs straight from top to toe as the stockings are pulled on. The best way is to carefully gather each leg from top to toe with both hands, and slip the stocking over the toes. Then pull straight up. Repeat with the other hosiery leg. If you wear hosiery for a second time without first laundering them they'll have stretched to fit the contour of your feet—be sure to

put them on to fit this contour or you'll have yesterday's baggy heel sitting on top of to-day's instep! You'll trip!

LINGERIE:

Though it is seldom seen, lingerie can provide profound personal pleasure. Lovely silks and laces in ultra-feminine shades of champagne and petal pink or daring femme fatale red, who is to know a temptress lurks inside that conservative suit? Luxury lingerie is so delightful to wear, why deprive yourself? Enjoy! It's your secret. Keep it that way!

SLIPS

- Even if a skirt or dress is lined, it will keep clean longer and will hang better if a slip is worn beneath it.
- A slip should not pucker or gather and create bulges. It should fit smoothly over the body.
- A full slip will give a smoother line under close fitting dresses. Half-slips are ideal for most other wear, particularly when wearing a dark skirt and a light colored top.
- Clothes look best when dark slips are worn beneath dark colors and light under light colors. Though it is fine to wear light colored lingerie under dark outwear, it is unsightly to wear dark lingerie under light colored outerwear.
- Summer weight, white or light colored skirts that are somewhat transparent require that an opaque or double-panelled slip be worn with them. See through silhouettes: it's fun to *see* one but not to *be* one!

BRAS

The unsung champion of the polished image. (Webster says "champion" means supporter or upholder.) A bra is a champion all right, but sometimes we don't give it a chance to perform. There are two dimensions to a bra: cup size and chest measurement. Chest measurement is taken around the chest *directly under* the breasts. Cup size is determined by the size of the breast itself. An "A" cup would be a small size breast and a "DD" cup would be a very large one. If a person wears a 34DD it means they have a slender body and very large breasts, whereas someone who wears a 40A has a stout body and very *small* breasts. The centre of the bra should lie flat against the breastbone and the cups large enough so that the bra does not pull away at the cleavage. If the bra pulls up in the back it is usually because it is too big in the chest measurement and too small in the cup, or the straps may be too short. The band of the bra should be level all the way around and should not ride up. A badly designed or poorly fitted bra will spoil the line of your clothes. There should be no bulging above or below the bra. Wear bras that give good support and that hide your nipples. All clothes need a good base. Though they are expensive, don't skimp on buying quality bras.

BRIEFS
Briefs should be large enough to avoid bulging and also to avoid cutting off the circulation in the legs if you're sitting for long periods of time. This can cause varicose veins.

Clothing care

For clothing to look its best, it must have care. Most of the time if good quality clothes are hung up properly they'll need a minimum of pressing.

- *Invest in some serviceable hangers*. Padded ones are usually not long enough to support shoulders on coats and suits. These need a strong, *contoured* hanger to help retain the tailored shoulder lines. Most people don't give enough attention to purchasing good quality clothes hangers. The only apparel I'd put on a wire hanger is a cotton shirt or blouse and then only because a wire hanger takes less room in the clothes closet. Use clip-on skirt and pant hangers. Folding slacks over a wire hanger spoils their shape and leaves them creased.
- Give your clothes ample room. Don't cram them in. If space is limited, remove the clothes you seldom wear and place them elsewhere (buy a garment box that is custom-made to fit under a bed).

- When you remove your business or dress clothes, don't immediately hang them in the closet. Hang them on a hanger on a coat rack or over a doorway, so they can air and let the creases fall out before putting them away.
- Give your clothes and shoes *at least a day's rest between wearings*.
- Open your clothes closets doors at night and let air circulate. Louvre closet doors are a help.
- To save your dress and business clothes, get in the habit of changing to casual clothes as soon as the work day is over.
- Check clothes for any stains or spots and remove them immediately with fabric cleaner before they can set.
- Give your clothes a thorough brushing. Open up the pockets, turn them inside out and brush out lint and dust. Mend any loose hems or open seams and replace missing buttons. If you don't do this now, when you think of it, you'll be trying to do it when you're in a hurry.
- Remove any items from the pockets before hanging away your clothes. They'll stretch the garment.
- Don't use *plastic covers* over your clothes. Plastic gives off a gas that discolors and deteriorates fabrics. White wools will quickly turn yellow under a plastic cover. Purchase or sew your own *cloth* garment covers. Or *throw an old sheet over the entire clothes bar*.
- Use a shoe tree for your shoes and don't store them in plastic. Leather absorbs moisture, so shoes need to dry. Puncture air holes in cardboard shoe boxes and store shoes this way. Label the box to identify its contents and stack the boxes on a shelf. They're easy to get at and shoes are organized and protected. There are custom made, cardboard containers that hold a number of pairs of shoes. If your shelf is wide enough these work very well (for handbags too). Look for these in the "notions" departments.
- Always use a pressing cloth when ironing wool. Wool scorches easily and becomes shiny from pressing.
- Keep all washing instruction hangtags and write the garment name on each one, so you'll know how to clean it.
- *Choose your drycleaner carefully*. Guide rules:

- There should be *no smell* of drycleaning fluids in your clothes. This is usually a sign of improperly filtered cleaning solvent.
- A prestige cleaner will stuff tissue paper in the sleeves of garments to avoid creasing.
- Small repairs are made routinely, and stains that can't be removed are brought to your attention.
- If your clothes hold their press, you'll know they were expertly handled.

- If you spill something on silk don't try to remove it by rubbing it. Silk is very delicate when wet so *blot don't rub*. Get it to the cleaners pronto and tell the cleaners what you spilled so they know how to treat it.
- *Pure cotton* and *pure linen* fabrics will shrink if they have not been pre-shrunk. When laundering, use the gentle wash cycle and *remove them from the clothes drier while they are still very damp*, or you won't be able to iron out the wrinkles.
- To avoid having to sew in shoulder pads after each time the garment is laundered, sew strips of velcro in each shoulder seam and on each pad. *But one caution:* The uncovered velcro may grab on to the garment's fabric while it is being washed and make catches. To remedy this, I cut small strips of velcro and place them over the exposed velcro in the garment until the shoulder pads are back in place.
- Decent people that you want to favorably impress will make allowance for or excuse inexpensive clothing, but they *never will disregard unclean, careless grooming. All clothing must be immaculately clean at all times; if it is soiled in any way don't wear it*.

Remember: Dress the part and you'll be the part!

With this book, "Putting on the Polish," you'll be able to in-
itiate these improvements yourself in the privacy of your own
home without anyone knowing you needed a little help. "Put-
ting on the Polish" is your resident image consultant. Always
right there to bolster your confidence.

THE MAN OF THE 1990's

... has a positive self-image and the confidence

to express it.

The man of the 1990's is dressing better, and one of the main reasons
is *competition*. There always has been competition in the work force,
but now career competition includes *women*. Men have found that
women have more experience in knowing how to dress. First impressions being as influential as they are, appearance can give *a woman*
the edge in getting the job, not because she's cuter or sexier but because the business world now recognizes her comparable skills and
her superior ability to enhance her appearance.

Pull up your socks, gentlemen! We all know it's still a man's world,
so you have the edge there, *polish that image!* Classic dressing is not
a foolish luxury, it's a necessity.

Evaluate that image of yours. Start with your wardrobe.
- *Take an inventory of your clothes:* Make a list of each and
  every item under categories of: Suits, Jackets, Slacks, Coats,
  Shirts, Sox, Shoes, Sweaters, Handkerchiefs, Gloves, and
  Belts.
- *Read the following pages on dressing for progress* and then
  we'll determine what part of your present inventory fits into
  your future polished image.

Men: Dressing for progress

Suits

Someone once said that the business suit is a uniform that identifies a person as one who works with his *head* rather than his *hands*. When choosing a suit for business or for special occasion dress, there are four factors to consider: *Cut, Color, Fabric and Fit*.

CUT

Suits are cut in 3 different styles: American, British, and European.

- *The American Cut* has lightly padded shoulders, medium width notched lapels, full cut, straight lines, single rear vent, low armholes. This is the most popular cut and is gaining favor all over the world.
- *The British Cut* is a little more fitted than the American cut with a tuck at the waistline, high side vents, angled pockets and lightly padded shoulders.
- *The European Cut* is very closely fitted, has padded shoulders, tucked waist, contoured to the body. This is the least popular and is very uncomfortable. In my opinion, not even the most perfect physique looks attractive in this exaggerated cut. Little wonder it is losing favor.

COLOR

Research reveals that various shades of *Navy Blue* are the *number one color* choice for business or dress suits. The second most popular color is a *Dark Gray* and other shades of gray met with highly-favored approval. For *summer* suits the *Tans* and *Khaki* shades are popular and appropriate. These colors are also conventional for slacks and separate jackets. *Brown* has *never* been considered a "corporate" color. It is not a color that is complementary to most men's complexions unless it is a very, very, dark chocolate brown. Since brown colored clothing has not met with acceptance in the business world, it would be advisable to avoid it. From time to time, fashion creators have tried to convince men that brown is going to be a winner but it has never happened, so it is too risky to invest in this controverial color. *Green* isn't even to be considered when you're dressing for progress.

FABRIC

When purchasing a suit, the *weight* and the *weave* of the fabric must be considered. The best investment is an *all-seasons' weight* of worsted wool. With our central heating systems and undercover parking, heavy and bulky fabrics are no longer necessary for business suits. An *all-seasons' weight of fabric* will serve year-round, and the substantial funds you invest in a suit won't be unproductive for part of the year. This is where vested suits are particularly useful, as the vest can be worn for more warmth in the colder weather. A fine wool worsted in an *8 ounce weight* (ounces per yard) is ideal. Shades and *weaves* of wool can differ dramatically. An *all-seasons' weave* is very finely woven wool *worsted*. *Wool* is called the "air conditioned" fabric because it is warm in winter and cool in summer. It is the year-round fabric to choose for a classic image. It's the oil in wool that gives it the ability to breathe, absorb, and hold its shape. This makes it ideal for suits. A dignified worsted wool pinstripe or flannel will wear for many years. A worsted wool gabardine in a hard-wearing twill construction is tight and smooth with a crisp finish and is available in all-seasons' weight (8 ounce per yard) or heavier 12 ounce weight. A tropical worsted is perfect for blazers. An 8 ounce weight in a country squire houndstooth check is a great mixer and adds variety to a suit collection.

FIT

It's surprising to see the poor fit of so many top quality suits being worn. Even some custom-made suits aren't up to par. *Fit is extremely important*. Whether purchasing a suit from the racks or having one custom-made, don't be intimidated into accepting anything that is not correct. There is so much misguided information being imposed on the unsuspecting consumer that some of it has become almost the rule. This doesn't make it correct. *When fitting a suit, here are some long-established and reliable guidelines:*

- Wear your best quality suit and a white or plain, solid pastel shirt. This will give the salesclerk or tailor a better perception of your build and of your socio-economic status.
- Wear the type of shoes you are going to wear with the suit. Don't shop in sports shoes.
- Take along all items you usually carry in your suit pockets.

Place these items in the suit pockets to see the fit of the suit before the alterations and final purchase of the suit are made.

- There should be no breaks in the shoulder line. Shoulders should be smooth and straight. You may need a little extra padding added to adjust one shoulder, as most people have one shoulder a little higher than the other one.
- If there are breaks in the jacket sleeves it is an indication that the shoulder padding is too soft. Over a period of time this will only get worse. Select another suit.
- The neckline of the suit should fit closely over the shirt collar even when you shrug your shoulders.
- There should be *no pull* at the button closing.
- *The length of the suit jacket* is correct when, with your arms straight down at your sides, your fingers can curl under the jacket hem.
- *The suit jacket* sleeves should end just below the wrist bone where your wrist meets the back of your hand. This will allow about 3/8 of an inch of shirt sleeve to show. This is why short sleeved shirts are never worn under a suit jacket. *Blazer or sport jacket sleeves should not be shortened this extra 3/8 inch. You may want to wear them for casual dress with short sleeved sport shirts under them and, with no shirt cuffs showing, the jacket sleeves will look too short for you.* If you intend to use a *blazer* only for business or dress wear you might want the shirt cuffs to show and this is acceptable. Many retailers overlook (or don't know!) this rule of proper dress, so be sure to let them know your preference. *Sports jackets* should not have the shirt cuffs show.
- The top of the suit collar should hit the shirt collar about a half an inch down from its top.
- *Lapels should be 3 1/2 inches to 3 3/4 inches at the widest point.* This conventional, medium width will not be out of fashion when fads come and go.
- Lapels should have absolutely *no puckers* in the stitching. *Don't let anyone tell you these can be removed with pressing, they cannot.*
- Lapels should lie flat against the chest and not curl or ripple. Pressing will not correct this.

- *Suit pants:* The waistband of the trousers should be snug but not too tight. You should be able to slide your hand between the waistband and your stomach.
- *Cuffed pants* should touch the top of the shoe and hang straight all the way around. Cuffs should be 1 and 1/4 inches wide.
- *No-cuff pants* should break over the front of the shoe and drop about 1/2 inch at the back. Trousers should rest lightly on the shoe front. The break or slight S-curve at the front crease should not be so pronounced that it looks slovenly. Because trousers tend to slide down a little as you move, be sure that the alterationist doesn't leave the pants too long. Pants that gather at the ankle give an untidy look. There should be only the slightest "break" in the trouser's front crease or the impeccable lines of the entire suit will be destroyed. Invest in a stylish pair of suspenders, they're terrific!
- *A well fitted trouser seat* requires the expertise of a highly qualified tailor. If the seat is not right, the trouser legs will not hang properly. Watch it!

SINGLE OR DOUBLE-BREASTED

Probably single breasted is the better buy. They are always in fashion and they suit all body shapes: tall or short, stout or slim. Only the tall and slim can wear double-breasted styles effectively. Something I dislike about double-breasted jackets and coats is that when they are open they look so untidy with all that fabric "hanging loose." Most people don't need that extra bulk, double thickness of material across their midriff. The latest double-breasted suits, however, do eliminate a lot of bulk and are handsome.

THE VESTED SUIT

The three-piece, vested suit gives a polished look. A vest can provide extra warmth. It is comfortable to leave a suit coat unbuttoned and this doesn't look very tidy without a vest. If you buy a three-piece suit you will have the option of wearing the vest or not. *Voila!* This gives the suit a whole new look.

- *Custom made suits* have always been the ultimate in men's clothing, and more and more *young* men are investing in them. They are initially expensive. I say "initially" because a well constructed custom-made suit will last for many years. Spread that price over several years and the cost-per-wearing is a very pleasant surprise. Divide that cost by the years of pleasure and hours of confidence such quality provides and you'll never again question its value. There's only one problem, you'll never again be satisfied with anything less.

- *Choose the best quality you can afford. At all times choose quality over quantity.* It is far better to always have *the same image of classic quality* than to have an inferior image in a lot of different ways! Buy 2 top quality suits instead of 4 mediocre ones.
- *Select classic styles, fabrics, and fit in navy, gray, black, or tan, solid or conservative patterns.*
- Invest in fabrics of all-seasons' weight and weave.

THE SOFT-STRUCTURED SUIT

A soft-structured suit can look very untidy even on a perfect physique. In business, when you're on your toes and ready to be productive, you won't look that way. Your suit will look like its standing at ease, drooping from your shoulders to your heels.

THE BLAZER AND/OR THE BLAZER SUIT:

Every man's wardrobe should have a blazer. It is the best investment possible.

- A *blazer suit* is especially versatile because both the jacket and the trousers can be interchanged with other garments to extend your wardrobe. If you're purchasing a blazer as part of a suit, it is best that it should have plain buttons instead of brass.
- A blazer suit, or a blazer worn with dark gray slacks, is quite appropriate for any dress-up occasion.
- If a blazer has brass buttons they should be of *pure* brass. A fine jewelry store can supply you with a set of pure brass buttons with or without your initials engraved on them. If you're having your blazer custom-made, ask your tailor to use a set of these buttons. Show your individuality.
- A tropical wool or a worsted wool gabardine are ideal fabrics for a blazer or a blazer suit.

- For summer, a distinctively tailored navy blue blazer is terrific worn with white flannel pants and cream colored silk shirt. Whether it's with dress flannels or cotton ducks there's something about a blazer that is fine, fine, fine!
- When developing an image-concious wardrobe, be sure you include a blazer suit in your collection.

THE SPECIAL OCCASION DRESS SUIT

If you can afford the luxury of one extra-special suit for dress wear, you'll find it does wonderful things for your enjoyment of the occasion. A suit you *never wear for business* gives you a whole new sparkle, just like your "Sunday best" used to do when you were a kid.

- The *fabric* and *color* of a suit is what categorizes it as to its appropriateness for dress or business wear. A dress suit is always dark: *black, navy, or midnight*.
- If a suit has a high percentage of silk in its content, it is more appropriate for special dress wear than for business. Silk gives it a lustre.
- If your budget will allow and you're going all out for dignified grandeur, a midnight blue cashmere suit is the epitome of elegance.
- A *white shirt is always worn with a dress suit*. Why not treat yourself to a custom-made silk one?

TUXEDO

- Call it a *Dinner Jacket or Dinner Suit* and you'll show you are polished. The purist would say that a tuxedo is a dinner suit that has been rented!
- Dinner Jackets come in all 3 silhouettes: American, British, and European. Lapels can be notched or peaked, or a dinner jacket can have a shawl collar.
- Adding your own individual touches can be done with a variety of vests, waistcoats, cummerbunds, or bow ties. The cummerbund can be plain black or in a color that matches the bow tie. I prefer to see a bow tie and cummerbund of the same color tone but a little varied in pattern so as not to look too contrived: for example, a deep blue cummerbund with a deep blue and black paisley patterned bow tie.

- Dinner jackets should be chosen in black or midnight blue. The pale blues and off-beat colors brand you as a bumpkin.
- Plain black *patent* leather slip-on shoes are the ideal for wear with a dinner suit, but a plain toed black slip-on shoe is acceptable. It's hard to believe anyone would be so coarse as to wear athletic shoes with a tuxedo but it *is* being done—for shock value, I guess.
- Shirts worn with Dinner Jackets should be white or ivory with a pleated front. No ruffles, frills, or colors, please, someone might expect you to perform a magic trick or play an accordian.
- Sox should be knee-length, black silk. When people do such unconventional things as going without socks with dress wear, it doesn't label them as being libertarians, it simply reduces their credibility.

Men's slacks

- Your wardrobe should have at least one pair of *gray flannel* slacks and a *taupe* or *tan* pair in a light tropical wool worsted.
- Classic trousers are cut with a straight leg that measures 9 and 1/2 inches at both knee and hem.
- Cuffed pants should have a 1 and 1/4 inch cuff. It should touch the top of the shoe and hang straight all the way round.
- Uncuffed pants should break *very slightly* over the front of the shoe and drop about 1/2 inch at the back. A pronounced break gives a slovenly, untidy look to the trousers. Wear suspenders!
- The waistband should be just snug. You should be able to put your hand between the waistband and your midriff.
- *The rise of the pant should be long enough to allow the pants to come up to the waistline, not sit under the stomach.* The rise is the length of the crotch seam from the top of the waistband at the front to the top of the waistband at the back. Most men do not check this, and there is nothing as unsightly as a big stomach hanging over a belt. *This really brands a man as being low class.*

Men's coats

Men that are very selective and knowledgeable about their suits, often pay little attention to the style and quality of their topcoat. Your coat sometimes is all that is seen. More important than anything else, it should certainly project a look of quality.

COLOR

Tan, khaki, or *beige* are the most classic colors for a man's topcoat. Surveys show that *navy* is acceptable but that *black* looks sinister. A *dark grey* in a chesterfield style is elegant. (*Too* much so for business?)

STYLE

- The most versatile of all styles is the traditional *Trench Coat.* In an all-seasons' weight (with a zip in lining for cold weather) this handsome coat is welcome for any occasion. This double-breasted coat with epaulets and loose shoulder-yoke styling in a water repellent fabric should be of *mid-calf length.* All shades of tan from light beige to deep khaki are the most popular and most wearable trench coats. If you can afford to buy only one topcoat it would be wise to select a top quality trench coat. *The epitome of quality and prestige is a Burberry.*
- A *Balmacaan style* coat is loose fitting, with raglan sleeves, small collar, and plain or fly-front closure.
- A classically tailored top coat in a tan colored luxury wool fabric is always in fashion and exudes a look of quality. Camel hair, alpaca, and cashmere blends are the finest.
- *Chesterfield style:* This is a single or double-breasted, semi-fitted, straight cut coat with a black velvet collar. Rather ostentatious for daily wear but certainly a classic number. Charcoal gray or black are the most acceptable colors.

Men's sweaters

Sweaters always have been and always shall be *indispensable.* They are available in many styles, from cardigans to pullovers to turtle-necks, and each style capably fills a specific function. There are a variety of fibers, from cotton to luxury cashmere.

- You'll get plenty of service out of a Shetland wool *crew neck sweater.*

- A classic *V-neck sweater* in a lightweight wool is important in any man's language and in any man's wardrobe. If you want to own the finest, one that has year-round appeal, choose an expensive cashmere.

Read the chapters on women's clothing purchasing and fiber types, for more specific information.

Men's shirts

COLOR

- *White* is the number one color choice for business wear. In addition to always being correct it takes a man directly from the office to an evening dinner engagement very "properly." But, please, *white must be white*. Cotton shirts with a blend of polyester very quickly acquire a dingy look. When this happens, discard the shirt; it can't be effectively bleached, since it has a percentage of synthetic in its content. Watch this carefully. If you stand beside someone wearing a truly white shirt, your shirt will appear to be "tattle-tale gray."
- *Pale blue* runs a close second to white and is a color that is complimentary to most men's complexions. Pale blue is an easier color to keep from looking discolored.
- *Light cream* is not only popular but looks superb under all suit colors.
- Pale pastels, pin stripes, and bold stripes are all great ways to lend dash to a solid colored suit. These take a little more skill to co-ordinate, but they'll provide individuality to your image.

FABRIC

- A *finely woven cotton broadcloth* is the number one fabric for shirts. This smooth surface with a slight sheen is appropriate for business or dress wear.
- A pure *cotton* shirt is the epitome of polish and of durable performance. Unless it is in the finest of weave, cotton tends to crease badly, but it is cool and very comfortable to wear. It's the ideal.
- *Oxford pinpoint weave* has a rougher texture, so is suited to the button-down-collar shirt which is of more casual style. Not as

versatile as broadcloth.

- Cotton blends don't breathe as well as 100% cotton but are easy care and don't wrinkle. There should be no more than a small percentage of polyester in the blend or you will get pilling of the fabric and whites will be almost impossible to keep white.
- The finest cotton fabric is a Sea Island Cotton, and a two-ply Egyptian cotton is also a prestige fabric. These are not widely available in ready-made shirts, but you should consider having them custom-made.

COLLAR STYLE

- The *collar* of a shirt is available in a variety of styles. Most collar styles are quite appropriate for business or for dress wear but should be chosen to suit the shape of your *face* and your *body build*. The *length and spread of the collar points* has the most influence on the style and suitability.
- A wide spread collar can make a narrow face look broader.
- A long collar can make a wide face look thinner.
- A very narrow collar is out of proportion to a large face and heavy jowls.
- A button-down collar is fine for most facial features but, though it is conservative, it is not always appropriate for evening occasions.
- A very wide, stiff, "Charles Dickens" collar is too uncomfortable for business wear and looks exceedingly ostentatious.
- Experiment with a number of shirt collar styles. Try them on and see which is best for you. Yes, they *are* all packaged up with pounds of cardboard and innumerable pins but when one's *image* is at stake, sir, one *must* persevere!

CUFFS

- Cuffs vary little in style in a ready-made shirt.
- The regular cuff is usually the one chosen for general wear, but French cuffs are especially nice for dress wear. French cuffs are turned back and fastened with cuff links and give the wearer an opportunity to wear a bit of appropriate jewelry.

Custom-made shirts

Top quality ready-made shirts have become so expensive it might be worth your time to check out custom-made ones. The *fit, selection, and exquisite quality* of these shirts make them very practical options.

- Depending on the fabric you select, custom-made shirts can be as inexpensive as a cotton/blend from $40; to Egyptian cotton at $85—$140; and up to the creme de la creme Sea Island cotton at $100—$200. The elegance of silk is skillfully rendered in styles that only custom tailoring could achieve. These fine fabrics are not found in a ready-made shirt. A good basic fabric to choose is a cotton poplin which has been pre-washed to limit shrinkage and creasing.

- Custom-made shirts are available in fabrics and styles suitable for dress, business, and casual wear.

- You can express your *individuality* by choosing from *3 shirt styles* (tapered, medium tapered, and loose); *5 cuff shapes*; and *12 different collars*. In addition to this you'll have *hundreds of fabrics in solids and patterns* from which to establish your own exclusive identity. Even the *pockets* on a custom-made shirt reflect superlative detail. You order combinations that are exactly what *you* want. This is not possible in a ready-to-wear shirt.

- *Fit is absolutely perfect*. As many as 10 to 12 different measurements are taken: 3 for the collar (circumference, back height, and front height); waist; chest; torso; arms; wrist; and cuff depth. A smooth fit allows you to put your finger between your neck and the shirt collar. On ready-made shirts, collars come in only 1/2 inch measures, but custom-made are exactly right for *you*, down to the 1/4 inch. Neat. Trim. More comfortable.

- *Choose your tailor carefully*. The custom-made shirt will reflect the skill of its producer. Ask to see examples of his or her workmanship. *Purchase only from long-established, well-experienced shirt-makers*.

- *First orders are usually for a minimum of 4 shirts*. This may seem a hefty blow to the pocketbook but it's well worth the investment. After the shirt-maker has your measurements on file you usually can purchase shirts one at a time or in larger quantities. It's as easy as a telephone call.

- The stitching in custom-made shirts is much more durable than machine made. The pearl buttons are stronger than plastic and will withstand the pressure of laundry mangles without breaking.
- Your initials distinctively featured on collar or cuff will add the consummate excellence you'll enjoy.
- With a custom-made shirt being as attractively priced as a factory-made shirt, doesn't it prove to be a more viable investment? Its rather wonderful to be able to enjoy all the added benefits of an individually styled and fitted shirt for the same price as a ready-made but in a *much superior fabric*.
- After owning, wearing, and being frequently complimented about this superb garb, I know you'll bet *anything but your shirt* on future wagers!

Men's socks:

- Socks for business and dress wear should be long, over-the-calf length. To be well-dressed, any bare leg showing is indecent exposure! Solid colors of *black, gray, navy, or beige* to co-ordinate with the suit or slacks being worn look the most refined.
- Select socks of finely knit wool or cotton in first class quality. Silk socks for evening wear.
- *Patterned socks*, or "fancies" as they are called in the industry, do have appeal if they are very subtle or subdued in tones of black, gray, navy, or tan. They are available in magnificent cotton blends at about $18 to $20 a pair. With careful selection these can add quite a bit of dash in a distinguished way. *Classic wear for business and dress is never garish*.

Men's handkerchiefs:

Plain *white linen* or *white pure cotton* handkerchiefs with hand-rolled edges will provide you with a perfect 144 square inches of polish! Buy the best available.

- The handkerchief that is placed in the breast pocket is strictly for "show," *it is not used*.
- This breast pocket handkerchief can be placed in the pocket

in 4 different ways:

- The *"square fold"* which shows about a 1/2 inch of the handkerchief at the top of the pocket.
- The *"loose points fold"* which is put in the pocket with the corners of the handkerchief showing about 1 inch.
- The *"4 point fold"* which is put in the breast pocket with the 4 corners of the handkerchief precisely arranged in 4 points, showing about 1 inch.
- The *"loose pouff"* has the corners concealed and the handkerchief loosely stuffed into the pocket with about an inch of pouff showing.

• Buy plain white handkerchiefs, so they can be bleached to snowy white perfection.

• The "functional" handkerchief goes in the pant pocket and *after it is used is never spread out and folded but is discreetly enfolded and returned to pocket*.

Men's shoes

Shoes are of prime importance. If your shoes are out of step with the rest of your apparel you'll have tripped up on a major point of influence. Shoes silently (and *not* so silently if they squeak) shout all kinds of messages about you. If your shoes are of a classic style and well polished they say the owner is that way too and is treading the path of success. Shoes that are run down at the heels, shabby, and/or inappropriate, stand there looking ashamed that they'll never climb the corporate ladder. *Your shoes, more than any other part of your apparel, really reveal who you are, where you came from, and where you're heading. You can't afford to wear shoes of inferior quality*.

CLASSIC TYPES

• The plain *black oxford* is the standard business shoe. This shoe is correct for business or dress. The lace-up style does not get loose and out of shape.

• The *wing tip shoe*, because of the extra piece of leather shaped like a bird's wing over the toe, has a somewhat bulkier look that is fine for business but is not suitable for evening wear. This is a great second pair of shoes to have in your wardrobe.

• *Slip-on shoes* are not the best choice for business wear, but if they are absolutely plain, of top grade leather, and not cut too low in front they will be "tolerated" by the gurus of propriety.

- Slip on shoes, particularly those of patent leather, look best worn with evening clothes.
- Penny or tasseled loafers and moccasins do not belong with a business suit, those are for more casual wear.
- Always buy top quality *leather*. The lining of the shoe should also be leather. The cheap material and strong smelling glue in inexpensive shoes soon take on a very offensive odor. The very minimum you can expect to pay for good quality shoes is $100 to $125. They will last for years. Anything less than that is false economy because you'll be having to replace a cheaper pair and end up paying more for 2 pairs that will never give you a polished image.
- Have your leather soled shoes treated with a rubber coating to protect them from wet weather.
- Always place shoe trees in your shoes to help them maintain their shape.
- Leather shoes absorb moisture. Give them a chance to dry and, by alternating with another pair, try not to wear your shoes more than two days in a row.

Men's underwear

What right does anyone have to inquire about your most private attire? Absolutely none! Just to help you *keep* it private, however, let me suggest:

- Crew neck *undershirts* should not be worn under dress shirts and should not show at a shirt's open neck.
- Briefs or shorts should be loose enough that they don't cut into the seat and spoil the line of your clothes.
- Have a sufficient supply of underwear to change it *every day*. This helps keep your expensive outer clothing fresh and ensures a hygienic "aura."
- *Pure cotton* underclothes are the most comfortable because they are absorbent and cool.

Men's accessories

Your top coat, your suit, your shirt and your shoes are the epitome of polished perfection. You're feeling confident and handsomely attired. Now, all you need is *your own personal signature* on this superb masterpiece. *That's what accessories do. They set you apart and make a positive statement about your individuality.*

TIES:

Your most noticeable and impressive accessory is your tie. It visually communicates your savoir faire.

- *Tie length is important.* The tip of the tie should just touch the belt. Shorter or longer than that and this flag of individuality will become a negative rather than a positive. Ties come in lengths of 54 to 57 inches. It would be a help if the haberdasher would *group* and display ties in the various *lengths.* A tie that is 3 inches too long or 3 inches too short will be impossible to tie to the correct length. We tend to only consider pattern and color when we select a tie but we should consider the wearer's height. When purchasing a tie, have you ever been asked what *length* is required? I haven't. It's evident that haberdashers should pull up their socks!
- The *standard width* of a tie is about 3 1/4 inches at its widest point and this is a safe width to buy. However, widths up to 3 1/2 inches are acceptable. Other widths come and go but a very wide tie dulls the polish.
- The *knot* of a tie should suit the design of the shirt collar, but the "four-in-hand" is the standard business knot. *A tie should be untied when it is taken off,* or the knot will soon show wear and grime.
- A *pure silk tie* gives the *sheen* and allowable flair and panache you infuse to animate an otherwise conservative business or dress suit.
- Choose patterns with bright color accents in the *small part* of the design. Large patches of color take over the picture and smother the intent. *Stripe* and *paisley* patterns are classics. Men's ties get more attractive every year and the opportunity for self-expression is extensive. Intense color can still be discreet. Excellence speaks for itself.
- *Bow ties* are acceptable for business but do you want to show all that shirt front? You may look like a rebel without a cause.

Why sabotage yourself?

- Prudently selected, your tie reflects power and confidence. Those *inner circles of business* will be so impressed they'll drag you in by your tie!

BELTS:

- A plain black leather belt will serve for every purpose. They cost from about $40 on up.
- Metal fittings on a good quality belt should be pure brass or gold or silver or they will discolor.
- A belt is worn *at* the waistline, level with the floor, *not cinched-in under the stomach*. If the fit of your pants won't allow them to come up to the waistline, *the pants do not have a long enough rise*. You should be buying a different cut. *A belt worn slung beneath the midriff will surely brand you as a rube.*
- Purchase a belt by the waist measurement, being sure that it is not so short you must use the last hole, nor so long you leave the end too far overlapped.
- A belt is in a conspicuous spot: front and centre. When it gets shabby, get rid of it.

SUSPENDERS

Whether they're patterned or plain, wide or narrow, suspenders not only add color and bravura to a conservative outfit but they keep your trousers up. *They must be the kind that button onto the pants' waistband, never the clip-on kind.*

JEWELRY

- An absolute minimum of jewelry and, especially, no diamond rings. Does that stifle your craving for opulence? Sorry, but if you want polish you won't find it in glitter, *and* you won't find a man's diamond ring at Tiffany's; their professional savvy says *no*.
- Satisfy your craving for jewelry by concentrating it all on *one* good piece of jewelry that is functional and distinctive: a *carat gold wrist watch*. Choose an exquisitely-understated watch of thin design with *a carat gold* or *a good quality leather strap*. If you require a watch for rough and tumble wear, have a second

one for those activities.

- If carat gold is not in your budget, choose a watch of simple design of *the best quality you can afford*. It would be unfortunate to detract from a well groomed image with a bulky wrist watch capable of performance twenty thousand leagues under the sea.
- A *signet ring* of good quality is acceptable for business wear.
- A man's plain, *carat gold wedding band* looks much more refined than one that is set with jewels.
- For dress wear, a ring with *certain* birthstones, such as a star sapphire or a bloodstone, is acceptable, but *never wear more than one ring on each hand* and that *includes* a wedding band.
- A ring should be in proportion to the *size* of the hand. Large hands require large rings.
- A carat gold *tie bar* is great for keeping your tie in place. A simple *tie tack* or *tie pin* looks proper but can be somewhat damaging to an expensive tie.
- A carat gold *collar pin* is excellent if you can wear your collar pinned in close.
- You'll need *cuff-links* for shirts with French cuffs. Keep them simple and of superb quality.
- *Don't mix your metals!* Whether you prefer silver or gold colored accessories, choose belt buckles, rings, watch, tie clips, cuff links, *all in the same metal*.

BRIEFCASE

- Leather in the best quality you can afford.
- Color: tan, black, or deep burgundy.
- Your briefcase should have the *slenderest* lines with which you can cope. It must, of course, be functional, but a narrow, trim-looking briefcase denotes power. Men at the top of the corporate ladder don't carry big, hard structured briefcases.
- There should be a minimum of metal fittings and they should be of good quality brass, or they'll discolor.

WALLET

- Black or brown leather.
- The most appropriate wallet is the flat, fold-over, inside

breast-pocket type.

- Keep your wallet trim and neat, not bulging with credit card receipts and other paraphernalia.

P E N

- In this day and age of credit buying, we're signing for this, that, and the other, so our *pens* are always on display. There is a fine selection of quality pens on the market. Invest in a beautiful gold one from Cross or, if that's too rich for your blood, consider a silver or chrome one. Magnificent black ones are "quietly" handsome, careful you don't show it off so much you get writer's cramp!
- You'll probably find that a ballpoint pen is most suitable for signatures where there are carbon copies involved. Nibbed pens don't provide enough pressure.
- A nibbed pen will give your signature much more character, as it forms thin and thick lines. Have a look at the superb selection of pens. They are magnificent. Talk about polish!
- Don't scrimp. A fine pen is a man's "jewelry." Make your mark in the most distinctive way.

U M B R E L L A
It's black, and it has a plain wooden handle.

G L O V E S
The simplest style in the finest leather.

Men's casual clothes
There are so many handsome, absolutely outstanding casual clothes for men that I couldn't begin to evaluate each fashion. Here's where you can sport your own identity. The easy-care of very elegant sports and casual clothes makes them quite practical for both participating and spectator sports fans. Meticulous styling gives a man a look of debonair refinement. Indulge yourself, but keep in mind that *it's better to have quality over quantity,* and this applies to your casual apparel as much as to your other wear. *You're the man with polish in every aspect of your life.*

Men's wardrobe analysis

- Take all the garments out of your clothes closet. Pile them on the bed or any convenient place.
- Get 2 large cartons. Label one: *"Reconsider,"* and label the other: *"Disposal."*
- Make a list. Head up a ruled page of paper as follows:

ITEM	1.	2.	3.	4.	5.	6.	7.	W	R	D

- You're going to pick up each garment one by one and, as you do, enter it on that list. Tell yourself to *be ruthless,* you want to eliminate the negative and *build* on the positive.

As you evaluate each garment, ask yourself

(1) *"Does it suit my present and future lifestyle?"* If you haven't been wearing it because it no longer is appropriate for the *appearance* that you want for a polished image, put it in the *"Disposal"* carton. Put a check mark under the "D" on the list. *Don't* return it to your wardrobe. If it does suit your present lifestyle, make a check mark under column (1) and go on to the question (2).

(2) *"Does it fit my measurements?"* If the garment is not a perfect fit but could be altered and it meets the criteria of a polished image, place it in the *Reconsider* carton. Make a check mark under the "R." If it fits well, make a check mark under number (2) and go on to question (3).

(3) *"Is it good quality?"* If it is getting shabby, has permanent stains, or doesn't meet the standards of your future image, here's where you must be totally ruthless. It doesn't belong in *your* life, so put it in the *Disposal* carton to sell, to donate, or to trash. If it's of good quality, clean, and wearable, make a check mark under number (3) and go on to question (4).

(4) *"Do I enjoy wearing it?"* If you don't think that the garment does anything for you, doesn't inspire your confidence, or is going to hang

in the closet and not be worn, place it in the *Disposal* carton and place a check mark under the "D" column. If it suits you for color and style and you enjoy it, check column (4) and go on to question (5).

(5) *"Is the fabric appropriate?"* If you've moved from a cold climate to a warmer one or vice versa, you may have perfectly good, top quality clothing that you seldom wear. This may be useful at some time. Place it in the *Reconsider* carton for further evaluation. Make a check mark under the "R." If the fabric is suitable for your wardrobe, make a check mark under (5) and go on to question (6).

(6) *"Is the style classic or, at least, current?"* If the garment is too flashy or obtrusive for a polished image, it's not for you. Place it in the *Disposal* carton and check the "D" column. If it's of classic or of an acceptable current style, check column (6) and go on to procedure (7).

(7) *A garment that has made it through all 6 evaluations deserves to be hung in your closet with pride. Evaluate each item in this way. This is the nucleus around which you're going to build and retain a positively polished and practical wardrobe that will place you on the road to progress and keep you there*

Take your *sweaters, shirts, sox, shoes, handkerchiefs, underwear,* and *all accessories* and evaluate them in the same way. Do not place anything back into your dresser drawers that you aren't going to use any more. Place them in carton "R' or carton "D." List only what you are going to keep, for example: 6 pr socks, 3 sweaters, etc. If you want a progressive image, it means *quality for all things at all times,* you can't have polish on a part-time basis. Even a handkerchief is significant!

You now have a list of all the apparel you own. Review it carefully. If you are in doubt about how you've evaluated any piece, look it over again. Your list will tell you if it is in your closet or in which carton it was placed. Perhaps you'd like someone else's opinion, just be sure you ask someone who *knows* what a polished image demands.

Arrange your clothes closet so your casual and dress/casual clothes are separated from your business and dress clothes.

Your major concern, where you'll concentrate first, is your business and dress wear.

The following is a list showing a well-balanced, classic wardrobe:

TOPCOAT:	*1 Trench coat*. The ultimate is a Burberry.
SUITS:	*5 Suits* in "Allseasons' weight" fabrics.
	Suggestions:
	1 Navy Business or Dress Suit
	1 Navy Blue Blazer Suit
	1 Dark Grey Suit
	1 *Mini*-Houndstooth Check Suit
	1 Khaki/Tan Tropical Worsted
	1 Suit Extra Light Weight Summer Suit
	Suggestion: A tan poplin
BLAZER:	1 Navy Blue All-seasons' weight.
SPORTCOAT:	1 Camel or Subdued Pattern
SLACKS:	4 All-seasons' weight
	Suggestions:
	1 gray flannel
	1 taupe worsted wool gabardine
	1 navy blue
	1 black

SHIRTS:	10	3 white, 3 lt. blue, 2 cream, 2 striped
SWEATERS:	2	1 Shetland crew neck, 1 V-neck
NECKTIES:	10	Patterned silks
SHOES:	3	1 Plain laced black oxford
		1 Wingtip black oxford
		1 Slip-on Black (Does for dress.)
BELTS:	2	2 Black Leather (1 dark ox blood?)
SOCKS:		12 pr. over-the-calf black, navy, gray, beige
UNDERWEAR:		12 sets white cotton shorts and vests
GLOVES:		1 pr. black fine leather
BRIEFCASE:	1	leather, slender style, black or brown
WALLET:	1	black or brown leather
PEN:	1	prestigious quality
UMBRELLA:	1	black, plain wooden handle

CASUAL DRESS CLOTHES:

Tasseled loafers; button-down shirts; silk sports shirts; polo shirts; white cotton ducks; etc. *Always buy very good quality rather than quantity*.

A man's total image: publicly always prepared

Many people have comparable skills, and competition in the job market is keen. Your appearance can be the selling factor that wins you the position. Approach every day as if you are going for an interview, you don't know when or where someone of importance may be evaluating your appearance. When I was a "Head Hunter," an Executive Recruiter, I always had my eye out for that special person to fill that certain, choice, corporate position. A well-groomed, conservative appearance is what first triggers interest.

HAIR
Cut and style are extremely important.
Consider every angle: back, front, and profile. Read the chapter on *Hair*.

FINGERNAILS
The flags of good grooming.
Read the chapter on *Grooming*. Almost every part of this book, "Putting on the Polish," is as applicable to *men* as it is to women. Read it from cover to cover and follow the guidance of this, *your own private "image consultant."*

Semper paratus: Always prepared

LOOK THE PART,
BEHAVE THE PART,
AND YOU'LL BE THE PART.

CHAPTER FOUR

EFFECTIVE
COMMUNICATION

CHAPTER FOUR

EFFECTIVE COMMUNICATION

Silent and Otherwise

What we silently say about ourselves is much more revealing than any words we speak. We know our clothes and grooming have influence but we need to be aware that our *bearing* is every bit as important. Our "body language" and attitude very profoundly affect other people's reactions to us.

Posture

Poor posture can project a message of laziness. Only the elderly can be excused for a stooped or twisted stance. All others are viewed in an adverse light: clothes hang badly, stomachs protrude, and the entire profile is that of a loser.

The remedy
For youthful posture, lift your head as though you are being hoisted to the sky by the hair at the crown of your head. Pull in your chin, contract your buttock muscles, and tuck in your pelvis. Draw your stomach in and lift the diaphragm. A helpful exercise is to practise walking with a book on your head. Try it.

When standing, keep your knees slightly bent. Locked knee joints can cause a swaybacked appearance and can create a bowlegged look that undermines an otherwise well-groomed figure.

Briefcases and shoulder bags twist the spine and pull your clothing out of shape. If you frequently carry either of these, don't carry them on the same side all the time, alternate sides to give your spine a rest.

When sitting, keep the small of your back against the chair's back with your feet flat on the floor. If the chair is too large or very soft, sit near the edge and lean a bit forward. (In an interview, try to choose a straightbacked chair, an overstuffed one can swallow you and overwhelm your self confidence.)

Women: If you *do* sit with your legs crossed, slant both legs to the same direction. Example: cross left leg over right, then move your right leg to slant to the *right* or cross right leg over left and move the left leg to slant to the *left.* This looks more graceful. *When not crossed,* with knees held together, legs slanted to one side can also provide a look of refinement.

Men: A man has much less limitation as to his sitting posture *as long as he doesn't slouch.* To assume that sliding down in a chair and lolling about gives a look of confidence and sophistication is an error of major importance. *Man* and *woman* should project a respect for their audience, *sit up and take notice!*

Body gestures: kinesics.

Body gestures give silent messages that may sabotage your image. Kinesics means the study of communication through body movement. It is non-verbal communication with a pronounced effect! Silent communication by way of grooming and apparel is intentional and planned. Communication telegraphed by way of posture and gestures is *usually subconscious,* you aren't aware you are revealing damaging information. I say "usually" because some gestures are very intentional, very meaningful, and easily understood. *We can learn to project body language that's more conducive to a polished image.* Let's analyze some gestures as to whether they're complimentary or detrimental, and let's consider some ways to improve our silent communications.

The handshake
The first unspoken communication two people are involved in sharing is a handshake. A timid little grasp with limp fingers projects an attitude of insecurity or inferiority, or worse: disinterest. This immediately gives an unfavorable impression.

SOLUTION
Step forward with a bit of warmth and take the extended hand in a firm but comfortable handshake which imparts sincerity, confidence, and *interest*.

Eye contact

Eye contact can be so expressive it has to be used discreetly. Eyes can reveal varying degrees of every emotion from love to profound contempt. We relate shifty eyes to dishonesty, when it may be inhibition. A bold stare may be perceived as insolence, when it's really a result of near-sightedness. Through our entire lives, from cradle to grave, our eyes send and receive the most genuine communications quite involuntarily. It is imperative that we be aware of our expressions.

SOLUTION
Look directly at with whomever you are speaking but, so as not to appear glaring, look *down* occasionally. *Don't shift your gaze from side to side, this looks evasive.* Give full attention to the conversation and your eyes will reflect your interest. *If you need glasses wear them.* A frowning, squinting, countenance can innocently send angry signals that inspire disharmony.

Crossed arms

Crossing your arms across your chest indicates you are on the defensive. You, and the person with whom you're conversing, won't know why, but suddenly a barrier has been erected: *a negative influence*.

SOLUTION
Break the habit of crossing your arms when in conversation with someone. Be approachable.

Touching face

Holding your hand to your face or over your mouth implies deceptiveness, according to communication experts. This gesture, even if not misinterpreted, is not attractive. If you partially cover your mouth with your hand or fingers, it muffles your speech. This is a gesture that is often engaged in by people that are middle-aged or elderly.

SOLUTION

For the sake of your image and for the benefit of a clear complexion, keep your hands off your face. Be youthful!

Clenched hands

Tightly clenched fists reveal a lack of confidence and show intense stress. This is even more pronounced if the thumb is tucked inside the fist. Unfortunately, the tighter the hands are clenched, the more tense we become and the entire body stiffens.

SOLUTION

If you are sitting down, place your hands wide open, fingers to-gether loosely, palms down against your lap. *It is difficult to be tense if the hands are relaxed*. Whether standing or sitting, consciously remember to open the palms and relax your hands, particularly in stressful situations.

Undermining mannerisms:

Scratching just never is done in public. I don't know if TV studios are infested with vermin, but it seems that all guests on talk shows are constantly scratching. Many people don't seem to realize that scratching the head also is objectionable and certainly detracts from a polished image.

SOLUTION

Determine what is creating the condition that makes you scratch. If it's dry skin or dry scalp, apply treatment. If it's simply a bad habit, leave the habit and the scratch to the race track.

Lip licking

Probably licking the lips starts as a nervous habit and creates a dry condition of the lips that necessitates more licking to moisten them— a vicious cycle and a deplorably unsightly one.

SOLUTION

A tube of Blistex either in salve or in stick form will heal the lips, and the medicated taste might help to remind you to break the habit.

Fidgeting

Constantly adjusting your tie, twisting your ring, playing with your beads, fussing with your hair, are all *negative mannerisms*. This fidgeting draws *all* the attention and robs you of your polished image.

S O L U T I O N
Concentrate on having refined composure.

Personality

Personality: the totality of an individual's characteristics; psychological, emotional, intellectual, and physical.

An individual's personality seems to be, if not innate, certainly established soon after birth. The smallest child can have a winning personality or, conversely, have no charm what-so-ever. Innate as it may well be, *it is possible to develop a gracious personality*.

- *Smile:* The shyest, most inhibited person can manage a smile. It's the least expensive and most effective face-lift in which you can indulge. A smile is like turning on a switch, it brightens where-ever you are and electric vibrancy begins to flow. *A pleasant and sincere smile combined with eye contact is more valuable than expensive apparel or impeccable bearing.* That doesn't mean you go around constantly grinning, being the resident idiot. It means the kind of smile that projects genuine warmth and interest. Savoir faire personified!
- *Be considerate: If you can forget about yourself and endeavor to put other people at their ease you'll have mastered the finest characteristic of a winning personality. You, too, will be at ease.* Being considerate is simply realizing that *almost everyone has a little insecurity in their make-up and would appreciate being put at their ease.* To do that you'll have regard for:
    - *Courtesy:* Know the rules of exemplary etiquette. That's what etiquette is: consideration for others.

- *Patience:* A winning personality exercises patience in all personal associations. Hurrying someone along that speaks hesitantly or rushing a situation to the discomfort of some-one else, are examples of impatient behavior and an unpleasant personality.
- *Loyalty:* Being supportive and loyal to friends, associates, employers, and employees, not only reflects a rare and important personality trait but will win you loyalty in return.
- *Tolerance:* Respect for other people's opinions, religious beliefs, ethnic behavior, or any other aspect of living, different than your own, reveals a well-adjusted, confident personality that is not threatened by disparity.

Think about each of these characteristics of an engaging personality. *Nobody is perfect,* but with a little perseverance we can knock some of the rough corners off an abrasive idiosyncrasy or two. A polished image demands a pleasant and *enthusiastic personality*.

Voice and speech

Ben Jonson said: "Speak that I may see thee."

How very true. A person can look attractive and be beautifully groomed, but when they open their mouth and speak we "see" the *entire* picture. *It is such a disappointment when that voice or manner of speaking does not enhance the initial appearance. In fact, the sound and delivery of the spoken word can destroy an otherwise polished image. Can even destroy a relationship.*

You have many different sides to your personality, and you have many different *sounds* to your voice. What do you have to say for yourself? *Do you sound successful?*

The mouth is not the source of speech, nor is the nose, but these two organs affect the sound and delivery of the voice. *The sound of the voice is actually produced by air.*

Improving the voice for a polished and cultured image:
There are three components that create speech. Using each of these most effectively will declare your culture and polish:
Breath, Sound (Resonance), and Articulation.

BREATH

- *The diaphragm* is a powerful muscle that lies under the lungs, pulling air into the lungs like a bellows. Your *posture* greatly affects the diaphragm. By sitting and standing erect, you give the diaphragm room to draw sufficient air into the lungs to project a controlled and resonant voice. Exercising the diaphragm improves your breathing and strengthens your voice. Do the following exercises standing comfortably erect. Don't take a deep breath just breath normally. (1) Take a short breath and, as you exhale, hiss through your teeth. See how long you can hissssss on this one short breath (count quickly to yourself). *Don't force your breath.* You probably can count to about 28 or 30. Keep practising and you'll soon be able to count higher as you improve your ability to control your breath. (2) Take a short breath and, as you exhale, count aloud as fast as you can and see how far you can count without taking another breath and *without forcing your breath.* You'll probably count to about 75–90. Practise this every day and you should make it to 125–135. *The more control you can master over your exhaled breath, the more you'll be able to develop your voice from thin and timorous to mellow and confident.*
- There are many places that you can practise developing the breathing muscles. Going up stairs, see how many stairs you can climb on a single breath *exhalation.* Out walking or golfing, see how far you can walk with *one single exhalation.* As you develop your ability to control your breath, your voice will be improved. You won't have to speak in little short gasps, there'll be strong muscle (diaphragm) control projecting your words effortlessly. An added bonus is that a few long, slow, controlled breaths can settle your nerves. Try it just before you go up to make a speech or go in for an interview. This is why women are taught to pant when going through natural

childbirth, controlled breathing can reduce pain and eliminate panic.

SOUND (RESONANCE)

- *The larynx (commonly called the Adam's apple)* is the large lump at the front of your neck. It is not as large in women as it is in men. Behind the larynx is the *voice box* which is made up of two membranes called *vocal cords*. As air passes by the vocal cords they vibrate, and this creates *sound. Men's vocal cords are usually about 1/3 longer than women's,* and this is why their voices are much lower and resonant. The longer the cords, the slower the vibration and this results in a lower *tone*. Women's shorter vocal cords produce higher pitched sounds, and this is why *women should learn to speak in more moderate tones or their voices sound high pitched and irritating.* Intelligent, informative communication can be impaired if delivered in an abrasive sound of voice. Women, as much as men, find this high pitched, nagging sound, aggravating. Radio and television producers have used it as a reason for not hiring women for on-air positions. This isn't to say that all *men's* voices are pleasant. *Far from it.* I only am acknowledging that *women,* because of having shorter vocal cords, *must do more work on their voices to deliver a more agreeable sound.*

- When sound is produced, it then reverberates as an echo. To do this, it must have an enclosed space for the echo to form. Your voice box and vocal cords determine the *pitch,* resonance determines the quality of the *tone*. If the echo is formed in the nose, the tone will be twangy and nasal. If the echo is projected from the chest, the tone will be vibrant and impressive. The words you deliver will be supported by a rich, agreeable sound. All speakers should pay attention to this important influence.

ARTICULATION

- To shape sound into words, we use our *mouths,* our *tongues,* our *teeth,* our *lips,* and our *cheeks*. A lazy tongue can neglect to form sound properly, and articulation is then distorted. Words sound slurred and are difficult to interpret. This is the way an inebriated person sounds because they don't have control of their tongue. Conversely, using the tongue and lips *too precisely* can produce sound that is clipped and pretentious. *Children learn to speak by listening to what they hear. If they hear carelessly formed words, that is the way they learn to say them.* The agility of the tongue is also influenced by generations of use of a particular language. For that reason certain nationalities have difficulty producing specific sounds, for example: it is easy to identify someone of a Swedish background if they say a "Y" sound for a "J," or those of a Chinese culture have a problem articulating an "L' or an "R." The commonest articulation error by people of other than an English speaking background, is saying a "d" sound instead of "th": "these," "them," "this," and "that" become "dese," "dem," "dis," and "dat." The tongue is placed *flat* under the upper front teeth (as though to bite it) to form a "th." If the tongue is *curled* against the roof of the mouth behind the teeth a "d" sound results. Most people do not even know they are doing this and aren't aware that it detracts from effective presentation. This isn't a biased criticism, it is simply a fact that, *due to genetics,* we each must labor to overcome *innate mannerisms* of speech. English speaking people have difficulty manipulating their tongues to produce certain sounds in other languages, and these are just as obvious to people of those nationalities. Whatever the language, the sound of the voice and the way those sounds are articulated will have great influence on one's image.

Practice effective breathing, sound projection, and articulation. Open a large magazine and holding it about four inches from your face, speak into it. Listen to the sound of your voice. Is it nasal? Is it too high-pitched? If possible, work with a tape recorder. Listen to your voice and evaluate its sound. *Work on producing a lower tone.* Perfect enunciation won't be appreciated unless it is delivered with a *sound* that strokes the ear and bids the listener hope for more.

- *A high pitched voice lacks authority and annoys.* Hold your hand on the centre of your chest just under the collarbone.

Speak in a high voice. There will be no vibration. Speak a little lower, then lower and lower. As you lower the pitch of your voice, there will be increased vibration which produces a more mellow tone. *When you reach a low tone that is natural and not harsh sounding, strive to keep this tone in all your conversation.* Read aloud with your hand on your chest, to get in the habit of speaking in a low pitch. Print the words: *"pitch low"* in red ink on several stickers. Put a sticker on your home telephone where you'll see it when phoning. Put a sticker on your phone at work. Put one on your appointment diary. Where-ever you are, remind yourself when you talk to *"pitch low."*

- *Don't shout.* Project your voice. Deliver it to the farthest corner of the room without shouting. Public speakers, particularly politicians, frequently raise their voices *higher* and *higher* in a shout instead of propelling the voice in a vibrant and authoritative natural pitch that lets the microphone magnify the intensity. *Pitch low* with emphasis.
- *Don't mumble.* Open your mouth and let the sound out.
- *Relax the throat.* Consciously think that, when speaking, the throat should always be *open* except when making the sound of "ng," "m," or "n," for example: say "so*ng*," "to*ng*ue," "bri*ng*"—feel the throat close? Now say other words and feel the throat open. When you are nervous, the throat tightens and the voice will come out through these taut muscles sounding strained and tense. Relax your jaw and tongue and work the throat muscles as if to yawn. If you're making a speech, take a drink of water. Relax.
- *Don't cough or strain, to clear phlegm from your throat.* Chew lightly on the back of your tongue and this will produce saliva. *Swallow* the irritation away. Hacking or "harrumphing" will only damage the vocal cords and cause more problems.
- *Speak at a reasonably fast pace.* It's tiresome to listen to slow, deliberate speech.
- *Practice saying a sentence with "W's," to keep from speaking through your nose.* "Wee Willie Winkie was wistfully wondering when worse weather would weaken weary wanderers." Memorize a sentence with "W" alliteration and repeat it

quickly several times a day to rid your voice of any nasal sounds.

What do you have to say for yourself?

- *An enthusiastic voice,* like a lively tune, lifts the spirits, yours and all those around you. Speaking with the shoulders slumped and your head down gives no room for breath support and your voice will sound tired and old. In any situation where you want to win approval, you'd be wise to present a dynamic attitude and your voice must contribute to that attractive vigor.

- *Don't fake it.* Whenever we try to present a front that isn't really our true selves, we lose immeasurably. To try to sound like a favorite actor or actress is so blatantly pretentious that you lose all credibility. A British accent is one which many people try to copy, in an endeavor to be la-di-da, but they never master it correctly and end up sounding like "prop-ah" fools. Be yourself. Why should you want to be anyone else? *You* are terrific.

- On the other hand, *you have an extensive vocal repertoire,* each one authentic, each one your very own. Be sure you present each vocal "personality" at the appropriate time. For example: the authoritative, completely businesslike voice you use at the office is softened and perhaps even seductive when used in a personal and private relationship. Reverse that and use a sexy, breathy voice when making a business presentation and every hope of being taken seriously will be doomed. *In an endeavor to be appealing, this is a mistake many young women make.* If your motive is to progress in business, or in any other aspect of living, it is important to *sound* the part that you want to be.

- *Don't be monotonous.* In addition to having your voice play supporting parts in various "roles," do different things with your voice. Keep your listeners interested, modulate the tones of your voice. *Think about what you want to say,* then say it without being verbose. Be concise but not abrupt.

- *Don't be a bore.* Some of the worst bores are the "I, I, I" kind that commandeer the conversation with constant talk about themselves; the "oh so funny" kind that, in trying to be witty, turn everything into a joke; the "relate every detail" kind that must be specific about the event, the place, the weather, etc., etc., etc. If someone has called you a bore, don't be disheartened. You may just be associating with people that can't relate to your intellect. Pay attention to the criticism, however, and gear your conversation to the appropriate level. It is never a person's intention to deliberately bore anyone.

PRONUNCIATION

It would be unfortunate if, after striving to develop a cultured and spirited voice, it were impaired by careless pronunciation. These are some of the most prevalent pitfalls that result from careless pronunciation:

- *Dropping the "g"*. It reduces your status quo when words such as "being" and "having" are pronounced as "bein'" and "havin'" or "keeping" as "keepin'."

- *Dropping the "h" in "wh."* Pronounce "when" and "while" and "which" and "wharf" and "white" as if blowing the breath. Practice this by holding a sheet of paper about 6 inches from your face. Blow the paper with the "wh" sound. Say the above words, if the paper doesn't move, you are probably saying "wen" and "wile" and "wich." This is lazy pronunciation. Practice saying the following sentences until you don't even have to think about blowing the "wh," it'll become habit:
  "Mr. Watt asked *wh*i*ch* way Mr. *Wh*ite went." "William considered *wh*ether it was wise to wear the *wh*ite wig and *wh*iskers."

- *Omission of consonants at the end of a word*. The tongue is naturally lazy. "Cts" and "sts" are difficult combinations. "Acts," "facts," "objects," "lists," "fists" are examples. Practice saying these words placing *extra emphasis* on the last three consonants. Then practice saying them naturally to avoid sounding affected.

  | mints—mince | wend—went | told—toll |
  | prints—prince | and—Ann | used—use |

tents—tense	band—ban	Bess—best
dents—dense	fold—foal	less—lest
goal—gold	lass—last	ask—asked
cents—sense	lend—lent	bold—bowl
pass—past	mend—meant	cold—coal

See how different the meaning of the word becomes when you omit the final consonants? It is important.

- *Mispronouncing "lm" and "sm."* Avoid the introduction of a vowel sound between "l" and "m" or "s" and "m" in such words as "elm," "helm," "film," "realm," "chasm," "enthusiasm," "communism," "baptism." "M" is produced with the lips closed, so close the mouth quickly after saying "s" or "l." Not "fil-um" but "film"; not "enthusias-um" but "enthusiasm"; not "communis-um" but "communism."

- *Interchanging consonants.* These consonants often require a lot of practice, because they so frequently are slurred over. Concentration on these consonants should be crisp but understated. It is a fine art to speak clearly but naturally, being careful not to *over*-enunciate. Practice the following:

(t-d)	better, letter	not	be*dd*er , le*dd*er
(p-b)	potatoes, principal	not	*b*otatoes, princi*b*al
(f-v)	have to, progressive	not	ha*f* to, progressi*f*
(s-z)	has to, because	not	ha*s*s to, becaus*s*se
(k-g)	recognize	not	reco*k*nize (nor reca-nize)
(ch-j)	just, mileage	not	*ch*ust and milea*ch*
(sh-zh)	adhesion, adhe*zh*ion	not	adhe*sh*un,

- *The sound "u" (yew) pronounced as "oo."* The preferred pronunciation is y + oo for example the word "duke" should be pronounced "dyook" not "dook." For a lazy tongue "oo" is easier than "yoo." The tongue has hard work when d, t, l, n, s, or "th" precedes "u." After "r" or "l" preceded by a consonant, and usually after "j" and the sound of "sh," the sound is "oo": as in blue (bloo), rule (rool), June (Joon), and sure (shoor). No wonder so many people have trouble pronouncing words correctly, English is a very confusing language!

Practice saying these words to get the "yoo" sound:

due (dyoo)	New York (Nyoo York)
feud (fyood)	tulips (tyoolips)
duty (dyooty)	beauty (byooty)
lute (lyoot)	tutor (tyooter)
muse (myooz)	stew (styoo)
news (nyooz)	avenue (avenyoo)
duly (dyooly)	constitution (constityooshun)
figure (figyoor)	education (edyoocashun)
neuter (nyooter)	inauguration (inaugyoorashun)
produce (prodyoos)	literature (literatyoor)
suit (syoot)	opportunity (opportyoonity)
reduce (redyoose)	supreme (syoopreme)
dude (dyood)	maturity (matyoority)
tune (tyoon)	fortune (fortyoon)
picture (pictyoor)	institute (instityoot)
capture (captyoor)	altitude (altityood)
stupid (styoopid)	enthusiasm (enthyoosiasm)
Tuesday (Tyoosday)	numeral (nyoomeral)
studio (styoodio)	vacuum (vac-yoo-um)

Practice these sentences:

"The wind blew the student from the zoo to the new institution on the avenue."

"The opportunity and duty of the duke was to institute education and manufacture in New York."

- *Running words to-gether*. Slurring is a common speech fault. The lazy tongue both runs words to-gether and drops sounds. The polished speaker makes each word easily intelligible and cuts the words apart. At all (adoll), had to (haddoo), give him (givum), at them (attum), by him (by-im), could you (cudja), caught him (coddim), on him (on-im), do you (dooya), put him (puddim), give me that (gimmee that), don't know (dunno), want to (wanna), at him (addim), let me (lemmee), did you ever (dija ever), is he (izzy), better than (beddern), going to (gonna), more than (morn), would you take them (woojatakum), can't you go (canja go), heard her (herder), what did you say (wujasay). *What DID you say?????*

- *Fillers: "Um, sorta like, y'know."* The use of slang, swearing, or "fillers" is conspicuous evidence of a limited vocabulary. The hesitancy of an "um" between every other word is either a bad habit or lack of concentration on what you're trying to say. To hesitate is not as noticable or irritating if that "um" isn't spoken. Be silent while you search for a word. Often this hesitancy is a result of trying to be overly impressive with your vocabulary. Far more intelligence is revealed by speaking smoothly and clearly in very simple every-day words than by *struggling with "ums" and "ahs" and "you knows"* in an effort to find words to express yourself more impressively. Get that tape recorder out and *listen to yourself.* Most people don't realize how burdened their conversation is with these detrimental fillers. Ask a friend to help you break this noxious habit. Since this is so common a problem, you can probably help him or her at the same time. Start with the filler, "you know." Every time either of you say "you know," point it out. You'll end up in side-splitting laughter when you realize how frequently it occurs. Do this with each filler until you rid your conversation of the culprits. The greatest help you can get in developing a more extensive vocabulary is to *read. People that speak exceptionally well are usually avid readers. Reading helps you to broaden your vocabulary, expand your intellect, and develop your opinions.* You'll speak with confidence and conviction, without the aid of fillers, because you'll have something interesting to say and the ability to express it. Read up on subjects that interest you so that reading becomes a pleasure not a chore. *Read your way to progress!*

Common errors in speaking

- *Raising your voice at the end of a sentence when not asking a question.* You'll sound like you're not sure of yourself and are asking for approval of your comment. *Drop your voice at the end of a sentence.* This has a ring of confidence.

• *Using the word "goes" instead of "says" or "said."* An example of this is when you say: "He was asked his name and he *goes*, 'I think it's Steve'" instead of he *says*, "I think it's Steve." This is not only a violation of acceptable language, it brands you as an emulator of the "crass approach" to speaking.

• *Saying "old adage" or "old antique."* The *old* is superfluous. Simply say "adage" or "antique."

• *Using an "er" with "more."* Examples: more greener; more heavier, simply say "greener" or "heavier."

• *Using "at about" for approximately.* It is either "at" which is actual or "about" which is approximate. Example: "I'll be there *about* 4 p.m." or "I'll be there *at* 4 p.m." have different meanings.

• *Using "advise" and "inform" incorrectly.* "Advise" is used to suggest something and "inform" is used to state something more definitely. Examples: " I advise you not to go there at this time." "I want to inform you that this product is inferior."

More commonly mispronounced words

piquant—(PEE'-kent)	comptroller—(kon-TRO'-ler)
indict—(in-DITE')	poignant—(POY'-nyunt)
queue—(kew)	chestnut—(CHES'-nut)
solder—(SOD'-er)	gunwale—(GUN'-ul)
quay—(KEE or kway)	fertile—(FER'-tul)
entree—(AHN'-tray)	en route—(ahn-ROOT')
chasm—(kasm)	chicanery—(shi-KAY'neree)
gourmet—(GOOR'-may)	formidable—(FOR'-mid-abl)
cuisine—(kwi-ZEEN')	ensemble—(ahn-SOM'-bl)
amateur—(ama-TOOR')	en suite—(ahn-SWEET')
succinct—(sek-SINKT')	catastrophic (kata-STROF'-ik)
psalm—(sahm)	vehicle—(VEE'-ikle)
clique—(KLEEK)	potpourri—(poe-poo-REE)
orgy—(AUR-jee)	mischievous—(MIS-cha-vas)
wrestle—(RES-el)	municipal—(myoo-NIS-a-pal)
genuine—(JEN-yoo-an)	February—(FEB-roo-ary)

pianist—(pee-AN'-ist) more refined than PEE'-an-ist

The English language is impossible:

ough is	*off*	as in *cough*
ough is	*ooo*	as in *through*
ough is	*uff*	as in *rough*
ough is	*ow*	as in *drought*
ough is	*ahh*	as in *fought*
ough is	*oh*	as in *dough*

Sough, hough did she dough? She coughed until her hat blough ough. Ough! Nough! Whought poughlish! (Thank yough, Bennett Cerf.)

Making a speech

There comes a time in every progressive person's life when the platform calls for their presence. Speech! Speech! Whether it's impromptu or planned, *be ready*. George Jessel once said, "The human brain is a wonderful organ. It starts to work as soon as you are born and doesn't stop until you get up to deliver a public speech."

Here are some of the best ways to ensure that your brain doesn't stall and words don't fail you just when you need them most:

The purpose of the speech
The successful speaker knows why he is speaking and what he wishes to accomplish with his speech. The five common purposes of a speech are: to **entertain,** to **inform,** to **impress,** to **convince,** to **move to action.**

> • *Decide what your purpose is. Then state your aim in a complete sentence, around which you will build your speech.* The politician, for example, may decide: "My purpose is to *convince* my constituents that XYZ program will be of benefit to everyone." The sales manager may decide: " My purpose is to *inspire (move to action)* the sales staff to get out and sell the new product." The club president may decide: "My purpose is to *inform* the members of project results." By building your speech around *one sentence* you are building it around *one thought* that is easily understood, easily remembered, and designed to

arouse interest. *Keep this sentence in mind as you construct your speech so you don't stray from the purpose.* Arrange your material under the main points and before including a quotation, an illustration, a set of statistics, or any other material you have collected, ask yourself: *"Is this on the subject, and will it help me accomplish my purpose?"*

Evaluate your prospective audience

- *What is their level of intellect?* Be careful not to talk over their heads nor to *underestimate* their ability to comprehend the subject.
- *What is their socio-economic level?* The subject matter should be relative to the target.
- *What age range?* If the audience is of a wide range of ages, appeal to the generation gap. If the audience is youth oriented, don't delve too far into the past for pertinent illustrations. If the audience is elderly, such topics as health care will spur their interest immediately. *Note their fields of interest.*
- *Will they be females/males/mixed?* An all male or all female audience can perceive certain subjects with quite diverse attitudes. Nurture those attitudes.
- *Will the audience be general or specialized?* Speaking to a group of professional architects, for instance, you would concentrate your subject on their *group* concerns. To an audience of varied trades and professions the subject would be more generalized to engage the interest of each *individual*.
- *Think what objections might arise* in the minds of the audience. This is important even when delivering a speech that is solely to entertain.
- *Is there any of your material that may offend someone in your audience?* A racial joke? A feminist put-down? Such comments may be quite innocent but *could undermine your entire purpose*. Analyze each sentence from every viewpoint and, where necessary, revise it.
- If certain material is relevant, not unnecessarily offensive, *needing to be said to achieve your purpose* but that might encounter objections, be alert to this. *Include, or be ready with, a convincing rebuttal.*

The Introduction

Remember *first impressions*. Be a *winner* from the start. Getting into the speech and getting out of it are sometimes the most difficult to do but are *the* major factors.

- If the opening sentences have *impact* they'll immediately seize the listeners' interest. Speaking on the subject of the benefits of sunscreening products, for instance, your opening might be: "This year four persons out of every hundred will have skin cancer. *(Pause) Will one of those four be YOU?"*

- To open with a bit of *humor* is also effective. It relaxes both the speaker and the audience and, if the joke is apropos of the situation, can win the crowd's approval. Everyone enjoys a laugh; for example, speaking on the subject of the difficulties encountered in learning the English language, your opening might be: "Noah Webster had an amazing command of the English language. Audience's were spellbound by his mastery of words. His English was perfect. "Well," said Will Rogers, "Mine would be, too, if I wrote my own dictionary!"

- What ever the introduction, it must be short and to the point. You'll lose your audience's attention by rambling on before getting to the "meat" of the speech and the purpose of its being.

- *Never apologize.* To introduce your speech by saying you didn't have much notice to prepare it, or any other excuse offered as an apology, will only weaken your image. You'll be off to a questionable start. No apology is needed. Either your speech will be quite adequate or it will miss the boat, either way an apology will not help. If you haven't time to prepare *or for any reason* cannot deliver an effective address, *don't do it.* Postpone the address till later or, if that isn't possible, if the speech *must* be delivered, *deliver it without apologies.*

The body of the speech

- Be sure every part of it enhances the *purpose* of the address. If this is so, your appearance, delivery, and enthusiasm will effectively "drive it home."

- Your material should *say something worth listening to, provoke curiosity, stimulate the imagination, and be composed of concrete language.*

- Two common speech pitfalls are: talking too much, and saying too little. Don't be guilty.

- *Asking questions* during the speech can inspire closer communication with your audience. If circumstances allow, audience participation is a real booster. *Don't lose control of the rapport,* however.

Visuals

- Since a picture is worth a thousand words, it is helpful to support your statements with illustrations. If the speech is of necessity quite a long one, it is imperative that some relief be interjected. Where it is possible to use audio-visual equipment *to your advantage,* do so, it breaks the monotony. But *never, absolutely never,* let yourself *be in the dark.* As the speaker, the audience must always be aware of your presence. If the slide presentation needs total darkness, have a subsidiary lighting arrangement directed on *you,* otherwise you'll lose the rapport you've built with your audience.

- Be sure the equipment is set up and running properly before the event takes place. Don't place the projector half-way up the aisle, it disturbs the audience. Place it at the back of the room.

- *If you use a blackboard, be sure to leave it blank and enter the points of interest as you mention them.* If the information is on the board, the audience will be so busy reading it they won't pay attention to your address. After you have finished with the blackboard, *erase the copy. The copy will compete with you for attention.*

- *Don't let the visuals become more important than the speech.* Visuals should play a supporting role, not take over as the star of the show.

- *As you use visuals, always look at the audience.* When you constantly look at what you are trying to show the audience, it becomes an activity between you and the visuals instead of between you and the audience. *Ooops!* You're losing your communication *and* your polish!

- *Use an overhead projector.* Wherever possible, use an overhead projector. It operates very effectively with the *lights on and you won't have the problem of losing the attention of your audience.* You will be personally in control of the machine and always facing your audience. Overhead projectors can be rented, they are easily carried with you, and you can make your own inexpensive transparencies. Check out this invaluable assistant that will *put the polish on both you and your speech.*
- *Never end the speech with visuals.* Use them early or as a break in the middle of the address.

The Conclusion:

- The prime qualities of an effective conclusion are *brevity* and *force.*
- In the conclusion, the speaker should leave the audience gracefully and drive home the main point. The conclusion should throw a new light on the subject, strike the keynote of the speech, serve as a climax, repeat important ideas, hammer home the essential, or impel to action.
- If the *purpose* of the speech is to inspire *action;* for example: subscriptions for a hospital, the sale or purchase of a product, or votes for a candidate, the speaker in his/her conclusion should persuade and convince the listeners to *act.* Action is more important than belief or conviction and is much more difficult to secure. You'll begin your introduction as a *winner.* You'll win the audience's loyalty and support with the material you present. *Now, win their gratitude by keeping the conclusion short.*

The preparation

- Besides preparing your speech, you must prepare your own personal appearance.
- Check everything pertinent to good grooming i.e. haircut, shoe shine, etc.
- *Establish what attire would be appropriate.* If you're delivering an address after a tennis tournament, for instance, and the audience will be in sports wear, a three piece business suit

might be out of place. An address presented at a formal affair with the participants in formal evening dress would leave you feeling most uncomfortable if what you chose to wear didn't "fit the picture." I know a man who, in a mistaken concern that he might intimidate a group of fishermen to whom he was delivering a speech, decided to wear a casual windbreaker, an open collar sport shirt, and jeans for the presentation. His important address was totally sabotaged by *his own* intimidation, due to his self-conscious awareness of his inappropriate attire when he faced 200 fishermen, *all successful business men, impeccably attired in suits*. Sometimes, for lack of *astute preparation*, one's best intentions can back-fire!

The presentation

Every speech or business presentation that you make has a great influence on your progress in life. *A speech has to meet all the criteria of style, even before it registers as having substance.* Your delivery in *tone of voice* and *body language* will have *greater impact than the words you state*.

Researchers claim that *55% of communication is from body language, 38% from the tone of voice, and only 7% from the actual words that are stated*. This is easy to believe if you stop to think how many ways you can tell someone something. "Please stop doing that" said in a *soft, gentle tone* with a smile and a beseeching expression (body language), registers much differently than *"Please! Stop doing that!"* in a *mean tone* delivered with a *frowning face* and a *pointed finger* (body language). Same words, same *substance*, but those *styles* are certain to inspire quite different responses.

S T Y L E

- Read the earlier chapters on "Kinesics" and "Personality." These apply not only in every day conversation but are particularly important when you're in the spotlight making a speech.
- *Wear dark colors. They give your image power.* Navy blue is especially good. Brown gives an image of doubt, and green is not well received.
- *Fasten your jacket, if you're wearing a suit.* At all times when you're standing, the suit jacket should be buttoned. Man or

woman, unless wearing a vest, this is a "rule." An open coat looks casual and unfinished.

- *Don't put your hands in your pockets*. Men indulge in this habit and it doesn't do anything for a polished image; for a speaker it's the pits.
- *As you walk to-ward the platform, glance at the audience and smile*. So many speakers put their heads down and look like cat-burglars trying to sneak up on the platform unobserved.
- *Don't stop to chat on the way to the platform*.
- *Walk on the platform as you normally walk*. Not little mincing steps nor long stiff strides. *You are being evaluated from the moment you're in view*.
- *If you aren't using a podium, walk straight to a position well forward on the platform*. Don't stand too close to the edge of the platform or your audience will be distracted, waiting for you to pitch more than your voice into the front seats. Look at the audience and acknowledge their presence.
- *Avoid haste in beginning to speak*. Take a deep breath (don't let it be obvious!), this will relax you and *let the audience settle down before you begin*.
- *Make sure that everyone hears your opening words*, but don't shout or begin in a high pitched voice.
- *Occasional eye contact with people throughout the entire audience* will be an advantage in "winning friends and influencing people." Eye contact is a plus, but don't ever *point*; it's rude at any time, but during a speech it's unforgivable.
- *Don't pace the platform*. Every unnecessary movement such as pacing and constantly swinging the microphone cord takes away from your purpose.
- *Practice correct posture and platform behavior, over and over again until the correct becomes habitual*. With plenty of practice, you can forget these details, they come naturally to a polished speaker.
- *Notes: Keep them to a minimum*. A few listed points to keep you on the subject and to ensure nothing of importance is omitted, is all you should require. Number your note cards and spread them out on the podium so you can refer to them unobserved.

- *Never memorize a speech.* It will come across as stilted and insincere. *Do* memorize your pointers, however, *know what you want to say.* A great speech delivered without the aid of notes is the epitome of polish and confidence.
- *Don't end a speech with "I thank you." The last sentence should have such impact you leave it uninterrupted to electrify the communication.* Depending on the subject matter, your last sentence should reflect the mood appropriate to the purpose. In raising hospital funds, for example, try this; *pause* before delivery of your final sentence, let the message register, then, in a voice of *quiet urgency:* "Do we act *now* to purchase these respirators, or do we just let these gravely ill children die?" *Pause, let silence aid the audience's concentration.* After a meaningful look at the audience to hold the moment, give a gracious nod to the audience and to the Chairperson, slowly gather your notes and (to thunderous applause!) leave the platform.

Radio interviews

- Because you can't be seen, your *words* must be more carefully selected; *you won't have facial and body expression as support.*
- When you address an invisible audience, *pause, inflection,* and *distinct enunciation* are even more important than in ordinary speaking.
- *The radio speaker must use notes or provide the interviewer with a list of questions to cover the subject. Every word and phrase should be carefully chosen and packed with meaning.*
- Avoid long sentences and unusual words. Speak as though you are in conversation with an individual.
- Time is of the essence and a few seconds here or there, without the help of notes, might catch you short of your mission.
- *Prepare your message in segments.* The most important points first. Should you run out of time, you'll have the major points

covered. *If you are reading your speech, don't rush your words as in ordinary delivery, speak a little slower, about 150 words a minute.* Time yourself accordingly. If you have a straight 5 minute radio time allotment, prepare around *75 lines of typewritten copy* (three pages of double spaced copy). This timing will leave a bit of leeway for a strong conclusion.

- Each radio studio may have somewhat varied equipment. The announcer will let you know what distance from their particular microphone is best. I've worked with "mikes" from the impossible (best if you stand on your head) to the technically supreme. The usual distance is about 8 inches from your mouth to the mike. Establish the position and then don't move from side to side or back and forth. Direct your voice a little to one side of the microphone to eliminate "popping" such letters as "p" or "t." Radio is where your good breathing skills will come to your assistance. Huffing and puffing, like the big bad wolf, won't blow the house down, but it'll surely have little pigs and all your other listeners running to switch off their radios. Move back from the mike to draw in a breath, and then return to the necessary position to speak.

- *Don't rattle paper.* Speakers seem to forget that every sound is magnified and the movement of paper is very irritating. Tapping the desk or unnecessary sounds should be avoided.

- *Don't hold your script between your mouth and the microphone.* Don't cover your mouth in any way.

- Try to sound as if you are talking, not reading. An even, not too loud, voice sounds more natural.

- *To give emphasis to a phrase, pause just prior to saying it, this is more effective than blaring.*

- *Smile, smile, smile.* Your voice projects much more effectively when your mouth is in a smiling position. It even comes through on the airwaves as more pleasant and friendly. Have you ever *heard* a smile? I have, and, with my many years in radio, I hope I've delivered a few. My favorite radio announcer, Al Jordan, has been *smiling* into microphones for over 40 years and his voice is still in demand. Put on the polish with a *smiling voice.*

Television interviews

- Television demands such close-up scrutiny, you'll have to call on your most polished *appearance, sound* and *personality*. Keep your ring twisting, face stroking, head scratching, and every other nervous little gesture, out of the picture.
- Relax. Sitting up like the sphinx, frozen in stone, isn't natural. Slouching and lolling to prove your confidence projects an attitude of indifference and arrogance, and that is worse. Sit comfortably with good posture, leaning forward a little portrays a look of vigor and interest. It also tucks a big tummy, or a middle age spread, back out of sight!
- Face the "live" camera. There will likely be at least two cameras being used for the shoot, but you'll have to *keep aware of which one is in operation*. It usually has a red light to indicate this, but your host or hostess will tell you what procedure they'll follow for your particular interview. *Look at your interviewer, and conduct the conversation as though the cameras were simply Peeping Toms*. Occasionally, when the camera does a close-up, you could turn and acknowledge the viewers if the gist of the conversation is apropos of that gesture. Try not to stare into the camera, as you could look like you're peering way off into the distance. *Television delivers a powerful message:* for *or* against. Sit in front of a full length mirror and evaluate your actions. Practice concentrating on your positives and eliminating your negatives before you subject yourself to the ruthlessly revealing TV screen.
- Wear dark, simply tailored clothing, nothing fancy or elaborate in pattern or design, but a light color next to the face. A dark suit with a white shirt or blouse is great. *Never wear small checks, narrow stripes, or iridescent fabrics*. They make the screen of the television *dance* and your viewers get dizzy.
- *Fasten your jacket or suit coat if standing but it is better to unbutton it when sitting*. Your coat will bunch up and look unsightly if left fastened. Be sure to make a habit of buttoning your jacket whenever you are standing, at all times, if you're not wearing a vest.
- *Don't stand, sit, or move too quickly*. Cameramen cry! The

camera must follow you smoothly and any rapid movements to sit or to stand can create problems.

Whether it's radio, television, the speakers' podium, or just plain every day living, the eyes of the world are upon you:

Present a polished image via sight and sound!

NOTE:

In an endeavor not to exclude the female sex in my speaking or in my writing, I use "they" or "them" to refer back to the singular. This may exasperate the gurus of grammatical perfection, but it makes reading much less awkward than having to cope with each male and female reference.

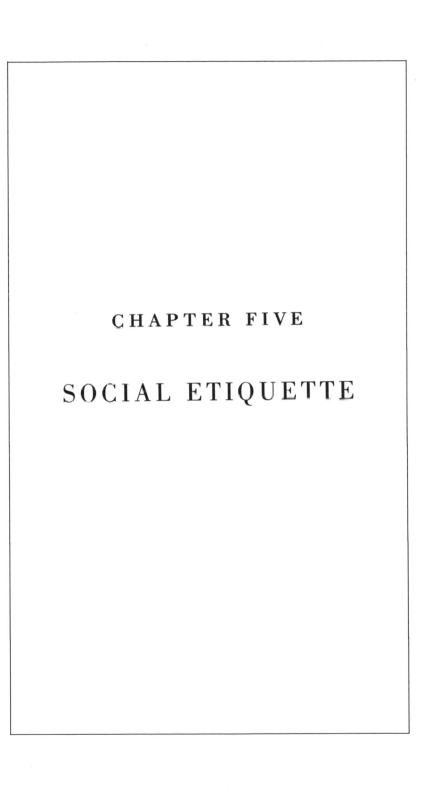

CHAPTER FIVE

SOCIAL ETIQUETTE

CHAPTER FIVE

SOCIAL ETIQUETTE

This book, "Putting on the Polish," is for special people like you. People that care about being considerate. People that subscribe to acceptable behavior.

Ah! Ha! And just who sets themselves up as authorities on acceptable behavior? **Society itself sets the standards.** For this book, and for my classes on image improvement, I've *researched* hundreds of articles, seminars, books, magazines, and manuals about British, American, and Canadian etiquette and image enhancement, and I *computerized* the information. **The underlying principles of these subjects emerged as the general and most customary rules for "Putting on the Polish."**

Everyone is comfortable with the person who is comfortable with him or her self. A knowledge of the social graces contributes to that comfort and confidence. It is not an attitude of superiority, but an awareness that "class" is a matter of *behavior,* not heritage or wealth. Being a "class act" is within the power of anyone who has an interest in self improvement.

To-day, as in the past, a polished image is an asset, almost a matter of survival!

Introductions

- *An introduction is the first impression you make on someone.* Look into the person's eyes and show genuine interest in the introduction.

- *If you are seated, it is a gracious gesture to stand.* The elderly, or people seated around a table, might find this difficult to do and a nod is sufficient. In the 1990's, men, women, and children treat each other with mutual respect.

- *Most people shake hands when being introduced.* It doesn't matter who offers their hand first except in the case of senior dignitaries and then you should wait for him or her to make the gesture, not initiate it yourself. It looks especially considerate when *children,* at an early age, are taught to stand and confidently shake hands. This gets them comfortable with the day to day gracious approach to living. If the person to whom you're being introduced is disabled and must shake hands with their left hand, you still use your right hand. Whether or not people shake hands, at least give a *nod* of your head.

- *When introducing someone, say: "I'd like you to meet. . . ."* or, formally, "May I present. . . ."

- *When being introduced to someone, say: "How do you do"* or *"Hello."* Words such as "Charmed, I'm sure" or "It's a pleasure to make your aquaintance" sound stilted and phoney. If you *mean it,* such words as "My pleasure!" can be quite appropriate. Don't respond with a careless, "Pleezta meecha."

- *Introduce someone using their first name, surname, and Mr., Mrs., or Miss.* Many people dislike being called by their first name by someone they have just met. This is important with older people.

- *When you meet someone, don't use their first name until you are invited to do so.* If you have taught your children this and they are invited by an adult to call them by their first name, you should allow them to do so. It is the prerogative of the owner of the name to decide what they want to be called.

- *When you are introduced to someone, repeat their name.* If you aren't sure of it, say so. Example: "How do you do, Mrs. Digby? Did I hear your name right?" It's better to do this than to use the wrong name or not use it at all. No one objects, it shows interest and sincerity. Use their name throughout the conversation, so you'll remember it later.

- *Always introduce your spouse if the two of you stop to speak to someone you know.* Women often complain that their husbands neglect to introduce them. If this happens, it is quite acceptable for a woman to say, "I'm Jack's wife, Rita Lewis." She might add, "Sorry, I didn't catch your name." This will help her husband, too, because that's probably why he didn't introduce her, he couldn't think of the other person's name! This also works well in reverse.
- *In chance encounters, it isn't always necessary to introduce the person you are with, but it is more polite to do so.* Consider the situation carefully.

Precedence in introductions

- *Dignitaries take precedence over everyone.* Not because they are superior people but to show respect for their office. "Senator Foghorn, may I present my mother, Mrs. Helen Green."
- *Elders take precedence over those younger.* "Gramp, I'd like you to meet Miss Smith. Ella-May this is my grandfather, Mr. Gordon Powell."
- *Women take precedence over men, except in either of the above two situations.* "Mavis, I'd like you to meet Mr. Fred Wallace. Fred, this is Mrs. Stewart."
- *Host and hostess take precedence over someone you take to their home as a guest.* "Mrs. Lake, I'd like you to meet my friend Miss Jordan. Mr. Lake, this is Miss Jordan. Carol, these are Janet and Bob Lake." If you usually call them by their first names, use them *after* the initial formal introductions.
- *Married couples should be introduced individually.* In the 1990's people don't lose their individuality when they get married. They may not use the same surname, the woman having chosen to keep her maiden name. The woman may prefer to use her married name socially and her maiden name professionally. They might also have different titles, for example: "Doctor Diane Carrington and Mr. Ross Townsend." If you're

in doubt as to how a woman prefers to be introduced, determine beforehand; ask her privately so as not to be confronted
with this uncertainty at a more public time.

Other introductions

- *Introducing someone to a group of people at a party.* If the
  group is small, 6–10 people, mention the person's name to
  the group, then go around the circle and introduce each one.
  If the group is larger, it is quite acceptable to introduce the
  person then ask each one around the group to introduce themselves one by one. Then, *see that the new arrival is seated*.
- *Children should always be introduced.* I repeat this because I
  think we treat children rather rudely. If young people and
  little children are treated with courtesy, they learn to be considerate themselves.
- *When is it permissable to introduce yourself?* At a social gathering it is quite appropriate to introduce yourself or your partner
  to another guest. *At a public gathering it is not always correct;*
  you really have to evaluate the situation carefully before you
  take the liberty of introducing yourself or anyone else. I follow
  the rule: *if in doubt, DON'T!*
- *After introducing people, give them a common ground to "break
  the ice."* Make a comment that inspires conversation. Example: "Diane has just returned from a trip to Australia."
  Surely the other person can think of something to ask about
  Australia.
- *Business introductions follow the general rules of precedence.*
  Senior executives take precedence over those of lower rank
  and down the corporate chain of command. Example: (The
  C.E.O.) " Mr. Harold Bigboss, may I present Mrs. Catherine
  Striving. Mrs. Striving, Mr. Bigboss is the Chief Executive Of-
  ficer of this company." Company order of rank sets the prece-
  dent, "ladies first" does not prevail in business.

Table manners

Ignorance of proper table manners can adversely affect your relationships and hinder advancement in your career. Much as friends may love you, they'll hesitate including you in their social arrangements if your table manners are objectionable.

More and more corporations are judging a potential employee's table manners, they are so aware of how important this can be. When engaged in Executive Search, in the final analysis of a prospective candidate, I always take him or her to a lunch and/or dinner engagement before presenting them to my client for an interview. In corporate executive positions, it is imperative that an employee is able to represent their company with impeccable social grace. If their table manners don't come up to par, I won't present a candidate to my client.

There are many instances where capable people have not progressed socially or professionally, simply because they have no idea how lacking they are in the social graces. In this book, I'll cover some of the most common problems and offer some suggestions for you to consider. These are just every day, down to earth situations where knowing acceptable behavior at the table, in a restaurant or at home, may be of assistance to you. Learn and practice these good manners until they become habit.

Common errors in table manners—Absolutely taboo

- *Speaking with food in your mouth.* There is nothing as unsightly and objectionable as this. If someone speaks to you while you have food in your mouth, finish it before you respond. They won't mind waiting, but they *will* mind watching you speak with your mouth full. *Never, never, never, do this.*
- *Taking a drink with food in your mouth.* You should finish the food in your mouth and *wipe your mouth* before taking a drink of a beverage. To look at someone's glass or cup covered with food on the rim is not very appetizing. *This is one of the first indications that a person is not very polished. Your mouth should be empty when you take a drink of anything.* Television performers show their lack of class by drinking with food in their mouths. Don't copy them and be unrefined.

- *Eating or drinking with sound effects*. Loud smacking and gulping and slurping and burping don't belong at the dinner table or anywhere within decent earshot. Children should be taught this at an early age so they, too, are welcome meal companions.
- *Chewing with the mouth open*. Eat in front of a mirror and see what an ugly sight this can be.
- *Pushing too much food into the mouth*. Take small amounts that the mouth is capable of handling. It is impossible to chew with the mouth closed if a great load has been pushed into it. This is a common sight (and I do mean *common!*) particularly when some people eat salad. Cut it into smaller pieces, if it can't be handled with grace.
- *Taking butter from the serving dish and putting it directly on to bread or food*. Use the butter knife and take a serving of butter large enough to spread the entire roll or slice of bread. Place the butter on the side of your bread and butter plate. *It is never placed directly on your bread or food*. If there is not a bread and butter plate (why isn't there?) then place the butter on the left edge of your dinner plate. If there isn't an individual butter knife or a general service butter knife, use your dinner knife to transfer the butter from the main butter dish to your *plate*, not to your bread or food. This keeps the main butter dish from gathering crumbs and becoming messy. This should be done with jams and other spreads, also. Jams and spreads are transferred from the main dish to your *side plate*, not directly to your bread.
- *Buttering a whole slice of bread or roll*. A slice of bread or a roll is taken on to the bread and butter plate or to the left side of the dinner plate. *The entire slice or roll is not spread all at once*. To eat it, a bite-size piece of bread or roll is broken off, buttered, and placed in the mouth. This is done with each individual bite. *Hold the piece being spread down on the plate, not up off the plate*.
- *Getting lipstick on cups, glasses, and eating utensils. Blot your lipstick very well so it doesn't come off on eating utensils*. If you're concerned that you won't look nice without your lipstick, believe me, you'll look much worse as a person with no

manners. As a guest, you won't be invited back if you ruin the table napkins with lipstick. Even those people who don't give a hoot for propriety, can't stand the sight of lipstick on dishes. Clean up your act!

- *Elbows on the table.* There is a lot of difference between resting a wrist on the table and leaning on your elbows. After the meal is finished it is all right to rest an elbow on the table but never with the arm up in the air. The hand and wrist should be down in front of you on the edge of the table.
- *Waving an eating utensil aloft.* It is a common sight to see someone gesturing with a fork in their hand, and that's just how it looks, *common.* It is even worse if there is food on that fork.
- *Beginning to eat as soon as you've been served.* Wait until the hostess, who is always served last or next to last if she has a husband, begins eating. If in a restaurant, wait until everyone at the table has been served. If the food is *hot,* your hostess, (or in a restaurant the others at the table) should tell you to go ahead and eat. If they don't, you must *wait.* If it is *cold food* that is being served you *always wait* and no-one should invite you to begin until everyone is served. As a hostess you should be alert to asking people to begin and not let food get cold.
- *Pouring gravy or ketchup all over your food.* It is an insult to the cook to treat food this way. Gravy is poured *only over the meat. Ketchup* is placed on the side of your plate. If you like to combine the potatoes with the gravy, dip the potatoes in the gravy (that has run off the meat on your plate) as you eat them.
- *Removing food from the mouth improperly.* Here's an easy rule to remember: *food is removed from the mouth in the same way it went into the mouth.*

  Example: Preserved cherries go into the mouth with a spoon, so the pips are removed from the mouth with a spoon. They are then placed on your side plate as unobtrusively as possible. Fresh cherries go into the mouth with your fingers, and the pips are removed from your mouth with your fingers. The exception to this is when eating something that may have very small bones such as fish or cornish hen. Small bones or pieces of bone can only be removed from the mouth with the fingers and it is quite appropriate to do so. Fish bones or other pieces of bone are then placed on the edge of your dinner plate.

• *Picking up and eating chicken held in your hands.* The only time this is acceptable is at a very informal picnic or barbecue. Chicken, and all fowl, is eaten with a knife and fork. The meat is cut away from the bones as you eat it and the bones are placed to the side of the dinner plate. No "if," "and," or "but," fowl is *not* eaten with the fingers. No, not even the drumstick! What we do in the privacy of our own homes with no guests present is another matter, anything goes. However, children should occasionally be asked to eat fowl with a knife and fork even at home to get them accustomed to eating fowl properly when in public or with guests.

• *Placing the knife and fork on the plate incorrectly.* Since this isn't offensive why should it matter? It matters because *the way the knife and fork are placed gives a signal.* Many people don't realize that there is a silent but significant message in how you place your knife and fork on your plate.

Figure A   Figure B

With your knife and fork placed side by side; the fork, with its tines turned up, placed to the left of the knife with its sharp edge turned to the fork, *Figure "A," signals* the hostess or the table attendant *that you have finished that course* and the plate can be removed. Don't be surprised when a waiter removes your plate and you haven't yet finished eating, if the utensils signal that you are, that's your problem! Placing your knife and fork on the plate as in *Figure "B" indicates that you have not finished eating. This is the way the utensils are placed when you pause during your meal.* If you have ever had a waiter ask if you are finished, when your plate is quite obviously empty, it is likely because you've given this incorrect signal.

• *Using serving implements incorrectly.* When a dish is served with both a serving spoon *and* a serving fork, the spoon is held in the right hand if you are right handed or the left if you are left handed. The fork is held in the opposite hand and, with tines pointing down, is used as a guide to get the food onto the serving spoon.

• *Holding knife, fork, and spoon incorrectly.* There are two accepted ways of eating:

(1) *North American Way:* Pick up the knife and fork, cut up one or two pieces of food, put the knife down on the plate, transfer the fork to the right hand and with the fork tines turned up, eat with just the fork. Then repeat this process through-out the meal.

(2) *The Continental Way:* Keep the knife in the right hand and the fork in the left hand and cut the food and eat it as you dine. With the fork (tines down) in the left hand, the meat is speared and some of the other food on the plate is placed on the back of the fork on top of the meat and lifted to the mouth. This is a more elegant method and, with practice, much easier to master. This method of eating is considered correct *in all countries.*

NORTH AMERICAN WAY

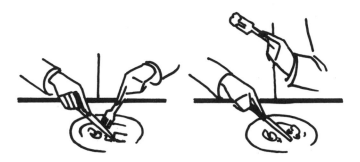

CONTINENTAL   WAY

Figure #1

Whether you choose to eat in the North American or the Continental way is less important than the way in which you handle your eating utensils. The correct way to hold a dinner knife is shown in Figure #1. *The knife handle is tucked into the palm of the hand. The index finger should not touch the knife blade.*

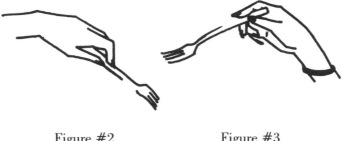

Figure #2   Figure #3

The correct way to hold a dinner fork when cutting food or eating in the *Continental* way is shown in Figure #2. The correct way to hold a fork when eating with it in the right hand is shown in Figure #3. The fork is held with the tines pointing up. *Hold the fork as near to the end of the handle as possible.* If you do this, you can pivot the fork as you carry the food to your mouth. Hold the fork so the handle rests on the middle finger, supported by the two outer fingers beneath. The thumb and index finger placed on top of the handle hold and guide the implement comfortably.

Spoons are held in exactly the same way as the fork. Hold the handle as far from the bowl as possible and pivot the implement to-ward the mouth. Serving spoons and forks are held this way also, not clutched in the fist.

- *Never*(oh please! never!) *use a toothpick. Don't place them on the table if you are the hostess.* If you have a problem with something lodged in your teeth that might show or that is bothering you, excuse yourself and go *in private* to remove it. It is unsightly to dig at the problem with your finger or your tongue, leave the table and take care of it.
- *Smoking during the meal.* Even in a smoking designated area, it is impolite to smoke during a meal or between courses. Wait until everyone is finished eating before you light up a smoke.
- *Cutting bread and rolls or buns.* Don't use your knife to cut bread or rolls, *they should be broken.*
- Never say, "I'm *full*," it sounds crude. Say you've had sufficient or "I'm very satisfied, thank you."
- *Eating too quickly.* Rapidly devouring your food is not only

bad manners but it has you finished when everyone else is still eating. Truly refined guests time their eating with those around the table. If you see you're much ahead or behind the others, change your pace. *Though some restaurants remove a diner's plate as soon as they are finished, that is not correct.* This method can leave one slow eater eating alone while everyone else's plates have been removed. Actually, all plates should be removed at about the same time. If you are ahead, save a little food on your plate to "dawdle" over and finish with everyone else. It is actually the hostess's responsibility to set a realistic pace, possibly slowed a little for the most tardy (most talkative?) diner. Elegant dining is never rushed.

- *Drinking from a bottle*. Though you may prefer your beverage straight from the bottle (pop, beer, cider), it is better to drink it from a glass when dining socially. These drinks are not usually served or ordered with an elegant meal. A table becomes quite cluttered and unattractive if bottles are served.

These are some of the most frequent errors in table manners. For further guidance see the specific topics.

Napkins
- Wait to see if grace is said, then pick up your napkin. Some people prefer to wait until the hostess or host takes up their napkin. Either way is correct.
- Take the napkin, unobtrusively unfold it and place it across your lap. Never tuck it in under your chin or into your waistband, nor place it anywhere but across your lap. Under the chin is for children *only*.
- A dinner size napkin is left *half* folded either in a triangle or a rectangle. The fold is placed to-ward you. A napkin folded into a triangle is more efficient to handle as a *corner* can more easily be lifted to blot the mouth.
- A luncheon or cocktail size napkin is unfolded completely.
- The napkin is left across the lap from the beginning of the meal until the end.
- At the end of the meal, the napkin is *not* carefully folded or scrunched in a ball but is loosely gathered to-gether and

placed to the left of your place setting. *Never place it on your plate*.

- If you leave the table during the meal, your napkin should be placed *on your chair, not on the table*. No-one wants to look at what may be a soiled napkin, and it looks untidy on a beautifully set table.

- Never use a napkin to mop your brow, or never as a handkerchief to sneeze into it or to tidy your nose. That is the epitome of vulgarity.

- *Blot* carefully with a napkin. Big swipes and wipes look boorish.

- With cloth napkins be particularly careful with lipstick. Blot your lipstick with a tissue before sitting down to dinner. *Leaving lipstick on linens, forks, spoons, cups, and glasses is unforgivable*. If you inadvertently get lipstick on utensils or drinking vessels, wipe it away as *inconspicuously* as possible with a *paper* napkin or with your own tissue if the napkin is cloth. This is rather a strange procedure at a dinner table, but *anything* is better than others at the table having to look at the deplorable sight of lipstick on eating utensils. Blot your lips so it doesn't happen over again.

- At a dinner table, handle a *paper* napkin in the same way as you use a cloth one.

- At a buffet or cocktail party, use the paper napkin as you do a cloth one but when you are finished with it look for a wastepaper basket to dispose of it. A capable host/ess sees that a basket is available. If not, ask the host/ess where s/he'd like it placed. Don't sneak it into a nearby potted plant, you rascal, you!

Table settings and meal etiquette

- Two basic rules prevail for the position of flatware at a place setting. The diner should find that:
  (1) The forks are placed to the left of the plate and the spoons and knives are on the right. (An exception to this rule is the seafood fork which may be placed next to the soup spoon.)

(2) The diner begins by using the implements on the *outside*, the farthest from the plate. As each course is served, the next outside implements are used, working in to-ward the dinner plate. (See: Dinner Table Settings)

- If you are presented with unusual food that you are not sure how to eat, either watch what others at the table do or ask your host/ess or waiter. To inquire discreetly is probably the safest solution because it is quite probable that others are not familiar with the right procedure either. If they *do* know, they'll be eager to show you their expertise.

- When being served by a servant or waiter, help yourself to as much as you want and replace the serving utensils *side by side* on the serving dish. It is polite to thank the person serving you.

- When serving dishes are passed along around a table, if the dish is not heavy or very hot, the person takes it, serves him/herself and passes it along. If the dish is cumbersome each diner should hold the dish for the next diner to serve him/herself.

- When placing food on your plate, it should not touch the outside rim. Plates were designed this way so the wide rim is there to hold bones and pips that are removed from food. It also gives an edge to hold the plate for serving. It is quite incorrect for anyone to serve a plate with food *on* or *covering* this rim, though many restaurants very often do so. Some dishes now do not have this rim but are of a scooped out design. That's unfortunate, because rimmed plates are much better.

- Never *ask* for second helpings; there may not be any. If *offered* second helpings, it's a compliment to the cook for you to accept and to have a *little* more. Of course, it's fine to decline.

- Try not to refuse a course of food unless for a good reason such as an allergy. If you do refuse, do it with as little comment as possible: "No, thank-you." If it's possible to simply pass the serving dish on, without any comment, that is best. However, it is more sensible to refuse food than to leave it on your plate wasted when someone else might have enjoyed it.

- Don't ask for tea or coffee to be served during the meal. It is customary for tea or coffee to be served *after* the meal and your request disrupts the plan.

- It's quite acceptable to ask for a glass of water or for more water, at any time during the meal. Blot your mouth *before* you drink (to keep the glass clean, remember?) and drink with a few sips not gulps. Never drink with food in your mouth. If the water is served in a stemmed glass, hold the glass *on the stem* just *below the bowl* of the goblet.

W I N E *(also see information under "wines")*

- If you do not want wine, simply say, "No, thank-you." Don't turn over the goblet, as some people do, but it's all right to *fleetingly* put your hand over the top of the glass so none will be poured for you.
- Wine is sipped. Between sips, the glass is returned to its proper position on the table.
- If more than one type of wine is being served, try to finish each serving before the next course and its accompanying wine. If you aren't able to finish, don't continue drinking the wine when you've begun the next course of food. The unfinished wine should be removed with everyone else's empty glasses. You may request to stay with that same wine if you see that there is some left. (I.e. white instead of red.)
- When wine is poured, the glass should only be filled to about 2/3 of its capacity.
- Even in these days of equality, ladies do not usually pour the wine. Guests at a dinner table wait to be invited to have wine or liqueurs, they don't ask, but the host/ess should be alert to the need for refills.

S A L A D

- Salad may be served from a main salad bowl with each diner given an individual plate. In this way, the hostess either has the salad plates beside her, fills each plate and passes it to the diner, or the salad bowl is passed around the table and the salad plate, already in place to the left side of each dinner plate, is filled. Then *use the salad fork*.
- If the salad bowl is passed around and you do not have a salad plate, put the salad on your dinner plate, *not on your bread*

plate. Your salad is eaten with the rest of your food, using your dinner fork, not a separate salad fork. If the main course is a cold meal, this is how the salad should be served. If the meal is hot, it is preferable to provide a side salad plate to keep the salad crisp.

- The dinner roll or specialty bread is *usually* eaten with the salad course, not with the main course.
- Salad may be served before, after, or with, the main course. The position of your salad fork will tell you what to expect.
- Salad should be served on a salad plate; individual *bowls* are for more casual dining. The pieces should be small enough that they can be eaten with a fork. *You should not need to cut a salad.* It is, however, better to cut it than to force large pieces into your mouth. The thoughtful hostess or chef should consider this when preparing the salad.
- The dressing may have been mixed with the salad in the bowl, or the dressing may be served separately. Because of restricted diets, this has become a popular way of serving salad, to let each person use as much or as little dressing as they prefer. If the dressing is served separately, it should be in cruets or pouring vessels *served on a small tray*, so the diner has no trouble with "drips" on the tablecloth.
- Pour the dressing over the salad on your plate. *Don't mix it all to-gether.* Eat the salad by dipping each piece in the dressing on your plate.
- If the salad is served on a side plate immediately prior to the main course and you haven't finished eating it, it's fine to ask to keep it to finish it with the main course.

SOUP

- Soup may be served in a soup plate (bowl) or in a bouillon cup. If in a soup plate, it is *only* eaten with a spoon. If in a bouillon cup or small bowl with handles, it may be eaten with a spoon *or drunk from the bowl*.
- If soup is drunk from the bowl, any solids in the soup are eaten with a spoon *before* the soup bowl is picked up.
- *Crackers are never broken into the soup.* They are eaten separately.

- The soup spoon is the largest one on the outside and to the right of the knives and should be first in line for service. (Unless there's a seafood fork.)
- The edge of the soup spoon is dipped into the soup bowl at the edge nearest you and is swept to the other side of the soup bowl. This way, any drips will fall back into the bowl and not on you or the tablecloth.
- Drink from the *side* of the soup spoon, not from the *end* of it.
- Tilt the soup bowl *away* from you when getting the last spoonfuls. Scoop *away* from you with the spoon.
- Place the soup spoon on the *serving plate under the soup bowl,* if none, leave the spoon in the bowl.

FISH

- There may be a fish knife and fork at your place setting. This is a short knife (see "k") and a fork similar to a salad fork but may have different shaped tines (see "l"). Though these implements are rarely set out, it's nice to be able to recognize them if you meet them on the table.
- You may fillet a fish all at once or gradually remove the bones as you eat it. The way considered to be more proper is the latter. In a restaurant, it is quite all right to ask the waiter to have the fish filleted before it is served to you. In someone's home it's a "do it yourself" project.
- Any bones that get in your mouth should be discreetly removed with your thumb and index finger and placed on the side of your dinner plate. They are too small to remove otherwise and this is the simplest method. *One* leading etiquette "expert" (?) says to use your fork for this, but that would be difficult and tacky.
- To squeeze lemon juice over the fish, with one hand use your fork to hold the lemon wedge, with the other hand squeeze the lemon. If the lemon is a slice instead of a wedge, place the slice over the fish and try to press out the juice with your fork. Let's hope people know enough to serve *wedges,* not *slices.*

SORBET

- Sorbet is frozen fruit juice served as chopped ice. It is a delightful way to refresh the taste buds *between courses*.

- Sorbet is not served as a dessert but is served after a strongly flavored dish, such as fish, to clear the palate for the next course.
- It is served in a small fruit or sherbert dish and is eaten with a teaspoon. The spoon is given with the sorbet bowl on a serving plate, not laid at the place setting.
- Sorbet not only refreshes your mouth, it aids digestion and ensures a *leisurely*, elegant meal.
- The sorbet dish is removed from the table when the diner is finished with it. The spoon is placed on the serving dish beneath the sorbet bowl, not left in the dish. If no serving dish, leave it in the bowl. *A used utensil is never put on the tablecloth*.

DESSERT

- If a dessert spoon *and* fork are given, they are served with the dessert or may be placed above the dinner plate in the place setting.
- It is quite proper to use the fork alone, but a spoon is used alone only for ice cream, sherbet, or sorbet.
- For pie or cake a la mode, the dessert spoon is held in the left hand, the dessert fork in the right. For berries or cut-up fruit, the fork is held in the left hand and the spoon in the right. One utensil is left on the plate as you eat with the other one.
- When finished, leave the spoon and fork, side by side in the finished position, on the plate.

COFFEE

- Coffee cups (with the spoon in the saucer) are not placed on the table until the end of the meal.
- Small coffee spoons are used with demi-tasse cups.
- These days, the host/ess usually has both regular and decaffeinated coffee ready and asks your preference. *Don't ask for what is not served*.
- There should also be milk and artificial sweetener served for those who do not use cream and/or sugar.
- It is customary to move to the living room for coffee and li-

queurs, but if everyone is comfortable, quite correct to remain
at the table.

LIQUEURS

- Liqueurs and/or brandy are offered as soon as the coffee has
been served.
- When offering liqueurs, the host/ess should let the guest know
what is available from which to choose. You wait to be offered
refills, you don't ask.

Restaurant dining

If you are the host/ess

- Choose a restaurant that you *know* and is appropriate to the occasion. Be sure there is an alternative food selection, if you
choose a specialty restaurant. Example: A seafood house that
also has fowl.
- Be there *before* your guests arrive, if they are not travelling
with you.
- *The Bill:* Arrange with the maitre d' to see that you get the bill.
It is more polished to give your credit card to the maitre d',
ask him to add the percentage tip you wish to pay, and then after the meal, you simply check and sign the bill as inconspicuously as possible. It should be understood, before going to dinner, that you are the host/ess. *Guests should not try
to pay the bill; it is rude to insist.*
- *Tipping:* 15% of the total of the bill, *before tax*, is the
customary rate. For outstanding service 20% may be given but
no more. Overtipping is improper. The wine steward's bill is
usually separate, and 7%, before tax, is sufficient here. Tips
may be left in cash on the table or added to the credit card
bill. If the service was not acceptable, *leave no tip* and tell the
manager of your complaints. Consider if it was the fault of the
service or the poor food. The attendant shouldn't be penalized

if it was not his/her fault and they've given good service. *Speak to the maitre d' privately, your guests should not be involved or embarrassed in any way.* It is preferable to phone or write a letter to the management after the event, rather than upset your guests.

- *Coatchecks are retrieved by the host and paid for,* as the guests leave. A host*ess* may ask a man in the party to look after helping with the coats, and she can discreetly leave the tip in the dish at the checkout. Usually fifty cents to one dollar per coat is the customary tip.

- *Smoking:* If diners in the party are all smokers, arrange to sit in the smoking area. If even one person is not a smoker, you should ask to be seated in the non-smoking area. *It may be a heart condition that can't stand the smoke, be considerate.*

- Rise when the guests arrive at the table. Make any introductions that are necessary.

- The guests should always be seated in the best seats, the view seats or the window seats.

- If someone is left-handed, they should let the host/ess know so they can be comfortably seated without knocking the diner beside them.

- It is the host/ess's responsibilty to look after the guests. Be alert to their needs. If someone isn't eating, quietly inquire if there is a problem. The host/ess, not the guest, deals with the waiter.

- As the host/ess, you choose the wine. It's fine to indicate one on the wine list *at the price range you prefer* and then ask your guests for their suggestions (they, of course, should notice the price and not choose something too much above or below it). It may be better to choose carafes or individual glasses if the situation warrants much variety in preferences.

If you are a guest

- Give your initial order to the host/ess, not to the waiter. After that, any further instructions, such as how you'd like your steak done and what condiments on your potatoes, are given directly to the waiter.

- Stand when other guests arrive.

- If you arrive before your host/ess, have the waiter take you to the table, but *don't take up your napkin, don't order a drink or eat anything, such as a roll, that is on the table*. If you expect to be waiting long, sit in the holding area and have a drink there.
- As a guest, it is gracious to ask the host/ess what he/she thinks you might enjoy in that particular restaurant. It isn't necessary to take their suggestion, but it gives you some idea as to what that restaurant specializes in, and pleases the host/ess. *Never order the most expensive dishes on the menu* unless the host/ess invites you to do so by making such comments as "Perhaps you'd enjoy the filet mignon."

General (guest, host/ess, customer)

- Never signal the attendant with a whistle, a call, or a snap of the fingers. Catch his/her attention with a slight wave of the index finger or a beckoning nod of the head.
- Call the attendant "Waiter" or "Waitress" not "Miss" or "Ma'am" or "Sir" or any quaint name. If an attendant introduces him/herself with his/her first name (refined establishments don't teach their staff to do this), do not use it. "Waiter" or "Waitress" is correct in every restaurant. If you are a regular customer and know the waiter or waitress well, you may correctly use their first name, but they should never use the customers' first name.
- When the orders are being taken, stop all conversation and give the attendants full attention. They have a lot of people to serve and wasting their time is inconsiderate. Each person gives their order for *appetizers and main menu*, to the host if you're a guest, to the waiter if you're the host or a customer. The dessert and liqueur orders are placed later, in the same way.
- Purses or briefcases are not placed on the table. It is unfortunate that no space is provided for a woman's purse. It is difficult to juggle it on your lap but that's the only place for it (under the table napkin). If possible take a small handbag that can be handled easily. *Caution:* (1) In a revolving restaurant don't place it on the window sill beside you. It'll go sailing

away to another table! (2) Be aware that, even in the most reputable restaurants, a thief can steal your handbag. Keep it securely near.

• Any problems are *quietly* told directly to the attendant, it isn't necessary to involve the host/ess: soiled cutlery, uncooked food, need for tableware.

• If you must leave the table to go to the washroom, simply excuse yourself and leave. Do not state where you are going. No one at the table should inquire.

• Don't pick up a napkin or cutlery that has fallen to the floor, *leave it there*. Ask the waiter for another.

• *Don't table hop.* You are with your guests or hosts. People dining at other tables did not come there to visit you. If you spot a long lost friend at another table, nod and let them be the one to come to you (on their way out), or send a note via the waiter giving your phone number or suggestion to meet after dinner. Dining rooms are not the place for grand reunions.

• Children and teenagers should be taught to remain seated throughout the meal in a restauarant or in a home. *It is very rude of them to wander around*.

• *Never blow your nose at the table. It isn't sufficient just to turn around; leave the table*.

• Turn off your message beeper, better still, leave it at home. Only a medical doctor on emergency call could be excused for using this machine during a social engagement. This is a crass interruption.

• Do not make, or arrange to receive, phone calls during a social engagement. *No one is that important* that they must be in contact with anyone at all times. You don't appear as important; you appear as pompous and inconsiderate.

Dining: Tilts and touchy times:

Spills

The host/ess should take no notice of small spills but should take care of large ones promptly. *Never make the "spiller" feel embarrassed. If it's a child's spill, remember children have feelings too*. Clean up a "dry" spill with a brush or folded napkin. A wet spill should be blotted up and paper towels put between the tablecloth and the table. If it is something that might stain, as red wine, rub salt into the stain and cover the "mess" with a clean napkin. If you aren't worried about damage to the table or cloth, simply blot up the liquid, cover it with a piece of plastic wrap (such as Saran or Handiwrap) and a clean napkin over that. (The plastic will keep the stain from seeping onto the napkin.) *Disrupt the meal as little as possible.* Small spills such as a bit of food dropped on the tablecloth should unobtrusively be quickly scraped up with your knife and put to the side of your dinner plate. Use a clean knife, don't add to the problem. Large spills may damage the table and the cloth, ask the host/ess or waiter for assistance, spare the other guests the sight of a messy table. If someone else spills, do everything you can to help.

"Foreign" objects in your food

IN A HOME

A dead insect: tuck it under something to the side of your plate and remember not to eat it!

A live insect: Pick it out of your food as privately as possible, ask to be excused, and go to the powder room to dispose of it. Killing it and putting it in your napkin would only ruin the rest of your meal. Killing it and dropping it to the carpet might soil the carpet. *Above all, try not to let the other guests see what has happened.*

A hair: Remove it as inconspicuously as possible or hide it under food at the side of your plate.

Broken glass: This should be quietly told to the hostess in case others will find pieces, too, and a serious accident can be avoided.

Other objects than the above should just be put to the side of the plate. They aren't offensive.

IN A RESTAURANT

Inconspicuously signal the waiter to come to the table, if you're a guest don't involve your host, *very quietly* ask the waiter to remove your food and have it replaced. He'll *see* the problem; don't discuss it. Try to keep from upsetting the other guests.

Saving graces

- *Catching drips from pitchers and pouring vessels: do not ever use your finger to wipe the spout of a container, that is objec-*

tionable and unsanitary. Before putting it down on the tablecloth, bring it to your host/ess's attention. Give him/her a chance to get a service dish to put beneath or something with which to wipe the spout.

- *Soiled cutlery:* As a guest in someone's home, the general advice is to ignore it. As a hostess, I would like to be discreetly told about it so I could replace it, however, *whoever sets the table should see that all dishes and cutlery are spotless*. In a restaurant, quietly ask for a replacement.

- *Cutlery dropped on the floor is not picked up*. Let your host/ess know so he/she can replace it.

- Walking to-ward a restaurant table a man precedes a woman *if there is not a waiter leading the way*. He pulls out the chair for the lady and sees that she is seated before going to his own chair. *If the waiter leads the way, the woman follows next*, and the man after that. The waiter pulls out the chair for the lady, and the man goes to his chair.

- *Hats* or *caps* are never worn by men while eating. A woman does not wear a hat in a home except at an afternoon tea or luncheon. A hostess never wears a hat in her own home. Women should not wear hats to any meals after 5 o'clock, unless it is a "cocktail" hat which is usually a very small creation of a bit of net and silk. Even a cocktail hat doesn't belong at a dinner table. Remove it.

- When served a tray of vegetables and dip: *never* dip, take a bite, and *then dip the piece back again*. Once you have bitten a piece of food it should never be returned for a second dip. People sharing the food do not want to share germs.

- If dishes of nuts and/or candies are served or set out around the room, *don't be a glutton* and help yourself to more than a few. Don't pick out certain choice nuts or chocolates.

- Don't rearrange the dishes on a table. The host/ess has his/her own methods and they should remain that way. Some changes should be made for the left-handed person to be comfortable, however, and *the host/ess* should make every effort to see that this is done.

- Don't help yourself first, when asked to pass food or salt and pepper shakers.

Entertaining with polish

THE SEATED DINNER PARTY

The invitation

- *Invite guests that have a variety of interests.* This makes a more versatile mix.
- *Don't invite more than you can comfortably seat.* Each person at the table should have *at least twenty eight to thirty inches of space.*
- *An invitation to dinner can be telephoned.* It should be offered about two weeks prior to the dinner, if possible.
- When inviting someone, don't put them in a vulnerable position by saying, "What are you doing next Friday evening?" They have no out if you suggest something they are not interested in doing. Come directly to the point. "Would you and Ken be available to come to our place for dinner next Friday evening?" Also, people always appreciate being told who the other guests, if any, will be.
- Invitations that are telephoned should be "short and sweet," there may be several calls to make.
- *The invitation should state:*
  The Time: (See the chart for suggested times.)
  The Date:
  The Dress: (Seldom casual for a sit down dinner.)
  The Address: where the dinner will be held.
  The Phone Number: of the host/ess.
  A benefit of inviting by phone is that you also can inquire as to whether the persons invited have any food allergies, etc., that you'd like to be aware of in arranging the dinner. The guest should inform the host/ess of such things as diabetes or low-fat diets.
- *Replies should be given immediately.* The recipient of the invitation should not make their acceptance "conditional," for example, on "Who is going to be there?" *Do not ask if you may bring someone along.*
- Once an invitation is accepted, the dinner engagement should not be cancelled for anything but a very important reason. The host/ess's dinner plans or the guests' appointment plans

should not be disrupted.

- It's wise to phone a day or two before the dinner to remind the guest(s) of the dinner *date* and the *time to arrive*. Invitations placed by telephone might be forgotten. This confirms who plans to attend.
- In extending the invitation you might want to suggest that transportation will be arranged for an elderly guest, or for a single woman.
- A well-organized host/ess keeps an "Entertainment Date Book" with a record of the parties s/he gives, the food served, the decor used, who attended, and pertinent comments. Success's may be repeated or repetition of decor or food can be avoided.

The dinner menu

- Usually *three courses are considered adequate:* first course, main course, and a dessert. For a special and leisurely meal, four or five simple courses may be served. (See list of courses.)
- *The important thing to consider is that the host/ess should not be away from his/her guests any longer than absolutely necessary.*
- The meal is planned according to: the budget; the ability of the cook (!); the time of year (what foods are in season and whether the weather is hot or cold); the equipment available; and the degree of formality.
- When deciding on a menu:

  (1) *Don't plan several elaborate dishes.* Courses that are *made ahead,* or that take little attention during the dinner party, will lend the most to a pleasant meal for everyone.

  (2) *Choose a balance of flavors and richness.* A creamed soup served before a main course of meat in a cream sauce would be far too rich a meal. A heavy main course should be preceded and followed by lighter courses.

  (3) *The courses should be varied.* A seafood salad as a first course with a broiled salmon main course would be too much of the same thing.

- *Restricted diets:* If some guests cannot eat certain foods due to religious or medical restrictions or a vegetarian diet, your menu does *not* have to omit these foods. Just be sure you have plenty of what those guests *can* eat.

- A good wine adds immensely to a meal, but have optional non-alcoholic drinks served to those who would prefer them. (See "Wine Service")
- A pitcher of ice water should be available. A very thin lemon slice added to each water goblet gives the ice water a refreshing lift.

Order of Courses

This is the *order* in which courses are served, but *not all* would be served at a meal.

Soup: Cold or hot.

Fish: Can be served as an appetizer, a seafood cocktail, or a main course.

Sorbet: Served to clear the taste buds only.

Meat and Vegetables: Main course.

Salad: Can be served as a *first* course, or served *with* the main course, or *as* the main course.

Dessert:

Savory: A small highly seasoned dish similar to, but a little larger than, an hors d'oeuvre. It is a British custom to serve a savory before the port wine, after and in contrast to the sweet dessert.

Example: Toasted Cheese Ball or Chicken Livers in Bacon.

Cheese: This is the favorite North American Savory.

Fruit: Cheese and fruit are frequently served at the same time. Select a cheese of strength and flavor that enhance the *fresh* fruit that is served.

Liqueur and Coffee

The more courses served, the smaller the portions.

Table settings

In addition to the cooking utensils, *four* types of equipment are required for a proper dinner party: China, Glasses, Silver Flatware, and Serving Dishes.

CHINA

The china should all match. The exception being the dessert plates and cups and saucers which, since they are served separately, could be different.

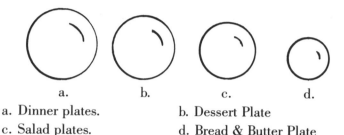

a.   b.   c.   d.

a. Dinner plates.   b. Dessert Plate
c. Salad plates.   d. Bread & Butter Plate

e.   f.

e. Soup plates   f. Bowls.

Glasses

Specific types of goblets are required for each type of wine or liqueur that is served. A water goblet is required for each guest.

Types of Goblets

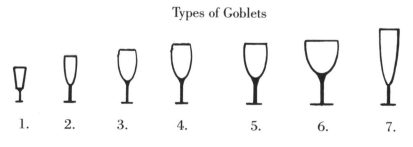

1.   2.   3.   4.   5.   6.   7.

1. liqueur   2. port   3. sherry   4. white wine   5. red wine
6. water   7. champagne

Silver flatware

The flatware must all match. Because most homes don't have servants, entertaining must be done with a thought for ease. Stainless steel flatware has gained favor because it doesn't require polishing and it can be put into the dish washer. *Stainless steel would be far more acceptable than tarnished silver.* It must be of very good quality to be featured at a dinner party. There are some truly beautiful patterns available in superb quality.

The bare essentials of flatware are:

a. Dinner Knives   b. Dinner Forks

c. Salad Forks   d. Teaspoons

e. Dessert Spoons   f. Soup Spoons   g. Coffee Spoons

h. Gravy Ladle   i. Sugar Spoon   j. Butter Server

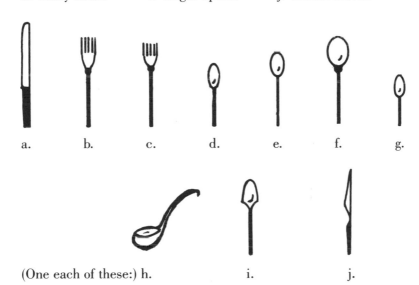

a.   b.   c.   d.   e.   f.   g.

(One each of these:) h.   i.   j.

Not essential but nice to have are:

k. Fish Knives   l. Fish Forks

m. Dessert Knives   n. Butter Spreaders

k.   l.   m.   n.

Table covering

Traditionally, the epitome of elegance is a solid white tablecloth, preferably of linen damask (pronounced *dam*'ask). These are expensive and difficult to keep *immaculate,* so, a great variety of tablecloths have become popular in white and a wide range of colors. Some main points about table coverings are:

- The tablecloth for a sit down dinner should be large enough to hang halfway to the floor.
- There must be absolutely no stains or spots on it.
- A "silence cloth," which is a padded table covering, should be placed beneath the table cloth. This protects the table and also gives a softer surface for dining. I place a thin plastic sheet between the silence cloth and the table. There is then no need to rush for paper towels for under the tablecloth if a major spill occurs, a simple surface blotting does the clean up.
- *Place mats are quite correct.* Be sure they are of an adequate size to accommodate the table setting you plan to use. The flatware should *all* be on the place mat, not some pieces on the mat and some on the table, or else the mat should be small and only under the dinner plate with the flatware all on the table. (See individual place setting illustrations.)
- The appearance of the table is of prime importance in creating the "mood" for pleasant dining. See the suggestions under "Gracious Entertaining."

Individual place settings

- Keep the table as uncluttered as possible.
- Place only the flatware and dishes that are needed for the first and main courses. This doesn't confuse the guests as to what implement to use.
- Cups and saucers are not placed until the coffee is served at the end of the dinner.
- If various wines and liqueur are being served, all goblets may be in place *or* the appropriate goblets may be given as the next wine is poured. I prefer this way, with the water and one wine goblet at each place to begin the meal with a minimum of clutter.

- *The table napkin* is placed either in the centre of the place setting or on the bread plate. It can be folded in a variety of attractive ways, laid flat, or placed standing up, whatever adds to the beauty of the table. Traditionally (and environmentally!) napkins should be of *cloth*. There are such gorgeous *paper* dinner napkins on the market that they, too, are becoming accepted. In the interests of hygiene, and the problem of stains, paper does have merit for more casual occasions.
- The bread and butter plate is placed to the left of the forks. Some people place it to the left and *above* the forks, this is harder to reach but either way is correct. If a cheese course is served, this plate may double as a cheese plate.
- The butter knife, with its blade side down, is placed horizontally across the top of the bread and butter plate. As it is used, it is placed back on the plate, never on the dinner plate or table.
- The following illustrations show place settings for a three course dinner with one wine (Fig. #8). A five course dinner with two wines (Fig. #9). The most. (You might find this on a cruise. Fig. #10.)

(Figure #8)
A THREE COURSE DINNER WITH ONE WINE.

The butter spreader is placed across the bread plate. The dinner knife and fork are next to the dinner plate. The soup spoon to the right of the knife. The dessert spoon could be placed above the plate.

(Figure #9)

A FIVE COURSE DINNER WITH TWO WINES.

a. fish fork   b. dinner fork   c. salad fork
d. salad knife   e. dinner knife   f. fish knife
g. soup spoon (dessert fork and/or spoon would be bought in with
the dessert)

Bread or rolls are not usually served with a dinner of several courses.
If they are served, the bread plate goes to the left of the forks.
A table is much less cluttered if the wine goblets are delivered as
each different wine is served. Liqueurs are usually served after the
meal with coffee at the table or in the living room.

(Figure #10)
A FORMAL DINNER (Some Cruise Ships)

a. fish fork	b. entree fork	c. main course fork
d. salad fork	e. fruit fork	f. fruit knife
g. salad knife	h. main course knife	
i. entree knife	j. fish knife	k. soup spoon
l. oyster fork	m. dessert spoon	n. dessert knife

GOBLETS

o. water	p. sherry	q. white wine
r. light red wine	s. white or red wine	t. port wine

A bread plate and cup and saucer are not included in a formal place setting. Coffee and liqueurs are served after the meal. Bread is not served. This is a very pretentious place setting and is *not* considered to be correct. Some cruise ships, in their strive for the ultimate luxury, present this overwhelming display. *It is more gracious to deliver the necessary utensils with each course as it is served.*

Serving dishes and serving utensils

GRAVY BOAT

This is a long narrow pitcher that has a a serving plate beneath it to catch drips. It may have a ladle or a spoon with it.

Figure #11
Gravy Boat

Figure #12
Gravy Ladle

VEGETABLE DISHES

Bowls are often of the same china as the dinnerware. You'll need at least two of these. Heat proof ones are ideal as they can go from oven to table (if they are handsome enough) and will hold the heat. Vegetable dishes with *handles* are the easiest to pass. Ones with lids are ideal to keep the food hot, and they can also be used as casseroles.

PLATTERS OR FLAT SERVING DISHES

Heat proof platters and trays of various sizes can serve many purposes. Several of these are needed for entertaining.

Bowls

Glass bowls for salad, dessert, and condiments, will be required in many sizes from very small to large.

The tea, coffee, cream and sugar service may be of silver or china. The cream and sugar set should have a tray.

Carving set

The carving knife and fork are usually a matched set which also includes a sharpening stone. This can match the silver flatware or be of any design from bone handles to stainless steel.

Salad servers
Because salad dressings tarnish silver, salad servers are often of other material. Both spoon and fork may be used or just the serving spoon.

Large serving spoons
Of various sizes, these spoons should be appropriate for the type of food being served.

Trivets
These are ornamental metal plates of various shapes on very short legs, used under hot dishes to protect the table. They may be of silver, brass, or wrought iron.

Glassware
- *Resist the urge to buy matched sets of everything.* Decide what you would actually use in stemware, and buy the best quality you can afford in sets of the major pieces. For instance, water goblets, two sizes of wine goblets, and liqueur glasses, would be a good start. Start with the stemware used most often, and add different shapes as the need arises.
- It is better to have an attractive, good quality set of glassware for four or six settings, than eight or ten settings of inferior quality.
- Clear glass will be the most versatile. Frosted and colored glassware limit table decor. Dark tinted glassware takes away from the beverage being served and doesn't provide the look of elegance that a fine table setting deserves.

Crystal
- Crystal is glass but not all glass is crystal.
- Crystal is made of flint and lead oxide which give it *sparkle* and a clear *bell-like ring* when struck. Ordinary glass has neither.
- The quality of crystal is judged by its clarity and brilliance and the percentage of lead in its content. The most expensive crystal has a high lead content, is handblown and hand cut.
- ***Beware:*** The public has just been informed that the lead in

crystal seeps into the liquid or food exposed to it. This happens in minutes and lead crystal should not be used to store food or drinks, we're told.

- Some of the most famous glass-producing areas of the world are: Ireland, where the beautiful and world-renowned *Waterford* crystal originated; France, where *Lalique* crystal is manufactured; *Orrefors* of Sweden; Czechoslovakia produces magnificent crystal; England, famous for Bristol glass; and, since the Middle Ages, *Venetian* glass is well known for its light and delicate qualities. America has many manufacturers of high quality glassware, from heavy lead crystal to colorful pressed glass.

- Cut-glass crystal is the most elaborate and the most formal of crystal design. It is also the most expensive.

- *It is better to purchase a good quality lead crystal in a plain design than a cheap cut glass that will simply look heavy and lusterless.*

- Choosing a pattern: Crystal patterns should enhance the dinnerware. If your china has a gold trim you wouldn't choose crystal with a silver trim. Heavily patterned china and silverware can balance with heavily patterned crystal. The 1990's favor very fine, *plain* crystal glassware. It goes with every type of china from pottery to the most formal presentation. Its delicate structure and clear uncluttered brilliance adds to the pleasure of any occasion. Crystal glassware is sold by individual piece. Its a wise plan to have a few extra pieces of the sizes you use most. Over the years, patterns come and go, so try to choose a pattern that is not likely to be discontinued in the near future, ask your retailer.

- Choosing crystal: The glass should balance properly when held between thumb and forefinger—not be top-heavy or it may easily tip over when filled. The rim should be perfectly smooth all around. To check for clarity, look straight down through the piece and be sure that it is colorless.

- Glassware, as with every other part of your *polished* lifestyle, should reflect quality and good taste.

Dinner procedure

Make a timetable and checklist for the event.

Date: _____ Time of Arrival: _____ Theme: _____

Number of Guests: _____ Seating _____

Invitations: (Names) _____

_____

The Menu: _____

_____

_____

_____ Special Diets: _____

Wines, Liqueurs, Beverages: _____

_____

Table Cloth: _____   _____ Napkins: _____

Silver: _____

Glassware: _____

China: _____   _____

_____

Serving Dishes: _____

_____

Candles: _____   _____ Flowers: _____ Music: _____

Decor Needs, Things To Do, & Shopping List: _____

_____

_____

_____

CANDLES

White candles are the traditional color for formal and elegant table decor. The creative and artistic approach to beautiful table settings of the '90's, employs the use of colored candles that co-ordinate with a chosen color scheme.

Candles add greatly to the mood of the occasion, just *be sure to have enough to supply adequate lighting to every part of the table,* or additional electric light to banish gloom.

To make candles burn slowly and evenly, with little or no dripping, put them in your freezer for several hours immediately prior to lighting them. I store my candles in the fridge or freezer so they're always ready. *Wrap them and lay them flat.*

A candle snuffer is inexpensive and will save your tablecloth from wax that flies when the candle is *blown* out. It is also easier to reach with a snuffer.

Candles are *not* used for daytime meals. In summer, when it may still be daylight at dinner time, darken the room by drawing the drapes. Candles are lighted before the guests sit down and are not extinguished until the guests leave the table. Candlesticks or candelabra may be used, but the candles must be above or below eye-level, so as not to impede the guests' view. As a rule, the shorter the candlestick, the taller the candle. Don't use leftover, half burnt, candles from another occasion. New tapers only.

FLOWERS

Flowers as table centrepieces should be low enough that they don't impede the view of guests sitting across the table from one another.

Artificial flowers have been used to advantage in some decors but they must be of top quality silk, *never* plastic. One real flower is much more effective than a whole bouquet of fakes.

MUSIC

Soft, *unobtrusive* music during the dinner meal buffers the silent moments and provides a pleasant background to the social atmosphere.

Taped instrumental music (not vocal) leaves the host/ess free of having to change discs or records.

Select light classical music that has no great variations in volume so it remains unobtrusive.

SEATING

Seating arrangments still follow the rule of the host and hostess being seated at each end of the table. This is not strictly adhered to unless formality is a prime requisite. A woman guest of honor sits to the right of the host. A man guest of honor sits to the right of the hostess.

With no guest of honor, the seats of honor are given to the most elderly people present.

After the above two "categories" have been considered, precedence should take a back seat to sociability. *People should be seated to achieve the enjoyment of everyone.* There's an old saying that "if they matter they don't mind, and if they mind they don't matter." If guests choose their own places, men and women should alternate but wives and husbands do not usually sit to-gether.

PLACE CARDS

If there are eight or more guests, it eliminates confusion if place cards are used.

At an informal dinner, just the first name on the card is enough. This should be handwritten. Cards for a formal dinner should give the full name: Mrs. Jack Endcl, Mr. Ken Cole, Miss Darleen Ansley.

BEFORE DINNER

- The host and/or hostess should be dressed and ready to meet the guests at least a half hour prior to their arrival. This gives time for last minute touch-ups and allows for any tilts that may occur. A relaxed attitude is part of being "polished."
- Guests are greeted at the door by both the host and hostess. The hostess shows them where to put their coats and the host offers them a drink.
- If a large number of guests are arriving, it is helpful to have the drinks, mix, and ice, out where guests can help themselves.
- Sherry is the customary drink and need be the only one offered. Gin, rye, scotch, other spirit, or wine, are other options. Sometimes, a friend will help serve before-meal drinks. Don't forget the ice!
- The guests may begin to drink as soon as they are served or serve themselves. They then are introduced to everyone.
- The host/ess should offer *late arrivals* a drink, but *if dinner is ready, the late arrival should refuse.* Dinner should not be delayed any longer than twenty minutes for late arrivals. They should slip into their place at table as unobtrusively as possible.
- *When dinner is announced, people should immediately go to the table. To dally, insults the hostess.*

- *Don't take your unfinished drink to the table.*
- The hostess goes to the table last unless there's a male guest of honor, then she would accompany him and go to the table first. The host follows with the female guest of honor. The ladies sit immmediately.
- The men should pull out the chairs for the ladies.
- The host takes his seat last.

SERVING DINNER

Table service without servants can be a problem, a very prevalent problem, with which the majority of homes must cope as graciously as we are able.

Here are some suggestions to ease the serving:

- If the first course is a cold dish, it should be in place at the table prior to the guests being seated.
- If the first course is a hot dish, it should be beside the host or hostess ready to be served. *The dinner plates should be previously heated.*
- There are three general ways of serving:

  (1) The hostess and/or host can take the food to each person. This method takes so much time that the food may get cold it also removes the host/ess from the table, which also seems less than ideal.

  (2) The food may be put on a sideboard, and guests help themselves, much like a buffet dinner. With this method, people are getting up and down from the table.

  (3) The food is placed on the table, and the guests help themselves and each other. This way the food is served quickly and there is minimal disruption.

- My favorite way is a combination of a *Serving Table* and *Method #3.* Within easy reach, I have most of the hot dishes on a tea wagon or roll-away side table where they're kept hot with electric trays, candle warmers, or chafing dishes. This removes the serving dishes from the dinner table, keeping it uncluttered and attractive while at the same time ensuring that second helpings are piping hot. It's a simple matter to roll the table back a bit, out of the way until it is needed. After the main courses, the serving table, carrying the serving dishes, is rolled to the kitchen, refilled with the final courses, and is back to the dining table pronto! This way the hostess is away from her guests just fleetingly and the food is always hot and handy. My little serving table is a great "Silent Waiter," and it never sticks its thumb in the gravy!

DURING DINNER

- Food is passed to the *right*, to the diner from his/her left side. The handles of the serving implements should be pointed toward the diner.
- Wine or other beverage is served to the right side of the diner, as that is where the glasses or cups are. *(See the information under "Wine Service.")*
- With a strictly formal dinner, there would be servants or hired caterers, so most of my comments refer to the informal dinner where guests and host/ess serve.
- The guests wait until the host/ess begins eating before they begin. The gracious host/ess will tell them to go ahead and eat and not let their dinner get cold, but the guest should wait for this suggestion.
- *Offering to help is a kind gesture that a host/ess appreciates and may accept.* If so, just one helper should be selected, not several, or it'll disrupt the dinner party. *If the offer to help is graciously refused, the guests should honor the request and not insist on helping.* I, for one, do *not* want my guests involved. Thanks, anyway!
- The host and hostess should not be away from the table *at the same time.* Alternately serving, pouring, and clearing, is a superb way to share the chores.
- Serving utensils are placed *beside* the service bowls and platters, at the beginning of the meal. They are not placed *in* the bowls until the first guest uses them, then, of course, they are placed back in the bowl after each use.
- Sets of salt and pepper shakers are conveniently placed around the table. Pepper *mills* usually aren't placed on an "elegant" table, it's a simple matter to grind fresh pepper prior to the meal to fill the shakers.
- If open salt dishes are used (almost never, they are so ineffi-

cient and ostentatious), the little spoon is placed in the salt dish after it is used. If there is no salt spoon, pinch some salt with your fingers and sprinkle it over your food. If using your fingers, don't return any excess salt to the salt dish, put it on the side of your dinner plate.

- After your food is served, don't immediately season it without trying it first. This is considered an affront to the cook. However, in these times of salt restricted diets, *the cook should use salt sparingly,* and the guests then should feel free to add more salt *after* they first taste the food.
- Diners should never push their plates away when they are finished eating nor should they stack the dishes thinking they are being helpful. Dishes are not stacked at the table. Period!
- *Dishes between courses are never stacked.* They are carried to the kitchen one plate and cutlery in each hand. Stacking makes *both* sides of the plates messy and more difficult to quickly rinse off. Also, fine dinner plates get scratched when stacked. This is a time that *one* guest may help the hostess remove the used plates, two at a time, *not stacked.*
- Care should be taken when cutting your food to consider the plate. Grinding into the plate surface with knives or forks is inconsiderate. Children should be taught at an early age not to bang on dishes.
- Never strike or tap on a glass or cup to get attention. This is not only rude, it is destructive.
- *If,* for some reason, *you must temporarily leave the table during the meal, your table napkin is placed on your chair not on the table.* Simply excuse yourself; it isn't necessary to explain your temporary absence.
- If coffee or tea is served *at the table,* all remains of the meal are first cleared away. With 8 or more guests, *the host/ess may suggest* that the guests change seats and visit with another table mate during coffee. Guests don't change seats unless invited by the host/ess to do so. This gives people a chance to stretch their legs. (Be sure to take your table napkin with you!)
- After a long session of sitting at the table, it is often more comfortable to have coffee/tea elsewhere. It also gives the guests a

chance to move around and to speak with other people.

- After the meal is finished, guests must wait for the hostess to suggest moving from the table to another room. Then they shouldn't linger at the table but should follow the host/ess.
- *Dishes are not washed until after the guests leave.* Only in the rarest case, where perhaps the hostess is very elderly or handicapped, are the guests allowed to help with cleaning up. This is a time to visit and to enjoy your company as the gracious host/ess, not the time to spend it in the kitchen as the maid. Dishes are rinsed and stacked in the kitchen, to be washed later. Guests and hosts relax and enjoy.
- When a diner leaves the table *after the meal is finished,* the table napkin is left neatly gathered (*but not folded*) on the left hand side of your place setting. A fresh napkin will be given when, and if, coffee is served in another room.

Pointers for the dinner guest

- Do not assist hired staff or caterers.
- Treat servants with respect and say "thank-you."
- Do not switch place cards. Sit where designated.
- If you happen to use the wrong utensil, don't be embarrassed, continue using it, and the alert hostess will replace it when that course is served.
- Don't lick the side of your cup or glass to tidy the side of it. This is a most unsightly habit.
- When offered more food, don't say you're "full." That sounds crude. Say you've had sufficient or that you're very satisfied, thank-you.
- Put your chair back in place when you leave the table, after a meal in a home or a restaurant.
- *Never turn over china to see what brand or pattern it is; this is the epitome of rudeness.*
- Don't put your feet on the rungs of the chairs or the table pedestal. Don't lean back on the chair legs.
- Don't ask for free advice from any professionals that are present.
- Don't hand out a business card unless one is requested.

- Don't ask to watch a special program on television.
- Do express appreciation for the good food.
- Be sure to phone and thank the host/ess for the pleasant evening.
- *Don't keep accepting invitations and never repaying the treat*. If you aren't in a position to entertain in your home, you can always take people out for a meal or a show or bring some special wine or send flowers. *If you won't do this, don't sponge!*
- *If there are no ashtrays at the table, don't ask to smoke. After dinner*, if you must, you may ask the host/ess to excuse you for a few minutes, that you're going *outside* for a smoke. This is preferable to forcing the smell of smoke in someone's home when they object. If the host/ess and guests have no objections to smoke, they'll invite you to smoke indoors and will get you an ashtray. It has become a situation that requires *consideration for all, those that smoke and those that don't*.

DEPARTURE

- *Guests usually leave between 11 P.M. and midnight*. If there are guests of honor, you should wait until they depart first. Since they may not be aware of this social custom, you'll do your hosts a favor if, at a reasonable hour, you make some *discreet* gesture or comment, "Well, it has been a very enjoyable evening. . . .", to indicate that the evening is over. It is quite correct for the hosts to close the bar, or to make a comment that gently says it's over.
- Host and hostess should accompany guests to the door to say goodnight.
- No lingering at the door. The host and hostess have other guests to attend to. Express your appreciation for the pleasant evening, say goodnight, and leave.
- A woman alone, very elderly guests, and anyone that is handicapped, should be accompanied to their cars.

THE BUFFET DINNER PARTY

The main appeal of a Buffet Dinner is its informality, but this type of dinner can be just as elegant as a more formal meal. With food attractively presented and beautiful table decor, a buffet dinner is the most gracious way to entertain a large number of guests. Even for a small group, it serves very well.

The Buffet Dinner Party follows the same rules as a sit-down dinner for invitation, arrival, and departure. Serving, seating, and the type of food served will differ.

The Buffet Dinner is less formal and has many benefits:

(a) More people can be invited since seating is much more extensive.

(b) Service is easier, as diners serve themselves.

(c) No worry about last minute extra guests or last minute "no shows," seating is flexible.

(d) The host/ess can more easily relax and enjoy.

Here are some tips for a successful Buffet Dinner Party:

COAT RACKS

- Coats may be damp from inclement weather, so planning to place them on a bed or in a closet is not always wise or convenient.
- For a large dinner party, it's a good idea to rent a rolling rack to set up near the front entrance for guests' hats and coats.
- In winter, a pretty, washable mat, on which to place guests' overshoes, will help to protect your carpet.

THE BUFFET TABLE

- *The buffet table decor should be as beautiful as you can make it*. Flowers, candles, fine flatware and china, lovely tablecloth and napkins, all lend color and sparkle. The Buffet Dinner provides a choice opportunity to be creative in decor. Since no-one has to peer over them, flower and candle arrangements can be tall and magnificent.
- If the table is placed against the wall, be sure the table is *long* enough accommodate all the food on the outer edges, so the diners won't have to reach too far *over the food* to serve themselves.
- The most efficient way is to place the buffet table in the centre of the room, so guests can circle it to serve themselves.

- For a large party, food and dishes can be arranged in *duplicate* up each side of the table, and guests form two lines. This provides faster service.
- For a smaller dinner party, food and dishes are arranged in one line.
- *The order of the Buffet Table setting should be:*

  (1) Large dinner plates, not stacked too high. For a hot meal, heat plates, but not too hot to handle.

  (2) The main course. If this is a hot dish, an electric tray, chafing dish, or candle warmer, will be of great benefit. Micro-wave ovens get foods hot, but they don't *keep* them hot. I still bless my electric Salton hot trays.

  (3) The vegetable dishes. These, too, should be kept hot. Hot food, turned cold, is not tasty.

  (4) Tossed salads. Beside foods such as salads, that require two hands for serving, leave enough room on the buffet table for diners to set their plates down to serve themselves.

  (5) Rolls, butter, relishes, salt and pepper, etc. Having served themselves the main meal, the guests know what condiments they want to add.

  (6) The napkins and flatware. Both hands are needed to hold a plate and serve one's self, so napkin and flatware are most easily picked up last.

  (7) Beverages can be on the buffet table or a side table. I like a rollaway table or tea cart, so the wine and other beverage can be taken to each guest or placed in a spot convenient to all.

- *Desserts, tea, coffee, cream, sugar, and liqueurs are usually placed on the buffet table after the main course has been cleared away*.
- Why not use a pretty basket to hold the flatware and napkins? Here is a handy way to fold napkins so they can conveniently hold the flatware:

(1) Take a large dinner size napkin and fold it in half with the open ends at the top. Fig.#15

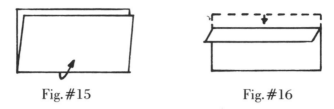

Fig. #15   Fig. #16

(2) Fold down the open top to about half way. Fig. #16

(3) Turn napkin over, face down. Fold napkin over 4 times from left to right to make a flat package or to give room for several pieces of silver. For a more compact, tighter package or fewer pieces of flatware, fold the napkin over 6 times from left to right. Fig. #17

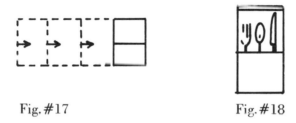

Fig. #17   Fig. #18

(4) Turn face up and put flatware in pocket. Fig. #18 These pile nicely in a basket or flat on a table.

- It's perfectly correct to use *good quality* paper napkins. Paper plates for a cold meal are also appropriate for easy clean-up. *A buffet dinner party for only a few people shouldn't need paper dishes*. Plastic cups are all right for cold drinks, but *spirits and wines deserve a glass*. It's not expensive to rent extra glasses if you haven't sufficient supply. This way, you'll have an ample supply and won't need to wash glasses during the party. For a large number of guests, you may not have enough of, or want to use, your best crystal goblets.

- The tablecloth should be large, reaching to the floor if possible or at least half way. It's wise to pin back the corners of the cloth to avoid accidents.

- Be sure your home is not too warm. Crowded rooms do not need much heat.
- By the time the guests arrive, *be sure your kitchen is spotless, counters cleared and ready to receive after-dinner dishes.* At buffet parties, guests tend to wander around more and may help carry dishes to the kitchen. The Buffet Dinner is one meal that help from guests is offered and accepted.
- At a very casual Buffet Dinner, food may be served from the kitchen counters. People love a kitchen!

SEATING

- Often, a Buffet Dinner doesn't provide seating for every person. In my opinion, this can be a tiresome way to enjoy one's self. I believe that, except at a Cocktail Party, everyone should have a place to sit, and preferably at some kind of a table. I stress: *There must be a place for everyone to sit comfortably to eat.* The foods served may then be regular "sit-down dinner" foods, not easily balanced on a knee. Even "fork" foods are more enjoyable at a table.
- Individual "T.V" tables covered with place mats, card tables covered with pretty tablecloths or place mats, folding chairs, whatever provides comfortable and attractive seating should be utilized. If extra card tables are used, see that each has a nice table-center: perhaps a few flowers or a candle.
- See that no-one has to sit alone in an isolated area. Dinner is more enjoyable with some social rapport.

HOSTESS

- The host and hostess should get around to visit with each guest, even if it's just for a few minutes.
- *Be alert to any service that is needed.* Particularly to show guests where to place used plates and to help replenish beverages. *Come to the aid of the party!*

FOOD FOR THE BUFFET DINNER

- Food laid *out for a Buffet Dinner should be displayed as attractively as possible.* This is part of the pleasure of the meal. Pretty serving dishes, candle-light, flowers, colorful table linens, creative design, all say, "Let's have a party!".

- *For a Buffet Dinner, it is imperative that there be plenty of food and beverages.* Since people help themselves and return for seconds, it's better to have too much than too little.
- *Plan a menu that can be prepared well ahead of time.* Casseroles that can be kept in the fridge or freezer will just need heating at the last minute. Many dishes can be made even days ahead.
- *The main course should be of meat, fowl, or fish.* Depending on the number of guests invited, perhaps two main dishes, one of meat and one of fish or fowl, would ensure appeal to everyone.
- *If a whole turkey, baron of beef, or roast, is featured on the buffet table, the host or hostess should carve it for each guest.*
- *A cold meal is the easiest to prepare and to serve.* If you don't have facilities for keeping food piping hot, it might be better to serve only cold dishes.
- *Individual portions,* such as Killarney baked potato balls, arranged on heat proof platters, are easy for the guests to pick up.
- *Be sure you have adequate oven and fridge space to handle the menu you plan.* Having many things to keep cold or to heat up at one time, might pose a problem. Plan the menu accordingly.
- *Have plenty of ice on hand and enough ice buckets to serve it.* Buy several bags of ice cubes.
- *Extra salt and pepper shakers at each individual table are handy for the guests.*
- *If not all guests will be seated at tables, be sure to have food that can be eaten with only a fork.* Trying to cut food balanced on a plate on one's lap is difficult. It's better to have fewer guests.
- *Dessert is put out on the buffet table after the main course dishes have been cleared away.* The table should be brushed and tidied for the next grand display. Tea, coffee, cream, and sugar, are also placed at this time, or can be carried around on trays to serve the guests at their table.
- *The Buffet Dinner can be as grand or as casual as you'd like it to be. The important thing is to have a happy time with family and friends.*

BUFFET DINNER GUEST ETIQUETTE

- The host/ess has made the table beautiful. It's a gracious gesture for the guests to gather around and "view the table" before the picture is disrupted by hungry diners. *This is an opportunity for the host/ess to explain the set-up* (i.e. duplicate lines of food) and the various dishes being served.
- The guests of honor lead the way in a buffet line.
- The host and hostess serve themselves last.
- If there are two lines of food, proceed down *one line only*. Be observant, don't disrupt both lines.
- Don't load up your plate. You may return to the buffet table for refills *after everyone has eaten*.
- Don't play Jack Horner and pick out the "plums." Hunting around in the food to find and take more than your share of the choice tid-bits is rude.
- When you are finished with your dinner dishes and napkin, the host/ess will let you know, or you should ask, where to put them. Be helpful and tidy.
- Serve yourself carefully, don't let spoon handles drop back into the serving dishes. Let the host/ess know if this has happened, so he/she can replace them.
- Don't loiter around the buffet table, others want to be served.

RESTAURANT BUFFET DINNER

BRUNCH — SMORGASBORD

Follow the information given for dinner in a restaurant, except for the following:

- If there are duplicate lines of food, go up one line only. Before you make your selection, it's wise to have a look at the entire buffet table first to see how it is set up and what dishes are served.
- Because people differ in the order in which they prefer to eat their salad: (1) you may start with the salad plate and take a selection of salads and return to your table; (2) if you prefer your salad on a side plate with your dinner, then fill a small plate with salad and a dinner plate with the main course or (3) take a dinner plate for the main course and return later to have your salad. What ever order you prefer to choose is accept-

able. That's what is great about a restaurant smorgasbord.

- *Leave your used plates at your place at the dinner table, the waiter will remove them, don't take them back for refills. Take fresh plates for refills.*

SOCIAL LUNCHEONS

Luncheons became rather "out of style" when women joined the public work force and weren't at home for such pleasant mid-day entertaining. Now, however, the luncheon has become a popular and delightful party again among lively *retirees* that have the time and the inclination for mid-day parties.

Luncheons are ideal for *seniors* who prefer daytime activities to late night ones. Retirees have fun with their beautiful trappings of dinnerware and linens and the budget to be as lavish as they please with the menu. Never mind the digestive system, surely we all may forget the calories, now and then! There *are* some compensations to retirement and one of them is getting to-gether with friends and family and having a scrumptious lunch in someone's home.

Social Luncheons once were predominantly a get-to-gether for ladies only, now, however, the order of the day is that both men and women make it a mixed event. Much of the time, the men share the preparation of the food; they have become such excellent cooks. The carefree, retirement years have become a *sharing* experience for husbands and wives. Nor are Single Seniors left out, they have their turn at wielding the mixing spoon and strutting their stuff with new recipes.

Social Luncheons are, of course, a great way to entertain on the week-ends or holidays when even members of the current labor force can make like retirees and relax with guests over a very special lunch.

- The invitation can be phoned as little as a week prior to the luncheon.
- A Social Luncheon can be buffet style or as a sit-down meal. It is served soon after the guests arrive.
- Luncheon menus are usually lighter than dinner menus. Some people prefer a substantial meal at noon rather than a big meal at night, so, suit the menu to the preference.

- A total of three courses is ample, or two courses and a light dessert. Wine may or may not be served.
- The menu can be hot or cold, as elaborate as hot casseroles or as simple as filled croissants and a side salad and a light dessert.
- *An attractively set table adds to the enjoyment.*
- Drinks may or may not be served, but if they are, popular *before* lunch drinks are Screwdrivers, Bloody Marys, Cider, Dubonnet or any other wine. Liqueurs are not usually served prior to or after lunch. Be sure to provide non-alcoholic beverages too.
- Lunch Begins: 12 to 1 p.m. Ends: 2:30 to 3 p.m.

Wine service

The knowledge and study of wines, *oenology,* is a most interesting and extensive subject. Recently, it is an ever changing one and so some beliefs about wine can be quite controversial. Not being an oenologist, I'll simply give the generally accepted terms and customs relating to wine, its service, and it's characteristics.

About wine in general

- Wines are distinguished by color, flavor, bouquet or aroma, and alcoholic content. They are classified as natural or fortified, sweet or dry, still or sparkling. For red wines the entire grape is used and for white wines the juice only.
- *Table Wines:* (e.g. claret, sauterne) contain from 8% to 14% alcohol by volume.
- *Fortified, or Brandied, Wines:* (e.g. sherry, port) contain added alcohol: their strength varies from 14% to 22% alcohol by volume. Most dessert and aperitif wines fall into this category.
- *Sparkling Wines:* Natural, effervescent wines, of which Champagne is best known, contain some carbon dioxide and

5% to 14% alcohol per volume.

- *Sweetness or Dryness of Wines:* Wines are assigned a number from 1 to 10 to indicate the sweetness or dryness of that particular wine.

  > 0 Very Dry
  > 1– 2 Dry
  > 3– 4 Medium
  > 5– 6 Sweet
  > 7–10 Very Sweet

- *Wine Diamonds:* Sometimes there are small crystals that form in wine: white crystals in white wine and red crystals in red wine, and they are known as "wine diamonds." This is a natural deposit in the wine that is nothing more than potassium bitartrate (cream of tartar). This doesn't mean this is an inferior product, on the contrary, it is almost certainly an indication that the wine is totally natural. Diamonds are a wine's best friend?

Countries of origin

- France is a leading wine-producing area both for quality and quantity; best known are the wines of Bordeaux and Burgundy (both red and white), the Loire and Rhone valleys, and Alsace.
- Germany produces some fine light, dry, white wines from the Rhine districts, the Moselle valley, Baden, Bavaria.
- Italy produces quantities of wines but much of it is of ordinary quality; however, Chianti, Lachryma Christi, Capri, and Falerno are esteemed, and Sicily makes Marsala which is usually fortified.
- The United States produces some excellent wines; California, the leading region, makes European-type wines from grapes of the Old World species.
- Canada, a new and very young country in comparison to the great wine producing countries of the world, is producing some respectable wines that are found to be very acceptable.
- Good wines are also available from Spain, Portugal, Australia, and Chile.

Storage of wine
- All wines should be kept in a cool, dark place and sudden changes of temperature should be avoided.
- Sparkling wines, table wines, and vintage ports should be stored on their sides to keep their corks wet and swollen, so air can't get in the bottle.
- Screw cap bottles and plastic stoppered sparkling wine bottles should be stored in an upright position.
- Table wines and sparkling wines deteriorate quite quickly after they are opened so should be used within three or four days.
- Fortified wines may be kept for longer periods after they have been opened, because of their higher alcohol content. Be sure they are well sealed.

Opening wine bottles
- Wipe the wine bottle with a damp cloth to clean it.
- The best opener is a corkscrew with long arms. As the easy-to-grasp top twists the screw into the cork, the two long arms are forced upward. When the screw has fully penetrated the cork, pressing down on the raised arms of the opener lifts the cork from the bottle. We've had this type opener for over 30 years; they last well and are a good investment.
- Open the wine bottles prior to the guests' arrival, in case there are problems with broken corks. Of course, sparkling wines aren't opened until served.
- *Red* wines should always be opened and allowed to stand a while. The newer the wine the longer it should be opened prior to serving (several hours). Older red wine needs only about an hour or less. Some experts disapprove of prolonged prior opening.
- After removing the cork, take a clean damp cloth and wipe the *inside of the bottle neck* where, on most wines, there is usually a collection from the cork. Wipe the top of the bottle and the outside.
- Some wines require decanting. See "Decanting Wines."
- Taste the wine. In a restaurant, the wine is tasted and approved at the table, but in the home it is *not*.

Decanting wines

- As wines age, they may produce a sediment. This is a natural occurrence. Let the wine stand in an upright position for a day *before it is going to be opened and served,* so the sediment can settle to the bottom of the bottle. Uncork the bottle, being careful not to disturb the sediment, and slowly, in a steady, continuous motion, decant the wine into another container. Stop pouring when the sediment begins to move to-ward the neck of the bottle. You may need to leave about two inches of wine in the bottle.
- A wine strainer is a handy thing to have.
- *Vintage port and old red wines are always decanted.* White wines, including champagne, are served from the bottle.
- Red wine often is poured into decanters for serving at the table. (Especially if it doesn't have a distinctive label!)
- Some wine connoisseurs say sherry and port should always be decanted. It's a matter of preference.

Tips about wine

- *Not all wines improve with age. It depends on the quality of the original product;* an inferior wine *can't* improve with time. A white wine should not be kept more than 8 to 10 years unless it is a *sweet* white wine of *superior quality,* that's good for at least a generation. Good quality red wines improve with age if they are properly stored. The higher the alcohol content, the better the aging potential. Know what you are storing and aging.
- All wine should be at least a year old before it is drunk.
- Room temperature does not mean 70 degrees when it comes to serving wine. This advice referred to old time conditions when homes were not centrally heated and when wine was stored in a cool wine cellar. Most wines should be cooled a little. (55°)

Purchasing wine

- Wine is a sensitive product. It is wise to purchase it from reliable vintners or Government Liquor Stores where it is handled knowledgeably. The corner grocery store or delicatessan, though convenient, may not store or care for the wine adequately.

Amount of wine to purchase
Sherry: One bottle will serve about 12 glasses.
Standard Size Bottle of Wine: Serves 6 glasses.
Litre Bottle of Wine: Serves 9 glasses.
Champagne: Allow 4 ounces per flute type glass.
Purchase extra white wine, some people prefer to drink white wine throughout the meal and prior to the meal.

Champagne

- Champagne must be served well chilled.

To open:

- Disturb the champagne bottle as little as possible, so the contents won't gush all over upon opening.
- Remove the wire from the top of the cork. After the wire is removed the bottle *must* be opened or the cork may blow off when no one is around.
- Hold the bottom of the bottle against you (30 degrees from the vertical) as you twist the cork and then press with your thumbs to push out the cork.
- Release the cork with as little "pop" as possible to retain the bubbles. It used to be the rage to see how loud a bang could be mustered when opening a bottle of champagne but now people know that it's much better to save all the bubbles to keep the drink lively.
- Aim the top of the bottle, so you won't hit anyone or anything when the cork flies out under pressure.

Types of champagne

Champagne ranges from dry to sweet in this order: brut (the driest), extra dry, sec, demi-sec, doux. Brut, having the lowest sugar content, seems to let more taste of the original wine come through.

The champagne glass

The champagne glass used to be a shallow saucer shape, but now a flute shaped glass is much preferred. The smaller surface retains the bubbles.

The champagne celebration
When we think of celebrating special moments, we think of champagne. Every part of the champagne "ritual" should be *shared*, from opening the bottle to pouring the bubbly, everyone enjoys the celebration.
Buy good quality, chill it to perfection, enjoy!

To dine with wine

Many of the rules for selecting certain types of wines to go with specific foods are justified. Though many people consider themselves "sophisticated rebels" who'll not be influenced by such guidance, there are very good reasons for these rules. Consider this:

Rule #1.   *Serve white wine with fish.*

Reasons: • The tannic acid in the majority of *red* wines can react harshly with the natural iodine in fish, not only for taste but for digestion.
               • White wine has a more mild flavor and doesn't overpower the delicate flavor of fish.

Rule #2.   *Serve red wine with red meat, wild game, chili, spaghetti & meatballs.*

Reason: These foods are more intense in flavor and need a more robust wine than a white can be.

Rule #3.   *No wine (red or white) with, or after, these foods: curries, asparagus, chocolate, oranges, grapefruit, artichokes, salads or anything made with vinegar.*

Reason: These foods destroy or distort the flavor of all wines. Red wine is particularly bad with artichokes, it makes a strong, metallic taste.

Rule #4:   *A white wine should be served before a red one. A light wine before a heavy one. A dry wine before a sweet one. A mediocre wine before a superior one.*

Reason: The taste buds react more favorably to this procedure.

Though these rules generally apply, there are exceptions, for example a pasta with a plain, bland-tasting sauce would be better with a white wine than a stronger tasting red wine. Chicken cooked with a red wine, such as is "coq au vin," should be served with a red wine. Match the intensity of tastes.

Aperitifs: Served prior to the meal.
- Can be served chilled or at room temperature.
- Sometimes served with a twist of lemon.
- Serve in a small tulip glass. Often served over ice in an old-fashioned glass, but a wine connoisseur would say this is an insult to add ice to fine wine!
- *Some aperitifs are:* Dry sherry, dry or sweet vermouth, red or white Dubonnet, Champagne.
- *Food to serve with aperitifs:* nuts, cheese sticks, nothing too substantial, just a snack to munch on.

White table wine: Served prior to, with, or after, the meal.
- White wine should be chilled.
- White wine is customarily served with the first course. It is so popular that many people prefer to stay with white wine throughout and after the meal.
- A white wine must be kept cool or cold, so a wine bucket with ice or a wine cooler should be used,
- White table wine is served in a *stemware* glass that ideally is a little smaller than a glass for red wine, and it has a more open shaped bowl. *The glass is held by the stem,* so the hand doesn't touch the bowl and warm the wine. It's perfectly fine to use the same size glass for white wine and red wine. Pour 3 to 3 1/2 ounces of white wine per serving.
- *Some white table wines are:* Chablis, Burgundy, Bordeau, Chardonnay, Rhine, Moselle, Riesling.
- *Foods to serve with white table wines:* Shellfish and mild tasting fish, such as sole; white meats, such as veal and chicken; fresh fruit, and desserts.

Red table wines: Served with main courses of robust flavor.
- Served at room temperature *no warmer than 65 degrees.*
- Beaujolais is often somewhat chilled.
- Red wine is served in a *stemmed* wine goblet a little larger than a glass for white wine. The top of the glass curves in to protect the wine's bouquet. The *glass is held by the stem* to keep the wine away from the warmth of the hand. Pour 3 to 3 1/2 ounces per serving.

- Red wine, unless it requires decanting, is placed on the dining table in its original bottle.
- *Some red table wines are:* Beaujolais, Pinot Noir, Bordeaux, Burgundy, Chianti, Zinfantel, Rhone.
- *Foods to serve with red table wines:* Stronger-flavor fish such as salmon; turkey; wild game and highly-seasoned red meat with a full-bodied Burgundy; other red meats with a lighter red wine such as a Bordeaux. Cheese is good with red wine and great with port.

Sparkling Wines: Served prior to, with, or after a meal.
- Served cold or chilled.
- Served in a *stemmed*, flute shaped glass. This is a 7 ounce glass but only 4 ounces are served or a little over half full.
- *Some sparkling wines are:* everything from a sparkling white, like Asti Spumanto, to the ultimate fine quality of Champagne. California produces some superb sparkling wines, look for those from the Schramsberg vineyard.
- *Food to serve with sparkling wines:* Not all foods go with sparkling wines, though this is a common belief. A sparkling red Burgundy is good served with roast beef. Champagne may be served with a dessert or as an aperitif. Champagne mixed with orange juice, served with an omelette for breakfast or brunch to launch a very special day, is quite a treat.

Dessert Wines: Served with dessert or after dessert.
- Some are chilled, some served at room temperature.
- There are sets of glasses made of *colored* glass specifically for serving dessert wines. Other wines shouldn't be served in colored glass, and, in my opinion, even dessert wines are better in a clear glass. Pour 2 to 2 1/2 ounces of dessert wine per serving.
- *Some dessert wines:* sweet white Sauternes, served chilled, is popular. Madeira and sherry are usually served at room temperature, but *we* like sherry chilled. Champagne is also served as a dessert wine.

Wine in a restaurant
- *The wine is not selected until after the dinner has been chosen.*

If some want white and some want red, it may be best to order a carafe of each in the house wine. In a reliable restaurant the house wine is dependable.

- In a prestigious restaurant or hotel dining room, the wine is served by the wine steward (sommelier). He is very knowledgeable and eager to be of assistance in recommending and selecting the wine. (*Note:* The wine bill will be separate. If the wine steward has been helpful and not aloof, as some tend to be, tip him 15% of the wine bill *before tax.*)

- In some elegant dining rooms, the prices of the food or wine are not shown on the menu. Perhaps they feel if you have to ask the price you can't afford it! Be sure you know their system ahead of time if price is a factor. You can get some alarming surprises.

- Where prices are shown on a menu, and the waiter or steward is helping you select a wine, *point at a price* saying "Could you suggest something in this range, please" without the guests being made aware of costs. Discussing the cost of anything should be avoided; it makes guests feel uncomfortable.

- *It isn't necessary to take the wine steward's suggestion.* Don't ever be intimidated by his vast (?) knowledge, *you* are the one in charge, not he. If, for instance, you ask to have a Beaujolais slightly chilled and he insists it should be served at room temperature (this often happens to us), tell him quietly but firmly that this is *your* preference, *chill it!*

- *If you are a guest, you should not suggest the wine unless you are invited to do so,* then it's discreet to suggest a couple in the *medium* price range.

- When the wine is brought to the table, it is shown to the person who ordered it, who, before it is opened, *checks to see that it is the brand that was ordered.*

- The waiter opens the wine and puts the cork on the table. *Pinch the cork to see that it is not dried out,* if it is, the wine has been stored carelessly and may not have kept well. If the cork is dry, taste the wine attentively. It isn't necessary to smell the cork, unless you're such an able sleuth you can detect imperfection with one little sniff. After pinching it, leave the cork on the table.

- The waiter will pour a little wine in the host's or hostess' glass for it to be approved.
- No one should flaunt their knowledge of wine by performing great rituals of swishing it about in their mouth; it's most objectionable to behold. Truly cultured people don't find it necessary to prove their superiority. Excellence speaks for itself. *Taste the wine in an unobtrusive manner,* and, because it is the same with wine as it is with people, you'll know if it's good or not; excellence speaks for itself.
- If the wine doesn't taste right to you, ask the steward to taste it; he will want to serve only fine fare and after tasting (*with his own glass*) will readily agree if it is the least bit "off" and will replace the bottle. This doesn't happen very often, considering the number of bottles of wine served.
- If you don't consume alcohol, or feel that you don't know enough about wine to determine its condition, it's perfectly acceptable to ask someone else at the table to be the taster.
- After the wine has been approved, the waiter pours a glass for each guest, usually ladies first, but it's much more efficient to go in order around the table, then he tops up the host's glass last.
- An alert waiter will see that glasses are refilled, but it's quite proper for the host to do so. At a large table it may be difficult to reach each one; if possible, catch the waiter's eye and quietly let him know your guests need service.
- The ordering and pouring of wine seems still to be a man's domain if there are both sexes at the table. It has become socially correct for women to select and order the wine (hurrah!) but *if there's a man at the table he should do the pouring.* I hope that rule doesn't offend anyone's sense of equality, but I'm one feminist who likes it that way!

The general etiquette regarding wine

- Wine is sipped, and the glass returned to the table after each sip.
- It is quite proper to refuse a drink of wine.
- Though some guests may be tea-totallers, it isn't necessary to

refrain from serving wine to other guests. Be sure there are non-alcoholic drinks too.

- A fresh glass is always given when you go from one type of wine to another for another course of food. If the diner hasn't finished a glass of the first wine, the glass is still removed, unless the diner wishes to keep on with the same wine. No one should ask to do this unless they know there is more available. This applies in a home or a restaurant.
- Wine from a carafe is not tasted and approved.
- It bears repeating (time and again!), that a wine glass has a stem for a very good reason; it is so the glass can be held with the warmth of the hand *away* from the wine. *The glass is held by the stem not by the bowl*. You'll notice a brandy snifter has almost no stem and has an oversize bowl. *You cup the bowl of a brandy glass in your hand to keep the brandy warm*.
- A wine glass is filled only to about 2/3 of its capacity. In a brandy snifter, serve one ounce to an ounce and a half of brandy, it is sipped very slowly.

Gifts of wine

- If a dinner guest brings a bottle of wine as a gift to the host/ess, it usually is not opened for that meal. Dinner wines have probably been selected appropriate to the food being served, so the host/ess won't want to disrupt her plans. *Don't be offended if your gift is not served*.
- If it's a special wine you want to bring as a treat to be served with dinner, ask your hostess well in advance of the occasion, so s/he can plan accordingly or can let you know if it would disrupt the plans.
- If you expect, or hope, that your gift of *white* wine will be served, be sure to have chilled it.
- After all is said and done, a gift is a gift and should be offered

for the enjoyment of the host/ess, whether it is opened and poured or kept for later.

- *If it is a large gathering where everyone brings the wine or drink of their choice, it is important that the host/ess sees that guests are served their own particular contribution.* It isn't enjoyable to have to drink a wine that doesn't appeal to you, when your bottle isn't opened or is served to someone else.

- *A Wine Shower* for a bride and groom is a great way to start a couple on a wine collection, or to add to their wine cellar. The various items that go with wines can be given also, such as a wine cooler, ice bucket, corkscrew, goblets; the list is endless.

Coffee service

- Coffee is not served with the main course of a meal. It is served with the dessert, or after the meal with a liqueur.

- Some people prefer decaffeinated coffee. Another option is certain coffees grown in Puerto Rico that have quite a bit less caffeine in them than has Columbian coffee.

- Never boil coffee. Boiling makes coffee very bitter.

- Coffee beans should be stored in a tightly closed container in the fridge or freezer. The beans are ideally ground immediately before use.

- If coffee is served in mugs, a saucer or a small plate should be provided for diners to place their spoons upon. If need be, ask for one. Diners never should place a used spoon on the cloth or place mat.

- Cream and/or milk should be allowed to warm to room temperature before being served, so as not to cool the coffee. Both cream and milk should be offered as cholesterol restricted diets may require milk.

- Coffee is served to the diner from the right side. Cream and sugar are served from the left.

- If coffee is served at the dinner table after the meal, it is all

right to move the cup and saucer to the centre of the place setting. At a formal dinner, however, the cup and saucer are not moved, but are kept to the right of the place setting
- If coffee spills into the saucer, the saucer should be replaced. In a restaurant ask for this service.

ESPRESSO
- Special equipment is needed to make Espresso coffee.
- It is served in demitasse cups or Espresso glasses.
- Milk or cream are never added to Espresso coffee, just sugar and a twist of lemon.
- Tasty ways to serve Espresso are with a dash of liqueur such as Tia Maria or Anise with a dollop of whipped cream.
- Espresso beans, because they are riper, do not have as much caffeine in them as do regular coffee beans.

CAPUCCINO
- Capuccino coffee is made by combining equal parts of Espresso coffee and hot milk with a little cinnamon and nutmeg.

Tea service

- Tea is the world's most widely used beverage, other than water. Though there is only one tea plant, the way it is grown, the type of soil, the age, blending, and grading, all give us many different tasting teas. Also, spices or flowers are added to some teas, and the tastes vary distinctively.
- *Three basic types of tea are: green tea* which is dried immediately after it is picked; *black tea,* which is more flavorful, is allowed to ferment before the final processing; and *Oolong* which is only partly fermented, is intermediate in flavor and color.

Making a perfect "cuppa"

- Boil the water. Never use water that has been boiled before, it must be fresh water.
- Fill a *tea ball* with one teaspoon of tea leaves for each cup of tea, and place it in a *pre-scalded* teapot.
- When the water almost reaches a full rolling boil, immediately pour about a cup of it over the tea leaves in the tea ball to activate the volotile oils in the tea which produce the flavor. Swish the tea ball around. *This water is then poured off.* This first rinse with almost boiling water also kills a lot of the germs that are in tea. Tea is a very dirty product!
- With the water at the rolling boil, not overboiled or underboiled, pour the required amount over the tea leaves that have been readied in the pot. The flavor that is produced by volatile oils in the tea leaves has been activated by the first hot rinse, and now will fully be released with the boiling water. The caffeine in the tea gives it its stimulating properties, and the tannin gives it its astringency.
- *Tea should be steeped not less than three minutes and not more than five minutes to be at its best.* The tea should be *"stirred"* with the tea ball, to get its optimum flavor. The tea ball should then be removed.
- Tea *bags* utilize only the "scraps" of tea leaves and cannot produce the finest "cuppa" tea.
- If the leaves have been put loose in the pot without using a tea ball, a tea strainer should be used.
- *Cream is not used in tea, as the fat distorts the delicate tea flavor.* Tea is either drunk plain, or with a bit of lemon juice, some like a little sugar, and the English usually like a little milk.

After-dinner drinks

WINES & LIQUEURS
After-Dinner Drinks: Served after the meal with coffee.

- Served at room temperature.

- Served in glasses appropriate for the type of drink as shown below.
- *Some after-dinner drinks are:*

  Sweet Sherry, Port, and Madeira: Fortified wines of rich taste and varying degrees of sweetness. Served at room temperature. Nicest, poured from a decanter into a stemmed, small crystal wine glass.

  Brandy, a spirituous liquor distilled from wine, is served in a small or large brandy snifter which is cupped in the hand to keep the brandy warm.

  Cognac and Armagnac come in a wide range of grades and qualities, vintage dated and non-vintage dated.

  Eaux de vie, which means "water of life," is a clear brandy made from distilled fruits. Two popular ones are Bertrand Framboise Sauvage (raspberry) and Bertrand Poire William (pear). Delicious!

Liqueurs: Served after dinner, usually with coffee.
- Almost all liqueurs are intensely sweet.
- Served straight, they are served at room temperature.
- Liqueurs are served in very small liqueur glasses.
- There are several popular liqueurs including:

  Orange: Grand Marnier Centennaire; Grand Marnier Cordon Rouge; Cointreau

  Mint: Creme de menthe; Walker's Peppermint Schnapps

  Coffee: Kahlua; Tia Maria; Sangsters Blue Mountain

  Anice/Licorice: Pernod; Ricard; Henke's Anisette

  Dairy Base: Bailey's Original Irish Creme; Creme de Grand Marnier; Carioca Rum Creme

  Herbal: Benedictine B & B; Chartreuse; Drambuie; Irish Mist; Morrison-Glayva

  Nut: D'Illva Amaretto Di Saronno; Malibu Coconut Rum

  Cacao: Creme De Cacao; Swiss Chocolate Almond
- Liqueurs, being so highly flavored and sweet, enhance the taste of other liquors, in fact, some are used almost entirely as *components* of mixed drinks.
- The alcohol content in liqueurs and brandies can be over 20%, so they should be sipped slowly and consumed with sensible restraint.

Beer and ale

- The term beer refers to a wide range of products which includes: ale, stout, lager, porter, bock, and pilsener.
- Almost all beers produced in North America are of the *lager* type.
- Beer is obtained by the fermentation of mash of various malted grains (predominantly barley), with or without the addition of hops or other flavoring ingredients.
- *Beer should not be over two months old.*
- Beers vary greatly in alcohol and sugar content. The "light" beers have less alcohol.
- Most people prefer their beer cold. Forty degrees produces the fullest flavor of the beer.
- Even the smallest bit of grease or oil ruins beer, as it kills the foam. Beer glasses should be washed with a detergent in very hot water to remove every smidgeon of grease or oil.
- Beer glasses shouldn't be dried with a cloth, but should be allowed to drain.
- Beer glasses should be rinsed in very cold water just prior to use, and the beer should be poured into a tilted, *wet* glass.
- Beer is served in glasses or in mugs.
- The Pilsener glass is for light beer; the smaller glass for ale; the beer stein (often made of pewter and with a glass bottom so the enemy could be watched!); and the beer mug, made of glass or of opaque porcelain.
- The foam on the top of beer is called the "head" or the "collar." Some people like a low collar with little foam, some like a deeper collar. The customary height of the collar is one quarter the height of the mug or glass.
- *Ale* is made from the same ingredients as beer, but a different strain of yeast is used.
- Ale is often of stronger alcoholic content than beer.
- Ale is served at a temperature a little warmer than that for beer.

Non-alcoholic drinks

SOFT DRINKS

With more and more people *wisely* choosing *not* to drink alcoholic beverages, *a polished host/ess gives special attention to providing tasty fruit and/or vegetable juices*. In the past, the tea-totaller was served anything that was handy, from a cola to a soda water. Most people greatly enjoy a carefully concocted cold drink in a fine crystal glass. There should be plenty of soft drinks to satisfy everyone.

- Drinks should not be too sweet or too rich; prior to dinner these would spoil the appetite.
- Be sure to serve non-alcoholic drinks in your best crystal, just as you do your wine and liquors.
- Make decorative ice cubes by filling the ice cube trays with water and dropping one piece of fruit in each section: a maraschino cherry, a pineapple chunk, a fancy twist of lemon peel, for fruit juice drinks.
- A Bloody Shame is a Bloody Mary with no liquor added. It tastes delicious chilled in a tall glass with either a slender stick of celery or a stick of English cucumber as a swizzle stick. Sprinkle a little celery salt on it.

How to serve and eat certain foods

CAVIAR

- Caviar, is prepared and salted roe of the sturgeon and certain other large fish.
- Thought by many to be the ultimate delicacy is the caviar from Russia where workers are highly skilled in its preparation and the sturgeon roe is of the most sought after quality. Because of its quality, only 2% salt is necessary to preserve it, so it is not salty or fishy in taste.
- It takes years for the sturgeon to yield these eggs, so caviar of the sturgeon is very expensive. Three of the finest caviars are:

Sevruga: Light to dark gray in color. The female sturgeon takes 4 years to yield these eggs. It is the least expensive.

Osetra: Light brown to yellowish in color. The female sturgeon takes 13-14 years to yield these eggs. Better than Sevruga.

Beluga: Light to dark gray in color. The female sturgeon takes 20 years to yield these eggs. *The most costly caviar.*

- The roe from salmon, cod, herring, tuna and gray mullet are also used as caviar, but are an inferior grade to that of the sturgeon.
- Caviar eggs should be shiny, translucent, grey, and *large* grained. (The eggs of caviar can vary in size from tiny grains to grains the size of a pea.)
- Caviar spoils rapidly in temperatures warmer than 40 degrees, so when it is opened it should be eaten immediately.
- Caviar is very oily, this keeps it from freezing.
- *Caviar should never touch metal, nor should it be served on it.*

SERVING
- Caviar is placed in a glass bowl (not crystal) over a bed of cracked ice to keep it cold.
- It is "piled" on rounds of toast or black bread. It isn't spread, as that breaks or bruises the eggs.
- The real connoisseurs of caviar prefer just a bit of lemon juice and parsley as a condiment. It can be served with minced hard-boiled egg whites, yolks, and onion (in individual bowls) to sprinkle over the top.
- Don't help yourself to a very big serving, caviar is an expensive specialty that is consumed sparingly.
- Ice cold, straight vodka served in a liqueur glass, or chilled champagne, are perfect drinks with caviar.

ESCARGOTS (SNAILS)
- *You should have the proper utensils, if you serve escargots: special tongs and double-pronged forks.* Guests' fingers will smell strongly of garlic if they have to grasp the shells with them.

- An escargot is very slippery, so care must be taken to grasp the shell *with the tongs held close to the plate* (not up in the air), then the snail is picked out with the small pronged fork.
- Using the tongs, turn the shell over, so all the tasty juice is poured out into your plate. Drop small bits of bread (one at a time) onto your plate to sop up this juice and eat it with your fork. This way the juice from the shell gets mixed with the garlic sauce and is even more palatable. Some people pick up the shell and suck out the remaining juice, but this isn't very polite in company, particularly if others at the table aren't eating escargots and must listen to the sound effects.
- Bread should be served with escargots, so every bit of the juice and garlic sauce can be enjoyed.
- When escargots are served out of the shell, they are eaten with a regular or seafood fork.
- When finished, the tongs and fork are placed side by side in the finished position on the dish.

LOBSTER

- The Northern or American lobster from Maine, Nova Scotia, North Carolina, and North European waters is the best, with the female being finer in flavor.
- Allow a half lobster or one small lobster per serving. A large part of the lobster is discarded.
- Buy live lobsters weighing from 1 and 1/4 to 2 and a 1/2 pounds. Lobsters larger than this may be tough. A 2 and a 1/2 pound lobster will yield about 2 cups of cooked meat.
- Before you cook a lobster be sure it is in a healthy condition; pick it up and stretch its tail out flat, *it should snap back*.
- Whole lobster is so scrumptious it should be served with *informal* dignity! Bibs and "dig in and enjoy" attitudes are the order of the meal, so every tiny bit can be pried and twisted and squeezed from this tasty creature. Plenty of napkins and finger bowls.
- The considerate host/ess will have cracked and cut the claws and bodies of the lobster prior to its being served. Some people prefer to "do it yourself."
- Lobster crackers and meat scissors can be shared, but each

diner will need a pick and a seafood fork.

- With one hand holding the lobster steady on the plate:

  (1) Twist off the claws. Crack each with a lobster or nutcracker. Use a pick to remove and eat the meat.

  (2) Break the tail off the body. This is where there is the most meat. With the scissors, cut the soft underside of the tail up the middle, so you can remove the big piece of lobster meat. With a fork, cut off smaller pieces and, one at a time, dip them into the butter or sauce that is provided.

  (3) Twist off the legs. Cut them in small pieces. The meat from the legs can be pushed out or picked out.

  (4) The body part of the lobster has the liver, "tamale" (tomalley) which is a green material; and, in the female lobster, the coral or "roe." Some people do not eat the material from the stomach cavity; others consider it to be a delicacy.

- *The "lady" (a hard sac near the head), and the intestinal vein that runs through the middle of the underside of the tail meat, should not be eaten.*

- A large bowl, platter, or lined basket should be provided for the discarded lobster shells.

- Each diner should have their own small container of butter in which to dip the lobster.

- Other dips used for lobster are mayonnaise or plain lemon juice. Ask which ones each guest would prefer.

Lobster thermidor

- This is a tidier way to eat lobster, and it may be served in a more formal manner.

- Prior to the meal, the cooked lobster meat is removed from the entire lobster. The emptied tail of the lobster is then filled with lobster meat that has been mixed with a creamy white sauce.

- The lobster tail is served as the container and no special scissors, picks or crackers are required, just seafood forks and a good appetite.

SHRIMP

- Shrimp range in size from the tiny ones of the West Coast and Scandinavia to the large ones from Europe: scampi, langoustines and Dublin prawns. There are also super size shrimp from India.

- Shrimp that are fresh should be *dry* and *firm*.
- Shrimp must be deveined before serving. This can be done before or after cooking.
- *Shrimp Cocktail:* is eaten with the smallest fork on the outside of the place setting. If the sauce is served separately, it can be poured over the shrimp or the shrimp can be dipped in it. Leave the lettuce.

P A S T A : *Spaghetti or Long Noodles*

- Spaghetti or long noodles are only served at very informal meals.
- The proper way of eating string pasta is to put the fork tines under *only a couple of strands* and lift them as you twist them around the fork forming a **small** ball. When the strands have been completely wound, with no ends hanging, the pasta is placed in the mouth. By picking up only two or three strands, the ball that is formed won't be too large. Pasta is never sucked into the mouth, this flips the sauce over everyone and is a rude way to eat.
- Some people use a tablespoon to help twist the pasta around the fork, but this isn't considered to be the proper way, by the knowledgeable gourmet. *If a spoon is used, it should be held down close to the plate,* not up in the air above the plate.
- String pasta is never supposed to be cut into smaller pieces to be eaten. Tell that to arthritic hands that can't nimbly twist the strands around a fork. In my opinion, it's less messy (and it surely can't be offensive to anyone) for a diner to cut the pasta strands and eat it that way. Go ahead, with my blessings and, if you like, with my accompaniment!

BAKED POTATOES

- Baked potatoes should be eaten from the skin. The inside of the potato shouldn't be scooped out and mashed. It's all right to leave the skin.
- *Potatoes baked in foil should have the foil removed before they are brought to the table.* Some restaurants make this error,

even cutting through the foil and leaving dangerous little bits of foil that wreak havoc with a tooth filling. If the foil has not been removed, it should be gathered with your knife and fork (quite easily, really) and crushed into a small ball, which is placed on the side of the dinner plate. It is *not* put on the tablecloth.

- Condiments such as chives, bacon bits, and sour cream or butter, may be served; one or all can be chosen.

BACON

- If bacon is cooked very crisply in strips, it is one of the few foods that may be picked up in the fingers. If it were cut, it would break into pieces.
- Back bacon or side bacon that is the least bit soft is always eaten with a knife and fork.

SAUCES

- Sauces are always served with a spoon, they are not poured. *A sauce is spooned over only the food for which it is intended:* gravy is spooned over only the meat, not the potatoes or rice; hollandaise sauce goes over the eggs or the vegetables; the juice or sauce with a particular dish is spooned over only that food, not everything on the dinner plate.
- Sauces are partaken of sparingly. A sauce is an enhancement to certain foods, for *all* to share.
- Sauces such as jellies, tartar sauce, and catsup are placed at the side of the plate, not over the food. As it is eaten, the food is dipped into the sauce.

CHICKEN

- It is never correct to pick up chicken in your fingers unless it is being eaten under very casual conditions, such as at a picnic.
- It's quite possible to get all the meat off the chicken bones with a knife and fork.

SMALL BIRDS *(Quail, Cornish Hen, etc.)*

- *Eaten with a knife and fork.* There are very small bones that get in the mouth and may be removed with thumb and fore-finger. This food is not picked up and eaten out of hand.

PATÉ

- Patés (pastes) are made from chicken or goose livers or other foods blended into a smooth paste.
- Paté is served in two ways: either in individual servings of a slice cut from a loaf, or as one large loaf from which the diners help themselves. In the latter, a small amount of paté is taken and placed on the bread plate. The paté is then spread with the butter spreader, a little at a time, on pieces of plain or buttered toast.

  Paté de foie gras in Europe is made from the livers of geese that have been force fed, which produces a very fat liver. Our humane laws do not allow this, so we opt for Paté de Foie de Volaille (Chicken Liver Paté).

  Pate En Croute is the supreme treat of all patés. It is paté baked in a pate (pastry or crust). *The crust is not meant to be eaten,* it is there to seal in the flavor and the juices while the paté is being baked. An individual serving is a slice about a 1/2 inch thick which is usually served on a small plate and is enhanced with an appropriate sauce or lemon wedges.

Fruits

All fresh fruit should be thoroughly washed and checked for bruises before it is served. If there is a fruit knife and fork at the place setting, both should be used.

APPLES AND PEARS

- It is best to quarter these, then peel and core each quarter as it is eaten. The fruit can be eaten with the peel. If no fruit fork and knife have been given, the fruit is eaten by hand.

GRAPES

- Take a cluster of grapes from the fruit bowl by breaking or cutting off a branch and placing the grapes on your plate. *Don't pick grapes one by one from the main fruit bowl.*
- The seeds are removed from your mouth with the thumb and

forefinger and placed on the side plate. Correctly, only *seed-less* grapes should be served.

ORANGES

- A superb way to serve oranges for a dinner party is to peel and slice them, arranging the slices neatly on a small plate and pouring a little orange liqueur (Grand Marnier?) over them.
- Oranges are peeled, and eaten by breaking off sections and eating them. Seeds are placed on the side plate.

MELON

- A half or quarter wedge of a melon is eaten with a spoon.
- Slices of melon with the rind on are eaten with a fruit knife and fork. The rind first is cut away, and the melon then cut in bite size pieces. If the melon is served with the rind removed, the melon is eaten with a knife and fork.

STEWED FRUITS
(with pips or stones)

- The whole fruit is put in the mouth with a spoon and the stone is removed from the mouth into the spoon and placed on the side of the plate.

AVOCADO

- Half an avocado filled with a dressing, is eaten with a spoon.
- Half an avocado with a salad filling, is eaten with a salad fork.

GRAPEFRUIT

- Grapefruit should be halved and cut between and around the sections with a serrated knife before it is served.
- A tasty way to serve grapefruit is to half it, cut around the sections, sprinkle the top with brown sugar and then *broil* the grapefruit just till the sugar melts. Add a maraschino cherry in the centre.

Cheese

- *Soft Cheeses* may be fresh (unripened), e.g. ricotta, Petit Gervais, Neufchatel, Primost, Greek feta; or softened by microorganisms, or "mold-ripened" such as Brie, Camembert, Livarot, Limburger. These cheeses develop flavor as they ripen. Of these, Brie (bree) is a favorite, especially served with fresh fruit.

- *Semi-Hard Cheeses* include mold-ripened crumbly cheese e.g. Stilton, bleu, Roquefort, Gorgonzola; and bacteria-ripened cheeses such as Gouda, Fontina, and Jack. Stilton is sometimes served from the round and the crumbly center is picked up with a spoon.
- *Hard Cheeses* are all bacteria-ripened and include cheddar, Edam, Gruyere, Swiss, Gjetost and Parmesan. Hard cheeses are the best ones for cooking.
- If serving yourself from a wedge of cheese, don't cut across the point, cut along the *side* of the wedge.
- As with every other food, cheese is transferred from the main plate to your own plate. Never take food directly from the main serving plate to your mouth.
- The rind of soft cheese such as Camambert or Brie can be left or eaten, which ever is your preference.
- *Cheeses should always be served at room temperature.*

Sandwiches
- Sandwiches usually should have the crusts removed before being served to guests.
- Small sandwiches are eaten by hand.
- Large sandwiches should be cut in half or quartered, and a *very* thick sandwich, such as a Clubhouse, is most easily eaten with a knife and fork.
- Hamburgers should be cut in half and eaten by hand or, if they are really "oozy," with a knife and fork. The most tidy way to devour a 'burger is to wrap it in a paper napkin or two.
- An open-face sandwich is eaten with a knife and fork.
- Monster sandwiches like Heroes or Submarines, are usually served cut into sections and may be shared by more than one person.

Individual Casseroles, Ramekins, Side Dishes
- Individual casseroles or ramekins should have a large serving spoon on the plate beside the ramekin, so the food can be

transferred to the dinner plate. If there is no spoon (tut! tut!), as a guest in someone's home you'd eat right from the ramekin. In a restaurant, ask for a serving spoon.
- Food is transferred from the ramekin in two or three helpings. Rest the serving spoon in the ramekin.

The cocktail party

The Invitation
- It can be phoned, but in extending an oral invitation don't use the words "cocktail party," say instead "come for a drink."
- A written card is preferable, so the guests have a record of the *specific times* that the party will *start* and *end* and which are stated in the invitation. (See Time Schedules)

Seating
- It isn't necessary to have seats for everyone. In fact, people should circulate at a cocktail party.

Bar Needs
- *Glasses.* Unless it is a very small cocktail party you don't need to use your best crystal. It is better to rent glasses to have plenty on hand and a variety of types: "old-fashioned" glasses, highball glasses, stemmed glasses, should suffice. *Never* use plastic glasses unless the party is being held pool-side where glass is banned due to possible breakage and potential danger to bare feet.
- *Liquors, wines,* and *beers* of your choice.
- *Mixers,* appropriate for the liquors chosen.
- *Soft drinks, fruit and vegetable juices* for those who prefer not to, or can't, drink alcohol.
- *About 3 drinks per person* is the average consumption. It is important to have an adequate supply of drinks.
- *Lemon* and *lime wedges,* "*zests*" (peel), *and juice. Maraschino cherries, cocktail olives* and *onions, salt, Tabasco, Worcester-*

shire sauce, tomato juice.
- *Ice bucket. Ice cubes. Crushed ice (or ice crusher).*
- *Martini pitcher and stirrer. Swizzle sticks.*
- *Water pitcher. Mixing pitcher.*
- *Corkscrew. Bottle opener. Ice tongs.*
- *Shot glasses.* One ounce, and ounce and a half sizes.
- *Trays, knives, spoons. Piles of pretty paper napkins.*

Punch Bowl

- A *punch* made with or without alcohol is always a good way to serve drinks to a large number of people.
- Select a recipe for a tasty punch. Float an ice ring in the punch bowl to keep it cold and make it pretty.

To Make An Ice Mold Ring:

(1) Take a decorative metal mold of a ring shape, place about a half inch of *colored water in the bottom of it and freeze to a slushy consistency.

(2) Arrange a layer of small fruits, i.e. maraschino cherries or strawberries, and little mint leaves *in* this partially frozen ice.

(3) *Carefully,* so as not to disturb the arrangement, pour just enough very cold *colored water over the fruit to freeze it in place. Don't pour too much or the fruit will float and lose its arrangement.

(4) Place back in freezer until this layer is frozen hard enough to hold the fruit in place.

(5) Pour about 3/4 of an inch of *colored water over this layer and freeze until of slushy consistency.

(6) Arrange a second row of small fruit *in* this layer of thick, slushy ice.

(7) Carefully pour just enough very cold *colored water over this fruit to hold it in place. Return the ring mold to the freezer until frozen.

(8) Fill the ring mold to the top with more colored water and freeze it for at least two days to be sure it is absolutely frozen hard and will keep the punch bowl cold as long as possible.

**Colored water:* it is best to put some of the fruit juice that is being used in the punch, in the water, so the punch will not be diluted as the ice mold melts. It makes a more attractive ring if red and/or green food coloring (or maraschino cherry juice) is added to the water and two colors are alternated in the ring. Be sure the colors and the flavors chosen for the ice mold enhance the components of the punch.

Note: To make clear ice cubes and clear ice molds, after drawing the water from the tap, let it sit for a while *before* freezing it. This releases all the bubbles and the ice will then be crystal clear.

Foods

- Serve finger foods or foods that can be eaten with just a fork.
- *A buffet cocktail party* has more substantial food in large enough quantity to be a meal. This food is laid out on a buffet table. There needn't be a number of courses. The invitation should indicate that it is a *buffet* cocktail party, so guests know food enough for a meal will be served.
- A *simple* cocktail party consists of *snacks* and a few drinks and is often staged *early* in the evening prior to going on to some other event, or as an open-house get-to-gether where guests come and go. At this type of cocktail party, food is usually passed around on trays. *Don't eat so much as to make a meal of it.*

Other arrangements

Coat racks

Have extra coat racks available (rented if necessary): one for women, in a bedroom; one for men, in a hallway.

Parking

If your drive-way and street are not spacious enough to accommodate all the parking, or if you live in an apartment building with limited parking for guests, give your guests prior notice as to where it is best to park. They may be able to get to-gether in car-pools to cut down on parking space.

Powder room and lavatory facilities

- Have plenty of fancy paper guest towels and waste baskets in which to dispose of them.

- Provide *unscented liquid soap* in attractive dispensers. Individual small soaps are nice but are messy and not practical for a large number of guests. Unscented soap will not compete with any fragrance the guest may be wearing. Soap dispensers are very sanitary and tidy. Guests appreciate this.
- Have a box of facial tissues in each lavatory. Also have extra bathroom tissue *in sight,* for replacements.
- *Check powder rooms and lavatories often to see that they are tidy,* some guests may be careless.

Host/ess' duties

- The host/ess should greet guests as they arrive, show them where to put their coats, show them to the bar and help them get their first drink, then try to see that they are eased into the party.
- Allow plenty of space around the bar to have room for mixing drinks. Have the bar at one end of the room, and the food at the other end of the room. This relieves the traffic flow and balances the group.
- If there is no hired bartender, ask a friend to tend the bar, but be sure that he is spelled off to enjoy the party. It is not wise at a large cocktail party to have guests help themselves, there is too much risk of overindulgence that creates problems.
- The host/ess should try to see that no one gets inebriated. Ask the bar tender to "soften" the drink of anyone overindulging. The hostess should ply the problem guest with plenty of food.
- The host or hostess (host/ess) mingles with the guests, not spending too long with each.
- The host/ess sees that food trays are replenished.
- The host/ess watches for any guest that may be standing alone or looking uncomfortable, rectify the situation by discreetly getting others to-gether.
- The more crowded the party, the better the rapport.

Guests duties

- Arrival times are more flexible at a cocktail party, but your hosts will appreciate you coming soon after the start. If everyone comes late, it's disappointing.

- Wait to be invited to have a drink from the bar. Order a standard drink, not some exotic concoction that takes a lot of time to mix.
- Circulate. Hosts and hostesses love a guest that moves around and mixes with people. You'll be asked back time and time again and called a "good mixer."
- Don't overindulge. You ruin your own image and make everyone else uncomfortable for your indiscretion.
- Don't loiter at the bar or buffet table, it creates congestion at these busy areas. Move away.
- If a woman's glass is empty, it is gracious for a man to ask if he can get her a refill. He doesn't leave her standing alone, he invites her to come along with him to the bar.
- Don't leave your used paper napkins or dishes just anywhere. Ask where they should be placed. Be tidy.
- *Do use the guest towels. Never use the family towels.*
- Don't commandeer the washroom facilities. There are many people waiting. *Leave it spotlessly clean.*
- Leave by the time stated. Some guests may have been invited to stay longer, don't wait till others leave.

Dinner dance (private)

Invitation
- Issued 3 weeks to a month previous to the event.
- It should be a written invitation. The hostess should reconfirm with the guest by phone prior to the event.
- The guest answers the invitation promptly and accepts or declines. A telephone reply is acceptable.
- The invitation should state the details of date, time, place, and give specific details of the event.

Arrangements
- Usually a rented hall or hotel ballrooom is reserved.
- Arrange for a *secure* coat room.

- Give the guests specific parking instructions.
- Catering, Bar, Flowers, Music: all must be booked. A reputable hotel will give excellent guidance for all these arrangements.
- Ask for tables to seat groups of eight. This makes smaller, more pleasant seating arrangements.
- *The host and hostess greet guests as they arrive and the entire event is treated as though the guests were in your own home. See that they are comfortable.*

Charity balls and public dances

- People make up parties and attend in groups.
- When you ask someone if they are interested in attending, it is important to *immediately indicate who is expected to pay*. If you intend to pay, open the conversation by saying, "We would like you to be our guests at the XYZ Charity Ball." If you want them to pay for themselves, say, "We are making up a party to attend the XYZ Charity Ball, the tickets are $100.00 a couple, would you and Dick be interested in contributing to this event?" *Note:*If ever you are invited to attend any event and *the asker is not clear as to who will be paying,* a discreet way to find out is to say, "What price are the tickets?" If the asker is intending to take you as their guest, they *would not tell the cost* and would reply they want you to be their guests; or would tell you the cost of the tickets and you can accept or decline. *Never ask the cost of the tickets, if you are a guest.*
- At the dance, people dance with others *in their own party only.* It isn't polite to dance with people from other groups, no matter how well you know them.
- Check what type of attire will be worn; full evening dress, or formal, informal, or costume theme.
- These dinner dances almost never include the cost of drinks. It is polite to buy your hosts a drink and to follow the trend of the table; if someone buys a round of drinks for everyone at

that table, then you should take your turn to do the same. It is quite usual for couples to buy their own drinks only. If a single woman is in the party, the men should see that she has a drink and she in turn should return the favor. This applies if there is a no-host bar. If the table has drink service there is no problem, a woman can ask the waiter to bring her drinks.

- *A man dances first with his spouse or partner*. If he is a guest, he dances next with his hostess. He then dances with the woman on his right, and next with the woman on his left. His main concern then is to see that his spouse or partner is looked after. It isn't necessary that he dance with each woman in the group, but it would be considerate to do so.
- The host should try to dance with each woman guest.
- A man should not leave a woman alone at the table.
- Its quite correct for a woman to ask a man to dance.
- If a man or woman refuses a request to dance, they shouldn't then dance that dance with someone else.

It's entertainment time!

Breakfast: between 8:00 A.M. and 9:00 A.M.
lasts about 1 hr.

Brunch: between 11:00 A.M. and 2:00 P.M.
lasts about 1 hr. to 1.5 hrs.

Lunch: between 12:00 P.M. and 2:45 P.M.
lasts about 1 hr. to 2.75 hrs.

Cocktails: between 5:00 P.M. and 7:00 P.M.
prior to a concert or dinner dance.
or between 5:00 P.M. and 8:00 P.M.
as a social party or Open-House.

To end the party close the bar.

Cocktail-Buffet: between 6:00 P.M. and 9:00 P.M.

It is quite usual for *certain* guests to have been invited to stay later after a cocktail party or cocktail-buffet party. *It is therefore important to leave by the stipulated time.* Don't think that just because some people haven't left that you too can linger, did you get an invitation to remain?

Dinner: begins 7:00 P.M. or 7:30 P.M. or 8:00 P.M.
(allow 1/2 to 3/4 hr. prior if cocktails served)
Dinner lasts for 3 to 4 hours depending on starting time and prevailing circumstances.

A party for children

A child's party is a real opportunity to teach children, from an early age, the social graces. Greeting the guests, entertaining them, accepting gifts, showing appreciation, being considerate, all these subjects can be broached in a fun, but influential, way.

Parties for little children under the age of four, usually include the children's mothers and it's a get-to-gether to celebrate a child's birthday. Plenty of cake and ice cream, and a few tranquilizer pills for the Moms, and you'll have staged a successful event.

For children from four and older

The Invitation

- *An opportunity for a child to learn kindness and consideration.* The child chooses which guests to invite. He or she will probably want some or all of his/her classmates. *Check to be sure that not only one or two classmates are left out.* If the number of guests is a problem, consider asking only girls or only boys, but never leave only one or two out. A lone child that is not included can be heart-broken by this cruel gesture. A party is a *big* event for a child, a topic of conversation for weeks before and after. If you've ever been that child that was not included, you'll know the excruciating pain of it. Find out from your child why s/he doesn't want that person. An invitation to this party may be an ideal opportunity to heal a broken friendship or to appeal to the sweeter side of the class bully. Do your best to teach your child tolerance and understanding of every type of personality and race.

  As a school teacher, I saw children discriminated against in this way. There is no adequate consolation to relieve this hurt that leaves its brand solidly burnt into an innocent child's soul forever. *Please teach your child this kindness.*

- Helping the child *make* the invitation can be a fun project that highlights the big event even longer. For example:

  (1) *Make paper hats,* one for each guest, write their name on the side. Slip a paper inside that says, "Here is your hat to wear to Mary Smith's birthday party on _____ at

_____ etc." Fold the hat, place it in an envelope, put the guest's name on it.

(2) *Send balloon invitations.* Inflate a balloon for each guest. With a felt pen write this message on the balloon: "Come to Mary's birthday party, date, time." Deflate the balloon and place it in an envelope for the child to deliver. On the envelope write: *Blow up this balloon for an important message.* Write the details of the party, time, date etc., on a slip of paper and enclose it with the balloon in the envelope so the recipient has a reminder.

- Each invitation should state: the *occasion,* (whose birthday), *date, place, starting time* and *ending time,* so the parents know when to pick up their child.
- The invitation should also state your phone number.

The party

- *Have the child greet each guest and take their coats.* Explain to the child-host the importance of making people feel welcome and comfortable.
- It's natural to be excited about the gift the guest brings. Teach your child to show that the guest's presence is more important than the present, not to grab the gift and neglect the giver. To say "thank you" and to put the gift aside, it isn't opened immediately.
- Explain to the child that she/he is the host and must behave that way. This doesn't spoil the fun, it makes the child feel important and grown-up to have the ability to entertain properly, seeing that everybody has a good time and is happy. Thoughtfulness has to be *learned by example and by habit,* it doesn't come naturally. Do unto others!
- Indoor games or participation sports outdoors are better than video parties. *Children don't learn the pleasure of socializing by lining up in front of a video screen. A party should have merriment and a chance to play to-gether.* Plan the party with your child, give it as much care as for an adult party. We give children so little consideration and then we wonder why *they* show so little in later life. *Create the wonderful memories we each cherish.*

- Make everything beautiful. Decorate the cake and table so everyone knows it's a very special occasion.
- You don't have to spend a lot of time or money on fancy food, kids are like anyone else, make them feel welcome and happy and the food will taste marvelous.

Gift opening

Save the gift opening until just before the lunch. Teach your child to *announce who the gift is from* (that is the giver's moment in the spotlight) and to show appreciation. A briefing is a good idea before the party, to *teach your child that the gift is given with the best of intentions,* he/she must try not to show any disappointment. Say thank you.

> If you have a polaroid camera, take a picture of the donor and the child-host as the gift is being opened. Give the picture to the guest. What a keepsake!

The guests

- The guest brings a gift. The gift should be wrapped and *chosen with care*. A gift should not be so costly that it outshines all others but should be something likely to really please. Never leave a price tag on a gift or tell the recipient the price of it.
- If guests are dropped off by a parent, the parent should see that a very young child is taken in and settled into the party, then leave immediately. Older children or teens can be dropped off and make their own entry. The fewer adults at a young people's party the better. Establish the time they'll be picked up and be there *promptly*.
- Young people should be briefed to use their best manners and to do what they can to make the occasion a happy one. (*A note of encouragement,* parents, you would be pleasantly astonished at how well your child behaves when out on their own. In the many I've entertained, an unruly child is a rare exception.)
- Before leaving, the guest should thank both the child-host and the child's parent.

The teenager's party

THE INVITATION

- Unfortunately this has become a very dangerous and frightening message. When word gets out about a teenage party, the hoods crash it and often ruin not only the event but the property too. *It is imperative that invitations to a teenager's party be kept strictly secret among the guests. Only guests that can be relied upon to keep to this rule should be invited. Keep the party small.*

The party

- It's a known fact that people react to environment and circumstances in a like manner, e.g. throw a party with junk food tossed to-gether in any fashion, hold the party in untidy quarters, wear slovenly clothes, and everyone will *act* that way: *carelessly*. If you want it to be a memorable and pleasant time, set the scene to encourage a more refined reaction.
- *Teenagers appreciate being treated with respect.* They may feel a little insecure, not yet having had a lot of experience in living. Give them a break, help them get that polish and confidence they need.
- *Help your teenager to stage an elegant buffet dinner.*
- Send written invitations to several friends, boys and girls.
- State on the invitation that it's a buffet dinner to celebrate XYZ's birthday. Dress: Informal (See Dress Code: Informal does *not* mean casual.)
- Use your best china, glassware, dishes, and silver. See that there are flowers and candles and special decor: dramatic colors for napkins and tablecloth.
- *Let your teenager do the planning.* This is great experience to gain for the teenage host and guests. Either the teenager can do the serving, etc., as adults do at their own dinner parties, or Mom can don a frilly white apron and be the maid.
- The guests wear their best party clothes and their best manners. Something this adult appeals to them.
- Gingerale, cooled in ice buckets or wine coolers, is a good stand-in for champagne. The stemmed elegant glasses make it taste very special. If young people aren't trusted with fine

glasses how ever will they learn to be comfortable with them?

- The buffet dinner should be in the *dining room*.
- There can be dancing to taped music after the buffet dinner, and this can be in the recreation room. Decorate the room and make it festive.
- It's easy to have a casual party with good food and dancing and this can be fun. It's also important to let teenagers have more structured social parties from time to time to gain the poise they'll need in the adult world they are fast approaching.
- Don't hesitate to let any teenage guest know that they can't use drugs or drink liquor in your home. It is not rude to insist on this rule, *it is the law*.
- Don't be present at the teenager's party. Adults can put a damper on it. Be near, but not *there!*

The teen formal dance and/or prom

Times haven't changed a lot. Boys still prefer to do the asking for a date. Of course, there's the old saying, "he chased her till she caught him," meaning there are subtle ways a girl can let a fellow know she'd like to be his date.

The dress

- If the dance is formal, as proms usually are, the fellow will wear formal evening dress, so the girl should wear either a floor length or cocktail length dress, not a knee length and *never* a mini.
- Hats are not worn with formal gowns except for weddings. Just because some clothing shops promote the wearing of hats (and even garters!) with a prom dress, *doesn't make it correct*. They are just trying to generate more sales. Any shop that does this is not acting in the customers' interests and should not be patronized.
- Gloves can be worn but must be the appropriate style for the dress. (See "Gloves.") If you do wear gloves, *remove them*

when you eat, and don't wear jewelry over top of the gloves, watches and bracelets go beneath.

- A small evening bag is necessary with formal wear. Don't use your regular handbag.
- Shoes should be strappy or lightweight pumps.
- *A shawl* is not expensive and it looks *much* better than a street length coat which looks tacky over a formal evening dress. Also, it won't crush your dress.
- All accessories should be simple and elegant. No big plastic earrings overshadowing a beautiful gown.
- Shiny, clean, well cut and styled hair is a major part of your polished image. No tousled, untidy hairstyles.
- Most important of all, the one "accessory" that will outshine all others and make you the Belle of the Ball is a dazzling *smile!*

Expenses
- *The girl* has her formal dress, shoes, and accessories to buy. If it's *her* prom she buys the tickets for herself and her date. The dinner may be an extra charge and, correctly, she should pay for this too if she has invited her date. The girl actually should pay costs for transportation, etc. The old double standard is fast disappearing. Now, *whether it's a female or a male, the one who invites is the one who pays.* Put the shoe on the other foot, girls, if a fellow asked you out on a date would *you* expect to pay the costs? Welcome to the 1990's!
- The exception to this rule is when a girl and boy have been dating regularly and she would be expected to invite him as her partner; then she buys the necessary tickets, etc., and her date might offer to pay the transportation. *The most important thing is that they both should know who is paying for what.* It is embarrassing to be caught off guard with no credit card and limited funds.
- It's a nice gesture for a girl to give her date a boutonniere, particularly if he is her "steady."
- *The boy* pays to rent a dinner suit (tuxedo). He should take a corsage for his date. (Find out what color dress she'll be wearing so the flowers will enhance it.)

- If it's *his* grad dance, he pays for all the tickets and transportation.
- These are the *basic* rules of propriety. Couples are realistic these days, there are so many variables, some have part-time jobs, some have costly student expenses. With tact and consideration for everyone concerned, the sharing of expenses can be arranged.
- Even if the girl has done the inviting and is paying *she does not pick up her date alone. (See **below)*. He goes to her home to get her and he also sees her to her door after the event. Social rules have not changed in regard to male/female courtesy. Men still, and I hope always will, want to protect and escort their ladies. Monetary rules needed to be changed now that women are wage earners, but most women appreciate courtesy from a male, no matter what his age.
- The boy or young man should speak with the girl's parents and let them know as much as possible about the evening's plans. He has their most valuable possession in his care.
- If a limousine is hired by a group of young people, one of the group should look after the financing of it, get receipts, confirm times, confirm addresses.
- No girl should be picked up before her partner. The ideal is for the fellow to have someone drive him to his date's home and have the limousine pick them both up there. The purpose of the limousine is so no one in the party has to drive.
- When the party is over, the limousine drives the fellows to their homes *after* all the girls have been taken to their homes.
- ***If no limousine service has been hired,* and the girl has invited the boy, one of the girl's parents (preferably her father) should drive her over to pick up her date for the dance. He should not pretend to be a chauffeur. The father should also accompany his daughter to her date's door. This let's the boy's parents know their son is with respectable people who care about one another. The young folks get in the back seat and the father or driver doesn't make conversation, he is as "invisible" as possible, this is *their* evening. When the young couple are picked up after the dance, they again get in the back seat, the father (or driver) takes the boy home and the

girl then gets in the front seat with her dad. She doesn't see the boy to his door, but a tactful father gives them some time to say goodnight.

The teen dance

- The dress for both boy and girl should be their Sunday best, not casual sweaters and separates.
- Don't be coerced into wearing off-beat, tacky attire, show your refined individuality. Why stoop to the lowest *common* denominator when you can show your maturity and sense of style?
- Treat your date like he or she is very special. If it isn't the date you had hoped to have, remember that your date was kind enough to accompany you, and others will admire your consideration and courtesy.
- For picking up your date see ** above. Follow the same procedure as the ** above. The father, mother, or some adult family member does the driving for young people who do not drive.

Baby showers

- A Baby Shower should *not* be given by close relatives of the new mother's family (mother, aunt, sister, mother-in-law, sisters-in-law, etc.), unless *only* the relatives are invited. Otherwise it is too obvious a request for gifts for a member of the family.
- Showers should be given by friends and co-workers.
- A Baby Shower is usually given for the *first* baby only (or for the first adopted child). Family members may decide to get together for each new addition and bring gifts, but friends are not *expected* to do so.
- A Baby Shower can be held prior to the baby's birth, but it is getting more general to hold the shower a few weeks after the baby is born. This gives the guests a chance to see the new baby and to buy appropriate gifts. The mother can better enjoy the party, too.

- A Baby Shower can be held at any time of the day that is most appropriate for the guests: a noon luncheon, an afternoon tea, an evening get-to-gether. The proud father might appreciate being included in a mixed couples shower for the new baby *or adopted child*.
- Make it a combination Baby Shower and a "girls night to relax." Have the fellows each make a dish for a pot luck feast and bring it to the party. While the women open the gifts and enjoy a visit, the fellows can get the food ready and then serve it.
- If a newborn is not well and there is concern for its health, *delay the shower until later*. It is too painful for a worried parent to have to endure a baby shower. Do let the parents know how anxious you are for the baby and that you'll all be getting to-gether very soon when the baby is well and you can all meet him or her. Take a collection and send the mother a bouquet of flowers to her home to brighten her day, she needs a lift.
- In the tragedy of a newborn's death, after a shower has been held, *the gifts need not be returned*, people understand the sadness of the event. Large gifts such as baby carriages, high chairs, and trust accounts, should be returned to the donor. In the event of the child's death, gifts for the baby are *never returned by the parents for a refund from the store, if they are returned they must be returned to the donor*.
- The birth of a baby is a happy event. In my opinion, you can hold as many showers as you like, *celebrate!*

The bridal shower

- *A Bridal Shower can be given about three weeks before the wedding*. After that, wedding plans take up most of the bride-elect's time.
- *A Bridal Shower is never given by any member of the immediate family: sisters, mother, mother-in-law elect, grandmothers*.

- Friends, co-workers, aunts, cousins, or god-mother, may host a bridal shower.
- *Anyone planning to host a bridal shower should get a list of the wedding guests being invited, because everyone that is asked to a shower should also be asked to the wedding and wedding reception.* The only exception to this is if it is a very small wedding with only the immediate family and close friends of the family attending.
- There can be different types of bridal showers such as kitchen-ware showers, bridal lingerie showers, linen showers, or general showers. The same people should not be asked to more than one shower, however, the bride's mother, mother-in-law elect, grandmothers, sisters, and bridesmaids *are* invited to each shower.
- Anyone accepting an invitation to a bridal shower must bring a gift.
- A wedding gift is given in addition to a shower gift.
- A "Bride and Groom" shower, with both men and women invited, is growing in popularity. This could be a *wine* shower with each guest bringing a bottle of wine to start the couple on a wine collection. Items such as wine goblets, corkscrew, wine cooler, etc., make good gifts for this kind of shower. The wines given should be of good quality and respectable label.
- Showers for brides that have been married before, or that have been living with their groom-to-be, are different only in the kinds of gifts that will be given. The bride will already have many household items. A close check will be necessary to see what is needed. That is what a bridal shower is for; to help the newlyweds get established in their home. Advise the shower guests accordingly.
- Bridal Shower gifts are not lavish. More expensive gifts are given as wedding presents. Shower gifts should be small but very *useful* presents.
- Most showers are designed to be a surprise to the bride, but I'm sure most brides aren't surprised. They'd be much *more* surprised if they didn't get one!

Dress codes

Dress for the most formal event

The most formal of all events is referred to as "White Tie." It is never worn before 6:00 P.M. unless for a wedding and is somewhat different then. (See Dress Code: Wedding)

Men's most-formal apparel: (Invitation reads: "White Tie")
"White Tie": (Tails)
- *A black tailcoat,* the tails of which reach just to the back of the knees, no longer, no shorter.
- *Matching black pants* with grosgrain or satin ribbon down the outside leg seams. No cuffs.
- *A white starched-front shirt* with a wing collar. (Wing collar shirts are *only* worn with "white tie" apparel.) Studs are used for buttons. French cuffs with very plain gold cufflinks. (Slim gold watch.)
- *A white pique waistcoat.*
- *A white bowtie.*
- *Black patent leather pumps* with grosgrain ribbon bows or plain black evening pumps or oxfords.
- *Thin, black silk socks, not sheer.*
- Optional: white kid gloves, white scarf, silk top hat. (Check to see if these are called for.)

Women's most formal apparel: (Invitation reads: "White Tie")
- "White Tie" events call for long, *floor-length, evening gowns* for women, preferably with full skirts.
- *Long white gloves,* 16 button or over the elbow. Never place bracelets or a wristwatch on top of your gloves, they should be worn under the gloves. They'll be seen and will adorn your arms when you remove your gloves to eat. *Never eat with your gloves on.*
- This is the most formal and elegant of occasions and calls for the utmost in decorum.
- A "White Tie" event is an opportunity to wear your dazzling *real jewels* but don't overdo it. Refinement is never garish.
- *Elegant hairstyles,* not casual wash-and-wear frizz.

- *Evening shoes* of a color appropriate for the gown.
- *Small evening bag*, satin, beaded, or kid leather.
- *Never a hat* of any kind.
- *A floor length evening coat, a shawl, or a jacket of fur or evening fabric in a short or 3/4 length.* Never a street or knee length coat over a floor length gown. No, not even if it's Russian sable!

Dress for the formal event

The formal event is referred to as "Black Tie." This is as formal as most of us will ever encounter. The invitation will read "Black Tie" or "Formal."

MEN'S FORMAL APPAREL

- *A black dinner suit* (tuxedo), no cuffs, single or double breasted. The collar of the suit coat can be of satin in a notched or shawl style. Midnight blue is also very proper and elegant, but other colors are not for those who want a polished image, except in summer when a white dinner jacket with black pants is also correct. Any kind of sequins or flashy trim on a dinner suit are considered to be crass. Superb quality in the fabric of the suit is everything.
- A vest *or* a cummerbund is worn with a single breasted dinner suit, ideally of the fabric and the color of the suit. When you get too creative with colored cummerbunds and vests, you start to look like a magic show performer. Restrain yourself!
- A white, pleated-front, shirt. No ruffles, please.
- A satin or silk bowtie, preferably black.
- Plain black slip-on shoes. Black silk socks.
- Jewelry should be plain. A big, bulky, wristwatch is never very attractive, save it for scuba diving.
- *Unless "Black Tie" is specifically stipulated, it is perfectly fine to wear a plain, dark, dress suit to a formal event.* A white dress shirt (not a button down collar) with plain or French cuffs is correct. Shoes and socks in black only.

WOMEN'S FORMAL APPAREL

- To be strictly correct, *only* floor length dresses are worn if the invitation stipulates black tie. Otherwise, for formal events the dress can be floor-length, cocktail-length, or knee-length, but never mini-length, we're talking *polish*, remember? Fancy evening trousers are fine for formal or black tie events.

- The *fabric* of a woman's outfit is what makes it appropriate for a formal event. Chiffons, silks, and other opulent fabrics that belong only for special occasions are perfect.
- Gloves are optional. (See "Gloves")
- For shoes, evening bag, jewelry, and hats, see the information on White Tie events, the same rules apply for these items for a Formal or Black Tie event.

Dress for the cocktail party

Dress for a cocktail party is influenced by what type of function the cocktail party precedes. For a cocktail party that is held prior to going on to a dinner dance, dress might be formal or at least more elaborate than would be required for a cocktail party held prior to attending a theatre performance. Dress for a cocktail party, then, is suited to the evening's main event and to the season.

M E N : *(Cocktail party)*
- A dark dress suit preferably navy blue. You'll *never* be wrong with a navy blue blazer and grey slacks.
- A white dress shirt.
- Black shoes and socks.
- In summer a white dinner jacket is fine, but it is worn with plain black pants *not* pants that have a ribbon trim on the outside leg seam unless dress for the party is formal.
- Some cocktail parties are more on the casual side and a considerate host/ess will guide his/her guests with quite *specific* advice as to what dress is expected. *The hostess should never be vague about the dress.*

W O M E N : *(Cocktail Party)*
- The *cocktail suit* is exceptionally attractive. It can be black or any other color, but the fabric (silk, velvet, satin) or the trim (fancy glitter buttons) should set it apart as something more dressy than would ever be worn to business.
- Short dresses of silks, satins, or special occasion fabrics look terrific. Low cut, summery fabrics of very fine cottons and

linens are suitable for summer cocktail parties.

- Strappy sandals and plain pumps, appropriate for the color and fabric of the dress.
- A small clutch purse or evening bag. Beaded bags or metallic mesh bags are fine if the event is prior to a very dressy occasion and the outfit warrants this finery, otherwise a small plain evening bag is best.
- If a street length coat will *completely cover* the dress being worn, it would be acceptable to wear it. If the dress is long or cocktail length, wear a shawl or evening jacket, a street length coat looks *awful* over evening wear that shows beneath it.
- Jewelry for a cocktail party is suited to the type of apparel worn which is apropos the event. A couple of good pieces of jewelry are enough.

Dress for weddings

Most Formal daytime or evening wedding

The Most Formal Dress, a "White Tie" wedding, *for a bride* and *bridesmaids* is the same for morning, afternoon, or evening. The *time* of day doesn't change the type of Most Formal Dress. However, it *does* change for the groom and the men attending the wedding. Men wear "Morning Dress" for a daytime wedding.

B R I D E : *Most Formal dress*

- A bridal gown with long sleeves, white or ivory in color, and *never* with a low cut, bosom revealing neckline, this is very bad taste for any wedding.
- A long train of lace or net. The length of the train is measured from where it touches the floor to the end of the veil. A sweep, six inch in length is the shortest; chapel length is about two feet; cathedral length, the longest, is over two feet and often very much longer, worn *only* for a cathedral wedding.
- Usually there is a separate face-veil that is turned back during the ceremony and can be completely removed for the wedding reception.
- Jewelry is limited to a necklace and small earrings.
- Very light-colored hosiery. White shoes of fabric or fine leather, preferably closed-toe pumps.

B R I D E S M A I D S :
Daytime or Evening Most Formal:
- Floor length gowns. Colors and styles are the choice of the bride, but no plunging, revealing necklines.
- Long, over the elbow, white gloves unless the dresses have long sleeves, then short gloves are worn.
- For the most formal wedding, the bridesmaids wear short veils or headpieces.
- Shoes of fabric, which may be dyed to match the gown, or fine leather pumps. Light-colored hosiery.

B R I D E G R O O M *and all men*
Daytime Most Formal:
- Daytime Most Formal Dress for the bridegroom is called "Morning Dress" and consists of: Dark gray or black morning coat, gray striped trousers, stiff white dress shirt, gray waistcoat, and gray ascot or striped tie. Plain black shoes and lightweight silk (not sheer) socks.

Evening Most Formal:
- See "Men's Most Formal Apparel" (White Tie). The bridegroom dresses in this way for a wedding that is held after 6:00 P.M.

M O T H E R S *of the bride and groom*
Most Formal Daytime Wedding
- Long gowns or street-length dresses of opulent fabric in pale shades, never white. The mothers of the bridal couple should be sure to wear the same length dress, not one wear a floor-length and the other a street-length.
- Hats and gloves.

Most Formal Evening Wedding
- Floor length gowns only, never white.
- Gloves but *no* hats. Hats are not worn to *any* event after five p.m.
- See "Women's Most Formal Apparel."

FEMALE GUESTS

Most Formal Daytime Wedding

- Knee-length dresses of silk, chiffon, any "special occasion" fabrics. Cocktail suits. Never white.
- Hats and gloves.
- Small clutch bag or evening bag.

Most Formal Evening Wedding

- Floor-length evening gown. Never white in color.
- See "Women's Most Formal Apparel."

Formal daytime or evening wedding

B R I D E : *formal daytime or evening dress*

- Wedding gowns are less elaborate than for "White Tie" (Most Formal Weddings) where the gown is long-sleeved and the train can be very long. For a formal, Black Tie, wedding the gown should be floor-length or cocktail-length and can have long or short sleeves. If the dress is sleeveless or is a strapped gown, a small matching jacket must be worn over it for the wedding ceremony. It isn't in good taste to wear a wedding dress with too much exposure. The jacket may be removed for the wedding reception.
- It's fine to have a train on the dress, but it should be no longer than chapel length (2 feet).
- The veil is a shorter length that is appropriate for the gown. An elegant wedding hat may be worn in place of a veil or head-dress for a daytime wedding.
- Gloves are optional but do give a finished look.
- Other items are the same as those stated for a "Most Formal Wedding."

T H E   B R I D E S M A I D S : *(formal wedding)*

- Floor-length or cocktail length dresses in colors and styles chosen by the bride.
- It isn't necessary that gowns all be the same styles (except for length) or the same colors.
- The headdresses should all be the same style: all wear veils, or all wear flowers in their hair, or all wear hats (only at a daytime wedding).

B R I D E G R O O M *and all men: (formal wedding)*
Daytime Formal
- Daytime Formal Dress for a man is a black or charcoal gray sack coat, sometimes called a club or stroller coat which is a long jacket, that is worn with striped trousers, a turned-down-collar dress shirt with French cuffs, a four-in-hand striped tie or gray tie. Black shoes and black, lightweight silk, socks. A navy blue blazer and gray slacks are appropriate for a man to wear for day, evening, formal, or informal events. This is, therefore, an infallible investment.

Evening Formal
- A black dinner jacket with matching trousers.
- See "Black Tie" or "Formal Evening Dress for Men."

M O T H E R S *of the bride and groom*
Formal Daytime Wedding
- Street-length dresses of satins, silks, and dressy fabrics or cocktail suits in light colors. Never white. Corsages are worn.
- Hats and gloves.

Formal Evening Wedding
- Floor-length or cocktail length evening gowns in light colors but never white.
- See "Women's Formal Evening Wear."

F E M A L E   G U E S T S
Formal Daytime Wedding
- Street-length dresses of silk, satin, chiffon, any "special occasion" fabrics. Cocktail or theater suits. Never all white.
- Hats and gloves. Corsages *not* worn by guests.
- Small clutch bag or evening bag.

Formal Evening Wedding
- Floor-length or cocktail-length evening gown. Never white in color. Corsages are not worn.
- See "Women's Formal Apparel."

Semi-formal daytime or evening wear
What is semi-formal? It baffles me as to how anything can be "semi" formal. In studying over 26 books on the subject of weddings, however, I've discovered that there is a *"semi-formal"* category that

emerges. In fact, that is the most popular type of wedding being staged to-day. A semi-formal wedding is when the bride and groom and their attendants wear formal clothing (long gowns and tuxedos) and everyone else dresses informally. (A category that should be called "Potpourri," wherein *some* of the wedding *attendants* wear formal attire and some wear who-knows-what, seems also to exist, but that's too outrageous to even consider!)

Let's leave it at this: For the *semi-formal wedding*, the bride and groom and their attendants follow the rules for *formal dress*. All others follow *informal* dress rules.

- Keep in mind that a dinner suit (tuxedo) is *not* worn before 6:00 p.m.. A groom and his attendant wear dark suits for a daytime semi-formal wedding.
- If the groom wears a tuxedo for an evening wedding, so does his best man or groomsman. The ushers may wear tuxedos or dark suits.
- The bride's attendant, or attendants, should dress in floor-length gowns if the bride's dress is long.

Informal daytime or evening wedding
B R I D E *and her attendant*

- Street-length dresses of dressy fabric or cocktail suits. The bride's should be more outstanding.
- A hat or some kind of headdress, perhaps made of flowers.
- Gloves, optional.
- A corsage or a nosegay of flowers.
- Though the wedding is informal, the bride and her attendant (*one only*) should wear something extra elegant and beautiful. As in other dressing, the *fabric* is what makes the dress or suit very special. Very dark or very bright colors are not appropriate for a happy but serious event as is a wedding.

T H E   G R O O M, HIS ATTENDANT, AND MALE GUESTS:

- Dark blue or dark gray suits for the groom and his best man. *White* shirts, colorful ties, black shoes and black sox.
- Dark suits and *white* shirts for male guests attending an evening wedding. Pastel colored shirts are fine for a daytime wedding.

M O T H E R S *of the bridal couple, and female guests:*
- *Informal does not mean casual.*
- All women attending an informal wedding should wear their "Sunday best." To wear a casual skirt and blouse or *anything* casual to a wedding, shouts a message loud and clear that you have low regard for the bridal couple. Though the insult may hurt them, it cast's no reflection on the bridal couple, but it does make that guest look inconsiderate.
- Even those in mourning should wear something pastel and pretty, this is a joyous occasion and everything possible should be done by guests and family to make it as pleasant as possible.

Civil marriage ceremony

Dress for a marriage that is performed in a municipal hall or judge's chambers is the same as for an informal wedding. Only the bride and groom, their parents, and the bridal attendants usually attend the actual ceremony. If guests get to-gether for a reception or party afterwards, the guests dress as for an informal wedding. Never casual, please.

Other Dress Codes:
What to wear to a private club

L U N C H
Women: A daytime dress or suit or business clothes.
Men: Business apparel. Always a tie (just in case!). Some clubs do not permit members and guests to wear playing clothes, such as tennis wear, for lunch in the club dining room. Be sure to check.

D I N N E R
Cocktail attire for men and for women.
Men always wear a necktie. Some private clubs do not consider that an ascot is a regulation necktie.

T E N N I S   C O U R T S
Some private clubs require *white* clothing for wear on their tennis courts. Always determine the rules and regulations of a private club, so that as a member or a guest you make no embarrassing errors in judgement.

WIMBLEDON

Should you be so fortunate as to attend the World Championship Tennis Matches that are held in Wimbledon at the All England Club for two weeks each summer, the proper attire is important. In the royal box, admission to which is only by invitation from the chairman and the committee, men wear jackets and ties and women wear smart dresses or elegant suits. Hats are optional. People attending in the Member's Enclosure, which is reserved for Club members and their guests, dress in the same way as those attending in the royal box. Elsewhere, spectators dress for comfort but tailored, attractive, casual clothing is suggested. No big-brim sun hats that block people's view, please.

Note: In addition to proper dress, proper behavior is also important: Spectators only move from their stands when the players are changing ends and *they should applaud only at the end of a game, a set, or a match*. To applaud in the middle of a rally distracts the players and is not considered good manners. It is also impolite to eat or to drink in the stands.

What to wear to cultural events
THE OPERA

Dress for the opera has become less structured recently. Opening nights and gala performances still often call for formal attire. It is only good manners to attend any public function neatly and *cleanly* dressed. Sitting at close quarters with people demands attention to good grooming.

Consider, too, the etiquette of fragrance. Though your perfume may cost $500 a dram, it might not appeal to those around you who must sit for hours with an objectionable scent delivering knockout left hooks to their olfactory nerves.

THE SYMPHONY

The same as the opera. A matinee performance calls for more informal clothes than does an evening performance but always *clean, and well groomed*.

Whatever the cultural event, people should not be intimidated as to their clothing. The important thing is to be there for the enjoyment and for the appreciation of this professional ability. Children should be exposed to the arts as part of their education and development of this appreciation, never let them think they don't belong because of a lack of fine apparel. Only *one* criterion is expected: *cleanliness*.

What to wear to a public dining room

Restaurants and hotel dining rooms have different rules and regulations regarding proper dress, ranging from casual to very formal. When people go out for an evening of luxury in dining and relaxation, part of the enjoyment is the elegance of the entire affair. If other diners are treating it like the corner fast-food "joint," it takes away from the special occasion atmosphere. It is wise to check with the restaurant when you make your reservation.

- Jeans are not usually acceptable (no, not even when you flaunt the designer label!) for men or for women.
- Most prestigious restaurants and dining rooms insist on men wearing jackets and ties. A turtleneck sweater may be acceptable in place of a tie, but it is safer to inquire than to be turned away.
- A man should check his topcoat, but if a woman is wearing a coat she may check it or may keep it with her. Most women prefer to keep it and drape it over the back of their chair.
- In a restaurant where even the most casual dress is acceptable, men in tank tops should at least cover them with a shirt. Showing hairy armpits, naked torsos, or bare feet in an eating place is boorish.

What to wear on a boat or yacht

- Rubber-soled shoes with a good grip are a must. The soles should be of white or red but not black composition, so they don't leave marks on the deck.
- If it's an extended trip, be sure to take your own foul-weather gear.
- If it is a large yacht, something a little more dressy for dinner wear may be called for, or perhaps there'll be some port calls that require these. Wider skirts are best for climbing aboard. Remember, no stiletto heels that will mar the deck or yacht club floors.
- Teach children to be careful with their footwear, too.

What to wear on a cruise ship

- *Passengers in first-class dress for dinner every night except the first night and last night.* On the first night they have just boarded and are in travel clothes and haven't unpacked. On the last night they have packed and are again wearing travel clothes. Dressing for dinner on a luxury liner usually means "Black Tie" which is formal dress.
- It is always in good taste to appear in dinner dress. For the Captain's Dinner, the formality of dinner jackets and evening gowns is expected.
- In tourist and cabin class there is not the formality that there is for first class travellers. Certainly a suit, white shirt, and tie for a man and a dinner dress for a woman are proper attire for dinner in every class of travel.
- If you know that the ship on which you travel holds a costume affair, it's fun to take a costume along. The ship probably has costumes available to rent. It isn't compulsory to wear a costume, however.
- If you're invited to dine at the Captain's table it is considered an honor, one which you do not refuse without a very good reason. Conduct yourself as you would at a private dinner party: wait for your host, "Captain Jones," to arrive before you begin to eat. Captains often are late for dinner.
- Clothing on board ship is casual during the daytime. Styles on the conservative side are best. Sports wear and swim suits should be confined to the sports and swimming areas. Swimsuits are *never* worn into the dining rooms. Sportswear can be worn into the dining rooms for breakfast and lunch but not at dinner time.
- Be sure to pack walking shoes for ports of call.

General rules for dress

- The old rule of no white shoes to be worn before the end of May or after the first of September, still does apply. It's a matter of white shoes looking inappropriate for other seasons.
- Always respect the occasion. To wear jeans and a t-shirt to a social event, no matter how casual, is not good manners. The clothes you wear to do work in the garden surely aren't appro-

priate to wear for a party. Casual clothes can be smart and attractive, they shouldn't be your grubbies.

- Women and girls shouldn't wear slacks to church.
- For men, short sleeved dress shirts look tacky. Rolled back sleeves look better and also with short sleeved shirts a man's suit jacket sleeves look too short because there is no shirt cuff to show and fill in the space.
- Men should not wear white socks with anything but athletic shoes. The exception is when an all white outfit is worn, white pants, white shoes, etc., and then they should be finely knit, dress socks.
- People with polish don't wear t-shirts imprinted with sayings. Polo shirts looks better than t-shirts.
- Men should never wear the jacket of a business or dress suit with a pair of casual slacks. Awful!

CHAPTER SIX

Putting on the Polish
IN YOUR HOME

CHAPTER SIX

Putting on the Polish
IN YOUR HOME

You don't have to be rich to put on the polish. The most humble of homes have often been the most inviting and pleasant to visit. As I've stated through-out this book, nothing is more important than cleanliness. To aim for the enjoyment of having material comforts is a worthy cause, but *a person who cares first and foremost about cleanliness will always be regarded as a person of value and good class.*

The finest of furniture, the finest of appliances, the most fashionable decor, will never substitute for *cleanliness!* It is surprising how much attention people will give to buying and surrounding themselves with the fanciest of trappings and give little thought to how *clean* their home looks or smells.

Appealing to the olfactory nerve

- If you have cats or dogs, you get accustomed to their odors and don't realize how objectionably strong the air in your home can become. Even the occupants' clothing takes on these odors. It's important to keep animals very clean or accommodate them in *comfortable* outdoor facilities. We love them so much and nothing deserves our love more, so for their sakes, too, keep those precious friends very clean.
- *Invest in plenty of inexpensive baking soda.* Baking soda eliminates odors from just about everything.
- Sprinkle baking soda over carpets, leave it for twenty minutes before vacuuming it up. It will freshen the carpet quite noticeably.
- All traces of fish, onion, or other odors can be removed from

hands, dishes, sink disposal unit, and appliances by washing them with baking soda.

- If you can't immediately clean spills on stove top or oven and you need to eliminate the odor before guests arrive, sprinkle the spills with salt, it deodorizes.
- Boil a saucepan of water with some cinnamon, ginger, and nutmeg (a bit of orange peel is great, too). It makes the air smell delightful.
- Perfumed air fresheners that just mask odors really don't solve the problem, they makes it worse. Lysol™ spray actually kills the bacteria that creates the odor and is more effective and sanitary.
- Putting the plugs in bathtubs and sinks helps to eliminate any sewer odors.

Polished investment

Just as clothing gives an immediate message about a person, so do home furnishings and decor tell a great deal about the quality of the occupants of a home. Be it a one room studio suite or a many roomed mansion, every pillow, picture, cup, or chair, reflect the lifestyle, taste, and quality of the occupant.

Always buy the best quality you can afford
- The best advice young people just setting up their homes can follow is to buy *quality*. It's far more astute to add a few pieces of furniture at a time and know that each piece will last you a lifetime. Not only *last* a lifetime, but will reflect the quality of you, its owner. Inexpensive furniture will have to be replaced many times over and you'll never have the comfort and beautiful appearance of good furniture, and, in the end, will have paid the same price.
- The absolutely unbelievable bargains in top quality furniture that can be found at auction sales make it economically available even for young newlyweds who have so many expenses and need so many things.

Buy classic designs

- Home furnishings, like wearing apparel, do not go out of fashion if you *buy classic designs*. Simple lines in contemporary or provincial styling, or timeless antiques will never be out of fashion.
- *Buy hardwoods, not soft pine, or veneer-covered particle board as is so prevalent in to-day's market.*
- It's fine to start with "assemble yourself" unpainted furniture to tide you over the beginning years. Some of this is so well made and attractive it makes a home look cheery and inviting. But, as you add the pieces you want to have forever, buy them carefully and buy the best quality you can afford.

Buy basics in subdued plain colors not patterns.

- The same as you do with wearing apparel, have the bright dashes of color in accessories. Pillows and ornaments are easily and inexpensively changed when you want to change your decor, but expensive basics like sofas and carpets are not.

The carpet should be chosen first.

- Carpeting is an expensive investment and must last many years.
- Consider a *color* that will stand up to wear and be versatile in future decor color combinations.
- *Carpets may be, knitted, woven, or tufted.* One process is not necessarily superior to another. Some of the main types of weaves are velvets, Wilton, and Axminster. *These are types of looms, not brand names* and are available in different qualities.
- A *wool* carpet is the most luxurious, but it cannot be treated with the stain releasing processes that have become so important (e.g. Stainmaster). Hand knotted Indian broadlooms of wool have become very expensive. Be sure to see that any wool carpet is mothproofed.
- *The acrylics, and monacrylics, are very similar to wool in softness and warmth.* They are resilient and wear extremely well. They take dyes very well, resulting in uniform, rich, coloring. They are mothproof and mildew proof. These are among the

most popular fibers for carpeting.

- *Nylon* is the best wearing, color retaining, and stain releasing. The fiber is in two forms: *staple nylon*, used in cut-pile textures, and *continuous-filament* which eliminates the tendency to pilling.
- *Polyester* and *polypropylene* are popular fibers with most of the same qualities as the other synthetics.
- There are also *blends of wool with synthetic fibers*. A leading carpet dealer told me that, in his opinion, this is not a good combination. The synthetic cuts the wool, and, because there is wool in the blend, the carpet cannot be treated with a soil release process.
- *Blends of man-made fibers can result in superb carpet because the desirable traits of each are combined*. The wearability of one synthetic combined with the resiliency of another can create a quality *superior* to that of the individual fibers used alone.
- *Determine a carpet's quality by the rule:* "the deeper, the denser, the better." The "face yarns," or the surface pile, take the impact of wear. *Dense pile wears the longest* because the tufts are packed closely to-gether, supporting one another, resisting bending and abrasion. *To test for density*, take a piece of the carpet between your hands and bend it back, you should not be able to see the backing of the carpet if the pile is dense enough. The more backing that can be seen, the lower the grade of the carpet. The more dense the tufting, the better the quality and the durability of the carpet.
- *Consider where the carpet will be used*. A spare bedroom that will get little traffic will require less "quality" than will a high traffic family room. *Wall-to-wall carpeting in the same color through-out a home looks marvelous and adds to the optical illusion of a far greater expanse*. It chops up the overall appearance of the floor plan if different color carpet is used in each room. *Some carpet manufacturers now produce various price grades of carpet in the same color and texture but in various densities for different rooms*. This cuts down on the cost but makes it possible to have wall-to-wall carpet in one matching color through-out.

- *Select carpeting from the middle price range upward.* It is wiser to buy a good quality room-size rug, which can be turned to equalize the wear, than to buy an inferior wall-to-wall carpeting.
- *Underlay, padding, or cushioning is very important.* It prolongs the life of the carpet and makes it much more luxurious to walk upon. This padding is felt, or rubber (foam or sponge, sponge wears better and is more resilient), or felt with rubber coating. The combination of felt and rubber is the sturdiest.
- *All qualities of new carpet will shed for awhile.* Vacuum it every day until the shedding stops.
- *High heels are a carpet's most destructive enemy.* If heels have pulled or snagged the carpet, cut off the snag just even with the carpet tufts.
- *The odor of dog and, particularly, cat urine cannot be removed.* It will be necessary to replace that part of the carpet. *You* might get accustomed to this odor but your visitors will be repulsed by it.
- *A carpet is the background of all your decor.* The finest quality furniture set upon an inferior grade of carpeting only accentuates the difference. The color of a carpet can unify the other components of the decor and is the most vital contributing factor.

Pictures

Pictures should be hung at eye level. In a living room, people are usually in a seated position, so pictures should be hung somewhat lower. Keep in mind, however, that the bottom of the picture should be ten to twelve inches above the back of a chair or chesterfield, so that it doesn't get knocked if a person leans back.

- *Small pictures should not be hung alone on a large wall.* Small pictures look better in groups.
- *When placing a number of pictures on a wall, keep the distance between the pictures half the width of the frame.* The frames of the pictures should form an imaginary line of a square or a rectangle to give the appearance of a planned, coherent group, not just a bunch of pictures on a wall. (Fig. #32)

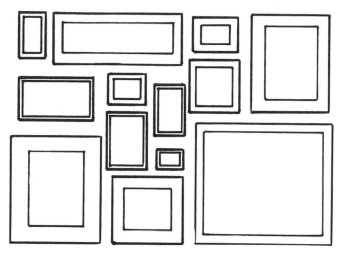

Fig. #32
Effective Wall Grouping of Pictures

The frames of the pictures on the *outside* of the grouping should create imaginary straight lines to give a look of a "framed" unit to the arrangement. Small pictures placed within this unified grouping gain more significance than if they were hung alone. At least two sides of the grouping should make a straight imaginary line, for example: the top and bottom lines, or the side lines.

- *When planning a wall arrangement of pictures, work out the entire arrangement before driving a nail,* or you'll have a pock-marked wall! Here's how:

  (1) Take sheets of paper and make exact patterns of each picture's outside dimension including the frame.

  (2) Place the pictures on the floor to arrange them. Move them around until you reach the look you want. You could arrange the paper patterns on the wall but the structure of the frames can change the balance of the arrangement, and by placing the actual pictures on the floor you'll get a realistic view.

  (3)Now measure the outside "frame" of this entire grouping and make small marks on the wall to *center* this arrangement where you want it placed.

  (4) Then, beginning with the lowest row of pictures, fasten the paper patterns to the wall in exactly that arrangement with a

bit of tape. Begin with the *lowest* row to ensure that you will have enough space.

(5) With a stiff metal tape measure, find the exact distance between the highest point of the hanging wire on the back of each picture when it is pulled taut, as it will be when the picture is on the wall, and the top edge of the picture frame. Make allowance for this distance between the wire and the edge of the frame when placing the picture hook on the wall. Be sure you keep to the rules of effective grouping by keeping at least two and preferably four of the sides in a straight line. Use a carpenter's level.

- If you're placing the pictures over a sofa, an item such as a lamp can balance the arrangement *(Fig#35)*.
- A picture grouping of any size looks far better with a piece or pieces of furniture placed beneath it to give it an "anchor." The anchor has to be of the same width as the grouping or you'll lose the effect *(Fig.#35)*.

FIG. #35

- *Don't have more than one large grouping of pictures.* Some vacant spots on the walls will relieve the eye and accent the grouping.
- *A wide variety of mediums, styles, and sizes can be combined*

with excellent results. Laying the articles out on the floor let's you see what colors, shapes, frames, etc., create the best effect. Such items as a wall barometer or a plaque can be included with pictures to give the arrangement textural impact.

- *Don't mix reproductions of paintings with original paintings in a grouping.* A reproduction, that by its self would look splendid, will probably look weak beside an original.

- It is not wise to include in a picture grouping a single work that is so large, so colorful, or otherwise so powerful that it dominates the grouping to the detriment of the other components.

- In a grouping, it is acceptable to have some of the pictures and items above eye-level since the grouping itself is like one large picture. Some arrangements can go almost to the ceiling and still be effective.

- Picture groupings that are in a *high, long, vertical rectangle* shape can make a room appear *higher.*

- Picture groupings that are in a *low, long, horizontal rectangle* shape can make a room appear *longer.*

Displayed photographs

- *The general rule is that no family or personal photographs should be on display in a living room.* That rule may be fine in a large home where there are many rooms and many places to display framed photos. In an apartment or a small home, I break that rule. I so much need to surround myself with images of the people that I love, I have their pictures where I see them a lot. Yes, they smile at me from my *livingroom* and this is one rule of proper etiquette to which I'll never subscribe, and I hope you'll do likewise. There are too few reminders of love in this world, and family and friends are the most precious kinds of love. Those pictures *stay!*

Bed linens

- A desirable *fine quality fabric* for sheets and pillowcases is a 100% combed cotton in 200 thread count. A blend of cotton and polyester soon pills, making it unsightly and uncomfortable to sleep on. Linen sheets and pillowcases are the ideal, but the price makes them beyond what many people care to pay.

- Absolutely magnificent patterns and colors are now available in bed attire. Indeed, a bedroom can be totally decorated around these beautiful creations. From dark, dramatic geometric designs to pale, delicate florals, it's a matter of what mood you want to create.
- *As with everything else, quality is the criterion.*

Blankets

- *Woolen or cotton thermal blankets are the best.* Blankets made of polyester and acrylics soon get very unsightly with pilling and a cheap shiny appearance. They also are not healthy to sleep beneath because of the field of electricity that a polyester creates. Electric blankets have recently come into some disfavor due to research that has found them to have adverse effects on some people's health. This is a matter of opinion, however, and many people would never part with their electric blankets.

Towels, guest towels, and soaps

- Towels and face cloths in 100% cotton are the ideal. There should be no more than 10% polyester in towels. Cotton is absorbent and of a texture that gives a healthy glow to the skin.
- Top quality towels and face cloths with a velvet finish have a sheen and a look of luxury.
- Monogramming towels with initials is expensive but attractive. With divorce being as prevalent as it is, it might be wiser not to monogram. "His" and "Her" labels on towels look tacky.

Guest Towels

- The polished host/ess always has guest towels handy for a guest or guests. Terry towels or fingertip towels of woven cotton are the ideal.
- *Guests should not use the family towels.* Why is it that no matter how many guest towels are placed very prominently for

guests to use, they insist on using a family towel? A towel is a very personal thing, and it is very rude to use anything but a guest towel.

- If you're a two career couple with no time for laundering extra guest towels, then be sure to have *paper* towels available. *There are some beautiful guest towels of paper on the market.* There is no excuse for not providing guest towels.
- Towels for guests visiting for extended stays are discussed in the chapter on "House Guests."

Soaps

- Liquid soap dispensers are the tidiest, most sanitary way to provide soap for family or for guests. There are liquid soaps available in many types of product from deodorizing soaps, such as Dial,™ to expensively perfumed soaps for more luxurious use.

Removing shoes

Recently, a young American woman remarked to me that she found very strange the Canadian custom of removing our shoes when we go into someone's house. I told her that not *all* Canadians do this, in fact, most of us think it's a pretty strange thing to do. *I ask people not to do this at our place.* To have people sitting around in their stockinged or (oh have mercy!) *bare* feet, is really objectionable. If they remove hot, damp, running shoes (phew!) it's deplorable. If people see that their shoes are wiped properly, they shouldn't need to remove their shoes.

If attending a party, guests should not remove their shoes, it looks awful. *The hostess that expects guests to remove their shoes should provide slippers.*

Putting the polish on the outside of your home

It is just as important that your yard and outside appearance of your home be as tidy as the inside. Perhaps *more* important because people don't have to look at the interior of your home but they *do* have to see the outside premises.

- *Keep all junk and clutter picked up and under cover.* It's infuriating to have to live beside neighbors who let their property get run-down and unsightly. It is a scar on the entire neighborhood.
- *Mow the lawns and trim the hedges.* Don't think that because you park an expensive automobile in the drive way your neighbors will be impressed, they won't. If your property is not well cared for you'll lose their respect. A person who wants a polished image conducts his *entire* life with discipline and consideration, and not only his/her dress is immaculate, so are his/her surroundings (and that includes their automobile).
- *Apartment and condominium dwellers, too, must think about the appearance of the outside of their homes.* Draping carpets or clothing over balcony rails, and using the balcony as a catch all, presents a tenement look to the outside of the building. Dirty windows and soiled curtains hanging all awry tell the passerby that some messy people dwell within.
- *Apartment and Condominium dwellers should think about their outside door.* Placing unsightly mats there and hanging plastic flowers on the door really downgrade a place. We have seen this in *luxury* apartment buildings and wondered at the lack of good taste. It forces other residents in the building, who share a common hallway, to also share this ugly display.
- *Fences can create a particular "eye-sore."* To erect a fence with no consideration for its *appearance* is to erect an insurmountable barrier to neighborliness. Give careful attention to selecting the type of fence you install. Discuss it with your neighbor. Your community will only be as tidy and attractive as each individual resident allows it to be. Show as much pride in your home as in yourself.
- Houses and buildings don't set the stature of an area, it's the people that live there that give a neighborhood a low class image simply by showing no concern for the upkeep of their property. It only takes one or two residents to create slum conditions. A lack of money for paint and repair is pardonable, but there should be no lack of energy to clean up the grounds and make things look neat. All this world needs is a little love, a rake, some soap and water, *and a whole lot of elbow grease!*

Polish starts with the family

"Abeunt studia in mores."
Practices zealously pursued pass into habits.

We come into this world with no sense of the social graces; as babies, we even answer "the call of nature" wherever and whenever we feel like it. We have to *learn* the kind of behavior that will allow our entry into civilized living. *If we learn and practice behavior that is courteous and considerate, it becomes habit. "Abeunt studia in mores."*

It all begins in our home with our family. The ones we love the most should certainly have our courtesy. Sadly, that old saying: *"Home: where we're treated the best and where we behave the worst,"* is often too true.

Manners can be explained in one word: consideration.

In the home:

(1) Learn to treat each other, from the youngest child to the elderly grandparent, with the same respect. Most lack of manners begins with the way we treat children. It's as if we don't think they have feelings. Children learn kindness and consideration from their siblings and adults. If they are never shown any consideration, how ever will they know what it is?

(2) Don't holler. Shouting messages to one another, being as boisterous as on a playing field, sets a habit of loud, uncontrolled behavior that doesn't belong in a home and certainly doesn't belong out in the public.

(3) Don't interrupt. We teach children and teen-agers not to interrupt but we interrupt *them* whenever *we* want, as though what they have to say is unimportant. You'll often find that the youngest member of a family grows up with the unpleasant habit of interrupting. It's simply a result of *their* having been interrupted so frequently that they *learn* do it, to get a word in edgewise!

(4) Don't intrude. Respect each other's private space.

- Knock on a bedroom door before entering.
- Let each family member receive and place phone calls with some degree of privacy.
- Never to open anyone else's mail.
- Never read anyone else's diary or open letters.

(5) Never embarrass one another in front of outsiders.

- Adults often correct and reprimand children in front of other people. Remember that little ones are as easily embarrassed as are adults. Private counselling is more effective, as it doesn't cause resentment.
- Don't tell outsiders the "family jokes" and personal stories you know about each other. "Trevor walks in his sleep" or "Donna wets the bed."

(6) Use good table manners at all times. Thinking you can behave one way at home and a more proper way in public, doesn't establish good habits. Slovenly table manners accustom children to a boorish lifestyle that is difficult to overcome in later life when they need the support of good table manners. For example, learning as a child to use a knife and fork properly becomes a lifetime habit.

(7) Properly introduce each other to guests and friends.

- This is where teenagers need a little guidance. They bring new friends home and don't take the trouble to introduce them. The friend stands there looking uncomfortable and quite often is made even more embarrassed by some parent saying, "Who's this guy?" To *prompt* young people to remember this important aspect of *consideration,* it is better to say, "I'd like to meet your friend," and then to make the friend welcome. An even worse scenario is when the visitor is totally disregarded and no-one acknowledges his or her presence. Children and teens exposed to this kind of courtesy soon reflect it in their own manners.
- When meeting people, at home or outside the home, even the youngest child should be introduced. Then, having been taught, the most gracious response is to offer a friendly handshake. Polish, personified!

(8) Practice loyalty to the family. Making detrimental remarks about any member of the family, in-laws, (out-laws!), relatives, step-family, only casts reflections on the tattler. If you don't show loyalty to a family member, how ever could you be expected to be supportive to anyone else?

(9) Communicate with family members. Don't let resentments build by secretly nurturing a difference of opinion or an insensitive remark. Learn to bring things out in the open. Problems in family re-

lationships can't be rectified if the offense isn't revealed. Almost every unfavorable situation in our daily associations is the result of a lack of communication. Quietly, with real *consideration* for every aspect of the discussion, communicate.

(10) Be a "giver" not only a "taker." Share. That's something members in a big family learn to do graciously. I come from a big family, and I know, without exception, each one of us would give each other anything we own or any help we could provide. Sharing inspires love. Love inspires sharing.

(11) Treat step-relatives and in-laws with courtesy. You may not like them and *you* didn't choose to have them in the family, but somebody you love *did* choose them, so, *for the sake of your loved one*, be pleasant.

The polished guest—Would you be invited back?

There are two kinds of guests: The kind that people are happy to see *arriving*, and the kind that people are delighted to see *leaving*. Just to be sure you're the kind of guest that inspires pleasure by arriving and a genuine "sorry to see you go" upon your departure, brush up on these pointers.

- *Be sure the timing of your visit is very convenient for your hosts.* Whether it's a visit of a few hours or few days, never just drop in, always give notice and ask if it's convenient. (We have some good friends that we're *delighted* to see at *any* time, without prior notice, so there *are* exceptions to the rule. I guess it's a matter of letting friends know that that's how you feel about them.)
- *Arrive and depart at the appointed times.* If planes or trains are late, or connections are missed, *phone*.
- *If it's an extended visit, give your hosts some time to be alone.* Having company drains one's energy and having an afternoon or an evening to catch up on things is always appreciated.
- *Share some of the entertaining costs.* Take your hosts out to dinner or buy some luxury food for a treat, take them to the theater, pay for some of the gas if you're doing a lot of driving, there are many ways to share expenses on an extended visit.

- *Bring along a gift for your hosts, or a toy for their child.* Children love a surprise, and *so do adults!* Be original, make it an unusual gift.
- *Offer your help.* If it is welcomed, get specific instructions on what you may do to be of assistance. *If it is declined, don't insist.* Some people prefer to do things themselves and really do not want help. Keep out of the way. Read a book. Go for a walk or amuse the kids, pick up the newspapers and do little chores that obviously need attention but that can't possibly offend an "independent" host or hostess.
- *Don't commandeer the bathroom.* See that it is free for people who must get ready for work. Ask what is the most convenient time for showering, etc. Learn the family's schedule, fit yours in accordingly.
- *If no-one in that home smokes, don't smoke.* Asking if it's alright for you to smoke, when you know that no one in that home does, really puts a host/ess on the spot. They want to make you welcome and very comfortable, so they might say yes to oblige. People that don't smoke find it detestable. It also may be a case of allergy or heart condition that forces a host to request no smoking. Go outside.
- *Never take a dog or cat along on a visit unless the hosts suggest that you are welcome to do so.* There may not be accommodation suitable for a pet.
- *Don't intrude in family "upsets."* Though most people refrain from quarreling in front of guests, there are times it just seems to happen. Don't run in a corner and hide as though the situation is deplorable. Be non-committal. Spats happen in the best of families, so don't act as though they never happen in yours.
- *Don't tattle on your hosts* or reveal information you learn while staying in their home. *Who* snores?
- *Keep your room and the bathroom meticulously clean.* Ask where the cleanser and cleaning cloth are located, so you can leave the shower, bath, and sink spotless. Don't leave your toiletries, etc., in the bathroom, carry them back to your own room unless you are given space in the family bathroom.
- *Take along the appropriate clothes for the visit.* If the host/ess

doesn't tell you, ask what the activities will be, dress-up, sports, etc., and also ask what clothes would be suitable for the weather.

- *Ask about the sleeping arrangements.* You may find it isn't really convenient, and that you'd be more comfortable in a hotel. If you are an unmarried couple, be sure to determine if the host/ess minds you sharing sleeping quarters.
- *If you have other friends in the vicinity that you want to see, let your host/ess know that.* Don't ask if you can have them over to the host/ess' home for a visit; leave it to the host/ess to suggest it.
- *Use decent luggage and keep it to a minimum.* Space will be limited, and an array of bags and boxes not only looks unsightly but makes a room untidy.
- *Don't complain.* It is so disappointing to a host/ess to do everything possible to arrange entertainment and to make guests as comfortable as possible only to hear one complaint after another. If that's the kind of mood you're in, or if you aren't feeling well, cancel the visit and *stay home*.
- *On the final morning of your stay, ask what to do with the bedding.* Should you strip the bed and make it up with fresh linens? This is always helpful.
- *Be sure to send a thank-you note.* If it has been a long visit, why not send flowers?

The host/ess with polish

How to treat an overnight house guest
The major rule is not to ask people to stay unless you really want them. There are times when one feels obligated to agree to having a house guest or guests, but, unless it's a dire situation, it is more considerate to decline inviting anyone if you would rather not have them. There is so much pleasure in having house guests that are truly welcome.

- *Take time to enjoy your guests.* The host/ess that spends too much time getting meals, cleaning up, and arranging entertainment, has no time to enjoy his/her company, so the purpose of the visit is unfulfilled. Share the work. Do some prearranging of quick-fix casseroles for meals; a happy visit is more important than fancy food that takes hours of preparation. Visitors go away feeling that they have been a burden when you slave every minute of their time with you.

- *Let overnight guests know the "idiosyncrasies" of the household.* For example: a small hot water tank that is soon depleted of hot water; showering, etc., has to be scheduled to give the tank time to re-heat. A family member who has to get to a job in the morning is inconvenienced if a guest, unaware, has used all the hot water. Let guests know the family's usual time of rising and of going to bed, but let the guests set their own schedule if they should want to go to bed and rise earlier or later than that.

- *Equip the guest room for comfort.*
  - A good reading light and some magazines.
  - An alarm clock (Just in case!)
  - A comfortable chair in the guest room is always appreciated, a place to sit with some privacy.
  - A radio would be nice to have.
  - Extra pillows and an extra blanket.
  - Your prettiest bed linens, drapery, and toss cushions, make it a home away from home.
  - A thermos of water and a glass or some paper cups.
  - A fruit basket with a few added goodies such as some nuts, candies, etc., is a welcome touch. Even small packages of cheese and crackers make a nice snack for a guest who may not feel comfortable raiding the fridge.
  - A thoughtful touch is to put some note paper and a pen in the guest room. Postcards of local scenes and some stamps make a handy gift for the guest visiting from afar to send to their friends.

- If your bathroom won't accommodate a guest's daily toiletries and cosmetics, make room on a shelf in the bedroom and give the guest a large tray. All the items they have to carry back and forth from the bathroom are easily toted on the tray. Another handy "conveyance," instead of a tray, is a large flat basket.

- *Unless it's unavoidable, guests shouldn't take over the bed of any family member.* Children's rooms are as personal to them as is an adult's room to an adult, so every effort should be made to respect a child's privacy. In limited quarters, it's quite correct for a guest to use a hide-a-bed or a roll-away cot. The exception, of course, is for an elderly guest. Some host/ess's prefer to give up the master bedroom, but proper etiquette does not obligate them to do so.

- *Have plenty of hand and bath towels for each guest.* If there isn't room in the bathroom to hang extra towels, be sure there is a towel bar behind the bedroom door. *Here's a hint for anyone needing additional space for hanging towels:* Fasten a shower curtain *rod* about 6 inches *outside,* and parallel to, the shower curtain rod already in place and use this to hang extra towels upon. *(Fig.#39)*

Fig.#39

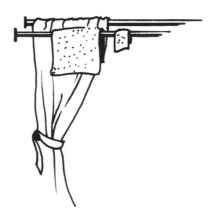

- *Always have an new toothbrush and comb on hand.* A guest caught short of having either of these items will bless your thoughtfulness. They are handy items to have for "impromptu" overnight guests also.
- *Let your guests know what clothes to bring.*
  - The attire appropriate for the *events* scheduled: sports clothes, walking shoes, evening clothes, *white* tennis clothes, and/or suit and tie.
  - The attire appropriate for the *weather* expected: raincoat, boots, very light or heavy clothing.
- *Let your guests know the sleeping arrangements.*
  - If they are aware that they'll be sleeping on a roll-away

cot, they might want to go to a hotel.

- If two people have been living to-gether and you do not want to explain the situation to your children (or to your own moral values), be frank, let the guests know in advance that they'll have separate accommodation at your house. *Never express any opinions as to the reason; simply say you'd prefer this arrangement.* It is important that people be in charge of the standards they set in their own homes and should not feel compelled to revise them to suit other lifestyles.

- *Show the guest where the coffee pot, tea pot, dishes, etc., are kept, and let them know they're welcome to help themselves.* The early riser or late-to-bed guest usually likes a snack and prefers to make it.

- *Help the guests to make the most of their visit.* If they have other friends in the neighborhood, try to arrange a get-gether or see that your guests have time to spend with them alone.

- *If everyone in the family is busy with jobs, school, etc., see that guests are entertained in some way.* It is rude to leave guests idly sitting around on their holiday. Lend them a car, or *take time off* for them.

Gifts: Giving and receiving with polish

(Also see: Business Gifts—International)

Giving gifts

- *As a rule, it is not good form to give money as a gift.* There are exceptions, but it usually gives the impression you couldn't be bothered to find an appropriate gift, or that you think the recipient is so mercenary all they want is money.

- *If you send flowers as a gift to someone, be sure the color co-ordinates with their decor or a corsage enhances the color of their gown.* To send a purple plant to someone with a peach colored living room is not the most thoughtful thing to do. If in doubt, send a mixed bouquet or white colored flowers.

- *If a gift you sent by mail has not been acknowledged, it is per-*

fectly correct to inquire as to whether it was received. If the recipient is embarrassed by the inquiry, they should have sent a thank-you note!

- *If giving a gift of wine, try to choose one that is favored by the recipient.* A good box of candy would be better than a cheap bottle of wine.
- *To end a gift exchange that has been a custom,* let those concerned know, *well in advance of the date,* that you want to discontinue the exchange.
- *Always make prior arrangements with a store so that, in case of duplication, a wedding gift may be exchanged.* If you prefer to keep the price of it private, tell the bridal couple you'll make the exchange yourself, and ask what they'd like instead.
- *It is not polite for a man to give personal items such as lingerie to a woman unless she is his fiance, wife, or co-vivant.* (Co-vivant is the name I prefer for a live-in partner.)
- *A man or woman should never give an expensive gift to someone they have just started dating.* It is poor taste, and puts the person in a compromising position.
- *It is also bad manners to give an expensive gift to anyone you don't know well;* it makes them feel uncomfortable at the inappropriate intimacy.
- *Gift certificates are always appreciated, but don't rely on this tactic year after year.* A gift certificate from a book store for the bookworm, or a gift certificate from a florist for flowers or a plant, to be cashed in when they are most wanted, are terrific gifts; just don't get in a rut and lose the intrigue of gift giving by being predictable.
- *Select a gift carefully.* You should be giving it to bring pleasure. If it obviously is quite out of sync with the recipient's interests, it is disappointing.
- *Always wrap a gift, that's part of the nice gesture.* Even a bow on a plant, or a fancy bag, makes it more special and exciting to receive.
- *Do not take a wedding gift to a wedding reception unless there is no other way to deliver it.* It is more considerate to drop it off prior to the wedding.
- *Always include a card with your full name.* The recipient of the

gift may know several people with your first name, don't leave him/her guessing.

- *It doesn't need to be a special occasion to send a gift.* Sometimes a gift means much more when there is no reason but *love* for sending it. If someone is having some problems, it's pretty wonderful to get a little gift to say someone cares and wants to bring a bit of sunshine into the day.

- *The gifts that can't be wrapped or seen but can be felt with great emotion, are the best gifts of all.* The little gifts, like a phone call to say you're thinking of him or her; little gifts, like baby-sitting for a tired new mother. These kinds of gifts make you feel so good it's a gift to yourself as well as to your friend. The gift of your *time* costs nothing but is the most valued gift there is; reading a story to a child; visiting a sick friend; where can these gifts be purchased? They are priceless.

Receiving gifts

- *Always write a thank-you note if you haven't been able to thank the donor in person.* It is very discouraging when no acknowledgment is received.

- *Gifts that are received by a bride-elect and then the wedding is canceled, should be returned to the donor.* The only exceptions to this is if the gift has been used or is engraved, then it must be kept.

- *When thanking a donor for a gift of money, in front of other people, say thank-you for the gift but don't mention the amount of the gift.* The discussion of money is always a delicate subject.

- *A wedding or shower gift may be exchanged, but the donor should be kindly notified that a duplication has necessitated the return.* The donor of the gift may want to handle the exchange personally. Many embarrassing situations have occurred in regard to gift exchanges. What if the gift was something the *donor* had received from someone?

- *Wedding gifts are not opened at the wedding reception.* They are opened later. Correctly, they should *not* be taken to the wedding but should be delivered prior to it.

- *If you receive a gift that is too extravagant and expensive from a recent acquaintance or "date," it is quite proper to discreetly and kindly return it* with an explanation that you would not feel comfortable accepting such a significant gift at this time.

- *If a dinner guest brings a bottle of wine as a gift to the host/ess, it doesn't have to be opened for that meal.* If it fits in with the dinner menu and the host/ess wants to open it, that's fine too.

- *If a guest brings a little gift to the host/ess and there are other guests present, the host/ess should not open the gift till later.* It may embarrass the guests that did not bring a gift and who needn't have done so. It would be gracious to *privately* thank the donor and to immediately phone the next day to express pleasure with the gift.

- *The gifts one receives that are not visible to the eye but are felt by the heart, should be acknowledged with a thank-you.* These are the most *memorable* gifts and often are the ones for which we neglect to show our appreciation. The little every-day gestures that make life more pleasant are sometimes not regarded as the precious "gifts" they are. How unfortunate. These gifts deserve the most sincere expression of thanks. Show your polish, write a note and say so.

CHAPTER SEVEN

Putting on the Polish
IN PUBLIC

CHAPTER SEVEN

Putting on the Polish
IN PUBLIC

Manners: don't leave home without them

At the theater

- *Be on time*. Many performances won't let late arrivals in until the intermission.
- *Pass in front of seated patrons carefully*. Hitting them in their faces with folded coats or big handbags is boorish. With your body turned to face those that are seated, hold your "paraphernalia" out of the way. Look at the seated person and quietly say "thank-you" as you pass. Be as unobtrusive as possible.
- *Help people to pass in front of you when you are the one that is seated*. Men and tall people should stand, because their legs are long, but anyone that remains seated *should slant their legs in the direction the passer-by is going,* to provide as much space as possible.
- *The seat you occupy is your designated space, don't go beyond it*. Placing your coat over the back of the seat, so that it falls in front of the person seated in the row behind you, infringes on their space. Leaning too far to the right or left, cramps the space of the person beside you. Only *one* arm rest is yours, leave the other one for the person beside you.
- *Don't talk or rattle candy wrappers and programs*. It's annoying when people disturb the sound. It not only is inconsiderate, it reveals your rough corners!
- *At the opera or symphony, don't nod, sway, or tap your toes to the music*. It is not good manners, and it shows you aren't aware of the customary behavior.

- *Don't applaud while the music is playing,* wait until the last note has faded away.
- *Don't eat strongly flavored foods before attending public events.* Having to sit for hours beside someone who reeks of garlic or strong spices ruins the entire performance. At *least* eat a breath mint.
- *If seated in a box seat, women sit in front and men sit behind them.* If the party is made up of all men or all women, they sit in whatever order they prefer.
- *When two couples attend a performance, the two women sit together between the two men.* A man and wife sit on either side of a lone woman guest. A wife sits between her husband and a lone male guest. Children sit between two parents or adults.
- *Dressing appropriately for public events is an important part of good manners.* See "Dress Codes."

Visiting in a hospital

- *Inquire about the condition of the patient prior to your visit* to determine whether or not s/he is well enough to want visitors.
- *Do not take flowers.* Nice as they are, no one has time to look after them and also there is no space. A patient in a private room may suddenly be taken to intensive care and flowers can't be moved about. Send flowers when the patient gets home. Flowers are wonderful ambassadors of friendship and cheer. If the patient is "long term," then flowers are more acceptable, *if* there is space, then make it a small plant as cut flowers need too much care.
- *When visiting, don't sit on the patient's bed or the empty bed beside it.* It can be excruciatingly painful to have the bed tilted or the bed covers pulled because someone is sitting on them pushing against tubes and other apparatus that are beneath. To sit on an empty bed in the room means a busy nurse or aid has to remake it, and they don't need any more work.
- *When giving a hug or a loving squeeze of the arm, think first, "Will it hurt the patient?"* Love and concern are what help a sick person recover, but oh, those touches against a needle in the arm or a tube in the nose bring tears to the eyes.
- *Try not to visit at meal time.* Eating a meal in front of visitors is

embarrassing for a patient.

- *Obey the visiting rules, and give other people time to visit*. Too many people at one time is exhausting.
- *Never visit a hospital if you have a cold or any communicable disorder*. Battling one illness is enough without being exposed to further problems.
- *Do send cards and letters*. They do more good than even medication can do. If the patient has a phone and is well enough, be sure to phone. Friends and relatives living at a distance can cheer a patient immensely with a long distance phone call.
- *Take magazines to a patient*. They are the easiest to read and are very welcome. Digest size is best.
- *Pay for a week of TV service* if the patient would enjoy it and you want to extend a special favor.
- *Look for ways to be helpful*. There is nothing so frustrating as needing something done and no-one to do it. Perhaps you could launder a personal nightgown for the patient, or run some errands. One is so helpless, and a kind relative or friend who relieves any problem is a friend in deed and a friend indeed! *I know*, my sister-in-law Winnie's chicken soup brought me back from the brink of death when I couldn't eat after surgery for abdominal cancer.
- *Don't say anything that might be disturbing for the patient to hear*. A patient in a coma or seeming to be asleep, often can *hear* quite distinctly, and listening to people remark on the seriousness of the illness is frightening when you're fighting for life.
- *If a doctor or nurse comes to speak with or examine the patient, leave the room*. Patients hate to be attended to in front of others, medical staff is accustomed to on-lookers and may not request privacy but, *please*, for the patient's sake, scat!
- *Don't peer at other patients as you pass by*. It might be fascinating to look at medical paraphernalia and various forms of human distress, but when one is the subject of the curiosity, with no way to throw a blanket over one's head, one really appreciates the considerate people who don't stare.
- *Wash your hands the first chance you get after the visit*. Hospi-

tals are rampant with disease germs. Every door handle and elevator button harbor all kinds of potential hazards; *keep your hands away from your mouth.* If this sounds paranoid, it isn't, most germs are passed from one person to another by our *hands*, then our hands touch our mouths, directly or by way of handling our food. Just one way to be a polished *visitor* instead of a polished *patient!*

As a patient in a hospital

- *Don't treat it like a hotel where everyone is at your service.* Do as much for yourself as possible.
- *Take a serviceable short or long robe with you.* Be sure it isn't a see-through beauty, but one that is presentable for walking down corridors when you are recuperating. A wrap-around robe tied at the waist is the most convenient. A robe that has to be put on over your head or buttoned up the front can be a real problem when coping with intravenous needles, etc. A long robe, though cosy in the winter, is a nuisance when using the washroom facilities.
- *Take slip-on, low heeled, bedroom slippers; comb; toothbrush; toothpaste; face moisturizer; hand lotion, and extra briefs with you.*
- *Do not take jewelry or valuables with you to the hospital.* Money for magazines or television service may be needed, so leave some with the nursing station on your floor. Don't keep money in your room.
- *Unless your doctor says not to, take along any prescriptions you are on in case they need to know what medication you have been taking. Show the medicine to the doctor, so they can lock it up.*
- *Upon leaving, give a token of your appreciation to the nurses.* A box of chocolates is a treat to share.

Attending a funeral

- *If it is a public funeral service, anyone may attend.* It would never be acceptable to attend out of sheer curiosity, however.
- *If it is a private funeral or memorial service, only those invited may attend.*

- *Whether or not to view the body of the deceased is a matter of personal preference.* If there is a walk-past, it would upset the family mourners to have people who were not close friends looking at their loved one. No one should walk past out of curiosity.
- *Dress should be conservative, in subdued colors.* It need not be black, but such styles as mini-skirts or "torn" blue jeans are far too casual for any church or religious service. A man should wear a shirt and tie and, preferably, a sport or suit coat.
- *Hats are usually worn by women attending Catholic funerals.* In an Orthodox synagogue a head covering of some kind is a must.
- *A person with polish would make inquiries to ensure they show respect for the customs of the service.*
- *It is considerate for the family of the deceased to place obituary notices in the newspapers of the various cities or communities wherein the deceased has resided.*

Attending religious services

- *Attending services of your own religious beliefs, you would be familiar with the customary behavior, but it may vary slightly from community to community.* For example, in some places it is permissible to chat and visit before the service, in some it is not. It is best to wait and see what behavior prevails.
- *If you are not accustomed to kneeling to pray, it is quite proper to just bow your head.* It is not necessary to participate in any of the rituals that are not familiar to you, but it is imperative that you show quiet respect while members *do* take part.
- *When the offering is taken, it is courteous to give a small donation even if it is not a religion of your own.* If you are too opposed to the doctrine to give even a small offering, what are you doing there?
- *Communion should not be taken unless you are a member of that religious denomination.* Some Protestant churches allow anyone worshipping in that service to take communion, but some do not. It is better to decline and to remain seated for that part of the service. Roman Catholic churches give communion only to their own members. Non-Christian faiths

should never share in communion since it is a symbol of a belief in Christ.

- *Dress can differ extensively in each house of worship and even from district to district.* Some churches do not allow women to wear slacks. It is wise to refrain from doing so in any case as, to some people, it indicates a lack of respect.
- *When attending unfamiliar religious services, ask for prior guidance regarding customs, regulations, and restrictions.* You'll feel more comfortable and you won't offend dedicated members. You may even find that it would be better not to attend. If visiting with friends who invite you to accompany them to a religious service, you are *not* obligated to accept. If you *do* accept, don't ridicule or make derogatory comments during or after any part of the service.

Attending and/or participating in sports events

- *A person's true character is often revealed when participating in sports.* A person with polish shows emotional restraint at a disappointing loss and doesn't engage in arrogance when experiencing a triumphant win. It's a fine personal attribute to be considered to be a good sport.
- Sports have become so commercialized that the rules of the game are etched in stone, but *the etiquette that should be shown is too often disregarded.*
- *Keep your self-respect.* To deliberately injure a player to gain the edge may win the game but brands you forever as a bully. That moment of revealing superior strength is fleeting, the lifetime of being branded *inferior* in sportsmanship is forever.
- *The loser should shake hands promptly with the winner* and a couple of words such as "Well done!" are not too difficult to express in even the worst scenario.
- *Obey the rules of the game, but even more important is to learn and practise the etiquette of each game:*

GOLF

- *Do not talk, whisper, or make any noise or movement when a player is putting.*
- *Stand in a position that does not distract a player that is ad-*

dressing a ball.

- *On the green, do not walk across the line between the hole and the player's ball,* the footmarks may affect the player's putt. If this happens, repair the green.
- *It is considered improper to ask a player which club s/he chose to make a certain shot.* Everyone has their method of play and may not want to reveal it.
- *Never criticize a player's method of play;* if they want lessons they'll hire a pro.
- *Women should never wear high heels on a golf course.* Wear regulation golf shoes or flat-heeled shoes.
- *Be sure the players ahead of you are out of your hitting range before you drive a shot.*
- *Let faster players play through, so you don't hold up their game.*
- *Help to search when an opponent has lost a ball.*

FOR ALL GAMES

- *Inquire as to the rules of the club regarding dress restrictions and hours of play, etc.*
- *Be on time but if you must cancel an appointment to play, get someone to replace you* or let the other players know as soon as possible, so as not to spoil their game.
- *Keep the club room and locker room clean and neat.*
- *Don't borrow toiletries or towels, always have your own equipment of every sort necessary.*
- *Do not swear or use rough language.* This is a sure sign of a person of low class.

SPECTATORS

- *Unless everyone is standing, don't stand up in* front *of people in an endeavor to see better.*
- *Never call out nasty personal remarks about any of the players or boo the opposite team.*
- *It is the epitome of rudeness to cheer the injury of an opposing player.* How barbaric can you be?
- *Never swear or use bad language,* it is offensive.
- *Don't make disparaging remarks to spectators* sitting near you in the stands. Cheering for opposing teams can be fun if the

challenge is kept courteous but can send everyone home feeling disgruntled if arguing in the stands has put a sour note on the event.

- *Be careful with drinks and food in the stands*. Spilling on people is the height of carelessness.
- *Pick up all your papers and popcorn boxes and other "junk" and put it in the garbage receptacles*. Teach your children to do the same. To simply think that the maintenance crew will tidy it is an attitude unbecoming to a person with class.
- *Be a pleasant spectator not an unpleasant spectacle*.

Using a private swimming pool

- *Never ask to use someone's private swimming pool. You must wait to be invited*. There are no exceptions to this rule. A pool is a very personal thing and if an owner wants to share it they will let you know.
- *Always shower prior to going in a pool*. To go in a pool wearing sun tanning lotions really upsets a pool owner. If there is no shower facility, use a garden hose.
- *Bring your own towels*. To expect someone to do extra laundry for your convenience is inconsiderate.
- *Never bring a dog or cat to a swimming pool*.
- *If you bring your children to someone's private pool, give them your full attention at all times*. No one else should have to look out for them, and accidents can happen in just minutes.
- *If you take your children to a neighbor's pool and you are not swimming yourself, stay with them*. It is not the responsibility of your neighbor to keep a constant vigil on your children.
- *Take a gift to the owners of the pool*. To use such an expensive facility is a privilege, show your appreciation. If poolside get-to-gethers are a regular event, contribute food and drinks to do your share of the entertainment costs.
- *If you have an open invitation to use a neighbor's pool, always inquire first if it is convenient*. If they are having guests do *not* use it. They will expect you to be polite enough to refrain from intruding when it isn't appropriate.
- *Turn down the volume on a radio or tape recorder if you are using one*. Don't be noisy in any way.

- *An invitation to use a pool on a regular basis does not mean you may use the owner's home also.* Confine your activities to pool-side only.
- *The owner establishes rules; the guests follow them.*

Owner or guest on a boat or yacht

There are some specific traditions and rules regarding boating, sailing, and yachting.

- *The "captain" (owner) always is the first to board the vessel and the last to leave it.* Allow him/her this traditional procedure.
- *Owners of yachts refer to their own craft as a "boat" or a "cabin cruiser" they do not call it a yacht.* When speaking of *other people's* craft they call it a yacht if it is of that structure. Discreet behavior is never boastful about your own possessions.
- *Neither owner nor passengers should drink alcohol to excess and should obey all boating regulations.*
- *Carry your luggage in a duffel bag.* It takes little room and it can be folded up and out of the way when emptied. Keep luggage to a minimum.
- *Take a spare paper bag to hold your soiled laundry.*
- *Boats have a limited supply of fresh water, use it sparingly.*
- *Use deodorants.* Be very clean; everyone is living in close quarters and it requires special attention to keep everything pleasant. *Deodorize shoes* and place used socks in a bag; it is surprising how many people don't seem to realize how offensive their foot odor can be.
- *Never dive from a boat that is moving.* The current created by the moving craft can pull you beneath the boat and into the propellers.
- *Obey the captain's orders immediately and totally.*
- *Keep out of the way of busy crew workers and don't speak to the captain when he is busy.*
- *Every one on board must do their share of cleaning and labor.* If there is a full maintenance crew on a large yacht it is still each person's duty to be neat and orderly.
- *Don't throw garbage overboard. Also never throw a lighted cigarette overboard as it may fly back onto the craft and cause a fire.*

- *If you smoke, go out on deck in the open air.* Filling closed quarters with smoke is unforgivable.
- *Take the boat a gift.* Anything from a good bottle of wine, to a set of towels for the shower. There are many gifts that would be appreciated, make it unique.
- *See "Dress Code" for appropriate dress. Pay particular attention to wearing the proper shoes.*
- *It's an expensive treat, as a guest be sure to express your thanks and appreciation. Bon voyage!*

Shopping etiquette

May I make a special note to new immigrants that have come to North America from very crowded countries. If ever you feel that we seem to make you unwelcome it is not due to bigotry or discrimination, it is often due only to the fact that we are not accustomed to having anyone push and shove their way to get where they're going. We get indignant and fail to stop and consider that you are not being rude, you are simply doing what you have learned to do in crowded living conditions. To make your life more pleasant in this, your new country, and to feel totally accepted and welcome, all you need to do is to *smile* and to become familiar with *polite* North American behavior. I say *polite* North American behavior because we can be as rude as anyone anywhere. It is only fair to make another note: many immigrants show the epitome of good manners, Japanese people, in particular, must be commended for their gracious behavior at all times. No matter what our racial origin or religious creed, *one thing is universal, consideration for each other will always result in having good manners.*

In the public, *when shopping,* for example, *we notice people's manners and are exposed to coping with the lack of them.* To deserve a polished image, each one of us must exercise considerate behavior.

ESCALATORS

- *When using an escalator, move away immediately when you reach the top or bottom.* The people behind you have no where to go when you block the top or bottom destination. Elderly people are the worst offenders. They get to the top and stop and look around to get their bearings instead of moving aside and doing their search from an unimpeditive vantage point.

- *When with a woman, a man steps on to an escalator before the woman when using the "down" escalator.* He is then in front of the woman to catch her if she should fall forward.
- *When with a woman, a man steps onto an escalator after a woman when using the "up" escalator.* He is then behind her if she should fall backwards.
- *Give people space on an escalator.* Crowding onto the same step with a stranger is usually unnecessary.
- *Don't let your children play on an escalator.* Older people in particular are easily knocked off balance when children push and shove past them on a moving escalator. It is dangerous for everyone.
- *Stand to the right side on an escalator.* Hold on to the rail with your right hand. One never knows when a sudden stop can throw everyone off balance.
- *If it is absolutely necessary to hurry, keep to the left as you walk up or down the stairs of an escalator.* Be very careful not to knock anyone off balance.

ELEVATORS

- *Male or female, the emerging persons nearest the door leave first when an elevator is crowded.* Trying to be polite and letting women go first can cause a real jumble and this serves no one well.
- Some women object to getting preferential treatment, but I believe *it's considerate for a man to let a woman leave an elevator first, if it can be done without impeding the path of others using the system.*
- *If a man removes his hat (in an uncrowded elevator) when I, a woman, enter an elevator, I feel very special.* I say, "Thank-you." He looks pleased! This is not a matter of superiority of the male or female sex, it's a gesture of respect. How can we as women not appreciate that?

• *Whether it is legal to do so or not, do not smoke in an elevator.* It not only fouls the air, people or their clothing can get burned and you could get sued!

GROCERY STORES

• *Don't sneak into the express lane with more than the maximum number of items.* This shows a disregard for other people's convenience. Most people will put up with your intrusion without comment, but they'll surely regard you as someone lacking in good manners.

• *If a shopper does go in front of you in the express lane with more than the maximum number of items, be polite.* Say, "Maybe you didn't notice but you're in the wrong check-out, this is the *express* lane." That should move even the most crusty individual. If it fails to, *keep your cool and your refined image*, it's no use *two* people being rude.

• *Let someone with only two or three items go ahead of you.* It's the *little* decencies that make a happy day.

• *Never argue with the check-out cashier about a store policy to which you object.* See the manager. The cashier can't revise corporate rules.

• *Do not help yourself to grapes, candies, fruit, nuts, all the goodies so easily "snitched" and quickly eaten.* Store staff and other customers are watching your *thievery* and one day you'll be embarrassed to be invited to the manager's office for the reprimand you deserve. Put the polish on your red face!

DEPARTMENT STORES

• *Salesclerks are usually as polite as the customers deserve them to be.* A snarly customer doesn't inspire a clerk to be courteous.

• *Salesclerks that visit with their friends and neglect customers usually cause the customer to become that snarly, however. This is a prevalent complaint.* To have to wait for a clerk to finish a personal phone call or wait while they file their nails is really infuriating. Worse than that, it's bad manners in addition to losing sales for the employer.

• *Customers should speak to the management if a store clerk is forced to point to where a product is located instead of taking the customer there and serving him or her.* That salesclerk cannot leave the checkout counter because of inadequate staffing. It is a situation that the management should rectify, *don't blame the clerk.*

- *Don't use ladies' wear departments as a form of entertainment.* If you are a serious shopper you need to try on clothing. Seeing what's new and different is fine, but trying clothes on with no intention to buy is inconsiderate. This is sometimes why clerks don't wait on the public properly, they don't know if you're buying or playing.

- *If you don't get good service, blame the management. Complain.* Either the staff is not properly trained or the number or quality of the personnel is inadequate. *Corporate carelessness in serving the public is bad manners that should not go unreported or, at the very least, should not be patronized.*

OTHER STORES

- *Handling food in an unsanitary way is not only poor manners it's against the law.* More people should complain when a clerk *handles money and then,* without washing his/her hands, *makes a sandwich.* Handling food and money should not be allowed. The same thing happens with ice cream outlets. The clerks have ice cream all over their hands and even up their arms and have handled money prior to serving the customers. Complain to the health department about this lack of hygiene. Let the management know you disapprove of it's discourtesy.

- *Let management and staff know when you are pleased with their service.* We often voice our complaints but all too seldom express our satisfaction. We each should remember our own manners and give credit where ever it's due. This encourages people to put their best foot forward.

Other public encounters

QUEUEING
- *Always move to the end of the line.* You won't need a book on etiquette to tell you this, every person in that queue or line-up will let you know very quickly if you have the audacity to push in out of turn.
- *If a couple is in a queue waiting for another couple to join them, it is best to wait one person behind the other.* When the later couple arrive, one of each of them can stand beside the first couple. The line-up would object if a couple arrives and takes a place behind the first couple, they'd make them go to the rear of the queue.
- *Never quarrel or talk about personal subjects while standing in a queue.* People standing so near you are embarrassed to have to listen to this.
- *It shouldn't be necessary to tell anyone not to kiss and fondle one another at any time in public.* This is behavior even the most ignorant person knows is not acceptable in public.

WALKING ON THE STREET
- *When walking two or three or more abreast, break up into singles to give room to those passing by.*
- Walk on the *right* on a street. Walk on the *left*, facing traffic, when walking on a road.

Neighbors

NEW NEIGHBORS
- *The established neighbor calls on the new neighbor.*
- *Within a day or two of their arrival, take them a hot casserole or some home-baked treat.* It's not necessary to phone first, it can be impromptu: It *is* nice to get a little warning, however, a phone call to say you'll be popping in with a treat is advised. Busy unpacking, they won't mind that you find them in disarray, they'll appreciate some good hot food. *Don't stay*, express your welcoming words and leave them to get settled. This is a great way to "break the ice" and, if you

leave a dish, it's a good excuse for the new neighbor to visit you to return the dish.

• *If you leave it longer than a day or two, phone first to be sure it is convenient to drop in and say hello.*

• *"Over the fence" introductions are casual and easy but a further gesture of friendship should be offered also.* "Come in and join us for a cold drink" is one way of getting to know each other.

• *New residents should wait for established residents to make the first gesture.* It's up to the old to welcome the new. A friendly hello must be offered always, but an invitation to visit must first be extended by the established resident.

• *Some people are very private and don't promote any sort of rapport with neighbor's new or old.* Though friendliness is a major part of personal polish, respecting people's privacy is just as important.

NEIGHBORS IN GENERAL

• *Communicate.* There are few problems that can't be solved by open communication. Allowing objectionable situations to become insurmountable barriers can be avoided simply by honest discussion.

• *Set a few neighborly rules and abide by them.* Taking turns at cleaning the driveway, for instance. Agreeing not to allow junk to accumulate in yards.

• *Don't use all the parking space.* Let each other know if you're having guests and need extra space.

• *Keep noise to a minimum.* No one wants to share someone else's choice in music. Turn down the volume.

• *Never pile snow or leaves onto the neighbor's property.* When scraping snow into piles, be sure not to cut off access to the neighbor's driveway or sidewalk. Feelings of goodwill could be nurtured by cleaning the neighbor's road when you do yours.

• *Keep any borrowing and lending to a minimum.* Invariably the day you want the drill, it's over at the neighbor's place and they aren't at home. Soon indignation rears it's ugly head and problem's arise. Borrowing and lending should be discreetly stifled.

• *Don't infringe on each other's time.* Asking for baby-sitting favors and running of errands should be a very occasional privilege and in times of emergency only. If favors are a reciprocal arrangement, be sure to keep the account balanced, some people tend to run over their credit limit.

• *Pets can create all kinds of resentment. Watch it.* The most tolerant neighbors can't put up with a constantly barking dog or a cat that digs up plants. Don't force them to resort to legal aid to resolve the disturbance. Most people love their neighbor's pets if they're disciplined and friendly.

• *To have a good neighbor, you must BE a good neighbor.* Look out for the security of each others' children and property. Neighbors can become as valued and as cherished as members of the family. It is usually a long term association, nurture its blessings.

• *Neighbors should mind their P's and Q's.* Respect each other's Properties, Perimeters, Privacy, Peculiarities, Priorities, and Peace and Quiet!

Travelling with polish

Automobile travel

- *Learn and comply with all the driving regulations that are in effect for that area.* To plead ignorance of the local restrictions is to no avail even when driving in an area unfamiliar to you. It shows a lack of concern for safety.
- *If a man and woman are taking a woman guest along with them for a short trip in a car, the two women both sit in the front seat with the driver or both sit in the back seat so the guest does not sit alone.* If the woman is driving, the woman guest sits in the front seat with the driver and the man sits in the back seat alone, or all three sit in the front seat, the man taking the position next to the door. (Phew! do you understand all that? Just be sure someone sits in the driver's seat!)
- *If two couples are taking a short drive, both men may sit in the front while the two women sit in the back seat, or the driver and partner in the front seat, and the guest couple in the back seat.*
- *Elderly passengers are always given the most easily accessible seat and are helped in and out.*
- *On a long trip by automobile, passengers should switch seats periodically,* so no-one must sit in the back seat all the time. It's considerate to offer to spell off the driver.
- *See "Shared Travel with Friends."*

TAXI

- *If a woman is out with a man and asks him to order a taxi for her to go home, she pays the fare herself.*
- *If a man is unable to accompany a woman to her home after a social engagement and he calls a taxi to take her, he must pay the fare.* He gives the driver the woman's address, asks what the fare will be, and pays it in advance with a tip included. He should wait the appropriate time and then should phone the woman to be sure that she got home safely. Only in the most unusual circumstances would a gentleman not see a woman to her home. Just to hand her the money to pay for a taxi home is positively crass.
- *The same procedure should be followed by a host or hostess that*

hires a taxi to see their guest(s) home or back to their hotel. Accompany them to the taxi and pay the driver.
- *A man gets out of a taxi first and then helps a woman by giving her his hand. He enters the taxi last.*
- *Passengers do not sit in the front seat of a taxi unless all seats are needed.* Wait for the driver to open the door; however, on a busy street s/he may not be able to do that, so act accordingly.
- *Have the fare ready so you don't cause delay.*
- *See "Tipping Rates."*

LIMOUSINE OR CHAUFFEUR DRIVEN CAR
- *The owner's seat is to the right, guests entering the limousine politely take seats to the left.* No one sits with the chauffeur unless all seats are needed, then a gracious host should take that seat himself. If the owner is a woman, she would ask a young man to take that seat or, if all the guests are women, she would take the seat beside the chauffeur herself.
- *Wait for the chauffeur to open the doors, and the owner should get out first.*
- *In a rented limousine, the host or hostess acts as the owner would do and takes a seat accordingly.*

CAR POOLS
- *Establish rules prior to participating in a car pool. Stick to the rules.* A clear understanding of the operation will avoid disagreements. Most problems that arise with car pools are a result of too loose arrangements and therefore misunderstandings.
- *If you aren't going to be ready for pick-up at the appointed time, phone and let the others know.* They can decide to either go on without you or to wait. If you're the driver, it's imperative that you arrange with another driver to take over that day.
- *Don't wear heavy fragrances.* Being exposed to strong scents while travelling in a closed vehicle can be objectionable.
- *Be sure you do your share* to make the arrangement as pleasant as possible, pay on time, etc..
- *Keep quiet.* Driving day after day with a chatterbox is hard on the nerves.

- *Don't discuss controversial subjects.* Religion and politics can raise great emotional reaction.
- *Don't gossip, complain, or discuss personal problems and relationships.* A daily description of someone's "soap opera" lifestyle is boring and embarrassing.
- *Never interfere with the driver or offer driving advice.* If you don't approve of his or her methods of operating a vehicle, find another car pool.
- *Respect the driver's vehicle.* Don't carry food or drink into the car; it might spill or be messy. Wipe your shoes to remove any mud.
- *The driver has a great responsibility to the safety of the passengers.* Also, adequate insurance coverage must be arranged.
- *The driver must see that passengers arrive at their destinations on time.* If it is difficult to meet this commitment, a driver should not participate in a car pool arrangement.
- *Radio or taped music should be mutually agreed upon.* Silence is better than exposing a passenger to a steady diet of sound he or she does not enjoy.
- *Never change the volume of a radio in someone else's vehicle.* If you find it disturbing or want it louder, discreetly inquire if you may adjust the volume.
- *In some car pools, driver's take turns using their vehicles.* Costs then are automatically evenly divided. Passengers that do not take their vehicle must be sure to pay their share *regularly*. It is a nice gesture for such a passenger to occasionally give an additional small gift to the driver. Vehicle operating expenses are so expensive, it is seldom possible to charge enough to compensate, so a token of appreciation is well received.

Train travel

- *Reservations for sleeping accommodation, compartment, or bedroom, must be made when purchasing the ticket.*
- *For all travel, keep luggage to a minimum.* This is important for train travel in particular, because you'll probably have to carry your own luggage. On an overnight train trip, take *one* bag containing only what you'll need while on board the train. Check the rest of your luggage. See: *"Packing for Travel"*

- *Greet the passengers sharing your seat or compartment but respect their privacy*. If it is obvious that someone wants to read or be quiet, don't try to make conversation.
- *As soon as you are settled on board the train, check with the porter regarding the reservations for your sleeping accommodation*. In case there is any error, don't leave this till bedtime, check it immediately.
- *If there is meal service on the train, also let the porter know what reservations you want for meals.*
- *Go promptly for your meals at the reserved time, and wait for the porter to seat you.*
- *The dining car is treated as a regular restaurant*. You leave a tip in the same amount and same manner.
- *Unlike a restaurant, however, you may have to share a table with strangers*. Be pleasant, but don't get too familiar or intrude. Most train travellers are friendly sorts and you'll have a superb time.
- *Always ask your seat-mates' approval before turning off a light, pulling down a window shade, or opening a window*. A polished traveller considers the comfort of others as well as their own.
- *There are only curtains separating most sleeping quarters so keep your voice low and your topics of conversation presentable to all ears*. Use earphones with your radio or tape recorder.
- *When meeting people in narrow corridors, turn your body to face the wall and give them as much space as possible to let them pass by.*
- *If drinks are served in the observation car, the steward is given a tip. See "Tipping Rates."*
- *When it is time for the porter to make up your berth, go and sit somewhere else so he is able to do so.*
- *Redcaps* (if you can find one, I think they should be given protection as a vanishing species) *should be tipped a dollar a bag if they have to handle your luggage between the train and the depot.*

Air travel
- *Wear clothes that are comfortable and that don't crease. Smart,*

casual apparel shows your polish. Being comfortable doesn't mean being untidy. Anytime you are out in the public you should look carefully groomed, and travelling is no exception.

- *Do not wear contact lenses unless absolutely necessary, and then they should be removed while in flight.* The air is so dry in a pressurized cabin that lenses get tight amd uncomfortable and can do damage to your eyes.
- *Wear comfortable walking shoes.* There is plenty of walking involved. Feet swell at high altitudes. If you remove your shoes, you might find it difficult to get them back on unless they are quite loose.
- *Don't wear a girdle or tightly fitted undergarments.* You'll cut off the circulation and be in pain.
- *Be scrupulously clean.* People must sit close to you.
- *Wear sox or stockings* in case you want to remove your shoes while in flight, no one wants to look at your bare feet and it would be rude to expect them to. A pair of roll-up, slip-on slippers are terrific.
- *Reconfirm your plane reservations a day or two before your flight.* Before going to the airport, check to see if the plane is leaving on time.
- *Get to the airport early.* You'll get a better seat if there's seat selection and your luggage is more likely to get on the same plane as you do. You won't get short-tempered due to unexpected delays and trying to rush. The trip will be much more pleasant.
- *Take a minimum of luggage. (See "Packing for Travel.")* Keep a small overnight case with you and carry it on the plane. *In it be sure to have:* reading glasses, medical prescriptions, tooth paste, toothbrush, soap, toiletries, change of underwear, nightclothes, phone numbers and addresses that you might need. If your luggage that is checked gets lost or transferred to the wrong destination, you will have the essentials with you that you can't do without. Plan that you may have to live out of your overnight case, your handbag, and your pockets for at least 4 days!
- *Do not attempt to carry extra luggage on board.* You may be asked to go back and check it and lose your flight. Some air-

lines have been lenient and people board with huge bags slung over their shoulders. This is a safety hazard to other passengers and to you.

- *Try to get a seat at the emergency exit locations.* No, not to be ready to jump out; these seats have more leg room. *Aisle seats are also good* for more leg room and for getting in and out of more easily.
- *Respect your seatmates' privacy.* They may prefer not to talk very much, then don't. You don't know their reason for travelling, it could be due to a death or illness in the family, it could be a grave business situation. Some people may just "want to be alone."
- *If you don't want to be engaged in conversation, take a book along and read it.* That lets anyone know not to disturb you with talk.
- *Except in First Class seating, you must pay for any wine or hard liquor that you order.* Be sure to have some small money with you, twenty and fifty dollar bills can be a problem to change. Have your payment ready when the airline personnel serve you.
- *Don't drink too much alcohol or drink it too quickly.* Alcohol has *twice* the intoxicating effect at high altitudes and you may get sick or behave in a manner unbecoming to a polished image!
- *You do not tip airline personnel for meals, drinks, or service.* Be sure to express your thanks, however.
- *If you need any of the following, just ask:* aspirin, blanket, pillow, ant-acid, medicine, tea, coffee, soda water, or a cold soft drink.
- *Prior to boarding, you should let the airline know of any special diet that you require.* Vegetarians, or diabetics in particular, should specify their needs.

How to avoid "jet lag"

- *Long distance travel traversing time zones disrupts the body's built-in clock.* This adversely affects the nervous system, the digestive system, and the body's wake-sleep cycles, resulting in dehydration, disorientation, lack of concentration, fatigue, indigestion, and emotional swings.

- *Drink plenty of water.* Try to drink a glass of water or fruit juice every hour. *Avoid drinking alcohol, coffee, or colas that contain caffeine, these drinks are all dehydrating.* The pressurized air in the cabin of the plane is exceptionally dry.
- *Moisturize you skin.* Don't mist your skin with water as some people do, the evaporation just makes your skin drier. For a long trip, either don't wear make-up or clean off your make-up after boarding and apply a good moisturizer, one with a humectant. A little bottle of glycerine and rosewater is great.
- *Eat lightly.* Don't eat rich foods, eat carbohydrates and proteins for energy. Your body swells from the cabin pressure and having a lot to eat will make you feel positively bloated.
- *For energy, take along your own high-protein snacks such as a bag of shelled sunflower seeds or peanuts.*
- *Get up and move around as much as you are able.* At least stand up and stretch, march on the spot.
- *Do a shoulder roll.* Shrug your shoulders to lift them to-ward your ears, squeeze tight, hold, relax. Then roll each shoulder in a circle. Then roll both shoulders at once and again alternately. This will relax the tightened muscles in your neck and back.
- *Try to sleep as much as possible if you will arrive at your destination in that time zone's morning.* You'll be ready then to stay awake for the day.
- *Try to stay awake for several hours before landing if you will arrive at your destination in that time zone's evening.* Then you'll be ready to go to bed. If you have difficulty getting to sleep, drink some milk or eat a high-carbohydrate snack before going to bed. Toast (no jam, the sugar in it will keep you awake) and a glass of milk works wonders. This increases brain *serotonin* which helps induce sleep.
- *Do not schedule any important business meetings or serious shopping for the first day of your arrival.* Disorientation and emotional upheaval from jet lag may affect your judgement. Sad stories abound about tragic business deals, imprudent art investments, and foolish behavior at sales meetings, that have each been a result of jet lag. Beware!

Packing for travel
Always take these items right with you
- *Driver's license*. Be sure the expiry date is current and in effect for the period of your trip.
- *Cash*. Local, and foreign currency if necessary.
- *Credit cards*. Check the expiry dates and arrange for additional credit if it may be necessary.
- *Tickets for airlines, trains, buses*. Confirm reservations a day or two before you travel.
- *Visa and Passport. Be sure they are in order.*
- *Medical Service I.D. Card and Medical Insurance.*
- *Traveller's Cheques. Cheque book*. Extra cheques.
- *Automobile registration and insurance coverage if you are travelling by car*. Check to see what other coverage you'll need if travelling out of country.
- *Money belt.*
- *Wallet*
- *Business cards*. If you're retired, engraved social cards are nice to have in place of a business card.
- *Photocopies of: birth and marriage certificates, social security card, medical insurance, passport, visa, credit cards, I.D. card, eyeglass prescription*. Keep these copies in a secure place. Leave a copy with a member of the family or a trusted friend, in case you must phone them in an emergency.

In a carry-on overnight case
Place the following:
- *A plastic-lined cosmetic case or shaving kit that can be hung up on a bathroom door. (Fig.#40)*

Rolled up

Open   *Fig.#40*

This is the most useful item possible. It can be used in cramped quarters on a plane or train. It organizes small items into compartments. It takes little room when rolled up. Women's come in a variety of colors and sizes, of cloth and plastic and of all plastic. Men's come in plastic or leather with plastic see-into compartments.

For the hang-up cosmetics bag
Here are some suggestions: make-up, make-up remover, moisturizer, deodorant, depilatory, razor and blades, hand/body lotion, curling iron, shower cap, tweezers, bobby pins and hair clips, toothbrush and paste, dental floss, mouth wash, fragrance, soap, brush and comb, shampoo, cotton squares, emery boards, nail enamel, polish remover, shampoo and conditioner, Q tips, hair spray, mirror, medical prescriptions, birth control pills, laxative, pain reliever pills, sanitary pads etc., vitamins, sunscreen, small sewing kit, scissors, safety pins, antiseptic, band aids, *lots of tissues*.

For the hang-up shaving kit
Here are some suggestions: razor and blades, electric shaver, shaving

soap or lotion, aftershave lotion, moisturizer, hand lotion, comb, deodorant, toothbrush and paste, mouth wash, emery boards, nail file, Q tips, shampoo/conditioner, hair spray, mousse or gel, magnifying mirror, soap, shower cap, tweezers, fold-up hair dryer, scissors, small sewing kit, safety pins, band aids, antiseptic.

For family travel

- *take an extra one of these roll-up plastic-lined bags to hold items of general use.* Having this extra bag means it won't be necessary to cart all the occasionally used items into the washroom on the plane or train but they'll be with you when you do need them. *Here are suggestions for those basic items:* sunscreen lotion, band aids, ointments, shampoo, hair conditioner, insect repellant, clothes hooks, nail file, emery boards, tweezers, antiseptic (peroxide), Q-tips, cotton squares, laxative, safety pins, soap, sewing kit, small scissors, motion-sickness pills, eye drops, foot powder (a vial of baking soda works very well), pain reliever pills, thermometer, water purification tablets, antihistamine, vitamins, laundry soap flakes, spot remover, Swiss Army knife.
- *Take small travel size products.* Get several of each and as they are emptied they can be thrown away. If the brands you prefer don't come in travel sizes, pour such products as shampoo and conditioner into small, unbreakable plastic containers. *A word of caution:* most plastic containers that come with cosmetics and shaving kits are *not leak-proof.* Purchase individual containers that are dependable or you'll have a ruined case full of spilled "soup."
- *Take a razor and blades instead of an electric shaver as electric power is not always dependable.*
- *Do not take a cordless butane hair curling iron.* They are illegal to carry on an aircraft. You may not be able to get butane refills.
- *Take a fold-up, compact, blow-dryer.*
- *For international travel, take an adaptor plug to convert power to suit the voltage of any electrical appliance you are taking with you.*
- *Take several plastic and zip-loc plastic bags.* Small items can

be placed in the zip-loc bags and larger items like wet cloths, messy shoes, or wet swimsuits, in the larger bags. Don't take *deodorized* plastic garbage bags or your clothes will *smell* of disinfectant and you can't put food in them or it'll *taste* of disinfectant.

- *Be sure to take an alarm clock.* Wake up calls may not *be* available or reliable.
- *Type or write a number of gummed address labels* with the name and address of each person to whom you plan to send a card or cards while you're on your trip.
- *Check these miscellaneous items:* corkscrew, compass, beach towels, washcloths, diary, pen, camera/film, binoculars, string tote bags, neck rest, flashlight, sunglasses, bottle/can opener, travel iron, maps.

Clothes for the overnight case
W O M E N
- Sleepwear, lightweight robe, stockings, underwear, slippers, one change of clothes i.e. blouse, etc.

M E N
- Sleepwear, lightweight robe, sox, underwear, slippers, extra shirt or top, handkerchiefs.

Travel clothes in general
W O M E N : *(checklist of suggestions)*
- Sweaters (cardigan, pullover), blouses, T-shirts, dresses, jeans, slacks, shorts, jackets, slips, bras, hosiery, underwear, swimsuits, dress shoes, walking shoes, athletic shoes, a dressy outfit suitable for day or evening wear, lightweight raincoat, umbrella.
- *Accessories:* scarfs, belts, small clutch purse suitable to use as an evening bag, costume jewelry, don't take any *real* jewels unless your social life will demand them, then lock them in the hotel safe, in a jewel case, upon arrival.
- *Build your travel wardrobe around two colors and black or white.* You won't need so many accessories to create a color co-ordinated look.
- *Base your travel wardrobe around one print then mix and*

match slacks, skirts, shorts and tops in solids.

- *For a holiday in the sun, have two swimsuits and a double-purpose coverup.* A shorty robe in brightly printed colors also serves as a bathrobe. A long, printed, sarong skirt is a beautiful coverup and does double duty as part of a patio outfit.

- *White clothes are crisp and cool looking but consider where they'll be worn.* If you're travelling on trains or dusty places they'll get soiled quickly.

- *A reversible wrap skirt, printed one side and plain the other, is comfortable and versatile.* Sew one for yourself, it's really quite easy.

- *The best materials for travel are cotton blended with polyester; cotton, silk, or wool knits; chiffon; seersucker.* Never linen, it creases so easily.

- *If you plan to "wash and wear," choose fabrics that dry quickly, knits do not.* Don't deprive yourself of knits, however, they're the most comfortable and crease resistant, just be sure you have other garments that can be rinsed and ready overnight.

- *For cold weather travel, don't pack bulky outerwear. Dress in layers, a pullover sweater beneath a warm cardigan. These take less room in your luggage.*

M E N : *(checklist of suggestions)*

- Sweaters (cardigan, pullover), sport shirts, polo shirts, washable slacks, dress slacks, walk shorts, underwear, swimsuits, walking shoes, dress shoes, athletic shoes, a navy blue blazer (is suitable for wear informally or formally anywhere), dress shirts, ties, belt, handkerchiefs, jewelry (cuff links).

- *For a holiday in the sun,* pack two swim trunks, sports shirts, two pair of shorts, a blazer, dress slacks and washable slacks, one dress shirt, ties, dress shoes and sandals, a cardigan.

Men's business travel clothes

- *Take two suits of the same color family.* Example: one black and one gray *or* one navy and one gray.
- *Take a navy blue blazer and*
- *two pair of dress slacks to go with it.* (one gray, one tan)

- *Take five dress shirts.* Be sure at least two of them are plain white for evening wear.
- *Take a sweatsuit to lounge and exercise in.*
- *Take two polo shirts or sports shirts.*
- *Pyjamas.*
- *Take six pairs black socks.*
- *8 sets of underwear.*
- *Take one pr. dress shoes and one pr. sport shoes.*
- *Accessories: Cuff links, belt, several ties.*
- *Optional: Raincoat, umbrella, tennis shorts.*

Women's business travel clothes

- *Take two suits in the same color family.* For example: one black and one gray, or one navy and one blue
- *Take five tops (blouses, shirts) for meetings.* Prints or plains that mix and match with the suits.
- *Take one fancy evening blouse* that can be worn with a dark suit skirt *and a beautiful belt* for a dinner engagement or dressy after hours event.
- *Take one pair of dress slacks* that go well with the jacket of one of the suits.
- *Take a cardigan and T-shirts or sweaters* for casual wear.
- *Take one sweatsuit* for lounging, jogging, or using the hotel's exercise facilities.
- *Take a double-purpose, short robe.* Use it as a bathrobe or as a coverup if you use the hotel pool. In that case you'd also take a swimsuit and thongs.
- *Take a plain pair of closed-toe pumps and a pair of comfortable walking shoes.*
- *Take scarfs, jewelry, belts, one handbag, a small clutch bag (not fancy), gloves for cold weather.*
- *Take the items shown in the "Cosmetics Hang Up Bag" and the necessary underwear, sleepwear, coat, etc.*

Before you travel

- Arrange with a trusted neighbor to keep an eye on your property and water your plants.
- Let them know *where* you're going and *when* you'll return. Give them a phone number in case of an emergency and the

number of a local relative.
- Give them a key to your house and garage.
- Get them to park their car in your driveway or to run their car up your drive to make tire treadmarks after a snowfall, so it looks like someone is home.
- Arrange for lawn to be mowed or snow to be removed while you are away. Burglars spot absentees.
- See that all windows and doors are secure and that a burglar alarm is operative. Let the police know you'll be away. Join neighborhood watch.
- Make arrangements for the care of your pet(s).
- Unplug electrical appliances, tv, etc., except the fridge and freezer and leave them as empty as possible in case of a power failure. Disconnect humidifier or dehumidifier.
- Discontinue delivery services, milk, paper, oil.
- Install an automatic timer that will turn on your lights in the evening and turn them off at midnight.
- Set the thermostat at a reasonable heat.
- List the registration numbers of cameras, binoculars, boat, fishing and sports equipment, so you won't have to prove to custom's officials that they belong to you and were not purchased on your trip. *Take the list with you.*
- Pull window drapes to the usual position they're in when you are home (sunny side of the house they'd be closed day and night, shade side they'd be open).

Travelling by automobile
- *check* brakes, tires, anti-freeze, signal lights, headlights, battery, spare tire. *Be sure to take with you:* registration papers, maps, driver's license, automobile insurance policy, first aid kit, fire extinguisher, car jack, spare tire, flashlight (blinker), gallon of water, extra set of car keys, windshield washer fluid, roll of paper towels, a small pillow, and a blanket.

Travelling with companions
Establish travel plans before you decide to travel to-gether. What type of accommodation: cheapest, medium priced, or luxury? How many miles to travel a day? Each pay own meals? What route to travel? Where you'll be stopping? Who drives? A trip always starts so friendly, make sure it ends that way.

When you stop at a hotel or motel

Check the means of fire escape

As soon as you arrive, check where the exit doors are located. Count how many doors there are between your room and the exit door down the corridor. If there is a fire, the lights may be out and with smokey conditions you won't be able to see. Get familiar with the layout of your room. Put a flashlight and your room key on the night table beside your bed so you can reach it easily. Have your slippers and robe handy. Look out the window and see where your room is located, is there a rooftop nearby and what is at ground level?

If there is a fire

Take the key and flashlight and crawl (beneath the smoke) to the door. If the door is hot DON'T OPEN IT. If the door isn't hot, open it very slowly to see the conditions in the hallway, close it quickly if it looks like you'd be safer in the room. Otherwise make your way to the exit. *Do not use the elevator under any circumstances.* If the door is hot, stay in the room. Try to phone the operator for instructions. *Wet towels and sheets and place them around the door to keep smoke from entering your room.* It's smoke that kills most people, not the actual flames. Close the hall transom. *Turn off the air conditioning system.* Go to the window but don't open it unless your room is getting smoky and you need fresh air. If there *is* smoke in your room open the window, or break it. *Make a tent over your head with a wet blanket.* Hold your head close to the window sill to get beneath the smoke that will be pouring out and to enable you to get fresh air, the blanket will help protect you from the smoke. *Don't jump* and try not to panic.

These are also useful instructions to follow if you are trapped in a house fire. *Teach your children what to do and check on the hotel's safety system, i.e. smoke detectors and exit doors that open.*

Travelling with children

- *Remember that they tire more quickly than an adult.* Consider their short legs if doing a lot of walking. If tempers flare it's usually a result of fatigue, try to see that they don't get that tired.
- *The perseverance of teaching them good manners at home will*

reward parents when they take their children out in the public. Courtesy begins in the family, practice becomes habit quite naturally.

• *Travel is the best education a person of any age can get.* Think of the child's interests not only your's.

Tipping
RATES AND PROCEDURES

• *The word "tips" comes from: To Insure Prompt Service.* It is quite in order to refuse to tip poor service.

• *Determine where blame for the lack of service lies.* Don't penalize an employee for something caused by the management, or vice versa. Tip accordingly.

• *The tipping percentage rate varies in some countries.* Ask your travel agent for tipping guidance.

• *Service is service, small town or city, tip fairly.* Some etiquette "experts" advise giving smaller tips to people in little towns or in modest business establishments. In my opinion, service should be rewarded at the same *percentage rate* in New York as in a village's beauty salon or wayside dining room.

• *Do not tip in private clubs.*

• *Do not leave an "insult tip."* To leave a penny or a nickel to show disapproval is rude. Leave nothing.

• *Be sure to deduct the taxes before calculating the tip.* This is sometimes forgotten resulting in excess tipping. Tip the wine bill separately.

• *The tip may be added to the bill or given in cash.*

TIPPING RATES
The following rates indicate the usual *minimum and maximum* for good to excellent service in most of North America. Within this range, tip according to service. The polished and knowledgeable person keeps within these ranges. For indifferent or poor service tip *nothing*.

Restaurant
• Head Waiter (Bribery?) $5–$10
• Table Waiter/Waitress: 15%–20%
• Buffet Waiter/Waitress: 10%–15%

- Wine Steward (Sommelier):   15%
- Busboy   no tip necessary.
- Counter Service: 10%–15%
- Bartender: 10%–15%
- Fast Food Delivery: $1–15%

Hotel or Motel
- Restaurant/Dining Room   same as above.
- Room-Service Waiter/ess   15%
- Coat-Check Attendant: $1 (for 1 or 2 coats)
- Valet Parking $1—$2
- Hotel Doorman $0.50 calling a cab
    $1—$2 carrying bags
    0 for opening doors
- Hotel Bellman $1 per bag
    Plus $0.50 for opening room
- Hotel Chambermaid: $1 per night
- Restroom Attendent: $0.50
- Concierge (if service used) $5—$10
- Desk Clerks   No tip.

Train
- Porter $1 per bag
    or $2—$3 a baggage cart
- Sleeping Car Porter $1—$2 per night
- Restaurant   (see "Restaurant" above)

Airoplane
- Porter $1 per bag
    or $2—$3 a baggage cart
- Flight Crew   No tip.

Taxi/Limousine driver
- (public)   15%
- Private   see "Household Staff"

Transoceanic Voyage: (Check with purser for tipping info.)
- Cabin Steward/ess $2 per day

- Headwaiter $5 per day
- Dining Room Steward $10 per day
- Deck Steward $5—$12 per day
- Wine Steward   15% of bill
- Bartender   15% of bill
- Staff "Gopher"   Minimum $1 per errand
- Tipping is done weekly (Friday night) on a long voyage. Plan to spend an additional ten percent on top of the cost of your ticket on tips. The rates indicated above are for first-class travel and may be somewhat scaled down for other classes.
- Bar bills are paid as the service is rendered, and a tip of 15% is added.

Cruise ship

- Tipping is done before ports of call (the night before going ashore) when on a cruise ship. Plan to spend about 15% on top of your ticket for tips.
- Bar bills are paid as the service is rendered, with a tip of 15% added.
- A ship's officers are never tipped.

Hair salon

- Hair Dresser   10%—20%
- Shampoo Person $0.50—$2
- Manicurist   15%
- Salon Owner—(Optional)   10%—15%

Ushers

- Theater or Concert   No tip.
- Sports Arena (if shown to seat) $0.50—$1 per group

Domestic staff: (permanent)

- Ask permission of your host or hostess.
- Seek your host or hostess's guidance as to amount.
- If *the maid* did personal laundry and/or pressing for you and other extra services give *$10—$15 tip*.
- Depending on the length of stay give *the cook a tip* of *$10* for a week-end stay, *$20* for a week's stay.

- Depending on how much you have used his service, give the *chauffeur $5 to $15*.
- And, *if the butler did it*, compensate accordingly!
- Pay these gratuities *in person* to each of these people and express your appreciation.

Temporary domestic staff
- *Baby Sitter:* Tip for extra service.
- *Household Help:* Optional. Tip for extra good service.
- *Caterers:* Tips usually included in the bill.
- *Bartenders:* Optional. Tip for extra good service

Do not tip the following
- Ships' officers.
- Bus drivers.
- Operators of "Bed and Breakfast" accommodations.
- Elevator operators.
- Train conductors.
- Police and Firemen.
- Airline personnel.

Foreign travel
- *You are a representative of your own country. First and foremost remember that your behavior brands all your countrymen as decent or indecent people.* We each should be the ambassador of goodwill that encourages our host country to respect us as individuals and as a nation.
- *Learn to say "Please" and "Thank you" in the language of the country you are visiting.* (See Appendix "A")
- *Never make disparaging remarks about a country to its residents, it is taken as a personal insult.* We might each have complaints about our own country, but none of us likes to hear outsiders criticize it.
- *Be more formal.* We Canadians and Americans are often more casual than are people in other cultures.
- *Don't use first names.* We shouldn't use first names anywhere until we are invited to do so.
- *It is an honor to be invited into someone's home and it is partic-*

ularly so in certain countries, treat it as such. Take a gift of flowers or candy. There are strict rules of protocol that must be respected with regard to the *wrapping* and giving of gifts in foreign countries. (See "Business Gifts—International)

- *Do not take photographs of people in their native dress unless you first ask their permission.* It is rude to assume that they would not object. Some will expect to be paid for allowing the photo.

- *Do not take photographs of anything that may be considered a security risk, for example, military equipment or areas.* You might raise suspicions that you're a spy!

- *Do not take photographs inside a house of worship without first getting permission.* Never take pictures during a religious service.

- *Tipping can be a delicate situation. Be sure to get specific guidance before visiting a country.* For example, in Japan when a tip is given it should be concealed in a small envelope or wrapped in paper.

- *In Moslem cultures, you should not pick up food with your left hand.* There is a very good reason why that is considered to be exceedingly bad manners.

- *In Arabic countries, women are treated very much differently than is the custom in North America.* If unaccompanied by a male, there are many places where a woman is not allowed to go.

- *In Arabic countries the drinking of alcoholic beverages is not allowed.*

"PLEASE" AND "THANK YOU" AROUND THE WORLD

COUNTRY	PLEASE	THANK YOU
GERMANY:	Bitte	Danke *Dahnk*-ah
ITALY:	Per favore	Grazie *Grahtz*-ee
FRANCE:	S'il vous plait	Merci *Mare-see*
ISRAEL:	Zayt azoy gut	A dank
SPAIN:	Por favor	Gracias *Grah*-see-as
JAPAN:	*Doh*-zoh/oh-*neh*	*Doh*-mo ah *ree*
	*gah-ee shee-mahs	*arr-*i*-gah-*toe*
GREECE:	*Pah-rah-*kah*-lo	*Ehf-khah-*ree*-sto
RUSSIA:	Pazhalsta	Spasiba *Spa-see-bow*
HOLLAND:	Alstublieft	Danku *Dahnk*-oo
MANDARIN:	———	*Shay-shay*
CANTONESE:	———	*Doe*-jay
ARABIC:	———	*Shu*-kran
PORTUGESE:	———	*Ohb-ri-*gah*-toe
SCANDANAVIAN:	———	*Tak
SWITZERLAND:	Use German, French or Italian	

*Phonetic spellings

Eating in ethnic restaurants

CHINESE RESTAURANT

- *Most food is ordered in large serving dishes and is meant to be shared.* It is best therefore to have two or more people in the group. The larger the group of diners, the more variety of dishes can be ordered.
- *Chopsticks should not be used unless you know how to use them properly.* Practice at home. Ineptly trying to pick up food and slurping and spilling should not be done in a public place.
- *It is quite proper to ask for a fork if only chopsticks are on the table.* To scoop up rice, the Chinese pick up their bowls and hold them close to their faces, this can't be done the way Westerners are accustomed to eating. Enjoy the excellent food, but use a fork unless you are an expert handler of chopsticks.

- *If you do use chopsticks, adhere to the rules.* Don't leave chopsticks in a bowl. Don't leave them pointing across the table, this is considered very bad manners. Don't cross them either, the Chinese believe it'll bring bad luck to the host.
- *Don't put used chopsticks on the tablecloth.*
- *Chopsticks are placed close to-gether horizontally across the top of the bowl, or on a chopstick rest if there is one.*
- *There likely will not be a tablecloth and wet cloths may be given instead of napkins.*
- *Lids on bowls are removed carefully and replaced at the end of the meal.*
- *If hot or heavy seasoning is not to your liking, particularly monosodium glutamate, request that it be limited or omitted.* The restaurant will oblige.
- *What we in North America refer to as Chinese food is quite different than that which you'll find in China.*
- *You'll also find that good manners in China are superbly proper.* No burping, as one common story would have one believe.
- *Dress conservatively and behave quietly.* Chinese people of good class are not boisterous people.

JAPANESE RESTAURANT

- *In many Japanese restaurants, diners sit cross-legged on the floor (tatami) to eat their meal.* Most, also have regular tables, too, for those who want them. When you make your reservation you should stipulate your preference.
- *Meals are ordered and served individually, not in large servings to be shared as with Chinese food.*
- *If chopsticks are on the table, you may ask for a fork.* You won't need a knife.
- *"Sushi" and "Sashimi," however, are most easily eaten with chopsticks.*
- *There are various kinds of "Sushi."* The main kind is *raw fish* wrapped around rice which then is often wrapped in seaweed. There are also egg sushi and vegetable sushi. "Sashimi" is rice with raw fish slices on top, served in a bowl.
- *Before the meal you may be given a hot hand towel (oshibori) to*

clean your hands. It is not good manners to refuse it. After you wipe your hands, put the cloth back on the tray without folding it.

- *Never take food directly from the serving plate to your mouth*. It isn't good manners anywhere to do this, take food to your plate, place the plate on the table and then begin to eat.
- *The main guest begins to eat first*.
- *If you are using chopsticks, never put the narrow end that you eat with into the serving bowls, use the clean wide end to serve yourself if there are no serving chopsticks*. If you are using a fork and there are no serving chopsticks, ask the waiter for a serving utensil. *Never* place your own fork in the serving dishes.
- *Do not leave your chopsticks in your bowl*. Don't leave them pointing across the table (a Japanese friend of mine tells me that is not good manners). Your chopsticks will likely be at your place wrapped in paper. Take the paper off carefully because when you are finished eating, you should place your chopsticks on top of the paper, just in front of you, along the edge of the table.
- *"Sake" is drunk through-out the meal from small cups. "Sake" is the chief alcoholic beverage of Japan*. (Pronounced sah-kee.) Somewhat sherrylike, it is made by fermenting rice.
- *Don't pick your teeth, anywhere or anytime, in public*.

National anthems

- *When a National Anthem is being played, always stand*. Certainly we know to stand for our own country's National Anthem, but it is important to stand for that of another country to show respect, as they should do for ours.
- *You do not sing when the National Anthem of another country is being played*. The words of the anthem are vowing allegiance to that particular country and you only vow allegiance to your own country.
- *Men should remove their hats when any National Anthem is being sung*. The exceptions to this are those men dressed in military uniform.
- *Everyone should stand at attention and not talk, laugh, smoke,*

or fidget no matter what country's anthem is being sung. It is good manners to show respect for an expression of national allegiance.

- *You do not applaud at the conclusion of the singing of a National Anthem.*

Toasting with polish

- *When you sit down to dinner, don't begin drinking your wine until you know if a "welcoming" toast will be made.* Wait till the host or hostess starts to drink their wine, then you'll be sure.
- *Any beverage can be used to give a toast.* If a person does not drink wine, a glass of water may quite properly be used to drink a toast.

WELCOMING TOAST

- *Unless it is a formal dinner, the host or hostess may sit to give the toast.*
- *The host or hostess raises his/her glass and says a few words of welcome to the guests.*
- *S/He then takes a sip out of the glass.*
- *The person being toasted does not take a drink. Whether the toast is casual, informal, or formal, never at any time do the people or person being toasted drink a toast to themselves.*
- *Without standing, one of the guests, or several in unison, then respond(s) with a short comment such as "Our pleasure to be here" and all guests raise their glasses and take a sip of their drink.*
- *No more toasts are made prior to the meal.*

FORMAL TOAST

- *Other than the welcoming toast, all other toasts are made at the end of a formal banquet or dinner.*
- *The toastmaster or toastmistress or host or hostess stands to give the toast.* Then, takes a sip of his/her drink.
- *The guests stand to respond, the person being toasted does not take a sip of his/her drink.*

WEDDING TOASTS

- *The usual order for giving wedding toasts is:*
  - *(1) Best man to bridal couple.*
  - *(2) Father of bride (or stepfather, uncle, brother).*
  - *(3) Father of groom (or step-father, uncle, brother).*
- *It now is quite proper and appropriate for the mothers of the bride and groom to give toasts in place of absent fathers, or in addition to the toasts delivered by the fathers.* Other immediate family relatives are next in line, then close friends, etc.

TOASTS TO GUEST(S) OF HONOR

- *The host or hostess gives the first toast to the guest of honor.* Other guests may then give their toasts to the guest of honor, but never before the host and/or hostess have given theirs.

TOASTS IN GENERAL

- *A toast is always short and sweet.* A toast is not a speech, it is a gracious recognition.
- **Other than for formal occasions, there need be no special procedure for offering a toast.* (*See rules for toasts in other countries.) Anytime you want to make someone feel appreciated and cared about, a toast dedicated to them makes them feel special. "Here's to Robbie, who did so well on his final exams" or "Here's to Mom for always getting us to the game on time" or "Here's to Dad for providing so well for all of us."
- *When delivering a toast, look at the person being toasted as you say your few words, take a sip of your drink as you continue to look at the recipient of the toast, give them a nod, then put down your glass.*
- *After a toast is given, all but the person or persons being toasted, raise their glasses and say, "To _____"* (the name of the person(s) being toasted) *and then take a sip of their drink.*
- *Always leave a little beverage in your glass, in case of more toasts; it is not good manners to hold up an empty glass.* If your wine glass is empty, pick up your water glass and drink the toast from that.
- *Never tap your wine glass to get attention. Rude!*

TOASTS AROUND THE WORLD

Cantonese:	Yum-sing	French:	Ah-votre-sahn-tay
Mandarin:	Kam-pay	Portuguese:	Sah-ude
Japanese:	Kam-pai	Scandinavian:	Skoal
Italian:	Sah-loo-tay	German:	Pro-zit
Spanish:	Sah-lood	Russian:	Nah-zda-roe-vee-ah

(Phonetic spellings)

CHAPTER EIGHT

CORRESPONDING WITH POLISH

CORRESPONDING WITH POLISH

Invitations and Replies

Formal Invitations

- Formal invitations should be sent at least three weeks to a month before the event.
- *Wedding invitations should be sent six weeks to two months prior to the wedding.*
- *Invitations should be printed, preferably engraved or thermographed, with black ink on white stationery. Never use a* typewriter to type formal invitations.
- *Formal invitations should state the following:*
    - *(1) Names of the hosts.*
    - *(2) Type of event.*
    - *(3) Purpose of the event.* (Not always necessary.)
    - *(4) The date of the event.*
    - *(5) The time of the event.*
    - *(6) The place where the event will be held.*
    - *(7) R.S.V.P.* (Beneath this, the host's address if different than the place of event.)
    - *(8) Additional instructions:* Type of Dress,
    - Parking Arrangements

> *Mr. and Mrs. Neville Malet-Veale*
> *request the pleasure of your company*
> *at a Buffet Dinner*
> *in honor of their daughter, Tracey*
> *on Saturday, March third*
> *from seven to eleven o'clock*
> *The Bayshore Inn*
> *Vancouver*
>
> *R.S.V.P.*   *Black tie*
> *PH: 000-0000*   *Valet Parking*

Fig. #43 A Formal Invitation

The above invitation would have the host's address printed under the R.S.V.P. if the host wanted a written reply. It is perfectly proper to ask for a confirmation by telephone even for a formal invitation, particularly if prior notice of the event has been short.

When holding a formal party for your own wedding anniversary, no mention is made of the reason for the event. (See Fig.#44)

> *Mr. and Mrs. Murray Bauer*
> *request the pleasure of your company*
> *at a Dinner Dance*
> *on Friday, the second of June,*
> *from eight to one-thirty o'clock*
> *The Petroleum Club*
> *Calgary*
>
> *Please respond.*   *Black tie*
> *00—Elbow Drive*
> *Calgary, Alberta*   *Valet Parking*
> *T2L 000*

Fig. #44   Formal Invitation to Your Own Wedding Anniversary

- *Preprinted formal invitation cards that have spaces for filling in the particulars are acceptable but are not as "polished" as those that are custom printed.* To avoid the delay of printing, however, anyone who does a lot of formal entertaining could have cards thermographed or engraved with their name and other constants on the card, and blank spaces left for the variables. *The variables then should be handwritten,* as they are issued and pertain to different events. *(See Fig.#45)*

Mr. and Mrs. Steven MacDougall
request the pleasure of the company of

at

on

at

R.S.V.P.   *12345 Hayley Drive*
PH: 000-0000   *Salem, Oregon 00000*

Fig.#45 Formal Invitation Printed/Fill-In

- *Do not use abbreviations on a formal invitation.*
  Example: Wrong: 2824 Pine St. N., Vancouver, B.C.
      Correct: 2824 Pine Street, North,
           Vancouver, British Columbia.
  (However, an address placed beneath the R.S.V.P and also the words "Mr." and "Mrs." may be abbreviated.)
  The time is written: "six-thirty o'clock"
  The date is written: Saturday, the fourth of April
- *R.S.V.P. stands for the French phrase "repondez, s'il vous plait" which in English means "reply, if you please."* The words "Please respond" may also be used; this sounds more North American, I like it.
- *It is quite correct to put either the host's phone number or address under the R.S.V.P.*
- *"Regrets Only" is another term sometimes used in place of*

R.S.V.P., meaning only those that cannot attend need to reply. In my opinion, invitations should be responded to whether or not you're able to attend. Promptly express your thanks and your reply.

- *A corporate formal invitation should always have a person's name or executive position on the invitation not just the name of the company.* An invitation sent in the name of a corporation seems too impersonal.

  Example: " Mr. Allan Jordan, President of XYZ Inc." or "The Chairman of Bones Inc." (See Fig. #46)

Mrs. Charmaine Wallace
President of Fine World Travel Inc.
requests the pleasure of your company
at a Cocktail Buffet
in honor of Dr. Guy Doplenty, Naturalist
on Wednesday, April sixth
from six to eight o'clock
The Frontenac
Los Angeles

R.S.V.P.   *Black tie*
PH: 000-0000   *Valet Parking*

Fig. #46 Formal Invitation—Corporate

- When there is more than one person hosting a formal event, the names are all listed on the invitation. If it is held at someone's home *their* names are listed *first*, then it is best to list the others' names in alphabetical order. State first and last names without titles: Marilyn Ward, James Kline.

Reply to a Formal Invitation

- *If a reply card is enclosed with the invitation it is simply completed and returned.*

- *If a phone number is included in the invitation, that is the way you respond*. No written reply is required.
- Whether you accept or decline, it is more polished to *enclose a short handwritten note* expressing your appreciation for being invited.
- *If no reply card is enclosed, a formal reply should be handwritten on good quality white stationery*.
- *A formal acceptance is neatly centred on the sheet:*

Mr. and Mrs. Tom Cryer
accept with pleasure
your kind invitation
for Wednesday, the third of July

- *To decline, a formal regret is written as follows:*

Ms. Dianne Parks
regrets that she is unable to accept
Mr. and Mrs. Reagan's
kind invitation to dinner
on Sunday, the thirteenth of May

- *No explanation is included in a formal regret*, but it shows polish to enclose a short note giving the reason (no details necessary) why you cannot attend.
- *Reply to an invitation promptly*.
- *Never express indecision, either accept or decline*. With no firm commitment, it is too difficult for a hostess to plan or to ask someone else in your place.

Informal invitations

- *Printed, engraved, or thermographed cards may be used but the wording is much less formal*.

Dianne and Larry Whetstone
would like you to join them for
Open House
Boxing Day from 2 to 8 P.M.

Please respond   *PH: 000-0000*

- *The above could be handwritten on white or creme colored notepaper enclosed in matching envelopes.*
- *Invitation cards from a stationery store are quite acceptable for informal events.*
- *Reply promptly and appreciatively.*
- *With an informal invitation you may offer your help.*

Thank-you notes

Essential to a polished image: (and a kind heart!)
- *After attending an event in your honor, it is essential that you send a handwritten thank-you note.* One letter to your host and hostess is sufficient, but if several people staged the event an individual letter should be sent to each of the major conveners. If a club sponsored the event in your honor, be sure to express your wish that all participants be informed of your appreciation. If the number involved is not overwhelming, a phone call to each would be a gracious gesture.
- *After attending a formal dinner party, it is essential that you send a handwritten thank-you letter.*
- *After staying at someone's home on an overnight or longer visit, it is essential that you express your appreciation in a handwritten thank-you note.* A gift of flowers might also be sent, but a note is mandatory.
- *After receiving a gift through the mail, it is essential that you send a thank-you note to express your thanks and to let the*

sender know the gift was received. It is the height of rudeness not to acknowledge receipt of a gift. *Teach children this.*

Thank-you notes are never inappropriate

- *Any time someone does something nice for you or lets you know they care, a thank-you note is always in order, a gesture of appreciation for their kindness.*
- *The letter should be handwritten, not typed.* It would be better to type a thank-you than not to send one at all, however.
- *A thank-you note should be sent within two or three days of receiving the favour, honor, or gift.* Make it more than an obligatory thank-you, mention something about the favour or gift to indicate your sincere pleasure and appreciation.
- *A written thank-you note is so much more significant than just the spoken word, it can brighten someone's day and there's no description for the warm feeling it instills in the heart of the sender.* Sometimes, such things as help in a time of need or small favors like running errands seem to be taken for granted. Quite unexpectedly, a thank-you note arrives and the receiver knows his or her efforts weren't in vain.
- *Commercial "thank-you" cards, many of which are beautiful with very effective words, are not a good substitute for a few of your own sincere words of appreciation. Always enclose a note of your own.*
- *"Thank you," so easy to say, so often not expressed!*

Letters of condolence

- *A letter of condolence is sent as soon as you hear of someone's death even if it occurred several months earlier.*
- *Letters should be handwritten.*
- *Use white, or creme colored stationery.*
- *Commercial sympathy cards should not be sent without also including a short letter of condolence.*
- *Inquire if there is any way that you can be helpful* and specifically suggest some way, such as offering to run errands.
- *If you did not know the deceased personally, but he or she was*

related to your friend or business associate, it is appropriate and considerate to express your sympathy. A simple "So sorry to hear of your mother's death, Jim. If there is anything I can do to be of help I would be grateful to assist in anyway possible. My sincere sympathy, Carole."

- *The printed cards that are supplied by funeral homes for the family of the deceased to send to acknowledge flowers, donations, etc., are not as appropriate as a short handwritten thank-you note.* Surely, dear friends deserve something more personal than a pre-printed card; they are mourning the deceased too.

Condolence replies

- *All letters of condolence, charitable donations, food, flowers, and favors, must be acknowledged by handwritten thank-you notes.*
- *If there is a great number to be acknowledged, a printed form could be used but must have a short handwritten personal message added.*
- *If there is a great number, other members of the family or close friends could help with the thank-you letters.* They would sign their own name and express the appreciation of the bereaved family.
- *Commercial "Sympathy" cards that do not include a personal note do not require a reply, but it is gracious to do so if you are able.*
- *Close friends and significant acquaintances* (i.e. your employer or fellow employees) *should receive handwritten replies, not printed cards.*
- *Replies to acts of condolence can be made over a period of a few weeks.* People understand the trauma of a bereavement and don't expect prompt replies, but as soon as you are emotionally able the replies must be given attention.

Priority list for condolence replies
(1) Acts of assistance. Contributors of food, cars, emotional support,

baby-sitting, errand running, message sending, funeral arrangements, etc., *must receive spoken acknowledgment immediately* and written acknowledgment later.

(2) Flowers and/or donations to charity, research, or foundations. Cards from flowers must be carefully retained for replies. Donations to a designated organization: ask the organization for a record of those that contributed so you can reply.

(3) Letters of condolence. These are replied to in the order of personal closeness to the bereaved. Example: A letter of condolence from a close friend would be before a letter from a co-worker.

(4) Cards with personally written messages. There are such beautiful commercial cards now so more and more people send them. Once considered to be incorrect and impersonal, if they are carefully chosen and there is a handwritten note enclosed, I feel these tokens of kindness are acceptable.

(5) People who attended the funeral. It is so gratifying when friends from near and far take time to show their sympathy. Try to thank them by phone or by a short note. They'll be pleased.

Personal letters

- *Use good quality stationery.* (See "Stationery.")
- *A personal letter begins with the salutation, followed by a comma.* Example: "Dear Elma," or for more endearing expression, "My dear Mavis."
- *Use blue or black ink, not pencil.*
- *Print the address on the envelope unless your writing is very easy to read.*
- *Use the same color ink to address the envelope as was used to write the letter.*
- *Typewritten or handwritten?* Technology and busy lifestyles have affected the inviolate rule that personal letters must be handwritten. Etiquette has grudgingly allowed the word processor to intrude. Research with psychological tests, however, has proven that the recipient of a handwritten letter experiences more intense reaction to it than to a typewritten one of exactly the same wording. For some unknown reason some-

thing *more* of one's self seems to be projected in a handwritten letter. Does a little bit of one's soul creep into the scripted pages? *Now* are you motivated to wield a pen?

- *Return address labels are useful if the envelopes are not pre-printed.* Try to match the labels to the color of the stationery. Place them on the envelope squarely and neatly, no natty motifs.

- *Letters to conduct personal business follow the same format as a letter written by a business office.* They must be concise but explanatory and structured in the customary format. (See Business *Signature*)

Closing

- *To close a letter, various terms are used depending upon the degree of intimacy you wish to express.* Example: "Affectionately," "Love," "My best regards," "Your devoted friend," "As always," "Faithfully." Discretion must be used, to not assume closer intimacy than that with which the recipient may feel comfortable. Being too formal is less likely to offend than being inappropriately too intimate.

- *Close a personal business letter with "Sincerely."* The old "Yours truly" is outdated.

- *"Respectfully" may be used to close a letter to someone of very high rank or exalted position.* This term may also be used by an employe to an employer or by a tradesman to a customer.

Signature

- *A legible signature reflects character and polish.* Signatures with flourish that cannot be deciphered are *not* indicative of importance, nor are they more difficult to forge as some people mistakenly believe. A strong, freehand, legible signature, is the trademark of an intelligent and confident person.

- *Establish a constant form for your signature.* Shall it be first name and surname or first two initials and surname, or what? Merrill E. Hubbell or Merrill Hubbell or M.E. Hubbell. Then keep to that form as a general rule. (Signing documents that require your *total* name are the exception.) If your second name is what you answer to, you might sign this way: M. Elmer Hubbell. The form is not important but the constancy is.

- *A woman may have occasion to change her signature due to marriage or divorce,* and that is why a woman in a business career often chooses to continue to use her maiden name which has been established and is recognized as *her* signature. Or, she may choose to *add* her husband's name to her own, Katherine Edwards becomes Katherine Edwards Warren thus keeping her established name in business still recognizable.

- *Signatures and titles:*
  A title is never included with your handwritten signature. Titles such as Mrs., Ms., Esquire, M.D., C.E.O., Professor, etc., are *not* included in your signature. In a business letter a title is typed (or hand printed) with your name beneath your signature:

Sincerely,

Donald R. Wallace,
Chief Executive Officer

or

Sincerely,

Rodney J. Stewart, Esquire

or

Sincerely,

Ivan Chelini, M.D.

Even where only a first name or a nickname is signed on a business letter, the full name and title are printed beneath.

- *A woman has more to consider when using her signature or making reference to her name and title.*
- *In a professional career, if she continues to use her maiden name after marriage, a woman should use the title "Miss" or "Ms." before her name, not "Mrs."* She would sign "Ethel Williams" and on personal (not corporate) business letters she would put in brackets beneath her signature ("Mrs. Richard Jocelyn").
- *A married woman uses "Mrs." only before her husband's name, i.e.: she is "Mrs. Kenneth Newport" or "Hedy Newport" not* "Mrs. Hedy Newport"; that signifies a divorced woman.
- *A married woman sending a letter to a business firm or a stranger, should sign it with her legal name.* If her stationery is marked with her full married name and address, her signature, Gail Neumann, is enough. If the stationery does not include this, a letter written by hand should be signed:

Sincerely,

Gail Neumann
(Mrs. C. Neumann)

and a typewritten letter would be signed:

Gail Neumann

Mrs. Charles Neumann

- *A divorced woman who continues to use the surname of her former husband, would use "Mrs." but would combine it with her own first name, i.e.: Mrs. Hedy Newport. She would sign "Hedy Newport."* A typewritten letter would have her name typed beneath the signature,

Sincerely,

Hedy Newport

Mrs. Hedy Newport

A handwritten personal business letter signed by a divorced woman would be:

Sincerely,

(Mrs.) Hedy Newport

- *A widow continues to use "Mrs." and her husband's first name and surname, e g · Mrs. Wilfred Cryer. She would sign "Olive Cryer" but an envelope to her would be addressed: "Mrs. Wilfred Cryer."*
- *An unmarried woman signs her name without a title, or in a business letter places the title in brackets. A handwritten letter would be signed:*

Sincerely,

(Ms) Darlene Ansley

A typewritten letter would be signed:

Sincerely,

D. Ansley

Miss Darlene Ansley

- *A woman does use her title Mrs., Ms., or Miss, when signing a hotel register or a debit to a charge account.*
- *The title "Ms." (pronounced Mizz) is preferred by some women*

and disliked by others. It is of convenience, however, when you address a woman and you don't know whether she is married or single. The title "Ms." is also an advantage when a woman doesn't want her marital status revealed. It is quite proper for a woman, married or single, to use the title "Ms."

- *When addressing a married couple that the woman has kept her own name, place the names on one line:*

    Mr. Robert Neumann and Ms. Marilyn Thompson

- *When addressing an unmarried couple that live to-gether, place one name beneath the other, with the woman's name placed first:*

    Ms. Ima Freespirit
    Mr. Will B. Single

- *A young boy is addressed as "Master" until mid teens and then later "Mr." is used.*

- *When professional titles are involved, follow these customary rules:*

    - Husband with a professional title, wife without:
        Dr. and Mrs. Lawrence Turner
    - Husband and wife both with professional titles:
        Dr. Lawrence Turner and Dr. Joyce Turner
                or
        The Doctors Lawrence and Joyce Turner
        Senator Leon Rice and Dr. Helen Rice
        Dr. Glen Pritchard and Dr. Mabel Casey
    - Wife with a professional title, husband without:
        Mr. William Leeson and Dr. Muriel Leeson
        Mr. Grant Burns and Dr. Hazel Whitby
                or
        Mr. and Mrs. William Leeson
        Mr. and Mrs. Grant Burns

The envelope

- *The address on the envelope may be written with each line indented a few spaces on the left or as a block with a straight margin on the left.*

Dr. Grace Smith,   Dr. Grace Smith,
15—High Street,   15—High Street,
Hillside, Oregon.   Hillside, Oregon.
Zip Code   Zip Code

- *Use a title or honorific Mr., Mrs., Ms., Miss, Dr., etc., before a person's name on an envelope address.*
- *The address on the envelope of a formal invitation should have no abbreviations (except for Mr. or Mrs.) names, streets, avenues, etc., are written out in full (except for the return address).*
- *Be sure to include the postal or zip codes on the address and return address.*
- *If your writing is not very plain, print!*
- If the letter is handwritten, the envelope should be hand written. If it is typewritten, the envelope should be typewritten.

Stationery

Communicate with quality. Your stationery reflects your polished image. Choose such quality watermarks as: "Classic Laid," "Cambric Writing" or "Strathmore Writing (25% cotton)."

A man's personal stationery
- *Choose white, ivory, cream, or pale gray in color.*
- *Single sheet approximately 7.1/4" x 10.1/2".*
- *The paper is folded in thirds to fit into a matching 7.1/2" x 4" envelope.*

A woman's personal stationery
- *Choose white, ivory, cream, or pale gray in color.*
- *Single sheet approximately 5.3/4" x 7.3/4".*
- *The paper is folded in half to fit into an envelope approximately 4" x 6".*
- *Also: Fold-over notes with matching envelopes.*

Family stationery
Use the same size paper as that shown for a man and have the address or a last initial or the family crest engraved or thermo-

graphed on it. This is by far the most practical way to invest in quality stationery. Women *prefer* to use this size rather than the small, traditional "women's" letter-paper.

Fold-over notes

- *Approximately 3 .3/4" x 5 .3/4" folded .*
- *Choose white, cream, or pale gray in color.* These may have a colored border (not black, that's for mourning) preferably blue or gray, nothing flashy.
- *Fold-over notes may be engraved, embossed, or thermographed with the family crest or monogram in the centre.*
- *Do not write on the top side of fold-over notes that* have been printed, engraved, embossed or thermographed.
- *If the fold-over note is engraved, don't write on the underside of the top page,* the engraving will make an indentation in the paper. This stationery is so handsome it would be a shame to disfigure the appearance of the note by writing on the top side.
- *Fold-over note paper is meant for short notes.* It is ideal for written invitations, thank-you notes, letters of condolence, or brief messages, etc. It is *not* meant for lengthy letters.
- *When a fold-over note is used for an invitation, the message is written on the inside bottom half.*
- *The fold-over note is placed in a matching envelope with the topside facing out.*
- *Fold-over note paper is essential in every properly stocked stationery supply.* With letter stationery and fold-over notes, every need is satisfied.

General guidance on stationery & its use

- *The paper may be plain with no printed letterhead.*
- *It can have a regular edge or a shorn look called a "decel" edge (expensive!).*
- *It may be imprinted with suitable letterhead.* Person's name (no title or honorific), address, postal or zip code (Fig. #48). Or just the name (Fig. #49) or initials (Fig. #50), this is more practical as stationery is too costly to have it become obsolete if there is a change of address. If one has a family crest, it could be used alone in the centre at the top of the sheet (Fig. #51), then no name or address would be added.

- *A letterhead or crest is used only on the first page of a letter. Plain, unprinted "second sheets" should be used for letters longer than one page.*
- *Stationery should never be ruled, oddly shaped, or highly scented.* Elaborate designs are tacky.

Personal stationery letterheads

NEVILLE MALET-VEALE
8—Oak Crescent City,
Zip Code

Fig.#48

Winnifred Mary Sinclair

Fig.#49

D.G.M-V.

Fig.#50

Fig.#51

- *Stationery ideally should be thermographed, engraved, or embossed, not just printed.*
- *The engraving or thermograph ink should be black or dark blue.* Fancy colored ink on fancy colored paper doesn't have the same look of "class."
- *Write on one side of the paper only.* If the paper is of heavy quality and the writing doesn't show through, both sides of "second sheets" may be used.
- *Keep your writing lines straight.* If you find this difficult to do, make a lined guide to slip under the paper to follow as you write.
- *Leave an even margin on each side of the page, at least one half an inch.*
- *Envelopes should be of the same finish and quality as the letter-paper.* Lined envelopes ensure privacy and are especially attractive, but very costly. Envelopes may have the crest or monogram engraved or thermographed on the flap. This done in blue or black ink, with the envelope lined in the same matching color, is very elegant.
- *If envelopes are printed with the return address, they should be printed on the front of the envelope not on the back.* The post office may not return an undelivered letter, if it's printed on the back.
- *Return address labels are not ideal, but acceptable.*

A basic stationery supply should include

- *Letter size paper 8.1/2" x 11".* Printed with address. Used for personal business letters.
- *Plain "second sheets" 8.1/2 " x 11".* To match the above.
- *Letter-paper 7.1/4" x 10.1/2".* Engraved or thermographed with *one person's* name and address, or monogram or crest, *OR* engraved with only the address, or family monogram or crest, to be used by *all* adult members of the family.
- *Plain second sheets 7.1/4" x 10.1/2".* To match the letter-paper above.
- *Fold-over Notes.* Engraved or thermographed for each individual or a general motif that could be used for every member in the family.

- *Envelopes to match the above stationery.* For personal business stationery: 4.1/8″ x 9.1/2″, for personal letter-paper:/7.1/2″ x 4″, for fold-over notes: 4″ x 6″
- *Social or Calling Cards:* Approx. 2″ x 3.1/2″
  Full name, home address, and phone number. Engraved or thermographed in black or blue ink.
  Best if color-matched to personal stationery.
  Socially, "Calling Cards" should be used *not* business cards. See Fig. #52 for examples.

CALLING CARD EXAMPLES:

Decima Malet-Veale
(Mrs. Franklin Neumann)

ADDRESS   **PHONE #**

Westcott Neville Malet-Veale

ADDRESS   **PHONE #**

Fig. #52

Socially, Calling Cards are proper, not business cards.

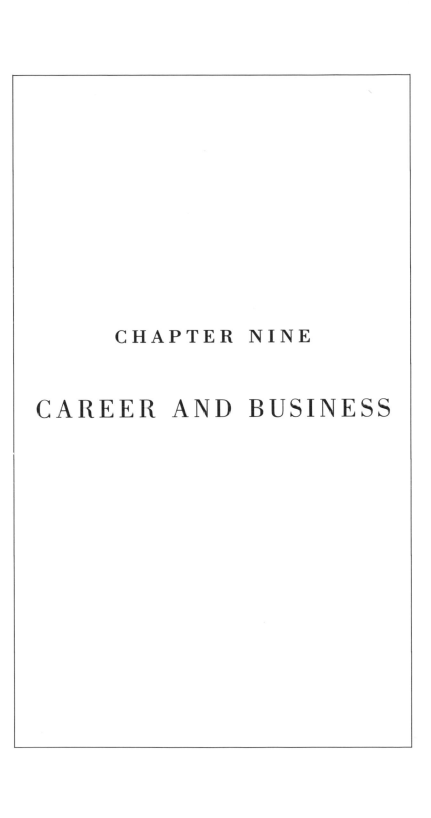

CHAPTER NINE

CAREER AND BUSINESS

CHAPTER NINE

CAREER AND BUSINESS

Investing in Your Career

The best investment in any career is:
To know your work and to look and act successful.
Knowing your work gives you confidence and polishes your performance. Looking successful grooms you for progress. Successful behavior projects a well mannered, refined image.

- ***Read everything possible that pertains to your work or that gives you assistance in self-improvement.*** Books, magazines, editorial material, advertising, consumer and trade publications, all are useful.
- ***Learn from those around you.*** Life is a never-ending learning process. It is called *experience*. Really *listen* to every person that you meet with every day. You'll be surprised at what you can learn from even, what may appear to be, the most insignificant contact.
- ***Be receptive to new ideas and improvements.*** Flexibility is a sure sign of growth potential.
- ***Enroll in educational classes and lectures.*** Increase your academic credentials.
- ***Speak distinctly with correct grammar and enunciation.***
- ***Don't swear, resort to tiresome cliches, or use fillers.*** "You know," "And-Ah," "I mean like."
- ***Be tactful.*** You'll never sell yourself, your product, or your service by putting someone on the defensive or by intimidating them.
- ***Be honest.*** Integrity is your most valuable asset.

A progressive approach to your career

(1) Look the part and you'll be the part.

- *Always dress in a manner that befits the position to which you aspire to be employed.* Too often people are influenced by their co-workers and peers and downgrade their own appearance to be one of the crowd. Progress does not come automatically. You must *look* like management material or an employer will never *see* you as being promotable.
- *Always be well groomed from the top of your head to the tips of your toes.*

(2) Behave the part and you'll be the part.

- *Be conservative in your personal conduct. At all times project an image of reliability and refinement.* Give attention to every facet of your being: your voice, your diction, your grammar, your manners, your public conduct, and your integrity.

How to look the part

Dress for progress

Appropriate apparel for business wear has been covered earlier in this book but here are these major reminders. *Common mistakes that are the most detrimental:*

W O M E N

- *Mini-skirts on the job. You'll never climb the corporate ladder in a mini-skirt.* You'll lose professional credibility.
- *Clothing that is skin-tight. It reveals a lack of refinement and brands you as a bimbo.* Take your career seriously, dress conservatively.
- *Clothing of inappropriate fabrics.* Such fabrics as denim, velvet, satin, lame, brocade, or anything trimmed with lace, sequins, or glitter do not belong in a business environment.
- *Lacy or any patterned hosiery.* These are wrong for business wear.

- *White shoes and/or white handbags.* These don't belong in a classic wardrobe at any time.
- *Strappy shoes or shoes with very high heels.* Flat or medium height heels are more efficient.

M E N

- *A belt tightly cinched in under the stomach.* This error immediately brands a man as a rube! Pants should have a high enough rise to reach your natural waistline, and your belt should be parallel with the floor.

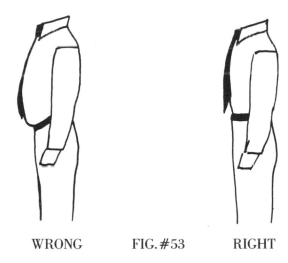

WRONG   FIG.#53   RIGHT

- *Ankle length socks. Socks should be over-the-calf length, of subtle design, and black, navy, or gray in color, never white.*
- *Clothes that are too tight.* These look plebeian, out of shape, and uncomfortable.
- *White shoes with business attire.* White shoes are never worn with business clothes.
- *Wearing casual loafers or shoes of inferior quality.* Tasselled loafers are not appropriate for business.
- *Suits of out-of-season fabrics* (e.g. seersucker, linen). Summer suits are worn only from June 1st to Sept.30th.
- *Short sleeve dress shirts.* Suit jacket sleeves are too short without a shirt cuff showing.
- *Cheap shirts of high polyester blend look extremely tacky.*

General errors in career attire

- *Wearing too much and/or inappropriate jewelry.* Women wearing jangling bracelets or men wearing big, chunky watches are the most common accessory mistakes.
- *Wearing boldly patterned fabrics.* Small checks and subtle, shadow patterns are acceptable.
- *Wearing double breasted suits. They look untidy when open.* Single breasted suits don't go out of fashion and are more businesslike for men or women.
- *Wearing white shirts and blouses of high polyester blend. They become discolored and unsightly after a few washings.* Buy *pure cotton* of a high thread count and *top quality*.
- *Investing in high fashion clothing trends.* Very wide lapels, massive shoulder pads, flashy color, all detract from a distinguished personal image.
- *Wearing shoes with run-down heels.* Check your shoes and have the heel lifts replaced often.
- *Wearing shabby, unpolished, out of shape shoes.* Buy top quality leather shoes and keep them well polished.
- *Wearing belts that are worn or frayed.* Belts are on display front and center, replace worn ones.
- *Wearing inferior quality ties and/or scarfs.* These downgrade an otherwise good quality outfit.
- *Buying quantity instead of quality. Always buy quality.*

The polished executive

A headhunter's idol—How to be one
A successful and progressive executive is always in demand in the employment market. Corporations are constantly alert in their vigilant search for competent management people.

Draw attention in a positive and favorable way.

Two other major factors are of utmost importance in attaining and progressing within a career. They are:

(1) Determine what kind of work you'd like to do and would have a propensity for doing.
- *Learn as much as you can about it and project your aims toward that goal.* You may not be able to break into that field of employment immediately but *every* job gives you beneficial experience. Glean every scrap of learning possible, and you'll find in future how often you draw on *all* past experience.
- *At all times be alert to opportunities that will help you reach your goal.* Develop a network of contacts in that field of work: obtain interviews with employment agencies and personnel directors.
- *In the meantime, concentrate on the benefits of the jobs you must do until you enter your dream career. Project the feeling that you love what you do.* This develops a positive attitude and gives you a highly regarded *positive image.* Being negative, thinking this stop-gap employment is beneath your dignity or capability, sends out negative, detrimental vibes that stifle your progress.

(2) Be aware of the pros and cons of business politics.
- *Learn the chain-of-command. As soon as you are employed by a business, ask for a personnel list. Get to know the duties of each employee,* from the top executives to the members of the general staff. *Become aware, also, of the real chain-of-command. The executive position doesn't always indicate who has the most influence.* The chief executive officer's *secretary,* because of

her expertise and good judgement, is often of profound influence in the business and has direct communication with the boss and administrative staff. Even someone far down on the management scale may have unsuspected but very influential corporate connections. (A relative?)

- *Learn who has influence and credibility. Who hires, who fires, who influences promotions, who is or isn't trustworthy, who must be "handled with care." Don't inadvertently lose valuable support.*
- *Discreetly ask questions, listen, be perceptive, and comment with caution!*

To achieve your goal of a satisfying career

- *At all times project a refined and polished image.*
  In public, dress conservatively and appropriately. No old blue jeans and t-shirts for travel or casual wear. Your appropriate casual wear should show as much quality and refinement as your business dress. You are under scrutiny at *all* times.
  In public, socially or at business, behave with well-bred reserve.
  In a junior position don't feel that you must dress and act with lower standards. If you look junior, you'll *stay* junior. Dress for progress and develop your skills, that way you'll reach your goal.
- *Associate with polite and respectable people.*
  Never let wealth be the measure of a person's worth. Wealth is not an indication of a person's *real* value. Evaluate and choose your friends for their integrity, decency, and enjoyable companionship.
- *Network with people of distinction and class. This will expose you to examples of acceptable behavior.* Also, this association will broaden your intellect and increase your opportunities for progress.
  Associating with coarse, vulgar people brands you as their equal. Your progress will be strictly limited.
- *Be as courteous with your business subordinates as you are with your business peers and superiors.*
  Being considerate of and helpful to those that are in positions junior to yours reflects sterling character. Flaunting superiority

or power in any situation is extremely unprofessional.

Never exhibit a patronizing attitude. That is insulting and alienating. You'll never live it down.

- *When you're starting a new job, don't be too chummy*.

  Be friendly and co-operative but reserved. Beginning a new job is an unnerving and lonely experience, so the first thing we're tempted to do is get very friendly with someone we find receptive. Wait. Get to know that person better. You may find you want someone quite different as a close friend.

- *Without letting it interrupt or interfere with work, get to speak with as many co-workers as possible*. Don't always go to lunch with the same person or group. Establish a number of sources from which to draw job-related information, connections, and beneficial guidance.

- *Don't be a Smart Alec*.

  Never comment about how differently and better something was done where you worked before. Learn the present routine and, if you really *do* know an improved method, find a way to suggest trying it without looking self-important.

- *Be part of the team*. An independent attitude can have adverse consequences, both personal and professional. If you isolate yourself, you'll be left out of informative corporate networking.

- *Develop a realistic sense of humor*.

  Constant jokes and frivolous treatment of serious situations have no place in a business environment but nor does a dour, inflexible, and humorless attitude. Many sensitive feelings can be spared and touchy predicaments avoided by looking at things a little on the lighter side. Laugh *with* a person never *at* a person.

  Learn to laugh at yourself. It's possible to turn an otherwise embarrassing situation into a feather in your cap by seeing the humor in it. You'll never look better than when you can be big enough to laugh when the jokes on you.

  To laugh to-gether is to bond to-gether.

- *Learn to effectively delegate:*

  The more you delegate the more you grow. Projects become more diversified and more thought-provoking with the stimulus of more than one creative mind.

Don't be afraid to share the spotlight. An executive that effectively delegates, enhances his or her own successful performance.

So they can function at full potential, give a free rein to those whom you know are capable, take full advantage of their expertise.

But . . . don't lose control. Always keep in close contact and personally guide a project to its successful conclusion. The buck stops here!

• *Read all your mail, memos, and routed material*.

Have respect for the potential power of information.

Inter-office memos that don't seem important, can come back to haunt you. Pay attention to content.

Even junk mail can get your creative juices flowing. Be open to new ideas and technical developments.

• *Designate some peak energy time for uninterrupted seclusion, to concentrate on major plans and projects*.

• *Don't be too available*. Ask the receptionist to: hold or screen all phone calls, arrange for drop-in visitors to call back, and ask not to be disturbed.

• *Honesty is not the best policy*.

Honesty is the ONLY policy.

Remember this at all times. You should not be expected to lie for anyone, nor ask anyone to lie for you. "Sorry, Mr. Bigboss is not in to-day" when he *is* in, may be an oft committed "little white one" but it's still a lie and you shouldn't be asked to say it. Just say, "Mr. Bigboss is not available."

• *Be prepared to work extra hours when necessary*.

A nine to five mentality will never bring success.

• *Be efficient. Putting in extra hours means nothing if you aren't productive*.

Don't con your boss into thinking you're a dedicated employee by staying late or working overtime. If you're efficient you should seldom need extra hours.

• *Recognize when you do need assistance and ask for it*.

If you find you are having to work too much overtime and you know you are efficient, your work load must be too heavy.

Make a list of your duties and ask for a meeting with your supervisor to determine what could be changed or if an assistant should be hired.

- *At all times balance your lifestyle. Your family and social life should not be jeopardized for your career.*

  A many-faceted lifestyle makes a better developed person. Thinking and dedicating yourself to nothing but the job is actually detrimental to your career.

  Humanitarian involvement with a service club or volunteer program provides worthwhile contribution and will give you profound personal satisfaction. A great way to clear your mind of corporate cobwebs and to help those less fortunate than yourself.

- *Don't only think positive.*

  Sensible negative thinking at times can be helpful. If you *prepare* for adversity you won't be so vulnerable if it should occur.

  With every project and important situation, consider the possible repercussions, objections, or adverse results and be ready with solutions or rebuttal.

- *Invest in a supply of top quality business cards.*

  Keep a supply of cards with you at all times. If the cards supplied by your employer are of inferior quality, *tactfully (very tactfully)* find a way to suggest how influential an impressive business card can be.

- *Don't mix your personal life with business.*

  Carrying your family problems to business is a big mistake. Try to resolve personal problems without involving your boss, peers, or co-workers.

- *Personal intimacy of any kind on the job is absolutely taboo.* Secrets shared or clandestine "love" trysts with co-workers can only result in *potential damage to your career.*

- *Don't complain about your job.*

  Never make the slightest derogatory remark about your duties. Indiscreet comments can reach your boss's ears by way of the grape-vine and cause irreparable friction.

  If you have a complaint, take it directly to your supervisor. Don't discuss it with anyone else.

- *Never go above your supervisor's head.*

That is who you were hired to work for and that is who deserves your loyalty. Important communication of any kind that you have with bosses equal to or senior to your supervisor, should always be shared with your immediate supervisor.

If your supervisor is the problem, ask for a meeting with someone senior but with your supervisor present.

• *Don't sabotage your image with undermining habits.*

Don't speak in an apologetic way.

Wrong: "Would you mind looking at this letter?"

Right: "Please look at this letter."

Don't speak in a tentative way by ending a sentence with a rise in your tone.

Wrong: Stating a fact as though it were a question.

Right: Drop the pitch of your voice at the end of a sentence to give emphasis to the statement.

Women; don't speak with a cute, "little girl" voice. You'll lose all credibility. The most proficient person, with unquestionable capabilities, won't be taken seriously when sounding so immature.

Don't resort to using trendy lingo. If you think using such phrases as "impacting on" and "this scenario" and "let's dimensionalize" give you an impressive vocabulary, they do not, they do quite the reverse. You sound uncultured aping these *tiresome* and often grammatically incorrect words. A plain, easily understood vocabulary is the mark of an intelligent person.

At all times speak in a natural, unaffected manner. Don't let the drama of your performance detract from the substance of your communication.

• *Recognize when you are ready for more responsibility.*

When you want and feel capable of promotion, ask for it. Busy bosses may value your work but take you for granted if you don't bring your potential for advancement to their attention.

If nothing is done to further your career, it may be time to look elsewhere. (See "Changing Jobs.")

• *Don't get overwhelmed with incidentals.*

Make, keep, and faithfully follow a "Master List."

Making a Master List:

Take each piece of paper on your desk and determine what has to be done with it. Then immediately:

(a) Toss it, if it has no value and needs no action.

(b) File it, if it must be kept but needs no action.

(c) Route it, if it needs someone else's attention.

(d) Calendar it, if it has specific date or deadline.

(e) Pile it, if it requires your attention, and then

(f) Master List every item in that pile by priority.

From now on, every piece of paper that crosses your desk will promptly be evaluated by a,b,c,d,e,f.

Cross-reference your calendar (appointment diary). This will provide you with full details of each appointment. Names, times, place of meeting, etc.

On your master list be sure to enter pertinent dates, times, and details in regard to each item listed for attention, and program the item so it gets completed in time for its delivery.

Example:

> *Oct. 15th:*
>
> *Compile sales projection figures for Acme meeting on Oct. 23, 2 p.m., Henry Black*

Before you leave work each day always check your master list and see what is your next priority.

As soon as you get to work the next day, work on and complete that priority.

Check it off your master list as a job well done!

• *Don't procrastinate in regard to extensive or difficult tasks.*

Attack a big project by breaking it down into several manageable parts. These smaller segments will seem less intimidating and more easily handled.

One by one, complete each segment.

Voila! A monstrous project completed without delay, off your master list and off your troubled mind.

Beginning your career as a receptionist

- *You are your employer's goodwill ambassador.* You set the image of the establishment, as the first person the public meets when visiting a business.
- *Your grooming must be impeccable, or the image of the company will be one of having shoddy standards.*
- *Your personality must be outgoing and gracious.* The visiting public will consider the entire company to be friendly and one with which they want to deal.
- *Your rapport with customers must be businesslike and helpful.* Learn as much as you can about the business, so you can adequately answer inquiries. To always refer every inquiry to someone else delays a customer and adversely reflects on your ability.
- *Don't give out unauthorized or incorrect information.* If you aren't sure of what is appropriate to tell, get corporate approval before you provide answers.
- *Be aware of your value to the employer.* When on the job behave in the dignified and refined manner that the position demands. No gum chewing, eating at your desk, slovenly posture, loud or crude talk.
- *Dress conservatively.* Project an image of efficiency and professional good taste. Follow the advice provided in the earlier chapter of this book, "Dress for Progress."
- *Telephone courtesy and efficiency are imperative.* Have the caller repeat their name and telephone number and double check that you've noted it accurately on the message form. If possible, use printed message forms that are bound in a book with carbon paper. These perforated forms are easily handled and the carbon copy remains in the book for future reference. If ever there is a question about someone's message, you'll have proof at hand. This is great support for a receptionist. (See the information on "Telephone Etiquette".)
- *Take all messages accurately and promptly.* The information you relay to individuals can have an important effect on their job performance, so it is imperative that all messages be adequately detailed.

Beginning your career as a secretary

- *A successful secretary is trustworthy and loyal.* Being privy to confidential information, demands total reliability and dedicated, discreet performance.
- *A successful secretary is capable of meticulous organization.* Others depend on your ability to locate files, documents, etc., at a moment's notice.
- *A polished secretary's telephone manners are polite and efficient.* You'll be required to screen calls and protect busy executives from unnecessary and unimportant interruptions. You'll require the ability to determine which calls are vital, and which can be delayed.
- *Telling a caller that the person they want to speak with cannot be interrupted at this time, requires the utmost diplomacy and grace.* A disgruntled caller can create havoc. If all else fails in your endeavor not to interrupt the person being called, see if a senior member of the staff will speak with the caller to support your position. (See "Telephone Etiquette".)
- *A polished secretary and her boss should not call each other by their first names.* This will give you both a more professional and respected image and keep the relationship on a business-like basis.
- *A discreet secretary keeps her personal life private.* Working so closely to-gether, people can become too familiar. Friendly and sincere consideration for your co-workers does not include sharing information of a personal nature. Your position of confidentiality may be at risk.
- *An executive secretary has an excellent opportunity to learn the operation of a business.* Contact with corporate intricacies teaches management skills and equips a perceptive secretary for career advancement. If you aspire to moving into a management position, the experience you gain as an executive secretary or administrative assistant will be of valuable contribution to a variety of choices: marketing, sales, advertising, personnel, or almost any facet of the corporation. If your long-range desire is to operate your own private business, this is a direct and viable path.

Choosing a career in sales

Nothing happens until a sale is made.

No marriage would take place without a person being sold on the merits of a mate.

No product or service would be accepted without selling someone on its benefits.

No book would be printed without selling a publisher on its potential worth.

Every successful business, every successful corporation, and every successful individual, relies on sales.

Nothing happens until a sale is made
but first you must sell yourself to yourself!

The successful sale of a *Product* depends on:

Product Packaging
Product Quality
Product Performance
Product Durability

You are the product. *Your Confidence gets the Attention. Your Apparel and Grooming determine the Packaging. Your Integrity and Refinement determine the Quality. Your Education and Experience determine the Performance. Your Flexibility and Dedication determine Durability.*

Your career as a sales representative

- *Always make an appointment for your sales call.* Dropping in is disruptive to business.
- *Make your sales calls when it is most convenient for your customer.* You want their full attention.
- *Don't take the prime parking space of the business on which you are calling.* To park in front of a store or business, depriving their customers of easy parking, will have the proprietor annoyed with you before you even enter the store. Park farther away.

- *Don't interrupt if another sales representative is with the buyer, even if it is at your appointed time.*
- *Don't put your briefcase or sample bag up on a table or counter.* Disrupting counter displays or impeding customer service makes you an unwelcome intruder.
- *Be well prepared, with your sales brochures and product samples organized and in perfect condition.*
- *Be brief and to the point.* Don't loiter.
- *Don't make promises, unless you're certain you and your employer can follow through and keep them.*
- *Never make derogatory remarks about your employer, your customers, or competitors.* This casts adverse reflections on yourself and damages your credibility.
- *Don't try to win favor with flirting or false charm.*
- *Be formal and conservative and you be won't be wrong.*

Beginning your career as a salesclerk

- *Smile! So few salespeople remember to smile.* Make your customer feel welcome and appreciated.
- *Don't rush to a customer the moment they enter the store or your department.* Greet them with a smile and a sincere "Hello" but *give them time to look around.* Customers are uncomfortable and overwhelmed with a salesclerk that constantly hovers over them.
- *Don't say "May I help you?"* The answer will almost certainly be "No" and you've lost an opportunity to inspire a sale. After a customer has had a *short time* to look around, find some reason to get into conversation with her. For instance, if she is looking at slacks, "Have you seen the latest style slacks with a stirrup leg?" or in the dress department, "These dresses in the new geometric prints have just arrived. Aren't they gorgeous?" Then be more direct and ask if there is something in particular for which she is looking; then help her find it.
- *When a customer is obviously waiting for service, serve him/her promptly.* Don't finish your chat with a co-worker or go on with your book work. That is unprofessional and unproductive.

- *Never inform a customer you can't wait on them because it is time for your coffee break*. Either delay your break or get another salesclerk; never mention a coffee or mealtime break.
- *Do not leave a customer to serve another, this is very rude*. If the customer you are serving is taking time to consider her purchase, you may ask her permission to wait on someone else, excuse yourself, wait on *one* other customer and *get right back* to the customer you were initially serving.
- *Don't contradict a customer's comments. You do not know the customer's expertise*. A cosmetician telling a customer she is wrong about certain skin care would look like a fool if that customer is a dermatologist!
- *Never intimidate a customer*. Being aloof or arrogant does not impress a customer with your importance or intelligence, it only alienates them.
- *Don't make immediate assumptions*. Evaluating a customer's socio-economic position by appearance only, is often a mistake. A poorly dressed person may spend all his disposable income on his prime interest. Those super-expensive cameras you sell, might be just what he's going to buy. Be polite and helpful to *all*.
- *Know your product*. A knowledgeable sales pitch will increase sales and win you loyal customers.
- *Be loyal to your employer*. Don't make detrimental comments about the company that employs you.
- *Never make unfavorable comments in reference to your competition or their products*. Even true statements comparing quality may sound biased. Point out any superior features that you know your own product has by asking questions: "Does the other product have this heat control thermostat?" Help the customer make her own comparisons by knowing your merchandise.
- *Be polite when the customer does not buy*. You may be profoundly disappointed and even anxious if your store desperately needs sales, but control yourself and be *especially gracious*, so the customer will feel she wants to return and do business with you.
- *It isn't necessary to be subservient to be polite*. If a customer is

rude, try to determine the cause and then offer a solution or a credible explanation.

- *Never get into an argument with a customer.* Politely refer them to a supervisor or manager.
- *Serve with dignity and you'll earn respect. It's the PERSON that gives an occupation its image.*

Changing jobs

That blessing in disguise!
There are two basic reasons for leaving a job:

(1) Voluntary
- *Leaving for a better career opportunity:* a promotion; higher salary; a larger company.
- *Leaving for personal reasons:* moving away; having a baby; personality clash.

(2) Involuntary:
- *Leaving due to changes in the company:* merge or takeover; bankruptcy; phase out of job.
- *Leaving because you're asked to resign: Fired!*

What ever the reason, you'll survive, actually thrive, if you regard the situation as a challenge not a calamity.

It no longer is considered desirable to stay in one job for a lifetime. Employers now recognize the importance and significant advantage of hiring a person with a wide variety of experience. You can't say you have 15 years of experience, if you have been in the same job for 15 years. You actually have *one* year's experience 15 times! To a potential employer that is an indication of limited ability to be promoted, or a lack of ambition. Neither of these traits have merit when an employer is considering a job applicant.

The message, therefore is: Don't be afraid to change jobs, but do it with good reason. Also, before you change, be sure to consider the following:

- **The best way to seek a new job is from an employed position.** *Employers are very reluctant to hire an unemployed person. An unemployed person is viewed as*

  (a) irresponsible for leaving a job before finding another, or

  (b) available because no other employer wants him.

  (The exceptions to this are: students; women returning to the work force after having children; people that relocate geographically and/or professionally due to a corporate merge, takeover, or phase-out of position.)

- *If possible, stay at least 18 months in a position. Less than that does not provide sufficient experience in the position to be impressive on your resume. Also, after that long you may find you don't want to leave!* It takes time to develop working rapport. A boss that may initially seem impossible can prove to be a very fair and considerate helpmate. Work that seems too mundane or too difficult, can become very enjoyable after mastering the procedures. *Don't make a snap decision to leave before you give the job a chance.*

- *An important consideration before you change jobs is to evaluate your present company pension plan and to compare it with the pension plan of the prospective employer. Plans can differ extensively and generate a difference of many thousands of dollars.*

- *Don't be blinded by an offer of a substantial increase in salary. Determine and compare the benefit programs offered.* Is there profit sharing? Would it be equal to your present profit sharing income? What medical and dental coverage is included? Consider future security. Is it a well-established company? Look at every aspect of income: bonuses, benefits, and future security. What are the self-satisfying benefits?

Job search

While you're still employed

- *If the situation is such that your employer would support you in your endeavor to change jobs, then it is all right to let your supervisor know of your intention to leave.* Some managers are broadminded enough not to hinder an employee's desire to move on to opportunities that aren't available where they are at present. Much as they hate to lose a productive and valued employee, they recognize the person's wise judgement to leave. They'll help. Knowing that you will still give your full ability to your job, they'll allow you reasonable time before termination while you search for another position. Bless them!

- *If the situation is such that your present employer would not greet your resignation kindly, or if the association with that company has been less than ideal and they'd not give you support in your search for another job, you'll have to wait to give your notice that you're leaving. Your job search will have to be conducted secretively.*

- *After you find another job, you will give adequate notice to your present employer of your plan to leave.* You can't risk losing your job before you have another one to go to.

- *When you have interviews with prospective employers, request complete confidentiality.* Explain why you do not want your employer informed of your job search, and your request will be honored. When it comes down to the wire and you are a candidate for a position, you may then have to give permission for them to contact your present employer. *Be sure you tell your employer before anyone else does.*

- *Enroll with caution with employment placement agencies.* Many use computer networks that broadcast widely. If your qualifications are unique and may be recognized or an agency does not exercise care, word of your search could reach the ears of your employer. Deal with only one or two *reputable* placement firms. Ask for a personal interview. Never mail your resume. If in the interview you find the firm does not appeal to you, *do not leave your resume or allow them to copy it,* go elsewhere.

When you've been fired.

First you'll feel like hiding and never facing the world again. There is nothing so soul shattering as being told you aren't wanted any more. Particularly if you know you didn't deserve to be terminated. *Control your anger.* Chalk it up to experience and realize that the higher you climb that shaky corporate ladder the more vulnerable you are, by fair means or foul, to getting fired some day.

Whether because of a corporate merge or take-over or because of economic conditions or because of that prevalent old reason: personality conflict, *every employee should plan and save for a period of unemployment.*

But first:

- *Recognize the warning signals, avoid the inevitable.*
- *Firings don't often occur as a flash decision.* There is usually either stated or implied warning that things are not going well.
- *If the problems cannot be resolved and your work environment is obviously deteriorating, do every-thing possible to leave before your inevitable firing takes place. Concede a no-win situation.*
- *Leave before you're asked to leave. The advantages are numerous. The employer will be relieved that there won't be the ill-will and upheaval that a firing creates.* Employers do not want a reputation of poor staff relations. You'll get better support having spared the company further unpleasantness. *Your own record with that company will be more favorable than a confrontation would reflect.* Leaving before adverse notations accumulate on your personal file means a less blemished work history. *Your job search from an employed position will be much easier and more positive. Your resume won't be handicapped with a firing.*

If there are no warning signals:
- *In a sudden, emotional confrontation, the blast "You're fired!" can be voiced impetuously, to the detriment of all concerned.* In such a situation, immediately ask to be excused from the meeting, so you aren't tempted to retaliate. Quietly state you'll wait in your office for further instruction when tempers are more rational. *Retain your dignity.*
- *Control your anger. You'll forever regret any harsh words or*

display of temper. Do everything possible to say nothing until your emotions are in check. It is best to condition yourself, prepare for a graceful exit and avoid the inevitable firing. In a later meeting, perhaps problems can be resolved, but the desirability of that is questionable. *It's probably time to negotiate a sensible parting of the ways.* Even if you're in the right, *you* are not in the position of power, pull in your horns and think only of your future career, of protecting your polished image, and of keeping some semblance of respect in the relationship. Leaving a job with animosity is destructive. *Never threaten to sue!*

- *Analyze the reasons for the termination. Without bias, face the facts.* If it's a lack of ability to handle the job or any reason that *you could not help,* your employer should not treat you with disgrace. *You should leave with your reputation intact.*

- *You should request and get support in relocating.* Too often, employees are overwhelmed with a feeling of shame, and they slink away without the assistance and adequate severance package they deserve. *Hold up your head, keep your self-esteem. Negotiate!*

Job search

IN GENERAL

- *Ask for letters of reference. Favorable letters of reference will be of great assistance in getting relocated.* If you've been fired, getting a supportive missive may be remote, but ask.

- *Nurture an agreeable relationship with your present employer.* This puts you in an advantageous light with prospective employers in the future.

- *Keep all doors open.* Don't have the attitude that you are leaving and you no longer have to care how you treat your job or co-workers. It's a small world, you never know who will appear on your "job scene" later, perhaps in a position of power. Always being polite means never having to mend fences.

- *Be sure you have an up-to-date and polished resume. Do it yourself.* Having some help with organizing the format of a resume is fine, but a resume must reflect *your own* way of expressing yourself. (See the information on *"Resumés."*)

- *Always submit a carefully composed cover letter. Every resumé requires an effective cover letter.* (See the information on *"Cover Letters."*)

- *Don't abuse or exploit business contacts.* Never inquire about employment with the clients or business associates of your present employer when they are in your place of employment. You will make them feel uncomfortable and you'll damage your image. They'll probably feel obligated to tell your boss that you approached them and are actively seeking a change of employment. *Your employer should never get that information from anyone but you.*

- *Remember those powerful business politics.* Your talents would have to be exceptional and of unique benefit to a company, for them to cross the ethical line of hiring an employee away from a business *ally.*

- *Applying for a job with competitors of your present employer also requires astute attention.* News travels rapidly along the business grapevine. The competition latches on to every bit of news of who's hired/who's fired/who's re-locating/who's a gem/who's a dud; they are acutely aware of it all. Proceed gingerly when exploring the competition for a possible job opportunity. *If they don't hire you, you won't want them to have all your credentials on their files. Discreetly ask pertinent questions and "feel your way" before making a formal application.*

Make your job search an organized, in-depth project. Seventy-five to eighty-five percent of job openings never reach the attention of the general public.

These job vacancies are not advertised or listed with employment agencies. They are filled by promotion of people on their present staff (which creates a job opening further down the line) *or these positions are filled by the company's personal contacts...*

that could be you!

Make those valuable company contacts. Here's how:

- *Take the yellow pages of the phone directory and list the names of companies that may require your skills.*

- *Then, try to get the names of the people in senior management positions. Check appropriate directories. Your public library is a good source.* They have the names of most companies and of their senior personnel listed in trade and professional directories. Knowing and stating the names of the people to whom you wish to speak or to whom you direct cover letters and resumés, makes a positive and effective impression.
- *Wherever possible, deliver your resumé in person and do not just drop it off at the reception desk.* Try to make an appointment with the person who does the hiring for the particular position or type of work you seek. (It isn't easy, I know. As an Executive Recruiter, I've had to discourage drop-ins myself. I wouldn't have had time for other work if I saw every job seeker on an impromptu basis.)

Here's a way to do it:
Looking your very best, call on the company in which you are interested and, if you can't get to the department head you want to see, *ask to speak with his/her secretary.* A private secretary carries a lot of influence. Your impressive appearance and your gracious personality may convince her to see that your resumé gets priority attention. Sometimes an amiable receptionist can do the same. *The point is, don't mail or just drop off your resumé. . . . make a favorable and positive impact, so you'll be remembered and called in for an interview. After two or three days, phone and ask if your resumé has been reviewed and request an appointment. Without being a nuisance, don't let them forget you.*

- *If you find it difficult to get past a receptionist or secretary to contact a prospective employer, make your phone call prior to the regular office hours.* Bosses are at their desks early, catch one before a "screener" is there to intercept your call.

Be brief and formal. A chummy "Hi, how're ya doin'?" will block your contact immediately.
First determine who has answered your call: "Good morning. May I speak with Mr. Clayton, your V.P. of Marketing?" If

that is who is on the line, continue with your message. If not, then still *state the purpose of your call:*

"I'm endeavoring to get information in regard to possible employment. My name is, Jane Doe. I have 4 years management experience in marketing and I am planning to relocate. I'm sure my qualifications would be of interest to your company. When could you see me for an information interview?"

You'll get one of several possible responses:

"Sorry, you'll have to call later during regular office hours." Reply: "Thank-you, I'll do that."

"We're not hiring right now." Reply: "Is it possible to have an interview, so you'll have my credentials on file to be considered for a future job opening?"

"What did you say your name is? How about 11 a.m., Tuesday?"

- *Persevere with discretion. Many job-search consultants will advise you to call businesses and persist in getting an interview. That might sound like positive direction, it isn't. Businesses get hundreds of phone calls requesting interviews. It is ludicrous to believe they could see them all.* The person who keeps persisting when told there are no openings is annoying and wastes a company's time. I must stress again, and again, that *the best approach is to deliver your resumé in person and if you look professional, someone will almost always take time to speak with you,* possibly arrange an interview, and very probably flag your resumé to give it priority attention when there's a job opening.
- *Always try to contact the person who directly manages the job in which you are interested.* Going *above* that person's head and approaching someone in a more senior position is not the advantage you might expect it to be. Managers like to find their own personnel, having someone thrust upon them may cause objection.
- *At all times, conduct your job search with business-like decorum.* Put yourself in the shoes of the prospective employer, what would *you* respect and find of value in a job applicant? Concentrate on that.

Sources of job leads

Classified ads in newspapers:

- *Ads that state the company name are the most reliable.* This enables you to do some research on the company to determine its function, location, number of personnel, length of establishment, and names of senior executives. Your application can then be directed to the right person *by name* and your *cover letter* will reflect your initiative in learning something about the company to which you are applying. This enhances your application.

- *Ads that don't state the company name and give only a box number to which to reply, are questionable.* They do this for a variety of reasons: They may not want their employees to know they are hiring. (This could be indicative of a staff problem and you'd rather not become involved.) They may not want their competition to know they are hiring. (That's a valid reason.) They often do not even have a job opening, they are simply accumulating resumés for future vacancies, *or* they want to determine who is available before they disclose their own identity. The biggest danger of all in applying to a box number is that it might be your present employer that is advertising. . . . *Ooops!* . . . or it may be a company with which you wouldn't want to associate. *Be warned.* Applying to a box number can have its drawbacks. You'd be revealing your credentials and the name of your present employer to an unknown factor and that could create serious repercussions. Also, you may never know *who* rejected your application!

- *An ad that states "Entry level opportunity" means exactly that.* If you are over-qualified, don't apply. Businesses have many reasons for being very reluctant to hire a person over-qualified for the job. An effective *cover letter might* get you an interview, but you'll have to persuasively state plausible reasons for your interest in the job.

- *An ad that states a specific job profile will be seeking applicants with relative expertise.* If your experience is in quite another field, don't apply *unless* you can submit a convincing *cover letter* that shows where your past experience can be of benefit, *and* you can give a credible explanation of why you are interested in the advertised position.

- *Read the ad carefully, then read it over again.* Compose your application as proficiently as possible, paying close attention to the points the employer is stating in the ad. Effectively relate those requirements to your qualifications. Stick to the subject and address the pertinent data.
- *Tailor your resumé to emphasize the details of your past employment experience that equip you for that particular job.* This is of utmost importance. (See *"Resumés,"* never send a *"fits-all"* resumé.)
- *Cut out a copy of the ad and attach it to your own copy of your cover letter.* Keep a file of all job applications with notations of interviews, etc.

Ads in trade magazines and publications:
- *Reply to ads in trade publications in the same way as to newspaper classified ads.* These are usually for more senior positions.
- *Subscribe to trade publications pertinent to the trade, profession, or industry in which you are at present (or aspire to be) employed.* This will keep you alert to trends and all aspects of your career. Check your public library, to select publications.

Utilize the media:
- *Business coverage in the newspapers is a lucrative source of potential job openings.* Information about business expansions, new businesses being started, personnel transfers and/or promotions, all may be opportunities for the alert job-searcher. Do some research, be first to apply.
- *News of mergers and acquisitions also keep you on your toes if it is your own employer involved. Often, due to the sensitivity of the procedure, the employees are the last to know.* Recognize the writing on the wall and be ready to relocate or to prepare to negotiate for a position with the new management. Forewarned is forearmed.

Membership in a trade or professional association:
- *A real advantage to all facets of your career is to belong to a club or association comprised of members in your particular oc-*

cupation. Networking with your peers provides many benefits, including assistance in *job placement. Join!* You'll enjoy the camaraderie and you'll receive bulletins, news letters, magazines, and other material that will keep you well-informed about the industry.

Professional conventions, trade and consumer shows:
- *Attendance at trade shows and conventions provides valuable contacts.* Even if you're out of a job, keep up your membership and *invest* in the expense of travel and accommodation to attend these events. Have business cards and copies of your resumé with you and get them into the hands of people who can aid in your job search. These people come into contact with a variety of businesses and are a lucrative source of inside information.

Employment agencies:
- *The support and excellent contacts that are possible through an employment agency are superb.* Choose an agency carefully and you'll find you'll get quick interviews and immediate responses, real time savers.
- *First you should be aware that you may have to pay a fee but you are under no obligation until they find you a position that you accept.* You can be sure they are going to work diligently for your sake and for their profit.
- *In Canada it is against the law to charge a person a fee for finding them a job.* The agency charges the employer a fee, usually 20% percent of the first year's salary.
- *A high percentage of companies use employment agencies for all their job placements. The job then is not advertised by the employer directly. The agency does all the advertising and handles the interviews.* You can see how important the agency can be to the person in search of a job.
- *When a company engages an employment agency to fill a job vacancy, that is called a "job order." The person looking for a job is called a "candidate."* A capable agency knows his client company very well and has unique expertise in filling the job order with a suitable candidate. This means the groundwork

has been done, and if you're chosen for the position you probably will fit in very well and enjoy your new employment.

- *A reputable agency will protect your identity* but you'll know the name of the prospective employer before agreeing to apply for the job.

- *An agency can point out weak or strong points in your resumé and advise you how to state them to advantage.* Though, I don't recommend having anyone write your resumé for you, I do encourage you to follow expert advice in composing it effectively. Following the information in this book, "Putting on the Polish," will be all an effective resumé requires.

- *A qualified agency can give you suggestions on how to improve your appearance for a job interview.* Take a look at the interviewer, does his or her appearance strike you as being professional? If so, then rely on their guidance and don't feel embarrassed if they are perfectly candid. They are trying to get you a job!

- *Well-established agencies use computer networks that provide the job searcher with very extensive coverage of the job market and possible opportunities.* If you are planning to geographically relocate, registering with an agency with nationwide contacts is a great help.

- *When you register with an agency, your application is kept on file and reviewed frequently for appropriate job openings.* You only need to register once and the agency will keep your file active until they place you in a job or you inform them you are employed.

- *An important advantage of working through an agency is that you can ask all the questions you want about the prospective employer without the fear of being too blunt.* The agency will answer your inquiries and act as the mediator in settling such negotiations as your starting wage, etc.

- *Remember: The agency is not there to find you a job. They are working for their client to fill a staff vacancy.* They owe you nothing. On the other hand, they must have high caliber candidates or they'd be out of business. *The applicant with appropriate credentials and personal polish is their only source of revenue and vital to an agency's success.*

- *Great as a reputable agency can prove to be, here are some hazards of which to be aware:*
  - Unlawfully, some companies use employment agencies to screen people for reasons that are actually discriminatory: racial reasons, reasons of age (too old?), reasons of sex (they want a man not a woman). When you *apply in person* and present a polished image, you can often convince an employer to change their discriminatory attitude.
  - *There are many unqualified and incompetent agencies in the job-placement market.* It is not a business that requires certified personnel. Anyone can set up a job-placement and resumé writing service. *Be very sure you check their reliability and expertise before you register.* Contact the personnel manager of a large company and ask him/her to recommend an agency (or agencies). Your resumé contains private information, don't pass it around indiscreetly.

The Headhunter and you

There are two types of recruiters or "headhunters":
Retainer and Contingency.

On a retainer basis:
- *A company pays for a recruiter's expertise on a retainer basis, whether or not the candidate they provide is hired.*
- Usually this type of recruiting is done by the same firm that the company retains as their accountants.
- These jobs are generally in the senior management bracket in the $75,000 and up salary range.
- One person is assigned to "head hunt" the desired candidate.
- If your credentials reflect senior level business experience, registering with this type of search firm is of substantial benefit. Most transactions with a retainer firm will be of superior quality. If they consider your experience appropriate for the

class of client they represent, the assistance they provide in grooming you for job opportunities will be the epitome of support in your search.

On a contingency basis:
- *A company pays for a recruiter's effort and expertise, only when a candidate they present is actually hired.*
- A recruiting firm operating on a contingency basis must work very hard to *get the job order* from a company in the first place. A reliable search firm will concentrate *their full attention* on finding the ideal candidate for the position.
- Working on a contingency basis, no placement/no pay, their profits and reputation depend *solely* on the placement of highly competent personnel. They must establish a track record of outstanding performance to ensure getting future job orders.
- There are, unfortunately, recruiting firms that think only of the immediate dollar and, known in the trade as "body shops", they conduct their business in a much less professional manner. They gather resumés and, without effective screening, indiscriminately market your credentials just anywhere. *Beware* of this type of recruiter, you'll recognize it by the set-up of its reception area. If it has a number of small booths (each with that ever present pen on a chain!) it probably is a "body shop." This is not a good place for the polished and progressive job candidate. I repeat: Deal only with reputable recruiting firms.

When a head hunter calls you:
- *They'll probably say something along this line:* "I'm with an executive search company and I'm looking for someone for the position of senior vice-president of retail operations. This position is with a high-profile corporation and offers compensation at a very attractive level. Since this is your field of expertise, I thought you might know of a qualified candidate." Primarily, it's *you* they have their sights on but the wise recruiter proceeds prudently.
- *You must be just as prudent.* You might be very keen on knowing more. There are few people that are not pleased with over-

tures from a reputable search firm, either for ego-stroking or career advancement reasons. Be very polite to the recruiter but *don't comment* about the inquiry. *Tell the caller you would be pleased to help but that you will have to take their phone number and call back later. This serves several purposes:*

(a) You get the phone number, the caller's name, and the name of the search firm and you can check to be certain it is a reliable company and a legitimate inquiry. The situation is sensitive!

(b) You get time to consider your response. If you are not interested in relocating but could submit the name of someone with appropriate credentials, you'll have time to contact that person and ask if they would agree to having you suggest their name.

(c) If you are interested in the position yourself, you'll have time to plan your strategy of getting more information about the prospective employer before indicating that you'd like a personal interview

(d) If the call is from a search firm that acts on a retainer basis representing a major clientele, you can consider yourself honored. They have been *retained* because of their professional ability. They wouldn't contact you without good reason.

- *Arrange to meet with the recruiter at the search firm's office or at a place that would give total privacy.* The corporate grapevine has big eyes and big ears. If you're important enough to be pursued by a headhunter, you're important enough to be grist for the rumor mill. To even be *seen* with a headhunter can nurture suspicion and jeopardize your present employment. *Be discreet.*

- *In the interview, get a detailed description of the job's responsibilities,* the compensation package, and the prospective employer's total profile.

- If the recruiter decides you're a leading contender for the position, you'll be subjected to further intensive scrutiny. You'll probably be taken out to lunch and/or dinner. If you are married, your spouse will be invited also. *The table manners and social conduct of each of you will be evaluated. Corporations are very image conscious. They want their employees, particularly those at an executive level, to reflect the corporate propriety.* Even entry level employees are evaluated for their polish, to ensure that they would be suitable for eventual promotion.

Many candidates lose career opportunities due to their lack of polish. *Study every part of this book, "Putting on the Polish," and equip yourself for progress.*

- *To be in demand:*
Develop superior ability in your chosen career.
Elevate your profile: write pieces for industry publications, be a guest speaker, serve on the board of a community charity, be honorable!

A polished and effective resumé

Never have anyone else do your resumé for you.

With many years experience as an Executive Recruiter (headhunter) and as a Personnel Manager, I can assure you that having someone else, even the most qualified person, compose your resumé for you is *not* the best thing to do.

A resumé is a profile not only of your education and your employment history, it also reflects:

> your ability to spell and use effective vocabulary
> your ability to pay attention to detail
> your ability to sell your qualifications
> your ability to focus on the position's requirements
> your ability to be concise and descriptive
> your ability to be neat and organized

and most important of all,

> *your confidence in your ability to write your own resumé!*

No "custom made" resumé, not even the most glossy one, will be as impressive as a resumé you do for yourself.

Why?

Here are several reasons why

- *Personnel Managers and prospective employers receive hundreds of resumés, so they must scan them quickly to determine if they are interested in the applicant. Custom-made resumés, those composed for you by a resumé writing service, are easily recognized.* We call them "Wall Street Wonders" and we are inclined to distrust their oft times exaggerated terminology.

- *Custom-made resumés, those produced for you by a resumé service, or resumés composed for you by a friend, use style and terminology that may be quite out of character for you. The resumé sounds one way and you actually speak quite another. It is like sending an imposter to represent you.* If you *do* get as far as being granted an interview, you may not be able to deliver the *intellectual presence* the resumé has so glowingly portrayed. The details of your experience may be correct but may be overstated in the commercial resumé service's endeavor to justify their fee. Often that fee will be exorbitant and the resumé of questionable value.

- *One form of a resumé cannot effectively represent you to a variety of employers. Each application for employment should have a resumé emphasizing your qualifications that fit the requirements for that particular job.* Having a number of copies of a custom-made resumé does not give you the necessary flexibility to *highlight* those certain aspects. For ultimate effectiveness, each position for which you apply must have a resumé specifically "tailored" and directed to that position.

- *One page is usually enough for a resumé and no resumé should be longer than two pages.* Employers spend about 15 seconds scanning a resumé to see if they are interested in the credentials. Unnecessary details cloud the issue and indicate lack of business proficiency.

- *Use good quality, plain white, letter-size paper.*

- *The layout of your resumé should be neat and orderly with at least an inch margin around all sides.*

- *A resumé should be typewritten unless the ad requests it be handwritten.* Some companies rely on handwriting analysis in screening applicants for a job.

- *Proofread your resumé over and over again.* Errors in spelling or typing are indicative of careless or shoddy performance and could disqualify you.

- *Avoid gimmicks and fancy presentations.*

- *Be specific. A resumé should include:*
  Your name, address, postal code, and phone number.

Your education including career related courses.
Your experience and employment history
Any miscellaneous information: languages spoken, military service, special skills, published material, academic or community awards.
- *Use one of the following two formats:*

Chronological format

This is the most frequently followed resumé format. It is the easiest for the prospective employer to read and the simplest for the applicant to compose. This format lists experience chronologically, beginning with your most recent job first. Dates of employment are placed in the left margin, then the name of the place of employment, then your position and title, then a summary of your *accomplishments* in that job. *If your work history is uninterrupted and shows steady progress this format is sure to be impressive.*

Functional format

A functional format uses headings to list, describe and/or explain your skills and qualifications. The *functional* format should be followed when a *chronological* format is not appropriate.

Under the following circumstances a chronological format should not be used. It will accentuate less favorable or weak points in your job application:

(a) If you have changed jobs frequently. A *functional* format won't accent instability.

(b) If your work history is sketchy. A *functional* format won't accent unreliability.

(c) If you have very limited employment experience. A *functional* format would effectively list related off-the-job experience.

(d) If you have extensive and varied experience. Headings in a *functional* format draw favorable attention and interest to qualifications.

(e) If you are applying for a major career change. A *functional* format provides more flexibility to correlate past experience with that which will be required in the desired new career.

The functional resumé does not change your work record, it presents it in a different way to draw attention to **what** *work you did, rather than* **how long** *you did it.*

Example of resumé using chronological format

RESUMÉ OF

BRAEDEN CUNNINGHAM
4360—Bonner Blvd.
Pittsburgh, Pa. 10962
Ph: (922) 555-0000

OBJECTIVE: A responsible position utilizing my experience in *retail operations* management, with opportunity for advancement to senior executive level.

EDUCATION: *U.C.L.A., Los Angeles, Cal.*
Master of Business Administration Degree 1981
Personnel Selection & Training Course 1984

EMPLOYMENT
HISTORY: *1984-90 Healthwise Drug Marts, Seattle, Wash.*
Retail Operations Ass't (H.O. 162 retail stores)
Established improved budget projections.
Set and *achieved* increased sales projections.
Designed and established cosmetics departments
  – cosmetics sales became 14% of total sales.
Initiated supplier volume-rebates & commissions
  – this increased stores' cosmetics revenue 11%.

1981-1984 Acme Distributors, Portland, Oregon
Merchandise Manager (H.O. 18 retails stores)
Improved stores' layouts—enhanced company image.
Developed effective staff training programs.
Increased profit margin by balanced inventories.

PERSONAL: Board Member, Children's Hospital
Pres. Sales & Marketing Executives Ass'n.

REFERENCES: On hand. Highly favorable. Provided on request.

Example of functional format resumé: (beginners)

RESUMÉ OF	Carmel Mallory, 32 Pricey Street, Tomahawk, B.C. V2P 4Z9 Phone: 000-0000 or 000-0000 S.I.N. 000-000-000

MARKETING TRAINEE

OBJECTIVE: Seeking entry level position which provides on-the-job training, with an opportunity for advancement in the areas of marketing, research, or advertising promotion.

EDUCATION: High School Certificate (Honors)
British Columbia Institute of Technology,
Vancouver, B.C. Graduated April, 1992
"Introduction to Marketing" Certificate

**SCHOOL
ACTIVITIES:**   Editor, School Newsletter, "Class Acts"
Vice-Pres., Sales & Marketing Club

**WORK
EXPERIENCE:**   Part-time sales clerk 1987-88 (Top sales award)
Summers 1986-92 Lifeguard instructor (Certified)

LANGUAGES: Fluent in English and French, learning Japanese.

PERSONAL: Willing to relocate, prefer Canada or U.S.A.
Immediate availability.

Example of functional format resumé (career change)

R E S U M E

OF

GWENDOLYN NORMAN
4—Gaylord Place
Toronto, Ont. T4R 6N1
PH: (416) 555-0000

OBJECTIVE: To obtain a position in advertising and sales promotion, leading to senior management level.

EDUCATION: *Carlton University, Ottawa, Ont.*
Journalism degree 1974
McMaster University, Hamilton, Ont.
Creative Writing Certificate 1972

COMMUNICATION SKILLS
- Wrote in-depth reports directed to management, evaluating the financial stability and growth potential of target companies industry-wide.
- Developed program outlines for industrial television videotapes.
- Designed & published a company magazine.

ADMINISTRATIVE SKILLS
- Supervised a staff of 12, meeting essential deadlines with efficient, congenial, teamwork.
- Negotiated lucrative client contracts.
- 6 years editorial & public relations experience.

EXPERIENCE: September, 1978   Public Relations Assistant,
to   Hubbell, Stuart & Parr, Inc.
October, 1982   1220 Mayfair Place, Montreal
November, 1982   Sales Promotion Director,
to   Worldly Transportation Assn.
Present   32 Commercial Drive, Toronto

To write an effective resumé

- *Emphasize your achievements not only your duties.* In what way did your performance in the job achieve beneficial results for your employer?
- *The person scanning your resumé wants to determine what you can do for an employer,* such information as:

> *Increased* sales volumes 32%.
>
> *Designed* more efficient product packaging.
>
> *Implemented* cost effective marketing plans.
>
> *Established* additional client accounts.
>
> *Negotiated* favorable labor contracts.

Use compelling words that make your resumé "speak" and effectively proclaim your corporate proficiency, value, and desirability.

- *Personal information such as age, height, weight, eye and hair color, should not be stated on a resumé.*
- *Personal information such as membership in a trade or professional association or significant volunteer involvement in a charitable organization should be stated.* These facts indicate favorable and important character traits.
- *Never misrepresent details regarding your education.* Academic achievement is quite easily checked and any distortion of the facts will disqualify you permanently.
- *Be sure to mention all continuing-education classes and business related courses in which you have enrolled.* Employers have a high regard for any self-improvement endeavor.
- *Don't state your reasons for leaving previous jobs.* This information should be revealed in an interview.
- *Do not list references. State they are available.*
- *Do not state salary received in any job, nor what you expect in the position for which you're applying.* (See "*Job Interview*" for further explanation of wage topic.) If an ad asks what salary expected, simply state, "Open to negotiation."
- An effective resumé gets the reader's interest immediately with *emphasis on the qualifications that will do the most for the employer.* Having captured this interest the applicant will be called in for a personal interview and that is when you can ex-

pand in more detail. Avoid saying anything that will get you screened out before you even have an interview.

• *Keep that resumé positive and concise!*

The all important cover letter

A well-written cover letter gets your foot in the door.

The most effective way to get your resumé into the hands of the person whose interest you are trying to capture is to send it with a *cover letter*. A prospective employer will read your resumé with enthusiasm if the cover letter inspires his or her interest.

To make a cover letter work for you, follow this guide.

(1) *Use good quality, plain white or cream colored letter size (8.1/2" x 11") paper.*

(2) *Type the letter, unless the ad specifically asks for a handwritten application.* A handwritten *cover letter* is quite acceptable, if you don't have a typewriter or can't get someone to copy it for you.

(3) A *cover letter* should be worded so effectively it convinces the prospective employer that you should be seen for an interview. It inspires them to read your resumé with much more interest.

(4) A *cover letter* adapts your resumé to a specific job and gives your resumé a "personality." A resumé simply states facts about your employment history, while a *cover letter explains* those facts in much the same way as you would do in a personal interview.

(5) *Never submit a resumé without a cover letter.* Whether personally delivered or mailed, *all* resumés should have a *carefully composed cover letter.*

(6) *Direct the letter to the exact person you want to contact.* Find out who is in charge of hiring for the job that you want. Phone the company and simply say you are sending a letter and you'd like to know the name of the person in charge of XYZ department, or go to the local library and see if it is listed in the business directories. Sending a resumé and *cover letter* to the Personnel Manager will seldom

get as favorable results. It may never be seen by the person you want to contact.

(7) A *cover letter* should be no longer than *one* page.

(8) *The title of the position for which you are applying should be written under the salutation.* "Re: Advertising Assistant (Senior Management)" (See example of *Cover Letter.*)

(9) A *cover letter* should open with a strong attention-arresting statement. (See example of *Cover Letter.*)

(10) *The first paragraph should clearly state why you are interested in the job.* It may be that you are changing careers and a cover letter can highlight the relative experience that would qualify you.

(11) *The second paragraph should give a capsule account of your work experience most relevant to the job for which you are applying.* Concentrate on *one* most impressive accomplishment that portrays you best.

(12) *The third paragraph should give any supportive personal information not shown in your resumé but that would make you a leading candidate for the job.* This way you end on a personal note, that changes your application from a piece of paper to a *person* the reader would like to meet.

(13) *Finish with a direct request for an interview.* If you have supporting evidence of your work, i.e. visible credentials such as a portfolio of advertisements, art work, etc., mention that you will bring it to the interview. Curiosity will be aroused and that's a plus for an interview.

(14) *Double check that spelling, grammar, punctuation, and typing are all flawless.* Don't scratch in any corrections, *type it again. It's perfect. It's you!*

Example of a cover letter

Gwendolyn Norman,
4—Gaylord Place,
Toronto, Ontario.
T4R 6N1

June 2nd, 1992

Mr. Gordon Nelson,
Vice-Pres. of Advertising,
SUPERBIG DRUG MARTS INC.,
1220 Production Way,
Toronto, Ontario. T6N 3H2

Dear Mr. Nelson,

Re: *Advertising Assistant (Senior Management)*

My *12 years experience in management positions*, which include *publishing a magazine* and *in-depth advertising duties* with two major corporations, would bring valuable expertise to the position of Advertising Assistant.

At present I am employed and, *due to competent administrative and communication skills, have had rapid escalation within the corporate structure*. I enjoy superb teamwork with my co-workers, but I am interested in relocating to a position with more concentration on advertising which will utilize *my degree in journalism* to a greater extent.

As a volunteer, I publish fund raising pamphlets for Children's Hospital and work one evening a week with the patients.

Would you please call me as to when it would be most convenient to *show you my advertising portfolio* and to attend a personal interview? I would appreciate your consideration.

Sincerely,

PHONE: 000-0000

Confidential, please.

Application form

When you appear for an interview, you will probably be asked to complete an *application form*. This may seem quite unnecessary to you since you've given full details in your resumé. *It is very important to complete this form without objecting. For these reasons:*

- *Employment agencies and large companies are so familiar with their own application forms that they can pick out relevant information with a quick scan of the page.* They don't have time to search every resumé for this information.
- *A person's resumé may not indicate certain key qualities that the prospective employer requires.* The applicant may indeed have these strengths but if they are not revealed in the resumé could lose the opportunity for a job.
- *The way in which the application form is completed tells the interviewer many things about the applicant:*
  Attitude. Do not object to filling out the form. This shows that you take direction with a pleasant and co-operative attitude.
  Neatness. Take your own pen to complete the form. Many times the ink in a pen can be globby and ruin your image of being neat and tidy.

Pointers:

Legible handwriting or printing. Don't be in such a hurry that you write carelessly. Be careful.

Be accurate and correct. Spelling, grammar, etc., should be perfect. Use your resumé to check it.

Answer every question. This shows you complete tasks in a proficient manner. If it asks for details of your work history, fill it in completely. Do not say "See resumé." Even if it's on your resumé, they also want it on the application form.

Questions that should not be answered such as color of hair, eyes (this can be used to screen out certain races), *age* (illegal on an application form), *marital status* (illegal), *religion* (illegal), *should be marked N/A* (not applicable, meaning not applicable to your eligibility for the job). Be sure to answer these questions with *N/A*, so it won't appear that you were careless and missed these questions.

The question asking about salary expected should be answered, "Negotiable." This does not eliminate you for the job before you've had a chance to determine and discuss the total salary package. *The question "reason for leaving a job" should not be answered "fired." In this case, answer the question with the word, "Personal."* This lets you discuss the reason in person in the interview.

The polished and successful job interview

It's in your power to ensure a favorable interview
> *by being confident*
> *by being prepared.*

Be confident

Relax! You're already being considered for the job, or they wouldn't have called you in for an interview. Keep reminding yourself of this. You have something that interests them. You aren't arrogant or pompous, you're polite, well groomed, polished, and confident. You're confident because you're prepared.

Be prepared

(1) *Prepare your documents:*
> **Two copies of your resumé.*
> **Two copies of your cover letter.*

(*If you have sent in a resumé and cover letter you'll only need *one* copy of each for yourself.)
Academic certificates. Performance reviews. References. Portfolio or samples of your work.

(2) *Prepare information about the job for which you are applying.* If you are going into an interview as the result of a classified ad, you won't likely have much information about the job. List everything you *do* know about it and *be familiar with what the ad states*. If you're dealing through an agency, you can learn a great deal more. This is one advantage that an agency provides. If the agency counselor doesn't have the information you want, ask him/her to contact the client and get the details. The more you know about the job, the better you can explain your ability to perform the work involved. The prospective employer will be impressed with the proficient manner in which you do your "homework."

Prior to the interview, find out the following

How large is the company?

It might be a one person operation, or too small to require your vast experience or offer you advantages.

How long has the company been in business?

This is very important. If it is a new company it may not offer enough security. Also, a new company might require you to do very involved "set-up" work which should be compensated at a higher wage rate. A long established company offers more security and opportunity for advancement.

How many divisions does the company have and where? You may be interested in transferring to another area. Being able to transfer within the company often appeals to a married person whose spouse is subject to frequent moves. You never know! The future is unpredictable, you might want a change.

How many employees does the company have?

This helps you decide if you want to work in a large or small company.

What volume of business does the company do?

Even a large company may experience a huge decrease in business and this is a warning that the position may be unstable. Applicants of the executive level want to know the volume of business to determine if it is relevant to their skills, and if it can provide adequate challenge to their expertise.

What types of customers does the business serve? Industrial, trade, or consumer?

To be satisfied in your job, you must feel your day to day contacts and involvements are of the type and environment in which you can thrive. Placing a "blue serge" attitude in a "denim overall" environment does not satisfy employer or employee.

Who is the president of the company?

You should always try to find out the names of the senior management staff.

What is the name of the manager of the department of the job for which you are applying?

Probably you'll have to meet with and eventually be approved by this person. Knowing his or her name gives you more confidence.

What is the name and position of the person to whom you would report?

This is the *most* important since this is the person who will interview you first and make the initial decision as to your being hired for the job. Your rapport with this person will help you determine whether or not you'd be happy working under his/her supervision. Knowing this person's name starts you off on a positive footing, the fast track to a successful interview.

What is the prevailing salary range for your type of work?
Government employment offices can provide this *vital* information. *Be sure you know it.*

Those are the questions *you* want answered *prior* to the interview. There are other questions you should ask *during* the interview. We'll discuss those later. *Now, for the questions the employer wants answered.*

(3) *Prepare your answers*

These are the most often asked interview questions:
There's usually the old standby question that's tossed out as the interview gets underway:

"WHAT CAN I DO FOR YOU?"
Don't let it catch you off guard and have to look for words to explain your presence. Be frank. An applicant with substantial credentials could confidently answer: *"Well, I'm here to see what we may be able to do for each other!"*
However, this answer from an applicant new to the job market would sound bold and presumptuous. A more realistic reply would be: *"I'm hoping you'll help guide me on beginning my future career."* An employer wants to assist a person who shows an eagerness to learn and who wants helpful direction. Even if you don't get the job, you've gained a mentor who would help you in the future.

"TELL ME ABOUT YOURSELF."
You should only mention job related strong points.
Be concise. Mention your greatest achievements. If you have little or no employment experience, tell about your academic achievements, i.e. good grades, scholarships. A letter of reference from a teacher or college professor would be beneficial.

"WHAT ARE YOUR QUALIFICATIONS FOR THIS POSITION?"
If you have relevant past experience, state the work you've done that qualifies you for this position.
Mention your most impressive skills first. Be ready with specific details of significant endeavors. That's what I mean by being prepared! If you have limited job experience, mention such favorable characteristics as the reliability you've shown in the baby-sitting jobs you've had or your dedication to your work on a school project. The employer wants an indication that you can handle the position. Be ready with convincing and *true* statements to support your aptness to qualify.

"WHY DO YOU WANT TO WORK FOR THIS COMPANY?"
This is where your research about the company will provide you with reasons that are credible and will show that you have indeed shown remarkable interest in the company as your prospective employer. This question is sure to be asked, so give it plenty of attention when preparing your answer. Review your answer often, before the interview, *know it*. If it's a new company or you could get little information about it, *show your knowledge of the industry in general* and make valid comments that indicate a genuine interest in working there.

"WHY ARE YOU LEAVING YOUR PRESENT (OR LAST) JOB?"
Never say anything adverse about yourself or your past employer(s). Be truthful. Make comments in a positive way, not a negative way. If you were fired, say your job was terminated. You could say, "My employer and I both felt that I would be happier in a job better suited to my skills." (Or to your temperament?)

Don't mention money as a motivation to change jobs. The employee who can be lured away with dollars is a risk to the employer. Express your desire for more challenge and responsibility, those are positive and commendable reasons for a job change. If you started your own business and are now unemployed because the business failed, don't feel humbled or humiliated, most employers respect the courage of an entrepreneur. State the fact of the business failure but stress the positive, say, "I know now, that I'm better at working within the structure of a company than independently self-employed." A prospective employer will regard this as an ideal opportunity to hire an experienced employee who is ready to settle down and make a valuable and extensive contribution to the corporate endeavor.

"WHERE DO YOU EXPECT TO BE FIVE YEARS FROM NOW?"

Some applicants think it shows confidence to say, "In your job!". It doesn't. It sounds tacky and arrogant and worse than that it sounds threatening. To mention a specific goal may arouse concern that the company could not provide that career path. It is more prudent to say, "I see myself as having set a record of steady progress and of capably handling added responsibility."

"WHAT ARE YOUR STRENGTHS?"

State job related strengths. Examples: Flexible, well organized, team worker, good grammar, eager to learn, good at follow-through, friendly manner. Specific strengths in a particular vocation are most effective: a salesman might state strengths as "strong closing ability" or "dedicated drive to get the order"; a receptionist might state strengths as "friendly composure on a busy switchboard" or "able to discreetly screen calls without arousing anger"; an executive level applicant might state strengths as "able to motivate and develop teamwork" or "well organized and astute in setting and achieving budget and inventory projections." *Consider what the job requires and then evaluate your strongest qualities that would contribute to that work.*

"WHAT ARE YOUR WEAK POINTS?"

Converted strengths are your best answer, i.e. "I'm too hard on myself when I make mistakes."
Never volunteer anything really negative (it'll surely come back to haunt you!). You might say "I used to be too independent but co-workers on my last job helped me to become a very effective team worker." Turn the adverse to a point of strength.

"WHAT ABOUT YOUR PAST EXPERIENCE?"

Never inflate your past experience. State it clearly and confidently but be truthful.

"WHAT SALARY ARE YOU EXPECTING?"

Don't be specific about a wage. Prior to your interview, it is important that you determine the prevailing salary range for your type of position. If you have a favorable work history with extensive experience, and feel confident that you are in the driver's seat, suggest a wage somewhat over the top of the scale. If you go too high you'll be disqualified as beyond the employer's budget. If you state a wage too low, you'll be rejected as not of the professional ability they had been seeking. It's risky being too specific, but you do deserve a wage relative to your qualifications. *There are many influencing factors to consider: your experience, is it extensive and in demand?; the economy, are jobs plentiful or hard to get?; the fringe benefits, bonus, medical/dental, profit sharing, pension plan, staff discounts, pleasant working environment, travel distance from home? Compensation can be a many faceted arrangement.*

Consider the total package, not just the wage. Discuss these topics with the interviewer. *State your willingness to negotiate.* (Employees should always refer to an *annual* wage, never hourly or monthly rates; that immediately categorizes you as a junior or temporary employee. Remember, *behave* the part and you'll *be* the part.) Employers know they must pay an adequate wage to keep a high-performance employee *but you are an unknown quantity. Your strongest bargaining point is to accept a reasonable wage, even if it is below your expectations, but with specific conditions. Whether a novice or experienced, you should state that you are willing to prove your capability by accepting the offered wage with a review and an increase at 3 months and again at 6 months, subject to satisfactory performance. Before you begin the job get written confirmation of this agreement.*

"ARE YOU WILLING TO RE-LOCATE?"

Be positive by saying it would depend on the benefits and circumstances at that time but that you would consider it. You may think you'd never want to move, but when the time comes for such a transfer it might interest and appeal to you.

Tricky questions: (they have no right to ask.)

"WHO WILL LOOK AFTER YOUR CHILDREN?"

This question is only asked of women, never of men. Strange? I understand the employer's concern, too much absence due to child care is very costly. *It is every employee's responsibility to have proper arrangements made, but it is every person's right to equal opportunity to be employed.* Try to satisfy this concern before the question is asked, by saying something like this, "I have arranged for reliable sitters and my mother (or whoever) has agreed to be available when needed."

"WHAT IS YOUR AGE" (Too old? Too young?)

The best response to a question you want to avoid answering is to ask a question. To the question of age say: *"Is a certain age a prerequisite for the job?"* The interviewer knows it's an illegal query and will probably drop the subject. Try that on the following "illegal" questions.

Answering an illegal question with a question

First let me say that if the question doesn't offend you or would not jeopardize your chances of getting the job, it is in your own best interests to answer it. Do everything possible to inspire co-operative rapport or you'll create hostility.

"DO YOU PLAN TO HAVE A FAMILY?"

Legal or not, in my opinion this question *should be answered and answered honestly.* It is grossly unfair that an employer should invest in costly training, only to find that the employee intended to work only long enough to qualify for benefits, and leaves before that training investment has been applied to the job. *A woman's record of reliability will be adversely affected, if she engages in this kind of tactic. There's nothing polished or honorable about this, a swindle is a swindle.* I'm aware that employers can be deceptive, and you may feel justified in beating them to the punch. Don't be tempted to stoop to that level. There are very reputable employers that will welcome your honesty.

"ARE YOU PREGNANT?"

Also an illegal question but it deserves an honest answer. (See the above question and answer.)

"DO YOU BELONG TO ANY UNION?"

Answer this with, "Oh, should I?" If this doesn't baffle the interviewer I don't know what would!

"WHAT ARE YOUR PLANS FOR MARRIAGE?"

A man is never asked this question. I wonder why? So, avoid the answer, ask a question: "Do you have to be married to work here?" Sound naive, *don't* sound impertinent.

"WHAT IS YOUR NATIONALITY?"

This has no bearing on your ability to do the job. Say: "Would you understand if I'd rather not answer questions about my family or my religion?" The interviewer will understand all right, and since you asked so *nicely*, won't feel provoked.

Coping with unfavorable aspects

The following situations will get negative reactions from a job interviewer. Be ready with plausible explanations.

Lacking specific skills: *Be truthful.* Stress your ability to learn quickly. If you've had any type of exposure to those skills or some knowledge of them, point that out.

Unstable work history: *Don't be defensive.* Emphasize that even when not employed you were gaining valuable knowledge. Did you back pack across Europe? Travel is very educational. End on a positive note, talk about your *stable* employment.

Job-hopping: *Some job-hopping is involuntary. If this is so, point out the reasons* i.e. lay-off, business closure, moved from another city, seasonal employment. If it was just a case of wanderlust, admit it and assure the interviewer that you are ready to settle down and want to make a long term commitment to your next employer. Stress that you are now more mature with different priorities. It is not wrong to point out that when one is just beginning in the job market it takes some trial and error to sort out which career path best suits your skills and desires. *End the explanation on a strong note: this job is the appropriate one for you.*

Changing careers: The objection from the interviewer about changing careers is that you'd have to be retrained. Talk about the many *highly developed skills you already have that will be just as valuable in the new career too.* Say: having business experience adapts you to fast-track learning.

Having been fired: Be honest. Not all people gel, and not all people are in the right job. Also, a great number of firings or terminations *are not the fault of the employee,* corporate politics engender some very unfair results. *A seasoned interviewer is quite aware of this.* Don't criticize your former employer or company. Say: "I now have a better understanding of successfully working within the corporate structure. We sometimes learn more from adversity than we learn from success, *but if* we learn, *we're more successful!*"

You are armed with answers and your careful preparation has you confident and ready for Putting on the Polish for the actual interview.

Put on the polish for progress

First impressions are crucial. It is an acknowledged fact that the experienced interviewer makes the decision to hire, or not to hire, in the first thirty seconds of the interview. From that point on, the interviewer looks for reasons to confirm that initial decision and *very seldom changes it.*

It's easy to understand that your ***appearance*** influences the greater part of that decision, and your ***behavior*** during those first few seconds is the other influencing factor.

It's true that you get no second chance at first impressions. The image you first establish in anyone's mind is the way they'll regard you forever after. . . .

but

it will bolster your confidence to know that *you* and you alone have complete power over those first thirty seconds. You *can* make a favorable first impression.

Your appearance and behavior are within your command!

APPEARANCE: *project the image of progress*

Grooming and posture have the greatest effect on appearance.

Expensive apparel will never be as important as careful grooming and good posture. In that first thirty seconds that the interviewer is evaluating you, *this is the order of impact* on those very crucial first impressions:

- *POSTURE:* Do you stand, sit, walk, without slouching?
- *HAIR:* Is it clean? Is it well cut?
  Does it look professional?
- *FACE:* (Men)
  Complexion clear and clean looking?
  Is face clean shaven? Mustache/beard trimmed?
  Nose and ear hair clipped? Teeth clean?
  (Women)
  Complexion clear and clean looking?
  Is make-up well applied? Too much/too little?
  Teeth clean?
- *EYES:* Is the expression direct, alert, and friendly?
- *APPAREL:* Is it appropriate for a job interview?
  Is it clean? Well pressed?
  Are shoes polished and in good condition?
  Is the shoe style appropriate for business?
  Is all the apparel of good quality?
  Does the apparel look professional?

The thirty second scan. Top to toe. Would you be hired?

The business dress code

Companies and businesses have a variety of dress codes. When you dress for a job interview, don't try to guess what that company's code may be. You can be sure of one thing, no company is impressed with dress that is trendy.

You'll never be wrong if you dress conservatively.

Earlier chapters in this book, "Putting on the Polish," have detailed information about apparel for men and for women, so here I'll summarize that and state *what national surveys of employment experts have shown to be universally the most appropriate dress for a job interview.* **This is the ideal.**

MEN: THE IDEAL DRESS FOR A JOB INTERVIEW

- *SUIT: dark navy, well pressed, no spots or stains, or a navy blue blazer with gray or tan slacks. A dark gray or black suit is also correct.* A sports jacket and slacks is not as impressive. Fasten the suit coat. (On a single breasted suit only one button is fastened.) You'll look and be more comfortable, if you *un*fasten your suit coat when seated, but be sure to immediately fasten it as soon as you stand up.

  The proper length for a suit coat can be measured in this way: let your arms hang straight down at your sides, curl your fingers up under the bottom edge of the suit coat, if it is the correct length for you this edge should fit exactly in the curl of your fingers.

  Put as little as possible in your pockets. A great suit can be sabotaged with stuffed pockets.

  Use your pockets correctly: Your wallet should go in the inside jacket pocket, *not* in the back pocket of your trousers.

  Don't put pens or pencils in the *outside* pocket of your suit coat or sports jacket. (Hey Rube!) Put them in the inside coat pocket.

  Be sure your trousers are the right length. Many men wear their pants too long and it makes them look *very slovenly*. Pants should "break" *only slightly* over your shoes at the front.

- *SHIRT: white, cotton, long-sleeved, dress shirt. A cream or pastel blue shirt is also acceptable. A fine-striped shirt under a plain suit can look great. Custom-made shirts are affordable and superb.* Never a short-sleeved shirt, and preferably not a shirt with button-down collar (too casual).

- *TIE: silk. Show your personality! Make it lively but classic.* The *tip* of your tie should just reach the top of your belt. No longer, no shorter.

- *SOCKS: black or navy blue, over-the-calf length.* Never ankle length socks that reveal bare legs. Fancy socks in *very* subtle tone-on-tone patterns in navy or black are reasonably safe, but anything with color mix or distinct pattern is taboo.

- *SHOES: plain black, good quality leather. Highly polished, good condition (no run-down heels). Laced. A wing-tip (brogue) is very handsome.* Loafers or moccasin styles are too casual. Patent leather shoes are only for evening dress wear.

• *BELT: top quality black leather.* Your belt is very obvious, see that it is in good shape, not looking shabby and showing wear.

• *JEWELRY: a plain, slim, wristwatch.* (A carat gold one, if possible, with gold band or leather band.) *Never more than two rings, including wedding band.* A diamond ring looks ostentatious.

• *HANDKERCHIEF: snowy white, pure cotton or linen.* (For goodness sake! *Don't* spread it out and *fold* it after you use it. *Gather* it to-gether and shove it in your pants' pocket out of sight.)

• *BRIEFCASE: black or tan, top quality leather, soft structured, slim, preferably the classic envelope.*

• *TOPCOAT or RAINCOAT:* a plain unbelted style coat, or the classic trench coat. A Burberry is the epitome of quality. (See *"Men's Apparel"*)

OTHER NECESSITIES:

• *A good quality pen.*

• *A leather wallet* (black, tan or brown).

• *A plain black umbrella with a wooden handle.*

• *Prescription eyeglasses (if required). Be sure your glasses are clean.* Remember how important eye contact can be, don't hide your eyes behind scratched and messy glasses. (Read the information on "Eyeglasses.")

• *A supply of top quality business cards.*

W O M E N :

• *SUIT: dark, with knee length skirt, well pressed,* simple-well-tailored-feminine styling, no massive shoulder padding (you aren't applying for a lineman's position). *A suit gives a professional look that can't be surpassed. It's the "uniform" of the business world. The recommended skirt length is just below the knee.* Fashion books may promote very short skirts for business wear, but if you're serious about a career, you'll save your mini-skirts for social wear. If you wear a short skirt to a job interview, it's doubtful you'd be hired. If you *are* hired, expect to be treated like a "toy" that gets advances but not advancement. Very long skirts look like you're more concerned with fashion than getting the job done. Business requires a no-nonsense attitude with no long skirts hampering and tripping up your performance. Be professional.

- *BLOUSE or SHIRT: white, pastel, printed, or plain.* A blouse does for a woman's suit what a tie does for a man's suit: gives it a dash of "personality." For the ultimate fit and tailored simplicity, a custom-made blouse or shirt is superb for a woman. (See "Custom Made Shirts and Blouses.")

- *HOSIERY: Dark toned to co-ordinate with dark shoes or a skintone shade.* Hosiery should be light colored if shoes are light in color. Never white stockings with black shoes or the reverse. Patterned or lace stockings are *not* appropriate for business wear. *Be sure your stockings have no catches or runs.* Be safe, carry an extra pair with you for emergencies.

- *SHOES: Plain pumps with a closed toe. Black, navy, or gray to co-ordinate with suit. Medium high, low, or flat heels. (Not over 2.1/2") Well polished, in good condition.* Check the heel lifts, replace them if they are run down.

- *JEWELRY: No "glitter." No outsize earrings. Keep jewelry to a minimum, in discreet good taste.* No more than two rings plus wedding band.

- *HANDBAG: Plain, medium size, leather, dark color. If you're carrying a brief case don't also carry a handbag.* Have a small, plain, dark leather clutch bag that holds comb, lipstick, mirror, checkbook, etc., and that fits into your briefcase. This will be handy when you want to shop without your briefcase. A big, cumbersome, over-the-shoulder satchel doesn't look trimly professional.

- *BRIEFCASE:* (See *"Men's Briefcase"*)

- *TOPCOAT or RAINCOAT:* (See the information on *"Coats"* under *"Grooming."*)

OTHER NECESSITIES:

- *A good quality pen.*
- *A leather wallet.*
- *Prescription eyeglasses. Be sure they are clean!* (Read the information on *"Eyeglasses."*)
- *A supply of top quality business cards.*

BEHAVIOR: *project the behavior of progress*

- *Don't be late.*
- *Arrive 10 minutes prior to the appointed time. Allow plenty of time for unexpected delays, but don't appear for the interview too early.* The interviewer may feel rushed. If possible, use the firm's public washroom to see that your hair is tidy and not windblown and to do a last minute over-all check. This gives you time to feel settled and composed. You'll have time to look things over in the reception area and observe the quality of the environment.
- *Be friendly to the receptionist and staff but do not interrupt their work.* Later, they may be asked to give their opinion of you, make it favorable.
- *You may be requested to fill out an application form, do it without objection.* (See "*Application Form.*")
- *Do not smoke.* Even if invited to smoke, *don't.*
- *It is better not to accept a cup of coffee, if it is offered.* You may not finish it in time and you'll find it awkward to handle during the interview.
- *If you have any parcels, umbrella, etc., leave them in the reception area, don't carry them into the interviewer's office.* (Remember them when you leave.)
- *If you are wearing a coat remove it.* Leave it in the reception area. Hang it up, if possible.

When meeting the interviewer

- *Smile! With a friendly expression, look directly into the eyes of the interviewer.*
- *Extend your hand in a firm (not knuckle-crunching) handshake.*
- *Don't sit down until invited to do so.* An interviewer may sit across the desk from you or may prefer to sit in a chair beside you. (See "*Interviewers' Methods.*")
- *Place your briefcase or handbag at your feet. Never place it on the interviewer's desk.*
- *Do not smoke or drink coffee, even if the interviewer does.* You'll find it disconcerting trying to balance a cup, review

your resumé, and give full attention to the interview, all at one time. The less clutter with which you have to contend, the better.

- *Call the interviewer "Mr.," "Miss," "Mrs.," or "Ms." and the last name, unless or until you are invited to use his or her first name.* (A polished interviewer wouldn't use first names in the initial interview.)

- *If you are seated close to the interviewer's desk, don't lean on it or over it.*

- *Don't handle items on the interviewer's desk, that is personal and "sacred" territory.*

- *Project enthusiasm. Sit up straight.* Some people think a slouched, settled back posture gives an image of confidence. Not so. It looks lazy and indifferent. Sit well back in the chair but lean the torso forward a little, this looks eager and alert. This manner of sitting also tucks the midsection back and gives a trimmer line to the body.

- *Don't interrupt.* No matter how important your comment, don't interrupt the interviewer.

- *Don't mumble.* Speak clearly and enunciate your words. Not "in" instead of "ing" (goin', doin', bein'). Not "pleezedta-meecha" instead of "My pleasure to meet you."

- *Use the interviewer's name throughout the interview.* This helps maintain a friendly rapport. Don't over do it. It's worse to use it too much than not at all. Using the name too often, sounds almost patronizing.

- *Don't try to be entertaining.* A little humor is usually welcome, but who would hire a clown?

- *Don't be a name dropper.* You may know some very influential people, but mentioning their names just to be impressive will do you more harm than good.

- *Listen carefully. Answer the question that is asked.* Many, many people give "roundabout" answers, saying words that don't pertain to the question asked. *Think before you answer.* (Put brain in gear, before tongue in drive!) *Be concise.*

- *Don't judge the entire company by the person who interviews you.* Sometimes interviewers use tactics that seem abrupt and officious, to catch the applicant off guard. They might be friendlier under different circumstances. On the other hand, if the interviewer is the person to whom you will report and who will be your supervisor on the job, *consider carefully whether you could work for this person.* If there is an abrasive attitude between you, it would be risky.

- *Be confident. Any anxiety or feeling of insecurity that is revealed to the interviewer will have a negative effect. For people to like you, you have to like yourself.*
- *Don't fidget.* Study the chapter on kinesics (body language) and follow that advice. Work on any adverse idiosyncrasies or imperfections. *Remember, you have been asked to appear for this interview, so you are already on the inside track. Show the kind of personality the employer would be pleased to welcome as a member of the staff.*

Now it's your turn to ask important questions

- *Do not ask about salary or holidays until you have been offered the job or until the interviewer opens the subject. (See "Preparing your answers.")*
- *"Why is this job open?"* Learn the fate of your predecessor. Was he/she fired, promoted, transferred, or did he/she resign? Why? How long had he/she been in the job? You want to be sure that you aren't taking a job that others had tried but with which they couldn't cope. *Is this a new position that will require specific organizational skills and expertise?* Can you handle it? Are there adequate guidelines? Having to establish a new position within a company is a difficult assignment. Is the compensation realistic?
- *Ask about the turnover of staff.* A high rate could be a trouble sign. You don't want to jeopardize your employment record with spasmodic work for an unreliable employer.
- *"To whom would I be reporting and for what area of expertise is that individual responsible?"* To be a serious player on a corporate team you have to understand the power structure.
- *"What attributes would you expect from me in this job?"* A competent interviewer should be ready with specific details. When it gets down to seriously considering taking the job, ask for a *written* job description. There should be a clear under-

standing as to the job's responsibilities.

- *"Am I going to be considered among the finalists for this position?"* (Ask this late in the interview.) *If the answer is no, tell the interviewer you would appreciate knowing in what way you failed to meet the requirements.* Say that knowing this will help you understand what you must improve to be successful in getting a comparable job. If it is due to a lack of qualifications for that specific position, ask if there is any other position open within the company that you may be qualified to fill. *If the answer is yes, you are going to be considered among the finalists,* express your thanks and ask the interviewer, *"When may I expect to hear from you?" If you want the job, it is important to ask for it.* This question makes your interest in the job evident, and you'll also learn whether more interviews will be required of you and with whom.
- *When the interview is over, don't linger or use the last few minutes making "small talk."* Simply say, "If I can provide any further information, please call me. I'm very interested in the job. Thank-you for your time and I'll look forward to hearing from you." SMILE, while you shake hands. *Then leave.*

After the interview

- *Write a "thank-you" letter.* This small courtesy shows your polish, and it can work miracles. The applicant who takes the time to say thanks is often well rewarded. *That letter also brings you to the interviewer's attention again.*

A thank-you letter should be *short* and contain the following:

When you are still being considered for the job.
(1) State that you appreciate the opportunity for the interview time that was given to you.
(2) *Call attention to the most important aspects of the job, and remind the recipient of your qualifications to efficiently perform those responsibilities.*
(3) Don't review your resume, they have those details.

(4) Close with your hope that you will hear from them that you have been selected for the position.

When you are not a successful applicant:
(1) Thank the interviewer for seeing you.
(2) If he/she has provided you with help in any way, mention this and express your appreciation.
(3) Keep it short.
In either instance, write a thank-you letter to the person at the employment agency if they referred you for the job.

INTERVIEWERS' METHODS

There are as many methods of interviewing as there are jobs in the market. Unfortunately, in employment agencies and businesses, you'll often find people that have little or no expertise at effectively interviewing or selecting candidates for employment. They may have impressive academic degrees but are not really equipped to select the most appropriate candidate for a corporate position. I point this out so you won't be discouraged and begin to believe that *you* are the one at fault. *Keep trying*. There are many very skilled interviewers that can proficiently evaluate people. They will recognize your strong points and place you in a job where you'll be effective and satisfied.

Being aware of the various methods used by experienced and inexperienced interviewers, may help you to cope more easily in a job interview.

The amateur interviewer

- *Keeps you waiting*. Is so self-important that he/she has little regard for your time and talent.
- *Is disorganized*. Can't locate your resume on an untidy desk. Has other applicants waiting, because he/she has not spaced the appointments judiciously.
- *Isn't professionally groomed*. Wears apparel that is too frilly, or too casual, not businesslike.
- *Engages in irrelevant chatter*. More interested in talking about him/her self than about you.

How to cope with the amateur interviewer

Listen to the banter and endeavor to get a friendly rapport established. This amateur isn't too concerned about your ability, only about whether or not he/she likes you. This inefficiency is usually only found at a small, independently-owned, employment agency. When you are eventually referred to that agency's *client* you will be more effectively evaluated, and you'll also better determine the details of the job. You might wonder, with good reason, what kind of a company would use such an agency, but make the most of it, turn on your charm, and *pray that you've listened well enough to be liked!*

The aloof professional

- *Keeps to the appointed time.* Not a minute early or late and expects the same of you.
- *Greets you with a glance that sweeps from your head to your feet with such analytical skill you'll feel he/she has discovered that little flaw in the left side of your underwear!*
- *Sits behind the desk to show who's the boss.* If he/she *really* knows how to appear commanding, the interviewer's chair will be higher than the candidate's chair. (The better to make you feel subordinate, my dear.)
- *Gets right to the subject at hand.* No putting you at your ease. Bang, bang, question after question, every one of which is on a carefully compiled list. With very little reaction to your answers, he/she will make notes about each response. It's almost a robot routine that leaves little room for discovering your unique qualifications and personality. You fit the mold or you don't stand a chance. This type of interviewer is usually inflexible and very insecure.

How to cope with the aloof interviewer

- *Don't be intimidated.* Listen carefully to each question and answer succinctly. Keep direct eye contact to show your confidence. Smile, but don't be subservient.
- *State your ability to proficiently handle the job.* This aloof interviewer means business and you mean business too!

The friendly professional

Absolutely charming and absolutely perilous!
- Is punctual and expects you to be also.
- Greets you with such a captivating manner you'll feel you've won instant approval.
- Sits on a chair *beside* you, makes you feel like an important, visiting friend.

- Makes you relax and makes you decide that this individual isn't a rigid business person. You might mistakenly regard him/her as an *amateur*.
- *Beware! This is no amateur. This is the most astute interviewer you'll encounter.* The interviewer may seem to be chatting quite superficially, but every question is designed to "delve" and draw out the *real you*. All that charm has you feeling so confident that you volunteer information that may reveal far too many warts. You'll *talk* yourself right out of the job. To recognize the difference between an *amateur* and a *friendly professional*, watch for this: an *amateur* talks about him/her self and want *you* just to *listen*, but the *friendly professional* intersperses the conversation with a few personal comments which inspire *you* to do a *lot* of talking too. This can be to your advantage or to your detriment, depending upon what skeletons lurk in your career closet.

How to cope with the friendly professional interviewer

- *Smile and be friendly.* This interviewer appreciates good manners and an outgoing personality.
- *Be very businesslike.* The Friendly Professional Interviewer may give the appearance of being casual but that is a facade, he/she actually *looks for and respects a candidate who conducts him or her self in a discreet and dignified manner*.
- *Don't let down your guard. Keep your comments directed to information pertinent to the interview. The Friendly Professional Interviewer won't feel you are being aloof, he or she will be impressed with your reserve.*
  This is the behavior you should apply in all interviews.

The polished interviewer

- *Does not keep an applicant waiting.*
- *Schedules appointments to allow adequate time for a thorough interview.* Doesn't rush the applicant.
- *Respects an applicant's privacy.* Never lines people up in a reception area, gives each person a secluded spot in which to wait.
- *Dresses to set an example of an appropriate business image, well-groomed and conservative.*

- *Meets applicant with a friendly approach and tells the applicant his/her name:* "Hello, Miss Davis, thank you for coming, my name is Helen Green, Mrs. Green." A man should only say his name and leave off the Mr., since the applicant knows to call him Mr., but a woman should give her title after her name or the applicant won't know if she is Miss or Mrs.
- *Sits up straight and treats the applicant with respectful interest.*
- *Looks directly at the applicant when conversing with him or her.*
- *Gives full attention to the interview,* doesn't engage in tidying the desk or looking in a drawer, etc.
- *Doesn't accept phone calls or interruptions during the interview.* This shows a total disregard for the applicant's time, it is exceedingly rude.
- *Uses the applicant's name.* Never uses such familiar words as "honey," "dearie," "young lady"; some male interviewers still do this (as a put-down?) and they undermine their own professionalism.
- *Speaks clearly. Listens carefully.*
- *Lets the applicant know when the interview has ended. Closes the file and stands up.* This usually is enough to prompt an effective close. A comment such as, "Well, that seems to cover the issue. Thank you for coming" will certainly accomplish a close.
- *If the applicant is being considered for the position, says so.* "You seem to be a strong contender for the position, Miss Davis, we'll be giving you a call in a day or two, possibly for a further interview."
- *Doesn't give the candidate false hopes. If is rejecting his or her application, gets this message across tactfully.* "Thank you for your interest in this position, Miss Davis. However, I feel your qualifications are not exactly what we are seeking for these particular responsibilities."
- *Gives helpful guidance if the candidate asks where he/she failed.* I.E. "If this is the kind of position you especially want, I'd suggest that you should concentrate on gaining stronger promotional skills. Have you considered a course in marketing?"
- *Walks the applicant to the door.* Particularly those that are *not*

being hired. Their egos have been bruised enough, shows
them every courtesy possible.

- *Lets the candidates that were interviewed know by letter when
  the position has been filled.* They gave their time for an interview, shows polish and thanks them. An applicant's time is no
  less valuable than that of an employer's, and often is more difficult to arrange.

- *Keeps all information about applicants confidential.* The fact
  they have applied for a job and all details revealed in their
  resumés and interviews should be regarded as absolutely private, never disclosed. (As an Executive Recruiter, I wouldn't
  even speak to someone, on the street, that I had interviewed
  for a job, in case it may evoke the questions "Who is that?
  How do you know her?" Sharing someone's career aspirations
  is a privilege to be respected.)

Employer: When you hire a new employee

No matter how junior his/her position, take him around and introduce
him to the various staff members with whom he'll be working. Show
him the major departments and where he'll be located. Leave him,
finally, with someone to get started. Make him feel welcome and valuable in his new job.

Putting on the polish on the job

*Are business manners different than social manners? In only a very
small way.*

Then what's all this fuss about etiquette in the world of business
having changed? Consideration for others has never changed, there
probably is just more concern about how to treat women now that
there are more of them involved on the job site. Some social rules
needed a little modifying.

How *do* you treat a woman in the work environment? *The same way
in which you treat a man, considerately.*

Certain attitudes have developed in the last few years, however, that have left people, in general, and men, in particular, confused. A few women interpret *any* act of etiquette on the part of a man as simply a desire to show his superiority. That's ridiculous. Men, then, are damned if they do and damned if they don't, and they are never sure what is expected of them. *Here's the answer. Be polite.* For the few women who object, well, gentlemen, show your good manners and try not to offend that individual preference. Don't let the occasional rebuff stifle your consideration, most women appreciate a man's (or anyone's) courtesy.

With social customs, women have been given some special treatment: men hold their chairs for them, help them put on their coats, and abide by the rule "women first." Very nice. Don't change it, *socially.*

But, is there anything wrong with doing the same for a man? No. Good manners haven't changed, they've just become affected by *equal rights* and I think that's terrific!

So fellows, hold that chair, and help with that coat, not because it's for a "helpless lady," we'll do the same for you even though you're a "strong man" who can do it for yourself. *Let's do these things because we're people who like being considerate of each other.*

We recognize, however, that, in reference to women, some social rules are modified for business. Let's call it:

Practical divergence

(1) *The social rule is that a man stands when a woman enters a room.*

In business, this is not necessary. A man would have to be a yo-yo, jumping up and down, to adhere to this rule.

(2) *The social rule is "women first."*

In business it's "seniority first." The person in the most senior position is considered first (*man or woman*): first greeted, first introduced, first seated (in the prime spot), and then on down the seniority line.

Okay, **people!** Welcome to the team!

Management that nurtures good manners, nurtures staff harmony and positive employee performance. The entire business profits. *Good manners start at the top and end up having a favorable impact on the bottom line.*

The hierarchy of business

- Every business has a distinct "pecking order." It is not only professionally rude but quite risky to step beyond that order of rank and authority.
- Learn where your specific position is in that hierarchy and behave accordingly, never partake of privileges designed and reserved for those of a higher status.
- Always deal directly with your *immediate* supervisor, never go above his or her head with complaints, queries, etc..
- *Be very polite, if you must disagree with someone of higher rank. Never express a contradictory opinion in front of visitors or clients. Do it in private.*
- Employees of equal status, sometimes create the most dissent within the pecking-order, in their endeavor to be the dominant power. Polite behavior will be the determining factor as to who is a true *leader*.

CLIENTS AND HIERARCHY

- *The visiting client's temporary place in the order of rank depends on whether he or she is providing a service or receiving a service.* Needless to say, *all* visitors are treated with utmost courtesy, but the client who is *receiving* a service is treated in a more formal manner.
- *The visiting client's rank in the company in which he or she is employed should also be considered.* A client of senior executive rank should receive the same degree of formality that he or she would merit in their home office.
- *Each client should be appropriately greeted and, if necessary, an offer made to hang up his/her topcoat.* After informing the appropriate individual that their appointment has arrived, the client should then be *escorted* to that person's office. If the person being called on is not ready, he/she should come and speak to the visitor, apologize for the delay, and see that the visitor is comfortable before leaving him or her to wait. Don't be "too busy" for these courtesies, nothing is more important.
- Visitors to a business should be treated as graciously as they'd be treated if calling at your home. Show proper regard for rank and *age*.

Business decorum

- *Don't be too casual*. Working with people day after day can generate feelings of relaxed familiarity. The old saying that "familiarity breeds contempt" is absolutely true. Congenial behavior doesn't mean taking liberties with the basic rules of etiquette.

- *Using first names should be carefully considered*. If that smacks of Victorian or prudish conduct, let me remind you that it has been proven that businesses that subscribe to a more formal approach have far less personnel problems with which to cope. *Law firms are superb examples of the refinement of formality*. Most other businesses are on a first name basis for general day to day contacts, but it generates feelings of pride and propriety to refer to each other as Mr., Mrs., or Ms. in front of visitors. *Whether a peer, a subordinate, or a superior, it's a wise practice not to use a person's first name until invited to do so*. This is especially important between a medical doctor and his or her patient. This being a *very personal relationship* between "business" associates, it should never be treated casually. *Doctors, please don't call any adults by their first names, ever*.

Inter-office communication etiquette

- *Don't shout*. Loud voices are disruptive and crude.
- *Don't swear*. The use of foul language indicates a lack of decency and reveals a limited vocabulary.
- *Don't gossip*. You'll lose your co-workers' respect.
- *Do send written memo's*. Communication that is conveyed in writing is more easily understood and remembered. It also provides a *record* of the message.
- *Use your intercom: Don't just drop into someone's office, inquire if it's convenient*. If you have no intercom, knock on their door and see if he or she is free to speak with you. If a peer or a subordinate does drop into your office unannounced, simply say, "Please, I can't be interrupted right now." If someone of superior position drops in, you'll have to put up with it. Here I'll remind personnel of *all* ranks, use your manners, no matter how important you are, *call first*.

- *Business communication does not include social chatting.* There is *always* some useful work to be done. Don't waste your time or anyone else's. That includes allowing friends to visit you at work.
- *Keep in contact.* Always let the front desk know when you will be out of your office and when you expect to return. When delayed, report in by phone.

Create an appealing office decor

- *Limit any personal trivia, ornaments, pictures, etc., to a minimum.* Business offices that are cluttered with irrelevant paraphernalia show a lack of good taste. Management should discourage such displays. A government office that I call on has a scrawled sign on one office wall that says, "How can I soar like an eagle when I'm forced to work with these turkeys?" That's crude. Maybe someone will inform that person that he is mistaken, the fact is, *he* is the turkey to display such a sign. People will question who is supervising that office, to allow this abuse of business decorum.

Personal habits that should be avoided.

- *Filing, clipping, or cleaning the fingernails in public should not be done. Picking at ears, nose, or teeth is exceedingly repulsive.* (It's quite permissible to request someone to refrain from doing this in front of you.) *Some men have the unpleasant habit of "adjusting their anatomy" and scratching here, there, and the other place.* Think about how embarrassing this is to your viewing public. Hands off!
- *Watch your mouth!* Use your handkerchief for that sneeze. Cover that yawn. No one wants to check the condition of your molars.

Learn to use those magic words that work miracles

- *They are: please and thank you.* Asking someone to *please* do some task is far more effective than simply telling them to do it. Showing your appreciation with a sincere *thank you* wins support and co-operation.
- *Be diplomatic.* Remember, put brain in gear before putting tongue in drive.

Putting on the polish for a business meeting

Never call a meeting when a memo would suffice.

- *Determine when a meeting is the only way to solve a problem or to discuss a project.* Statistics reveal that a business meeting that involves a dozen people of executive level, costs a minimum of $1,000 per hour. *It must achieve a worthwhile purpose that could not be accomplished by a memorandum.* Meetings with no serious purpose lose credibility. People gasp, "Not *another* meeting!" instead of saying "This must be important" and acting accordingly.

- *If a meeting requires the approval and/or participation of any of your superiors and peers of equal rank, it is imperative that they be consulted prior to the meeting being arranged.* Meetings with subordinates, unless of unusual corporate involvement, don't require prior approval, but upper management should be kept informed with copies of the agenda. They often contribute useful guidance that adds to the meeting's success.

Set an agenda. This is the meeting's master plan

- *An effective meeting needs specific guidelines.* What do you want to accomplish?

- *List the major topics first.* Attention is keenest at the beginning of a meeting. Listing most important topics first, ensures that time won't run out before they are covered.

- *With each topic, name the person or persons who will contribute information pertaining to that topic.* This has every person actively participating and responsible for providing pertinent information. This also determines which individuals are needed to be present and establishes a vital *team* attitude.

- *After each topic, schedule time for free and open discussion to take advantage of brainstorming.* List this on the circulated agenda, to alert each participant to prepare to be *totally* involved.

Distribute the agenda.

- *Notice of the meeting (time, date, place) with a copy of the agenda should be distributed early enough to allow adequate time for preparation (and travel?) prior to the event.* (Before the meeting *date* is set, conduct a preliminary check to ensure that all participants will be available.)

- *Inform only those that are to attend the meeting.* It is up to these individuals to inform any other personnel that are indirectly involved. *The meeting should include only the most essential participants,* as this will keep attention concentrated on the prime objectives and avoid the superficial discussion and abstract interest of anyone only remotely involved.

Plan the chairperson's guideline

- *The Chairperson or leader is solely responsible for the success of a meeting. Personnel that are more senior may be present but, during the meeting, the Chairperson is in charge.*
- *The guideline backs up the agenda with explicit objectives.* A well-organized leader, who knows what he or she expects the meeting to achieve, inspires confidence and initiative in those participating.
- *Using the agenda as a master plan, list specific notations of areas to discuss within that plan.* Keep all discussions concise and directed to the subject.
- *The Chairperson must be capable of effectively handling the interchange of information* that leads to *the solving of problems* and *the achieving of goals* while *restraining any emotional reactions among the participants. This requires a flexible specialist.*

Timing of the meeting and of the agenda.

- *The best day for a meeting is a Wednesday.*
- *Determine the amount of time needed to cover the agenda.* Allot time for each segment.
- *Set a realistic time limit and stick to it.* Meetings that drag very far beyond the set time limit usually reflect ineffective leadership.

  There are, however, extenuating circumstances wherein unforeseen problems may emerge that require prolonged attention. An alert leader recognizes that more time is needed to resolve that particular situation and *schedules a further meeting.* If there are immediate deadlines to be met, the meeting may have to continue beyond the designated time limit, but this should be a very infrequent occurrence.

- *If a two hour meeting is scheduled, set it for 10:00 a.m. to be concluded at noon, or set it for 3:00 p.m. to be concluded at 5:00 p.m.* These are the customary breaks in the work day that will help to limit the meeting's length. Morning meetings are most dynamic.

- *In a marathon meeting, one that lasts more than two hours, breaks must be planned.* Fifteen minutes break after the first two hours, 30 to 45 minutes break after the second two hours, fifteen minutes break again after the third two hours.

- *Break on time and insist on punctual return after each break.* Remind everyone of the time that the meeting will be resumed. Give obvious signs when you are getting ready to reconvene. *Begin exactly on time, whether or not everyone is present.*

- *Don't try to cover too much in one meeting.* If the subject matter is extensive, plan a series of meetings scheduled according to *priority of stages.*

- *Provide adequate time for each segment of the meeting and strictly adhere to these guidelines.* Don't let the meeting stray on to other subjects.

Meeting facilities

- *Choose a meeting room that fits, not too large nor too cramped.* It should be comfortable but not too lavish. Not drab, psychologically uplifting.

- *The room should accommodate every person equally, so each can clearly see the Chairperson and all visual aids (i.e. screen).* No one behind a pillar.

- *Close the drapes on the windows.* Views can be too distracting. Avoid having any distractions.

- *Remove any extra chairs from the meeting room.* With every chair occupied you will know there is full attendance. Unoccupied, extra chairs are negatives.

- *See that there is good lighting for everyone.*

Meeting seating

- *Wait to be seated. There are well established rules as to the placing of people in even an informal meeting. Know your place.*

Conventional seating: (Figure #53)

- *At a rectangular boardroom table, the Chairperson is seated at the end of the table farthest from the door to the room. If the entrance is at the centre of the side of the room, the Chairperson sits at the end of the table that is to the left of the entrance.*
- *The most senior personnel and/or distinguished guests are seated next to the Chairperson to the right and to the left.*
- *This protocol should be followed down the table: the higher the rank the closer they sit to the Chair.*

Optional seating arrangement: (Figure #54)
This method is used when:
- *two small, inter-office groups meet*
- *meeting with a small group of visitors*
- *it is the arrangement preferred for a meeting with foreign delegates. (They sit facing the door.) The two "teams" are seated across from one another with the most senior in rank in the centre, the next in rank to his/her right, the next to the left, etc. (Fig.#54)*

BUSINESS MEETING SEATING

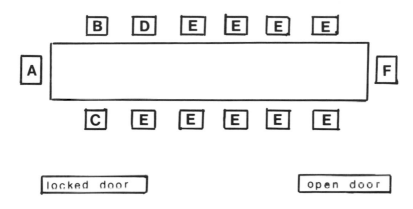

Fig. #53

A: The Chairperson
B: Person highest in rank or visiting V.I.P.
C: Person 2nd highest in rank

D: Person 3rd highest in rank
E: Other participants
F: Reserved for those giving presentations.

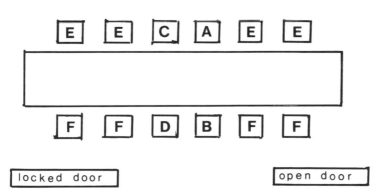

Fig. #54

A: Highest ranking visitor
B: Highest ranking local
C: 2nd highest ranking visitor

D: 2nd highest ranking local
E: Participating visitors
F: Participating locals

Note: The visitors are seated *facing* the entrance.

Meeting procedure

- *The Chairperson should see that a water pitcher and glasses, notepads and pencils, and all materials such as document files, hand-outs, and visual aids, are in the meeting room and ready.*

- *No one should sit down until the Chairperson invites them to do so.* Individuals stand behind their chairs.

- *While everyone is standing, the Chairperson makes any introductions that are necessary, introducing the most senior guests first, other guests in order of rank, then senior personnel from the home office, and others down the line.* It isn't necessary for each to shake hands. Business people want to save time. However, treat the situation with whatever degree of formality it commands.

- *The front desk should be informed that there are to be no interruptions.* The front desk should be given a list of those attending the meeting, including visitors, in case of any urgent calls. A visitor may be expecting a call and this should be acknowledged.

- *A secretary should be delegated to record the details of the meeting.* This is important for future reference and to resolve any misunderstandings.

- *The agenda is closely followed with participants keeping to their designated time frame.* It is not good manners to take more than your allotted time.

- *If necessary, the Chair tactfully reminds speakers when their time is up.* Catch his or her eye and give a nod and a short sideways sweep of your hand to indicate a cut-off gesture.

Effective leadership

- *Be confident. Confident of your ability to lead. Confident that the goal will be achieved.*

- *Present all background information pertaining to the topic of the meeting.* Solutions and projects require an in-depth review of the basic situation.

- *Encourage every person to participate.* In drawing out a shy person don't put them on the spot by saying, "What do you think, John?,," instead say, "How does this affect your advertising department, John?" Focus the question on the *department* not on the person, a shy person will respond more confidently.

- *Don't be fearful of conflicting ideas. Welcome them.* Properly handled, opposing stances can develop into the most valuable contribution to a meeting's success. SAY SO!
- *Express your respect for their opposing views, and ask for their co-operation in evaluating each stand. Then, without bias, ask each member to state their opinion in regard to each disagreement. Everyone else pays attention and evaluates that stand.*
- *Carefully review the pros and cons of each opinion.* If you stifle controversy, individuals will leave the meeting feeling frustrated and unable to effectively perform. A capable leader can control intelligent participation in debate and can turn destructive competition into co-operative energy directed to teamwork where *all* will benefit.
- *Specifically ask if there are any further objections or pertinent observations that should be discussed.* There often is one negative person that grumbles later that the plans won't work. If you're aware of that attitude, ask that person directly for their comments. Get every opinion out in the open.
- *Guide the meeting to it's successful conclusion, by asking questions and encouraging answers.* Remind people to *think* about the question and to give a concise, straightforward answer. Never ridicule.

Conclude the meeting

- *Take complete charge. State that there will be no further discussion.*
- *Review what was accomplished.*
- *State the decisions reached.* This prevents any misunderstandings and mistaken conclusions.
- *State the areas of disagreement.* Ask everyone to give particular thought to ways of solving these differences before the next meeting when they will be given further attention. It's the rare meeting that solves *all* problems, don't disregard them.

- *Inform of future follow-up*. Decide if and when the next meeting will be held, and remind each person of their designated responsibilities in the interim.
- *Close with a positive comment expressing confidence in the project*.
- *Thank everyone for their contribution and assistance*.

Distribute a summary of the meeting

- *Within a day or two send each participant a written summary of the meeting: decisions reached, follow-up action, etc. Copy superiors and/or those concerned*.

Meeting etiquette

- *Dress appropriately*. Wear your best dark suit. This gives an appearance of authority and makes you feel more confident.
- *Be immaculately groomed. Clean*.
- *Don't wear strong fragrance*. Sitting at close quarters, others may find it objectionable.
- *Be prepared*. Have all material, reports, etc., ready and well organized, so as not to impede procedures.
- *Be punctual*.
- *Speak loudly enough to be heard by all those present*.
- *Pay attention*. Don't fidget, doodle, rattle papers, or talk to your neighbor while the meeting is in progress.
- *Don't chew gum, smoke, or take food or drink into the meeting*. Any snacking should be done *out* of the room.
- *If you must leave the room, do so with as little disruption as possible*. Quietly excuse yourself and don't explain the reason for your absence.
- *Express your opinion in the meeting. Don't complain afterwards if you haven't pointed out your objections prior to final decisions*.
- *Exercise emotional control*. Lively debate can be productive if done courteously and impersonally.
- *Keep an open mind. Learn by listening. Be flexible*.

Telephone etiquette

Face to face conversation has the benefit of facial expressions and body gestures that *greatly* influence the message conveyed to the ears. A smile makes a curt comment less offensive, and a warm, friendly expression in the eyes softens all words of communication.

The message is taken at face value.

Not so with the telephone. Those same words and tones of voice sound very different when they are heard only by the *ear*. The ear interprets a message exactly the way it sounds. With conversation on a telephone, the ear can't see the smile behind abruptly spoken words, so the speaker sounds cold and unfriendly. Words spoken in banter, without the tempering benefit of facial expressions, can sound sarcastic and insulting on the telephone. The message and the messenger then inadvertently cause irreparable damage.

On the telephone the message is taken at sound value. The brain can't "hear" what the ear can't "see."

In both social and business situations, telephone etiquette is absolutely vital in establishing effective and accurate communication.

The rules of telephone etiquette
When placing a telephone call whether for business or social reasons, there is an inviolate rule that proper etiquette demands. That rule is:

The caller should immediately identify him or her self.

The person placing the phone call knows to whom s/he wishes to speak but the individual answering the call may not recognize the voice of the person who is calling. The polite caller says, "Hello, this is John Smith calling, may I speak with Mrs. Barbara Norris?" or more casually in a social call to a friend, "Hi Mary, this is Dora Beck."

Don't be indignant and don't refuse if whoever answers the phone, says, "May I ask who is calling?" That's proper. It's your error, it's up to you to identify yourself.

If, for very confidential reasons, you cannot reveal your name or phone number, and the call is of utmost importance, try to determine when the person you want to reach will be available and state a specific time that you'll be calling later. In situations of extreme secrecy, such as merges and take-over negotiations, code names for the principals involved should be arranged to eliminate problems of telephone contact.

Identify yourself. That's the *name* of the game.

A second rule, not as crucial but certainly important to the ear-drums, the nerves, and a polished image is:

Pitch low and regulate the volume.

A high-pitched, squeaky voice right up next to the ear is nerve wrack-ing, a voice delivered with very loud volume is ear splitting, and a timid whisper is difficult to decipher. In this book, *"Putting on the Polish,"* you'll have read the information on developing a pleasing voice, and maybe you'll have a sign by the phone to remind you to *pitch low!*

Answering a business phone

- *A greeting and the name of the company is stated:* "Good morn-ing, Donovan Construction." *Say the name clearly and not in a singsong manner.* If the corporate name is extra long, some companies *prefer to answer the call with their phone number:* "Good morning, this is 555-0000." Either is correct.
- *If the person being phoned is not available, ask if someone else could be of assistance.* If not, then ask if they'd like to leave a message.
- *When taking a message record the following information: Cal-ler's name, Company, Phone number, Caller's message, Date and time of call, Your own initials, Instructions: (Please call, Returned your call, Will call back, etc.)*
- *Use printed message forms. It is wise to use bound message forms.* Available at stationery stores, these forms are in dupli-cate with carbon paper inserts. The top copy goes to the per-son called and the other copy remains in the book for future reference. This method eliminates many hassles between "caller" and "called" and the ever incriminated "front desk."
- If the caller leaves a message stating he'll be calling back later in regard to a specific subject, a proficient secretary will pull any files pertinent to that call, so that when her boss returns the call, all information is readily available. That's polish!
- *If you transfer a call to another office, be sure you are transfer-ring the call to the appropriate person.* It is most annoying to be

telephonically chased from office to office in an endeavor to speak to someone.

- *Do not disclose company information.* For example: Simply say, "Mr. Thomas is not available until next Tuesday." instead of "Mr. Thomas is in Australia arranging to open a branch there." If anyone insists on more information than you feel you should provide, get someone in senior management to speak with the caller.
- *Do not lie for anyone.* If someone doesn't wish to take a call, simply say he or she is not available.

Other business phone courtesies

- *All levels of seniority should place their own calls when they are not too busy to do so.* It might sound important to have a secretary place your call but it takes valuable business time and if it is practised solely for your ego, it is not productive.
- *If you leave your office, don't leave your phone unattended.* Inform the switchboard of your absence or have someone take your calls for you.
- *When taking calls in someone else's office, identify yourself.* "Hello, Mrs. Stromberg's office, Miss Fox speaking" this let's the caller know they are not in contact with the person they called. Then ask if you can be of assistance or can take a message.
- *Be sure the line is closed before you make comments.* Put the call on hold, don't leave the line open, if you must put the phone down to check something.
- *On a multi-line pushbutton phone, be sure no one is on a line before you enter it.* Also take care in answering the right line on an incoming call.
- *When you're in someone's office and they must take a phone call, signal that you will leave to give the person privacy.* If it isn't confidential he/she should gesture for you to stay. If he/she *does* want privacy they should nod "yes" and say "thanks."
- *Do not accept telephone calls when you are in an appointment with someone.* Have the front desk hold your calls or, if calls come directly, answer the call but take their number and say

you'll call back. Only in urgent circumstances should you take your appointment's time by accepting calls.

- *When answering the phone, don't use just your first name.* A man says "Bill Kent speaking" a woman says, "Judith Newman speaking" you do *not* say Mr., Mrs., Miss, or Ms. The caller should call you by title, "Hello, Mr. Kent," "Hello, Ms. Newman." Now that there is a title "Ms.," it is easier to address a woman if you don't know if she is married or not. If a woman objects to being called "Ms." she can *tactfully* say, "It's *Mrs.* Newman, please."

- *Don't put anyone on hold for more than a few seconds.* Get right back to them and either take their call or, if you're going to be delayed, take their number.

- *No matter how busy you are, you yourself place your phone call to anyone in an equal or senior position. You don't ever have your secretary place these calls.*

- *Only phone an employee at his or her home when it is unavoidable. Do not abuse the privilege.*

Teleconference meeting etiquette

- *The teleconference meeting is useful for exchanging information and co-ordinating plans between two or more regions when the shortness of the meeting does not warrant the cost and time of travel to meet in person.* A few people in each geographic area can cover the subject at hand via conference telephone facilities.

- *The teleconference meeting time is arranged well enough in advance so participants are prepared.*

- *Notice of the topics to be discussed and the relevant information required should be transmitted by facsimile prior to the teleconference meeting.*

- *Participants must be punctual and prepared.*

- *There must be a Chairperson to exercise the same controls and leadership as in a regular meeting.* These qualities are even more important in a tele-conference call where more than one person speaking can garble the sound and create confusion.

- *First, the Chair introduces each participant by a roll call, in order of seniority.* The participant answers with his or her name, corporate position, and area: "Ed Brown here, V.P. Marketing, Chicago," "Dez Hubbell here, Cosmetics Co-Ordinator, Canada."

- *If there are several people in each area in on the teleconference, each area should have a leader to see that all participants get their messages across.* Pass notes to the leader, rather than every person trying to speak at once.
- *Each time you speak you must identify yourself, as some voices sound the same.* "Ed Brown, Chicago, we'll have to revise those dates, that's when we hold our gift show."
- *Signal the leader when you want to speak, never interrupt.*
- *Before the meeting concludes, the Chair goes down the roll and asks each person if they have anything further they'd like to say or any questions to ask.* It is important that every member be given the time and opportunity to contribute.
- *The Chair then summarizes the conclusions reached, and thanks all members for their participation.*
- *A follow-up memo of a summary of the meeting is circulated by fax transmission, within a day or two.*
- *Another approach to conducting a teleconference meeting is to designate only one spokesperson in each area. Other personnel involved are present so the spokesperson can ask for their input, but only one person relays the message.*

General telephone etiquette: Business and social

- *When calling, let the phone ring at least 7 times.*
- *Identify yourself. Pitch low!*
- *Always ask if it is a convenient time to talk.* To assume that a person has nothing to do but converse on the phone is inconsiderate. Even with a business call that is not urgent, you should first determine if the recipient is able to take the call or if you should leave your number or call back.
- *Social phone calls should not be made before 9:00 a.m or after 9:00 p.m. or during regular meal times.*
- *Don't answer a home phone with your phone number.* This is not only impolite, it is also hazardous for reasons of security.
- *Don't answer a phone call with "Yes" or worse "Yeah."* That is about as unpolished as you can get! *Say, "Hello," "Good*

morning," or "Good day" but, for security reasons, say nothing more until you identify who is calling. To say, "Hello, this the Taylor residence," lets an *unknown* caller know who you are and that can be a security risk. Legitimate callers must identify themselves or don't speak to them.

- *Don't put a caller on hold for more than 15 seconds while you take another call.* Excuse yourself, take the second caller's number to return the call later.

- *Have a notepad and pencil at the phone at all times.* Don't waste people's time while you search for these.

- *If you dial a wrong number, don't just hang up, apologize.* Then say, "I'm trying to reach number 555-0000, have I dialled correctly?" This way you won't dial the same number again in error. Never say, "What number is this?," they shouldn't tell you.

- *If someone calls you in error, a wrong number, don't act annoyed.* You'll dial a few wrong numbers yourself in your lifetime, or are you infallible? However, if the caller asks, "What number is this?" *do not give your number*, simply say, "What number are you trying to reach?" If they quote your number, ask with whom they want to speak and you'll probably find you have to tell them there is no-one there by that name. If they quote another number, tell them they have the wrong number but *never mention your number*. You don't know the motive for their call.

- *Speaking with an unknown caller, never reveal that you are home alone or working in the office at night alone.* If a caller asks if your husband or roommate or, at the office, if anyone else is there, *simply say, "No-one can come to the phone right now."* Never let on that you are alone. Ask for their phone number. A legitimate caller won't refuse to leave it.

- *Turn down background sound of radio, t.v., etc.* Trying to conduct a conversation with this sound interference is difficult.

- *Don't chew gum or food while talking on the phone.* Sounds are greatly magnified when close to the ear.

- *When a call is mistakenly disconnected, the person who placed the call should be the one to place it again.* If you follow this rule, both parties won't be dialling each other and getting busy signals.

- *When placing a long distance call, consider the time difference in geographic zones.* You wouldn't want to disturb someone in the middle of their night.
- *When placing a long distance call and you aren't able to contact the person you want, don't ask to have the person call you back collect.* Say that you'll call back later and state a specific time. Most people are reluctant to call collect and feel obligated to return the call at their own expense. Avoid this delicate situation.
- *Be discreet in cutting a call short.* It actually should be the person who places the call who *ends* the call but some people don't know this or choose to abuse it. Don't use some false excuse like "someone's at the door, I must go now." If there *is* someone at the door, it's polite to offer to return to the phone. Draw a phone call to a close by making a comment that obviously signals to the other person that the call should be concluded. The person *called* ends it by saying, "That was kind of you to call, Julie, I'll talk to you again soon." and if that doesn't work could add "I must go now, I'm kind of rushed today." The *caller* ends it by saying, "I'll be in touch with you soon, I haven't much time to talk to-day, I'm kind of rushed." Closing a call can be difficult, especially if you're calling a Gemini, we *love* to chat on the phone or anywhere else!
- *Children should not be allowed to answer a phone until they are old enough to do so properly.* Callers don't find it "cute" to hear a child's voice on the line. On the other hand, when a child is taught to capably take a message and be polite, it reflects *very* favorably on the parent(s). Example:
Child: "Hello"
Caller: "Hello, this is John Fox, is Mrs. Baker there, please?"
Child: "Yes, Mr. Fox, I'll get my mother for you, just a moment, please."
or
Child: "No, Mr. Fox, my mother can't come to the phone right now. May I take your number and have her call you?"
Teach your child never to give strangers, or voices they don't recognize, any more information.

Telephone answering machines

- *Recognize the fact that most people hate to contact a telephone answering machine. Do everything possible to make it less annoying.*
- *Do not try to be funny or clever with the recorded message on your machine.* Only a lowbrow subjects a caller to this nonsense. Show your polish, simply state: *"Thank you for calling 555-0000, we're not able to come to the phone right now. Please leave your name and phone number and the time that you called and your call will be returned as soon as possible."* This is short and wastes nobody's time.
- *Do not say that you are out. Burglars like to know that and they just might drop around.*
- *Don't use background music.* Whether it's a business or a private answering machine, people may not like your choice of music and also it makes the message harder to hear.
- *Phone your own answering machine often. See how it sounds and if it is operating properly.*
- *When speaking to an answering machine, speak clearly and slowly and keep your message brief.*
- *Don't just hang up without leaving a message.* At least say, "Hi, it's George, I'll call again later."
- *Don't leave rude messages.* A tape can be forever!

International business etiquette

When conducting business abroad you should pay particular attention to the following:

(1) *Names of persons with whom you'll be meeting.*

(2) *Titles of persons with whom you'll be meeting.*

(3) *Gestures and habits when speaking.*

(4) *The way you dress.*

(5) *Regional rituals and business etiquette.*

(6) *Social and entertainment etiquette.*

People's names

Be familiar with the names of the *persons with whom you'll be doing business*. Learn how to *use* the names properly and how to pronounce them correctly. Chinese names are the most unusual.

People's titles

In some countries, titles are of *paramount importance*. Learn and use them correctly.

Gestures and habits when speaking

Phrases that are well known here can be baffling to a person from another country. Examples: "a ball park figure," "that's his bag," "blew his top," "it won't fly." *This is impossible to understand in another language.* (Gestures are discussed under each country's heading.)

The way you dress

Man or woman, you will always be correct in a dark business suit for a business meeting.

WOMEN

- When attending a business meeting, women should never wear plunging necklines, skirts shorter than knee length, or apparel of any kind that is not moderate.
- In a meeting, a woman might look a little severe wearing a dark business suit when other women present are wearing silk saris; then, a dress in a feminine but business-like design may be more appropriate.

- On the street, shorts, athletic shoes, mini-skirts, and form fitting sweaters, are *not* worn by a woman who appreciates being respected.
- Formal events that state "Black tie" or "Smoking" call for a *full-length* evening gown for a woman.
- Women should not wear slacks or pant suits to a business meeting or to prestigious restaurants.

M E N

- Men should not remove their suit coats in an office when with visitors, on the street, or in public places. That's a rule of polished behavior everywhere, in North America too.
- On the street, men should not wear tank tops, athletic shoes, or wide open shirts with many chains.
- Formal events that state "Black tie" or "Smoking" call for a *traditional* dinner suit (tuxedo). Don't be flamboyant with a high fashion tuxedo of unusual design. The *classic* dinner suit is correct.

Regional rituals and business etiquette
(See the information under each country's heading.)

Social and entertainment etiquette
(See the information under each country's heading.)

(Also see: *"Travelling With Polish."*) *No matter where you travel to conduct business, do plenty of research about that particular area.* The best source would be that country's *embassy* which is usually very helpful and certainly knows the appropriate procedures and proper behavior in that region. To determine the correct use and pronunciation of names, contact the office with which you'll be dealing, the cost of a phone call or a facsimile transmission is incidental when compared with establishing respectful business relations.

General rules for business everywhere
- Always make an appointment. No drop in visits.
- First names are not used until you are invited to do so. Sometimes that familiarity may never be granted.

- It is wise to avoid talking about religion, politics, money, or topics of a personal nature.
- Don't be afraid to ask for guidance if in doubt about what to do in certain situations. It is better to ask than to offend.
- Hands in the pockets, smoking, gum chewing, feet up on furniture, swearing, back slapping, obscene or ethnic jokes, are all unacceptable behavior.
- Don't be critical. Never make comparisons of your own country with that of the country you are visiting.
- *Money*: Endeavor to learn the monetary system and don't ridicule it. Don't flash money around. It is good manners to *be discreet about any show of wealth*.
- Learn the local tipping rules, ask your travel agent.
- Allow plenty of time to get to meetings. Travel is congested and can be delayed.
- Respect the country's national anthem, *always stand*.
- If in doubt that you are able to converse adequately due to language difficulties, *hire a translator*.
- Be careful of hand and body gestures, you may offend.
- *Let the other person begin the business discussion*.
- *A business card is of prime importance everywhere. Don't choose colored or cleverly designed cards. On the card there should be: Company name. Your name. Your position* (this should not be abbreviated). *On the reverse side of the card have the same information but in the language of the people with whom you're doing business. Have this done in the country you visit, they'll know the exact terms to use*. In some countries this is an overnight service. Or, forward a supply of your cards to a printing firm *there* to process and to deliver to your hotel to await your arrival.)

Conducting business in GREAT BRITAIN

- *Great Britain is England, Scotland and Wales. Note: The United Kingdom is these three plus Ireland*.
- Be conservative in dress and in behavior.
- The British are not impressed with wealth, but they quickly evaluate your "breeding" by your behavior.

- Shake hands, that's customary.
- Don't sit until invited to do so. (That's universal.)
- The business day is 9:00 a.m. to 5:00 p.m.. Only *urgent* business is done before or after those hours.
- Protocol is of paramount importance.
- *Titles matter*. There are many titles in the Royal Family, then there's the Peerage which consists of the Peerage of England, of Scotland, of Ireland, of Great Britain and of the United Kingdom; after which there are many other titles including academic ranks. If there will be titled members in your meetings, check the public library for correct manner of address. Pay attention to how other's in the meeting address the titled, and you do the same.
- Be careful of hand gestures. The "V" sign with palm turned *toward* other people means "Victory" but the same sign with palm facing to-ward yourself has a very rude meaning. *Be safe, don't make gestures!*
- Say "British" instead of "English" and you'll meet with general approval.
- People from Scotland are called Scots or Scotsmen not Scotch (that's a drink). The language is Scottish, the tartans are Scottish, but the people are *Scots*.
- Be punctual, a few minutes late is excusable, but never be too early for an appointment.
- Don't make derogatory remarks about the Royal Family, coming from an "outsider," that is a cardinal sin.

Conducting business in FRANCE

- It is customary to confirm your meeting in writing.
- As with most of Europe, the French are very formal.
- Shake hands with those of equal or lower position than your own but *wait for anyone of senior rank to offer their hand first*.
- Be punctual.
- The business day is 8:30 a.m. to 12:30 noon when the French usually break for lunch and resume business again from 3:00 p.m. to 6:30 p.m..
- Lunch and dinner are leisurely meals with profound regard shown for food and superior wine.

- No breakfast meetings.
- Don't speak French unless you speak it *fluently*.
- (See "Business Gifts" and "The Language of Flowers.")

Conducting business in WEST GERMANY

- Recently *East Germany* and *West Germany* have undergone substantial change and, though the Berlin Wall is no longer in existence, rules of etiquette remain constant.
- The official name of *West Germany* is "Federal Republic of Germany." The abbreviation, BRD, is not as favorably accepted.
- Always state *East* or *West* when referring to *Berlin*.
- Business is punctual, formal, and to the point.

Conducting business in EAST GERMANY

- *The official name for East Germany is "The German Democratic Republic." (This may have changed.)*
- *When in East Berlin call it Berlin.*
- *Business is conducted in a formal manner.*
- *It is customary to shake hands when you arrive and also when you leave.*
- *Check security rules before visiting East Germany. You might find that there have been some changes.*

Conducting business in JAPAN

- *Send advance confirmation of your meeting and a proposed agenda.*
- *The customary greeting is to bow.* Don't bow unless someone bows to you. The back and neck are kept stiff as you bow from the waist with your arms held loosely at your sides. In a formal, high-level meeting, bow deeply to the elderly and to those of a higher rank than you, let subordinates bow lower than you do. Give a short extra bow if you wish to indicate even more respect. *Always lower your eyes.*
- *Be punctual and be very formal from the moment you enter the place of business.* Don't strike up a conversation with front office personnel, it would be improper to interrupt people at their work.

- *The business meeting probably will begin with tea being served. This is a ceremony, don't refuse it.*
- *Hours for a business meeting are not restricted.* The meeting may carry along well into the evening hours but will move from the office to a club or geisha house. (You probably won't discuss much business in the latter, but it's all in the *name* of business.) Don't decline the evening invitation, you *must* go.
- *However, women do not attend entertainment at a geisha house or a sumo wrestling ring.* In fact, women are few and far between in Japanese business.
- *It is not polite to call a Japanese by his first name.* A man's first name is used *only* by his family and long-time friends. To be correct, you would say, "Sumoto san" instead of "Mister Sumoto." San is Sir.
- *A business card is very important. It is treated with great respect.* It would be an insult to take a man's business card and scribble on the back of it as we so often do in North America. The *quality* of a business card has distinguished significance everywhere, but particularly in Japan. *Don't keep your business cards in your pants pocket, they should be kept in a pocket of your jacket. A Japanese would not like to be given a card that came out of your pants!*
- *If you are invited to a Japanese home, first take off your gloves and hat before you take off your shoes. Place your shoes neatly side by side with toes facing the door in which you entered.*
- *Gift giving requires real expertise.* The exchange of gifts has so much meaning, careful attention must be given to the selection and presentation of a gift. (See *Business Gift Giving.*)
- *Be aware that the Japanese do not say no in public.* For this reason, business decisions can be difficult to determine. Just because you don't get a negative answer, don't feel confident the answer is "yes," pay close attention to all responses and look for ways they might be letting you know the answer is "no," without them having to specifically say the word. In their endeavor to always be pleasing, the Japanese will wine and dine you in superb fashion, but that does not indicate your business proposals will be concluded in your company's favor. They are very astute, confident, honorable, and intelligent business people.

- *Even in the most discreet way, never mention the Second World War.*

Conducting business in Australia

- *G'dye! You're in the friendliest, least status-conscious country in the world.* People of all ranks, academic achievement, and working endeavor, are given equal attention and courtesy. In Australia that courtesy is proper but "uncluttered." Don't pull rank, mate, it wouldn't be appreciated.
- *Be punctual.* Australians might be casual but they don't take liberties with people's time, and nor should you.
- *Democratic as they are about equality, they still treat women as second class citizens.* A visiting business woman is given the same treatment as a man in a business meeting, but don't expect to be included in any entertainment afterwards. Australian men prefer getting to-gether with their *male* buddies.
- *Business meetings are conducted with astute directness.* In many ways, British procedures and propriety are followed.
- *In the hot weather, business dress may be more casual. A shirt and tie are worn with long shorts, knee high socks, and highly polished oxfords.* This doesn't mean that you can wear a pair of shorts and a sports shirt, an Australian's summer business dress, like regimental dress, is very uniform.

Conducting business in the *PEOPLE'S REPUBLIC OF CHINA:*

- *Greet people with a bow.* Physical contact was once frowned upon, but recently a handshake is accepted.
- *To the Chinese, "saving face" is still essential. Let them go through the door first, let them sit first, let them be the leaders.*
- *Do not call anyone "Comrade."* Only comrades call each other comrade.
- *Titles are of the utmost importance. Don't just call each man "Mister,"* use his correct title and his name, *"General"* or *"Committee Member"* or *"Factory Manager."*
- *Remember that in China the family name is first. Don't make the mistake of calling "Chang Lee" "Mr. Lee,"* he is *"Mr. Chang."*
- *Hire an interpreter. Look to the interpreter for guidance in behavior,* for example, a business meeting does not begin imme-

diately, there are formalities to be considered.

- *Be punctual. Meetings are decidedly organized.*
- *Do not wear white or blue apparel.* In China, white or blue clothing is reserved for those in mourning.
- *In conversation avoid any reference to Taiwan.*
- *Gifts should not be given.* (See *Business Gifts.*)
- *Tipping is not customary in China.*

Conducting business in HONG KONG

- *Business is done every day of the week.* Hours of business are not restricted. Morning or night, it's "business as usual."
- *Business is conducted in ways that closely reflect the British influence in procedures.*
- *Most business people speak English.*
- *Be reserved and formal. Speak quietly.*
- *The usual greeting is a handshake.*
- *Use your manners. To say "thank you" say "doe-jay."*
- *Business women are treated as equals.*
- *Don't wear white clothing, that is for mourning.*
- *Tea may be served. Whenever you are partaking of food or drink, wait until your host begins.*
- See *"Business Gifts"* and *"The Language of Flowers."*

Conducting business in ISRAEL

- *Business hours begin on Sunday morning and cease on Friday at sundown. The Sabbath is sundown on Friday to sundown on Saturday.*
- *Titles are not important, business is conducted on a first name basis.*
- *Business dress for men is quite casual, often no tie.*
- *The greeting word and parting word is "Shalom" which means "peace."*

Conducting business in ITALY

- *The business day is from 9:00 a.m. to 1:00 p.m. and from 4:00 p.m. to 8:00 p.m..* Lunch is the main meal of the day and lasts about 3 hours.
- *It's important to use academic and business position titles:*

technical fields "ingegnere"; law "avvocato"; liberal arts "dottore"; most medical doctors and professors "professore."
- Shake hands and shake hands and shake hands!
- Italians are friendly and relaxed, but business procedures are quite formal.

Conducting business in the U.S.S.R.

At this writing, the USSR has changed so radically we won't hazard a guess as to the rules of business. Russia will remain the largest country in the world and will become a major trading country and important business associate.

Conducting business in the MIDDLE EAST

- At this time, diplomatic relations with the Middle East are seriously unsettled, so guidance is limited to the following general observations:
- *Do not call it the Persian Gulf. In the Middle East it is called the Arabian Gulf.*
- *For Muslims the business week is from Saturday to Thursday.* The Muslim day of rest is Friday. Government departments are closed. A business meeting can be arranged for a Friday, however, as it is not against the law. It is proper to respect a Muslim's day of rest, so let *them* suggest Friday as a meeting day, don't you suggest it.
- *The ninth month of the Islamic calendar is Ramadan and usually no work is done after noon during this period.* Ramadan begins eleven days earlier each year, so check to see the exact dates involved. A Muslim fasts during Ramadan, so do not invite him to *lunch,* but you may *invite him to dine after sunset.*
- *During the first month of the Islamic year it is not respectful to give parties or elaborate dinners.* That is the month Mohammet's grandson was murdered.
- *Appointments are necessary. However, it is quite customary for Arabs to conduct business with a number of business appointments at the same time.* Other businessmen and even friends may be present, be ready to function under these distracting conditions.
- *Eat with your right hand only. Pass your business card with*

your right hand only. The left hand is used for bathroom activities, so is *never* used to take or give anything. Do not put your left hand on the dining table.

- *Do not show the soles of your shoes when facing your host. This is a personal affront.*
- *With the exception of Iraq, no alcoholic beverages are allowed in Arab countries.*
- *Men: An Arab businessman might hold your hand as you walk to-gether. This is a gesture of friendship.* You may feel uncomfortable but do not refuse to hold his hand, that would be an insult. (If a visiting Arab does that here in North America, tactfully explain to him the significance of that gesture and explain why you may not wish to hold hands.)
- *Do not compliment an Arab on anything he owns, he may feel obliged to give to you.* (Need a Rolex watch?)
- *Islamic rules demand that all activity be stopped for prayers five times a day.* An Arab may leave a meeting and go to a mosque or he may pray at his office. When he kneels and faces Mecca, it is not necessary that you do the same, but *do remain quiet*.

Other customs around the world:
- *In several countries it is considered impolite to converse with your hands in your pockets.*
- *In Eastern Europe, both hands should be seen while you are eating at a table.* It is not polite to rest one hand in your lap, rest it on the table edge.
- *Men should treat women with traditional courtesy.* With so many women in the business world in North America, the social graces have been somewhat changed for man/woman business manners, but this is not the case abroad. *With women in other countries, a man should be as gallant in business as he is socially.*
- *In Taiwan, it may be necessary to remove your shoes in some homes.* (Do what your host does.)
- *In Taiwan, do not discuss mainland China.*
- *In Thailand, you must remove your shoes in a home.* Do not step on the doorsill, Thais believe that you might disturb the good spirit that lurks there.

- *In Thailand, you are greeted with a short bow.* This is called a "wai." At chest level, the hands are held to-gether, as in prayer, as you bow.
- *In Thailand, do not touch anyone's head.* That is the highest part of the body and must be respected. Don't pat a child on the head (as most of us are so accustomed to doing).
- *In Austria, don't call an Austrian a German.*
- *In Denmark, the guest of honor is seated to the left of the hostess.* You are expected to give a toast to the hostess while dessert is served.
- *In Denmark, you must not touch your drink until your host raises his glass and says, "skoal."*
- *In Denmark there is no tipping in restaurants, hotels, or taxis.*
- *In Belgium, cheeks are kissed as they are in France except they are kissed three times.* First one cheek, then the other, and then to the first again.
- *In Ireland, even local phone calls are metered, so offer to pay for the cost of your phone call.*
- *In the Netherlands, don't call it "Holland."* Holland is only a part of the Netherlands.
- *In the Netherlands, don't ever say "Dutch," that is not respect-ful, say "Netherlander."*
- *In Spain, most businesses shut down during siesta from 1:30 p.m. to 4:30 p.m..* Restaurants close even longer, not opening until after 9:00 p.m..
- *In Brazil and Greece, do not make the gesture of what we use as the "okay" sign, which is making a circle with the thumb and forefinger. This is a a most obscene gesture in Brazil and is rude in Greece.*
- *In France the "okay" sign means what it looks like, zero.* The question, "Did you catch any fish to-day," can get totally op-posite answers with this gesture, in France it would mean "none," in America "plenty."
- *In Greece, be careful of how you nod your head. Our nod "Yes" means "no" in Greece.*
- *In some countries, pointing at someone with the index and little finger (with the other fingers and thumb curled into the palm) can mean you are putting a curse on them.* Superstitious

people may be exceedingly upset by this cruel gesture.

- *In Mexico, it is the custom to bargain with prices.*
- *In Egypt, watch that gesture of tapping your two index fingers to-gether. It might give the message "let's go to bed to-gether."*
- *In England, they say "thank-you" in the place of our "you're welcome."*
- *In England, it is crude to say "fanny"; say "bum" or "bottom" instead.*
- *In England, you might be asked if you'd like to be "knocked up" in the morning. It simply means would you like a wake-up call.*
- *In England, if they say someone is "homely" it means they like their home, it doesn't mean they are ugly.*
- *In Canada, most people do not speak French. There are far more English speaking people in Canada.* Outside of Quebec there are only small minority groups of French speaking people. The French that is spoken in Canada is much different than the French spoken in France. So far removed for so many decades, the Canadian French has become a unique language.
- *In Canada, make no derogatory comparisons between the eastern provinces and western provinces. Being the second largest country in the world, Canada covers such vast geographic expanse between the east and the west that lifestyles and climates across the country vary quite extensively, and sensitivities to east/west comparisons are keen.*
- *Canadians are indignant when people are mistakenly informed that the climate in Canada is cold. The climates range from very mild year round in southern British Columbia, to cold only in the four winter months in all the other nine provinces. Anyone who thinks Canada's climate is cold has only visited one part of this huge country and in only one season of the year.*
- *This means: We should try to learn about every part of this wonderful world and should learn to respect it's wide variety of regional traditions and customs.*

The international "language" of flowers:

Everyone loves flowers and to "Say it with flowers" is a universally acceptable and gracious thing to do. Be aware, however, that certain flowers have a traditional and very specific meaning in some countries.

- *In most countries, do not give 13 flowers.*
- *In most countries, a gift of roses has a romantic connotation.*
- *In almost all countries, red roses are the gift of lovers.* Beautiful as they are, take care that your gift of red roses is meant to convey a message of profound love.
- *In some countries, yellow roses are the gift of true and close friendship.* How special!
- *In many countries, an even number of flowers is considered to be an omen of bad luck or misfortune.*
- *In France, Belgium, Italy and most of western Europe, do not give chrysanthemums, they are given at times of death.*
- *In Japan, do not give the 16 petal chrysanthemum, that is reserved for the Imperial Family crest.*
- *In England and in Canada, because they suggest death, give white lilies only at Easter time in mourning the death of Jesus.*
- *In Hungary, flowers should be presented wrapped.*
- *In West Germany, East Germany and in Poland, flowers are presented unwrapped.*
- *In Kenya, do not give flowers except as a gift of condolence.*
- *In Brazil, do not send purple flowers, they are associated with death.*
- *In Mexico, to some people, different flower colors have different meanings: do not send red flowers as they can cast a spell, or yellow flowers which mean death. White flowers are good, because they banish evil spells.*

And something else about flowers:
- *It's a nice gesture to send cut flowers a day prior to a dinner engagement at someone's home.* This gives your host or hostess time to arrange them.
- *One, single, very beautiful flower can be just as splendid as a large bouquet.*
- *Check with the hospital before you take flowers to a patient.* A

hospital may not allow flowers or plants due to some patients' respiratory problems and/or the hospital's concern of the bacteria some plants may introduce.

- *If flowers are sent to a funeral, they are sent as a tribute to the dead, not as a condolence to the living. The card should read "In loving memory" or "In fond memory" or "In memory" but should not read "With deepest sympathy." The flowers are sent to the funeral chapel, addressed to the deceased not to the mourner.* The cards from these flowers are collected by the undertaker or a member of the family, so that a record can be kept to later send letters of thanks.
- *If you wish to send flowers to the bereaved,* send them to their *home* and address them to that person, then your card can read "With deepest sympathy." An announcement in the published obituary may say "No flowers, please" but that means for the funeral.
- *It is an especially nice gesture to send flowers to the bereaved a week or two after the funeral with a card that says, "Thinking of you" or "Just to cheer you."* Kindness, when it's needed most.
- *Flowers are not usually sent to a Jewish funeral.*
- *Flower arrangements on a dining table should be of low enough height not to obstruct peoples' views of one another.*
- *Try to send flowers or plants that enhance the color of the recipient's decor.* A purple flower in a perfectly co-ordinated peach colored living room may lose some of its floral charm.
- *Flowers should be worn with their stems down.*
- *Artificial flowers that are used in a room's decor should be of the finest quality silk, never plastic, and it is highly questionable whether or not they are a suitable gift. I would certainly suggest that you refrain from giving them in other countries, if ever.*
- *It's perfectly correct for a woman to send a man flowers. Unfortunately, I must qualify that statement and say, in any country that considers a woman as a man's equal.*
- *Flowers, like beautiful music, are understood around the world. They speak the language of goodwill, love, and friendship. They are always welcomed.*

International business gifts

- *Do not give gifts at your initial business encounter.* It could be interpreted as a bribe.
- *Gifts imprinted with your business logo are in very bad taste.* A *small* symbol or emblem on a gift may be all right but you shouldn't expect the recipient to be pleased to do your advertising.
- *Gifts can be purchased at a much reduced price from a duty free store when you are travelling out of the country.*
- *Don't gift wrap your parcels until you reach your destination.* The customs inspectors will remove the wrapping and you'll have to wrap the gift again.
- *Gifts that are symbolic of your own country or region of your own country are the most cherished.* Gifts made from the wood of local trees or from local gem stones. A blown-glass vase from a noted artist in San Francisco; something made of marble from Georgia; some smoked salmon from British Columbia, Canada.
- *Do not enclose a business card with a gift. A plain small card with your compliments and your signature is much more gracious.*
- *Gifts must be appropriate to the country to which they are given, for instance, you would not take perfume or wine as a gift to someone in France.* (It's like taking a block of ice to an Eskimo.)
- *Don't give gifts that are either too cheap or too lavish.* Something small of exquisite quality is most appropriate.
- *In some countries even the wrapping or the color of the wrapping paper has a meaning. Take care.* If in doubt take your gifts to a gift wrapping service, they would know what is correct.
- *In Germany, do not use paper or ribbons that are black, brown, or white to wrap a gift.*
- *IN JAPAN, gift wrapping is of paramount importance. Don't use black, white, or red, wrapping paper. Pastel colored rice paper is ideal.* Get your gift wrapped at a department store, they'll do it best.

Avoid gifts in multiples of four, in Japan the number four has unfavorable significance. (Two's are lucky!) Always wrap the gift. The Japanese prefer to open their gifts in private. *Business gifts are obligatory in Japan at year end or Toshidama (January 1st.) and at mid-year, Chugen, which is July 15th. Let a Japanese offer his gift before you give yours.*

- *Don't give an Arab anything with the picture or symbol of an animal on it, it may mean an ill omen.*
- *Don't give a clock as a gift to a Chinese. Bad luck.*
- *In India don't give any gifts made from the hide of a cow. The cow is sacred in India.*
- *People in most countries consider that the gift of a knife, scissors, or anything sharp, is an omen that the friendship will be cut.* To break this "spell," you must give a coin with the gift.
- *As you travel to do business or as a tourist anywhere in the world, take time to learn the local customs and social graces.* ***Universally, there is nothing more significant than consideration for others.***

THERE! YOU HAVE IT.

AROUND THE WORLD,

RIGHT NEXT DOOR,

OR

AT HOME, SWEET HOME,

PEOPLE LIKE AND RESPECT YOU

FOR

Putting on the Polish!